Data-Driven Customer Engagement

Ralf Strauss

Data-Driven Customer Engagement

Mastering MarTech Strategies for Success

Springer

Ralf Strauss
MarketingTechLab GmbH
Hamburg, Germany

ISBN 978-3-031-64294-4 ISBN 978-3-031-64295-1 (eBook)
https://doi.org/10.1007/978-3-031-64295-1

This Springer imprint is published by the registered company Springer Nature Switzerland AG
The registered company address is: Gewerbestrasse 11, 6330 Cham, Switzerland

"The further path to data-driven marketing requires the permanent change of processes, structures, IT applications and competences ... what appears to be an effective means today may already be obsolete tomorrow. The Marketing Tech Monitor provides orientation for this in terms of content, quality, and conceptual depth."

—Michael Schuld (Chief Commercial & Marketing Officer, *MediaMarktSaturn Retail Group*)

"The State of MarTech and data-driven marketing in D/A/CH ... Required reading for every marketing or digital/online marketing manager!"

—Uli Klenke (Chief Brand Officer, *Deutsche Telekom AG*)

"Data protection requirements and changes to data-driven sales present similar challenges to established companies. The Marketing Tech Monitor offers a wide range of ideas and new opportunities to meet these challenges."

—Dr Ina Offergeld (former Head of Sales IT, *Volkswagen Group*)

"The future belongs to Marketing Tech Monitor, which envisages and understands—an absolute must-read for all marketing professionals."

—Tim Alexander (Global CMO, *Deutsche Bank*)

"We observe that consulting requirements for us as an agency group have changed in recent years; comprehensive MarTech know-how has become a 'must'. The Marketing Tech Monitor is a great initiative to give all market participants a good understanding of the status quo as well as developments going forward."

—Daniela Tollert (Chief Growth Officer, *GroupM Germany*)

"Marketing Tech is also becoming increasingly important at the top management level. The Marketing Tech Monitor has established itself as a true lighthouse in the sea of offers and tools for data-driven marketing and sales ... an absolute 'must read'."

—Dr Uwe Stuhldreier (Board Member Marketing & Sales, *HUK24*)

"Hardly any other topic has occupied the marketing discipline as much in recent years as the successful handling and use of data. While marketing processes are already being intelligently automated on a broad front in Silicon Valley or Singapore, the reality in the German-speaking countries is often still rather analogue. The Marketing Tech Monitor not only helps to understand the status quo in D/A/CH, but also provides targeted recommendations for action to improve the use of MarTech in one's own company."

—Prof. Dr Marcus Schoegel (*University of St. Gallen, Switzerland*)

"Bridging the gap between future data-driven customer interaction and IT application scenarios, for example in the areas of CRM / customer experience, marketing automation, AI or even data science/marketing analytics. An annual North Star for orientation with a lot of depth and quality in the content."

—Robert Ader (Global CMO, *Porsche*)

"Data and technology are the foundation in a digitalised world. If you want to reach people, you need MarTech. Automatisms and AI will ensure that mediocrity will exist for free in the future. However, only the combination of creativity and technology leads to excellence. So, anyone who wants to not only reach people but also touch them will need both in the future: technology meeting creativity."

—Christian Raetsch (CEO, *BBDO Group Germany*)

"Artificial intelligence, data analytics, and automation in customer interaction have long been on everyone's lips in marketing. The crucial thing is to act. The Marketing Tech Monitor provides good approaches for concrete operationalisation."

—Anja Stolz (Member of the Board, CMO & Head of Omnichannel, *R+V Insurance*)

"The Marketing Tech Monitor is the annual highlight and standard work for every marketing decision-maker. No one can get around a technologically sound development plan anymore. Here, straight talk is given without embellishments and the complex topic is competently illuminated. The steadily growing MarTech community speaks for itself and the increasing relevance of the topic at all decision-making levels."

—Florian Poepleu (Global Head of Marketing & Sales Processes and Digital Solutions, *tesa*)

"Bridging the gap between strategy, data, and IT applications in marketing ... much needed."

—Adriana Nuneva (Chief Digital Officer, *CWS International*)

"Must-read for all developments in data-driven marketing ... with depth in content and cross-functional insights."

—Kai Schmidhuber (Managing Director, *ALDI SÜD Germany*)

"Marketing—whether online or offline—and accompanying IT applications are in a permanent mode of change. The permanent strategic imperative is 'change'. The Marketing Tech Monitor is the beacon for the further development of one's own organisation and for further digitalisation."

—Dr Thomas Schwetje (Member of the Executive Board, Head of Digital & Customer, *Coop Switzerland*)

"In building our overarching strategy for marketing, sales, service and digital, we took our cue from the Marketing Tech Monitor. There is nothing comparable in breadth and depth regarding current MarTech topics."

—Alexander Almerood (Senior Director Marketing & Sales, *BionTech*)

To my beloved family and my wife Brigitte—thank you for all your support, help, and loving coaching . . . without you, this entire journey over the last years would never have been possible.

Foreword

The Power of the Brand

In a time of unprecedented challenges and risks, it is more important than ever to understand the role of marketing and its impact on society.

Antiracist yoga rain jackets (as in the case of *Lululemon*), impact and "purpose-driven" sustainable green solutions, as well as various climate-protection products—marketing shapes social change and has been doing so throughout history. Today, everything is driven by the economy. The development of marketing in recent times can be divided into three basic evolutionary stages:

First, there was the (chaotic) "information society" in which brands were supposed to conquer the hearts and minds of consumers. Emotions were the focus, and concepts such as true love marks emerged. But it soon became clear that more than just emotional ties between the brand and the consumer were needed.

The "knowledge society" heralded the second stage of development, that of "woke brands", by using social and environmental concerns as the basis for new business models. During this time, companies began to adapt their stories not only to the needs and emotions of customers, but also to the pressing challenges of our time.

We are now facing a third and final stage of development, driven by a digital tsunami. With *ChatGPT* and AI, as well as blockchain infrastructure technology, centralised institutions in health, finance, education, and possibly politics are about to fall. Quantum technology is destined to become the most socially and economically transformative technology that humanity has ever experienced. Rapid developments in areas such as biotechnology and nanotechnology are driving the search for God-like abilities: deus ex machina. Immortality, godhood, and bliss are to be achieved on the path to technological singularity. The coming technological changes will transform our lives, our society, and our economy in ways we cannot yet fully comprehend. In an unprecedented dynamic, they will improve problems in all areas such as climate change, energy, health, or security and make the previously impossible possible.

This new era is about achieving omniscience and developing world-class products that improve people's problems while promoting a more humane capitalism. Brands are becoming more honest: What problems is the company trying to find better solutions for? Because it is about progress—infinite positive progress for humanity through better solutions to problems at hand. Marginal costs of intelligence (knowledge) as well as marginal costs of energy are racing towards zero, and a new culture of performance and enterprise is emerging in which Erhard's "*Prosperity for All*" is to be achieved by making the planet and people integral to the incentives for growth. In short, our grandchildren should be better off than we are. The times of finite solutions and products are being replaced by a grandchild-friendly attitude. It is all about infinity.

The number of opportunities in marketing today is huge, and the number of challenges to overcome is no fewer. In this new era, we need to ask ourselves how we can tell the stories that inspire us to make the world a better place and how we can create incentives to bring about behavioural change. The last 50 years show impressively: the story about renunciation and limitation does not work. These are two critical issues, especially in affluent Western regions. But what happens when three quarters of the world's population also aspire to progress? What do they do?

Case studies and technological insights for finding the answers are provided in the *Marketing Tech Monitor*—a comprehensive guide to help understand and successfully implement current trends, technologies, and strategies in MarTech. Valuable insights into the exciting world of marketing and the changes ahead are also included.

However, the most important question remains: what are you doing? Society becomes more social as the amount of output from business rises, and the world finds its "ecosophy" when ecology and philosophy synergise. In short, our operating system—the economy—must work. Never have we been able to shape the future as much as today. Humans are taking evolution into their own hands.

In the coming years, may the stories of the marketeers inspire us to improve the world and create a more humane capitalism based on the principles of the eco-social market economy. After all, it is stories that shape people. The *Marketing Tech Monitor* pairs such stories with technological and data-driven knowledge sharing. The long-awaited enlightenment is reaching its zenith, but still needs the story to animate people and brands. Countable and tellable. Explainable and experienceable. So, a final evolutionary stage of marketing is blossoming in which a society of the minds can emerge. We are facing years during which the task will be to understand the story we tell as a union of myth and enlightenment.

This could be the motto: "Technological utopianism of the future, with scientific optimism of progress and human growth as the way forward". We are at the dawn of a new era of marketing where brands do nothing less than teach people how to think and create better products and incentives for behavioural change.

It's a paradigm shift and a new narrative. Marketing must now teach people to think.

Yours sincerely,

Frankfurt, Germany
May 2024

Anders Indset

Foreword

The Evolving MarTech Landscape

It's a wonderful time to be working in marketing. It's a challenging time to be working in marketing.

It's a wonderful and challenging time to be working in marketing for the same underlying reason: change. We're living in an era of constant, pervasive change in the marketing profession. New technologies, touchpoints, and tactics. New customer expectations. New competitive threats. New ways of running our teams, our department, our organisation, our ecosystem. While change can be hard, it is also the source of great opportunity. Every new change opens a window for us to get ahead of our competitors, delight our customers in remarkable ways, and pioneer original marketing concepts that grow our business. Leaning into this change isn't easy. But it can be immensely rewarding.

Several of the biggest changes underway in marketing technology today are in the areas of commerce, operations, and creators.

In commerce, the volume and variety of transactions that we're able to conduct with customers through purely digital channels are expanding rapidly. And this isn't just in consumer businesses. B2B customers are conducting more and more of their business online, too. In the process, the lines between marketing and sales are blurring. An explosion of new "SalesTech" tools now complements the "MarTech" stack.

In operations, the rise of "ops" roles in companies are spanning nearly every department: marketing ops, sales ops, customer service ops, partner ops, revenue ops, data ops, and so on. This is above and beyond the traditional IT and business ops functions that continue to grow and evolve, too. Department-specific ops roles are not taking away work from IT. Rather, the size of the total pie is growing dramatically through digital transformation. There's more digitally powered ops work for everyone in the organisation. I call this new wave of domain-specific operations roles "Big Ops".

Just as big data is about the volume, velocity, and variety of data flowing into our business, Big Ops is all about the incredible volume, velocity, and variety of digital operations being run with that data. It's the sum of all the different apps, algorithms, automations, agents, analyses, etc. that are running in parallel in our organisation. While Big Ops certainly increases the complexity of our environment—driving the need for more technical and operations-focused talent within the marketing department—it also enables whole new capabilities for marketers. The integration of marketing systems and data with the digital flow of the rest of the organisation—sales, service, product, finance, supply chain—gives us dramatically more insight into the best ways to communicate with customers and the best ways to personalise their experiences with us.

Finally, there are creators. We're witnessing the rise of the "creator economy"—individuals or very small entrepreneurial teams earning a living by creating content and micro-apps on their own. In some cases, they're earning a very good living. They monetise their work through online commerce, subscription services, advertising, and/or sponsorships from brands who leverage them as influencers. There's tremendous opportunity for marketers to work with these independent creators. But potentially an even greater opportunity exists to bring the creator culture and capabilities inside our organisations. The rise of low-code and no-code tools empowers marketers and business users to create more things on their own without the costs or constraints of specialists. From creative assets to workflow automation, from data analysis to campaign experimentation, the power marketers now have at their fingertips is amazing. And it's continuing to advance at a rapid pace.

These are big changes. Big challenges. But big opportunities.

It's a wonderful time to be working in marketing.

Best,

Boston, MA
May 2024

Scott Brinker

Preface

In Search of MarTech Excellence

Despite all the prophecies of doom, the market in the field of marketing technology (MarTech) continues to grow steadily—the number of providers is still increasing by almost 30% annually, the software licence market on the customer side by around 20% annually . . . as before. The precarious thing from the company's or customer's point of view: in contrast to earlier, rather time-stable CRM projects, the requirements, and thus also the IT applications, will continue to evolve. The new channels and interaction mechanisms, new (legal) conditions, an "increase" in automation and analytics (AI) ensure that yesterday's tried-and-tested methods and tools can (and will) become obsolete just one day later. While the basic architecture and the data model will (hopefully) remain the same, new channels, interaction scenarios, and (peripheral) applications are constantly being added. An end is not in sight . . . and working in beta mode and permanent learning-by-doing can hardly be avoided, according to the credo of the legendary ice hockey player *Wayne Gretzky*: "*You miss 100% of the shots you don't take.*" The "big expedition" into a data-driven marketing & sales universe continues.

However, the large number of projects and workshops also shows that there is still a great deal of uncertainty on the part of marketing decision-makers. Arbitrary and constantly changing or newly invented acronyms meet an audience that, in many cases, has been socialised in classic brand management or which must still digest painful experiences in joint marketing and IT projects, for example in the introduction of customer relationship management (CRM). On the one hand, there is the dogma that "digital is the new normal", a legion of start-ups that are just waiting to cannibalise the existing business model and more than 14,000 different IT applications (with an upward trend) in the entire marketing and sales environment. On the other hand, this is often countered by a multitude of painful and cost-intensive experiences (and personal wounds) from joint marketing/sales and IT projects in the past (such as painful CRM implementations), uncertainty about the "right" way forward for the company, coupled with agencies and service providers who often virtuously combine theoretical, abstract *PowerPoint* orgies with insufficient implementation experience.

For instance, contrary to all CRM discussions over the last 25 years, about 35% of senior marketing executives in Europe complain about the lack of an adequate CRM tool in their own company. Another 50% or so are of the opinion that they do have a CRM tool but consider it to be of limited use and not very useful for achieving their business objectives. This means that CRM in the form of personalised audience management is likely to experience a renaissance in 2024 and beyond … hand in hand with the strive for first-party data. However, the large number of workshops and projects over the last decade also shows that there is a lack of basic principles and concepts, such as a common language and terminology, for instance understanding the customer journey. Outside-in, not inside-out, based on the individual perspectives of sales reps. Thus, arbitrary, and rather platitudinous discussions about "customer data platforms" or "customer experience management platforms" are often considered fairy dust within the discussion about data-driven marketing, without, for instance,

- the same common understanding of which application scenarios and thus requirements these should fulfil in each case,
- which internal/external process landscapes they are based on, or
- how they could or should fit into a company-specific master construction plan.

Consequently, new terminology meets users with very different conceptual understandings. The constant striving of providers to position themselves as uniquely as possible in the market and to distinguish themselves from competitors is leading to a constant stream of new terms from software vendors. At the same time, many of the projects have started to fail or have not achieved their initial goals. The reasons are just as trivial as they are serious: a lack of depth in content, the desire to make a "career-boosting move" as quickly as possible and to distinguish oneself from others internally. The lovingly celebrated trench warfare and dysfunctional political intrigues tend to act as accelerators in this respect—according to the motto: it is better to first claim a subject area for oneself with the help of "fancy" and elaborated *PowerPoint* charts and a lot of testosterone and then subsequently face the cruel project reality in implementation … with a simultaneously increasing pressure to change.

This book is yet another appeal for a further content-driven discussion about processes, based on the strategy and going down to the level of applications and data. It is not about "old vs. new" or "innovation vs. tradition" or "brand vs data/technology"—rather about how instruments are (or must be) orchestrated again and again along heterogeneous and context-related customer needs. In other words, it is not about "A *or* B", but "A *and* B". This poses completely new challenges for companies—from a cross-functional "way of working" to having the necessary competences and staffing, common goals, and IT applications.

In a study by *MediaSense*, only 11% of CMOs state that they have already successfully mastered digitalisation in marketing.[1] The biggest challenge: to unite the orchestra of MarTech, know-how, business processes, and data into a common symphony. The moral liturgy in most trade media celebrates the Sunday speeches of the MarTech providers, mostly without critically questioning them further. As in the early years of the Klondike Gold Rush, the valuable data claims in most companies today are (again) inadequately secured—ranging from issues like ad fraud, to unused data, to inadequate activation, and low adaptation of existing (and already licensed) systems . . . while at the same time the *Google*, *Apple*, *Facebook*, *Amazon* (GAFA) data miners sip champagne in the VIP lounge.

It is a brave new world. There is often a lack of fundamentals, such as a common language (terminologies used) and target pictures, as well as methods for working out the respective context, such as: "*what level of granularity is required for use cases or requirements*? *What is meant by a CDP and in which context does it really make sense to apply it*?" As before, content-empty discussions about CDPs or the customer experience are often simply fairy dust within the discussion about data-driven marketing and sales for the future. A stream of new terminology (syntax) collides hard with quite different conceptual understandings of content (semantics). Clarity is not being created—instead, fuel is being thrown into the fire of confusion. New channels and interaction mechanisms, new (legal) conditions (such as GDPR), an "increase" in automation and analytics (paired with AI) ensure that yesterday's tried-and-tested methods and tools can (and will) become obsolete just one day later. While the basic architecture and data model (hopefully) remain intact, new channels, interaction scenarios, and peripheral applications are constantly being added. There is hardly an end in sight. No way out.

The challenge for every manager in marketing, sales, or customer service:

- To filter out which trends and topics are relevant, and which will fade away like "dust in the wind". For instance, *Metaverse* and *Web3* have received a lot of attention recently, but currently have little of anything new to contribute, both from the point of view of the companies surveyed and in terms of their content and concept. They are still a longer way away from mass use. Artificial intelligence (AI), however, has left the hangar of innovations on hold, with *ChatGPT* having been at the forefront of the hype. Away from a rather technically motivated discussion about data and towards concrete use cases and "business benefits".
- In addition, it is and will remain our aim to give normative recommendations for action. In other words, going beyond providing a purely enumerative description to giving concrete recommendations for action for all "cheerleaders" on the way to data-driven marketing. This requires a broad network of experts, company representatives, and software providers who repeatedly discuss with us in depth which topics are relevant and have (or will have) real business impact. A big

[1] MediaSense: MediaSense Launches Wave Five of Media 20:20 Research; London, March 1, 2022.

thank you for all their "brain power" to almost 75 experts who contributed over the years!

- Walking the tightrope between the different topical spheres and functional domains—in other words, between strategies and concepts for data-driven customer interaction from a business perspective to technical implementation, data modelling, and change. This applies to the setting of a "demarcation line" in terms of content—both in structure and language style—between a mandatory tutorial (to clarify content) and (normative) recommendations for action based on real life.
- To distinguish which concepts have a more long-term character (e.g. change management methods) and which are more short-term in nature (e.g. new partnerships in ID management) . . . or are simply over-hyped.

Following *Peters' and Waterman's "In Search of Excellence"* idea, we try—as a claim and obligation for ourselves—to create a navigation aid on the way to data-driven marketing with the yearly *Marketing Tech Monitor* as a (normative) North Star since 2019. We welcome all questions and further discussions . . . because here, too, the following applies: we will only (be able to) further develop the necessary contents, concepts, best practices, and process models through critical, content-related discourses.

Yours sincerely,

Hamburg, Germany Ralf Strauss
May 2024

Acknowledgements

We would like to thank our partners on the Marketing Tech Monitor over the last years such as Tealium, entirely, Uptempo, Marmind, Adform, Oracle, Teavaro, Customer Excellence GmbH and others, as well as the many colleagues who took the time to participate in the quantitative study as well as the qualitative interviews, project discussions, and case studies, including all of the almost 200 colleagues from the CMO Community and the Digital CMO Community, as well as Dr Oliver Schmitt, Christian Spannbauer, Sebastian Weber, and Ute Lauer (Deutsche Lufthansa), Stephan Götze (DB Systel), Dr Matthias Rasztar and Maximilian Steudel (Dr Oetker), Michael Maurantonio (Ad Fraud Detection), Patrick von Gönna (dock36), Dr Alexander Falser (Kaufland), Tim Alexander, Renata Dadic and Andre Reintjes (Deutsche Bank), Sarah Bredenwischer (Pfalzwerke), Pascal Seifert (Kyocera), Felix Hattemer, Carolina Balzereit and Stephanie Niedung (HABA Family), Dr Dirk Rohweder (Teavaro), Nina Haller (ExperienceOne/GWA) and Veronique Franzen (Publicis/GWA), Dr Ralf Nöcker (GWA), Anders Indset (andersindset), Sven Stühmeier (Vodafone), Mario Bertsch (dm Drogerie Märkte), Alexander Willkomm (mParticle), Dr Uwe Stuhldreier (HUK24), Alexander Ewig and Marc Warninck (AIDA Cruises), Frank Trefzer (Tealium), Thorsten Schapmann (Beiersdorf), Dr Thomas Schwetje and Adrian Steiger (COOP Switzerland), Stephanie Wölfel and André Hoffschröer (Ernsting's Family), Florian Poepleu (Tesa), Petra Ahlert (Cisco), Alexander Ermisch (Taico), Matthias Ehrlich (Ehrlich Strategies), Cathrin Duppel and Andrea Geisler (formerly Rotkäppchen-Mumm), Tina Bergner and Ralf Ellermann (Rodenstock), Robert Ader and Patrick Gärtner (Porsche), Dr Axel Berger (Zalando), Peter Kotzur (Rehau), Peter Harzer and Dr Martino Sarazino (QIAGEN), Maren Huth (Brita), Katja Ohly-Nauber and Andreas Ehspanner (Mercedes-Benz), Dr Jens Thiemer, Martin Eibl and Wolfgang Groß (BMW Group), Dr Peter Opdemom, Roman Reichelt and Thierry Pool (formerly Credit Suisse), Adriana M. Nuneva (CWS International), Galina Herzig and Andreas Büning (Carglass), Rik Strubel (Westwing), Sven Schoderböck (formerly Musikhaus Thomann), Wolfram Bartke (HOKATA Online Marketing), Lars Schickner, Vera Neboisa (Sharp NEC), Marcus Koch (Pilot), Myron Kohut (Austrian Post), Annika Remberg, Dr Nicolai Johannsen and Stephan Huth (OTTO), Carlos Yniguez (formerly Bitburger Digital), Wolfgang Weber, Thomas Schäffer and Bianca Sünkel (CX Omni), Dr Simon Menke (OTTO), Kerstin Pape (Tennispoint), Dr Augustine Fou (Fouanalytics), Michael Reidel (Deutscher Fachverlag/Horizont), Tanja Backhaus and Lan Leiskau (Handelsblatt Media Solutions), Felix Jahnen (Krombacher Digital), Thorsten Müller (Reckitt Benkiser), Dimitri Herber (Warsteiner), Nils Stamm (Allianz Direkt), Stefan Wolk (Fielmann), Rolf Schumann and Raimund Bau (Schwarz Digital), and Marina Sverdel (RWE).

A similar thank you goes to Scott Brinker (Editor Chiefmartec/VP Platform Ecosystem, HubSpot, Boston/USA) and Frans Riemersma (MarTechTribe.com) for all their input on the development of the MarTech landscape. A special warm thank you goes to Frans Riemersma for all deep dives and his insights based on the MarTech databases.

Similarly, a big thank you goes to Dr Simon Menke (Otto Group)—for sharing all deep insights into legal frameworks in data and online marketing. To be honest, I will never understand to the full extent . . . even you tried hard to teach me.

A big thank you goes to the best team in the world—with Mareike Milde, Carsten Thierbach, and Katja Brandt for all their support. You rock!

Contents

About the Author

Ralf Strauss is Managing Partner of MarketingTechLab GmbH and Customer Excellence GmbH, two consultancies specialising in marketing, sales, service, and digitalisation. He is also an initiator and chairman of the CMO Community founded in 2006 (www.cmocommunity.de), initiator and chairman of the Digital CMO Community founded in 2015 (www.digitalcmocommunity.de), former President of the German Marketing Association (DMV) and Chairman of the Board of the European Marketing Confederation (EMC).

Previously, he was Senior Vice President of the Volkswagen Group between 2011 and 2012, where he was responsible for the digital transformation of marketing and sales. Before joining Volkswagen, he was Global Head of Product Management CRM Marketing between 2008 and 2011 and previously SAP's Head of Marketing in Germany and Central Europe for many years. Before joining SAP and Volkswagen, he already had several years of experience in marketing, sales, and digital projects in management consulting before joining SAP Germany as Head of Corporate Strategy and Development in 2002.

MarTech... The Via Dolorosa into Data-Driven Customer Interaction

1

1.1 MarketingTech: Systematisation

MarTech refers to a variety of more than 14,000 applications as of May 2024. Therefore, a systematisation is needed which differentiates into 5 different functional areas: from the (1.) data layer to (2.) analytics as the foundation. On the process level, (3.) Marketing Resource Management starts with all functions around planning and steering, being translated into (4.) orchestration into (5.) multi-channel campaign management.

MarTech, *MarketingTech*, or *CustomerTech* refers to a variety of different technologies that are used by companies to support and automate activities and processes through modern IT applications. The spectrum of applications subsumed under this term ranges from classic CRM scenarios (e.g. segmentation or campaign management) to customer data platforms to customer journey analysis or AdTech solutions (Fig. 1.1). Even if a categorisation can hardly cope with the multitude of different application scenarios and tools, it still helps to analyse individual functional dimensions and to answer the question of how far these individual technologies functionally overlap. The omission of such a *functional blueprint* (incl. comparison with targeted future business capabilities and detailed requirements) otherwise usually leads to an "over-munitioning" of technical platforms. The consequence is:

- competence disputes between functional areas ("*Which system should be leading in which process section or functional domain?*"),
- possibly the acquisition of applications that do not cover or only insufficiently cover the intended scenario, or
- over-licensing of IT applications and, subsequently, escalating implementation, interfaces, and maintenance costs.

The ultimate objective should be to create an overarching strategy and subsequent marketing technology landscape that all functional areas can access coherently, and which serves as a kind of structured "central engine room". In this context, we also

R. Strauss, *Data-Driven Customer Engagement*,
https://doi.org/10.1007/978-3-031-64295-1_1

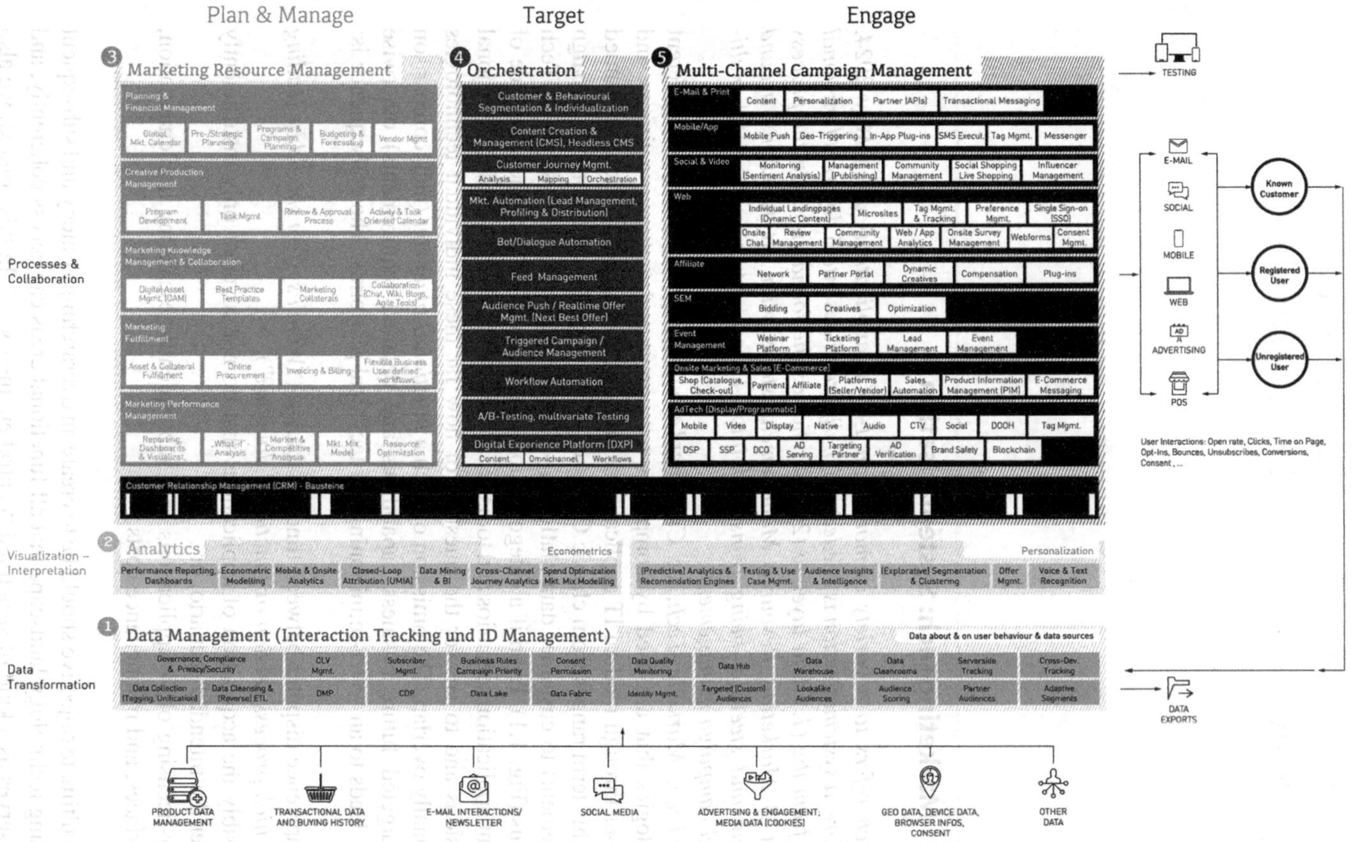

Fig. 1.1 MarTech blueprint—building blocks 1 through 5 of a MarketingTech landscape (schematic) (In a similar way see Forrester: Enterprise Architecture Technology Reference Model for Marketing, Boston, 2023)

had to say goodbye—with a heavy heart—to the idea of using the benchmarking database to work out a "best practice master construction plan" from more than 1400 MarTech maps. Business models, target groups, processes, or even applications are ultimately too different to filter out a single 'silver-bullet solution".

At the lowest level (*building block 1*), structures and data hubs form the foundation for collecting and processing data of all kinds, for example via *Customer Data Platforms* (CDPs). The most used are *Data Management Platforms* (DMPs), which aggregate anonymous user data and offer it for sale. Increasingly, DMPs are being replaced by CDPs or are being functionally merged with them. The emergence of CDPs (and public clouds) has decoupled the data layer from a channel-specific application and activation (e.g. in E-Mail engines and programmatic shopping tools), although campaigning is included in some CDPs. CDPs "morph" in a way similar towards other applications. In addition to core functions such as data management (e.g. the normalisation of customer history on the basis of party data), ID management or native integration with other databases and providers is provided, so that they overlap with components in the area of analytics and orchestration (e.g. via customer journey mapping and campaigning), audience segmentation, or marketing automation (in the direction of *Multichannel Marketing Hubs*). Providers like *Tealium* have more than 1000 native connectors for this, including their Data Connect for a no-code, automated data feed. While, from the software provider's point of view, many marketing tech applications are thus increasingly losing sight of their original focus on function, on the part of the user companies there is a trend towards *decomposition*: application and data layers are increasingly being separated from each other as a design principle of the software architecture in order to allow maximum freedom and flexibility in the processes and applications required for this—following the basic idea of *service oriented* or *composable architecture*.

> *… future marketing automation and E-Mail platforms will not have databases.* (Alfonso, 2021)

The spectrum of analytics applications in *building block 2* ranges from simple reporting to the analysis of attribution throughout the customer journey, to the optimisation of all measures and channels alongside defined KPIs (*Marketing Spend Optimisation /Mix Modelling*).

The planning process starts in *building block 3* and is based on data and analytics from *Marketing Resource Management* (MRM). This includes all applications for planning, budgeting, and financial accounting, such as marketing calendars, workflows, task lists, and budget management—including synchronisation with the cost centre in ERP via interfaces, WBS elements, or internal orders.

The orchestration of customer interactions in *building block 4* includes, among other things, simple segmentation, the dynamic provision of content via *Content Management Systems*, and Next Best Offers (NBOs) as a targeted approach towards a user at the right time with the right offer based on real-time analytics and A/B

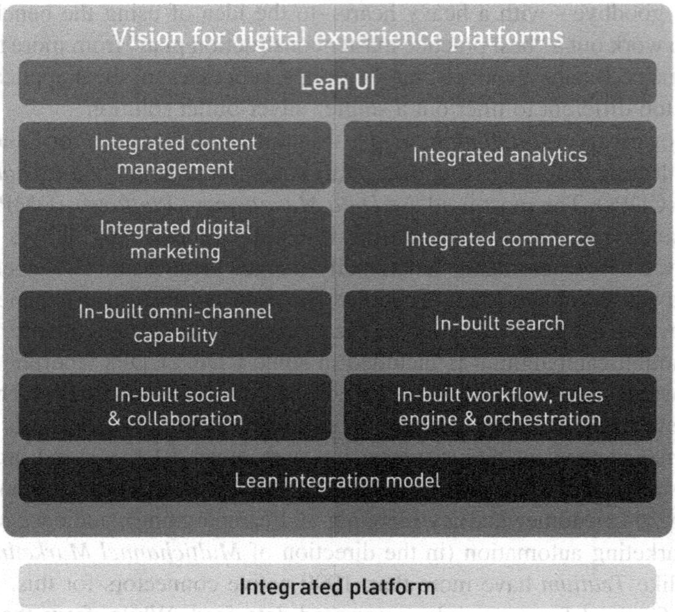

Fig. 1.2 Evolution of Portals and CMS systems into Digital Experience Platforms (DXPs; target picture; Marketing Tech Monitor 2021) (See also Third Door Media: Enterprise Digital Experience Platforms, A Marketer's Guide, February 2022)

(or multivariate) testing (content vs audiences). *CRM* suites take on an overarching role in this case (often bundled within a "Marketing Cloud"), since most often they have multilayered modules and functions—from MRM to Segmentation to Loyalty Management and Campaign Execution Management, including sub-elements of a CDP. More recently, (Web) *Digital Experience Platforms* (DXPs) have become an integrated technology approach based on a general platform that allows personalised access to information and applications via different digital touchpoints. The core functionalities include (Fig. 1.2):

- content management, incl. DAM, as well as PIM functions.
- content delivery, presentation, and orchestration (CMS).
- personalisation, cross-platform.
- analysis and optimisation logics.
- (rudimentary) management of customer data.
- commerce functions (incl. payment gateways), CRM functions (e.g. campaign management and MRM).
- using no-code development platforms.

Most of the applications positioned as a DXP have their origin in (Grannan, 2020):

- *Content Management Systems* (CMS): A collection of anonymised audience segments along the entire funnel, such as *Oracle CX Content, Adobe Experience Manager, Sitecore Experience Platform,* or *Kentico*. DXPs from this provenance tend to focus on web-based analyses, user segmentation, targeting, and E-Mail campaigns. Strengths are usually found in sophisticated tracking functions.
- *Portal-based DXPs*: These are particularly suitable for maintaining long-term customer relationships in the after-sales/service area, especially if these have evolved from earlier (self-service) customer portals. As with *Backbone* or *Liferay*, the focus is on analysis (via metrics à la NPS), the factors that encourage customer loyalty as well as new product purchases. Similarly, portal-based DXPs support application scenarios for the integration of further target groups such as partners, suppliers, or franchisees. The main functions are content management, targeting, support for mobile devices, workflow, and forms, but also self-services. The strengths usually lie in a deep integration of divergent functions and a user-individual (vs aggregated) storage of customer data.
- *E-commerce-based DXPs*: In addition to the product-related content in the front-end of an e-commerce store, these applications usually also offer functions related to inventory management, the shopping basket, payment integration, check-out, or fulfilment (connection to order management in the ERP system). Many e-commerce products such as *SAP Hybris* or *Demandware* have been supplemented with content management functions to support the promotion of products (catalogue). Weaknesses are usually found in inadequately implemented targeting functions, a CMS that is difficult to use, and only limited suitability for deeper integration scenarios in a more extensive MarTech architecture.

In addition to more traditional interaction mechanisms, *building block 5* includes AdTech components such as *Demand-Side Platforms* (DSPs) in a comprehensive *Multichannel Campaign Management* system. DSPs allow the efficient purchase of advertising inventory across different supply channels (e.g. ad networks, ad exchanges, and SSPs) from a central platform, including closed DSPs (e.g. from *Google* or *Facebook*) as walled gardens. *Supply-Side Platforms* (SSPs) take over the best-possible monetisation of existing advertising inventory for publishers. In real time, these offer advertisers advertising contacts that are most suitable for them in each case. SSPs simplify and improve the automatic management of advertising space for publishers and the selling of space at optimal prices, based on algorithms.

The basis of success in programmatic advertising is *header bidding*, as a sell-side technology that enables publishers to offer ad impressions on several advertising marketplaces such as ad exchanges, ad networks, or SSPs. This contrasts with the classic waterfall model, in which different advertising marketplaces are switched one after the other.

Consent management will continue to be highly important over the coming years—thanks to the EU GDPR and ePrivacy Directive, as will social media with *TikTok* and *Twitch*, among others.

Dynamic Creative Optimisation (DCO) refers to the technical and content-related process of personalising advertising. DCO campaigns can display advertising material that is composed of many small elements such as headlines, images, content, and call-to-action buttons. From the sum of the individual elements, ads are generated that can address users individually and in a differentiated way dynamically, in real time and optimised for multiple devices. Often, DCOs are connected to price feeds that, in addition to communication, also provide individualised prices or are used in retargeting.

In *Tag Management*, tracking pixels and tags are managed and controlled with the help of special containers. The tag manager is the crucial point for exchanging data with third-party systems such as analytics, social media, or media agencies. Users can administer tags and define rights for data transfer without having to intervene in the programming of an individual website every time a change is made.

Attribution Systems track the customer journey across different placements and touchpoints and then analyse the impact of the respective contribution. Newer developments additionally model offline information within the customer journey using a unified marketing impact analysis *(UMIA)* for holistic marketing spend optimisation. The next step will probably be further AI-enhanced tools for decision-making support as a kind of management information system (MIS), which incorporate the rankings from data science models.

> *We need to map holistic customer journeys ... and need measurement routes that can be transparently measured across channels.*—Benedikt Schaumann (Head of Consumer Communication Services, Nestlé).

Finally, *ad verification systems* provide test modules, such as whether a campaign has been delivered visibly or in a (brand) safe environment, whether the advertising material has been presented on the screen with the expected or booked visibility, whether a booked exclusion of competitor brands has been observed or whether the campaign is running in the booked regions (geo-targeting).

1.2 Empirical Foundation: The *Marketing Tech Monitor*

The empirical foundation is the yearly Marketing Tech Monitor since 2019. Here, every year between 1400 and 1600 marketing managers and CMOs have been surveyed for their strategies, usage, and hurdles on the way into data-driven marketing and sales, resulting in 280–370 completed responses each year. The quantitative survey was complemented each year by ca. *30 personal 1:1 interviews, summing up to almost 182 qualitative interviews since 2019.*

As part of the *Marketing Tech Monitor*, between 1400 and 1600 CMOs, marketing managers and Board members for marketing and sales, as well as digital/online marketing managers have been targeted every year since 2019 based on the databases of the *CMO Community* and the *Digital CMO Community*. This always resulted in between 280 and 370 completed responses each year. In parallel, a total of around 182 qualitative expert interviews have been conducted to provide more in-depth information over the years. The focus was alternately on different focus topics, such as:

- the use of technologies, in-house vs outsourcing, the role of agencies and walled gardens, and the question of "platform/suite vs best-of-breed",
- the trends in the use of different applications (e.g. inventory, required upgrades and tenders), the planned use in future within the context of "marketing performance management", as well as the pressure on marketing organisations to provide the required capabilities and know-how,
- providing a forum for questions about strategy and target pictures, control instruments (KPI frameworks), data use, necessary project organisations for implementation, as well as the challenges during implementation,
- integration architectures, efficient project organisation, benchmarking, first-party data strategies, marketing spend optimisation/data science, or even blockchain, and
- marketing budgets, the cooperation between marketing and IT, different maturity levels in architectures, customer journey analysis and mapping, or even the use of artificial intelligence and loyalty programs.

References

Alfonso, D. (2021, February 11). *4 disruptive, uncomfortable, yet inevitable MarTech trends*. MarTechToday.

Grannan, M. (2020, July 9). *DX platform: Strategy, software, or both?* Forrester, Blog.

The Strategic Imperative . . . Providing the Groundwork

2

2.1 Cascading from Strategy to Applications: The MarTech Cube

Companies successfully using MarTech or CustomerTech require to cascade from strategy, KPI frameworks, across processes, down to the application level. The focus should not be on the optimisation of a singular layer (horizontally), but rather the optimisation across the 10 different layers (vertically). In essence, to bring together a cross-functional orchestra instead of a plenitude of (functional) soloists.

Many concepts for the digitalisation of marketing are heavily based on the operational introduction of individual, singular, and rarely integrated IT applications. When it comes to choosing a marketing tech strategy, companies are faced with the challenge of having to select from a myriad of around 14,106 different applications (as of May 2024) (Brinker & Riemersma, 2024). The much-vaunted consolidation is still a long time coming, and categorisation is also becoming increasingly difficult, as many platforms bundle and designate the most diverse functions in their own way (Brearton, 2022).

> *It is really funny to state . . . everybody expected a consolidation of tools in the martech space . . . but the opposite happened and the number of tools increased even furthermore* (Brinker, 2021).—Scott Brinker (Editor, chiefmartec.com).

Zylo, a SaaS governance software for monitoring and licence management, showed in the *SaaS Management Index* from 2022 onwards that small and medium-sized enterprises have an average of 217 applications, while larger companies have 330 applications and corporations up to 609 IT applications (Zylo, 2022, 2024). On average, eight more applications are added to the MarTech stack . . . every month. On average, companies only use half (49%) of their SaaS licences. In plain language: 51% of applications sit on the shelf . . . fully paid for, . . .

R. Strauss, *Data-Driven Customer Engagement*,
https://doi.org/10.1007/978-3-031-64295-1_2

but unused. On average, a company wastes US$ 18 million/year, an increase of 7% p.a. The costs for larger companies (with more than 10,000 employees) add up to an incredible US$ 127 million/year. Only 27% of SaaS applications are under the control of IT—and this has continued to decline at a rate of 35% on average over the last few years. The growing sovereignty over IT spending in the business department correlates with the effective use rate of the applications. In other words, the apparently well-considered (painful) investment decision within the business department subsequently also fuels the effective use of the applications. The nucleus of all MarTech discussions thus increasingly arises from the business strategy, professional demand, and pressure and operates less as an "IT project".

Picking tools is no rocket science . . . the market is full of them . . . the magic is in the intelligent integration and activation of their possibilities.—Kirsten Nachtigall (Vice President Marketing, RTL Germany).

A strategy-driven approach to implementing data-driven marketing and sales cascades across ten fundamental levels as a "*MarTech cube*" or "*CustomerTech cube*" (Fig. 2.1):

- The (1st) *strategy and business level* examines how value (e.g. products or services) is created between different business partners. In this case, two complementary development paths can be found at the core:
  - *Customer centricity (external orientation)*: The customer as the starting point of all value chains; the best-possible catering to customer needs and wishes in the respective context and across touchpoints in the context of sales/marketing, but also service/dialogue (next evolution).
  - *Performance management (internal orientation)*: As marketing operations management, the internal efficient orchestration of all processes, budgets, personnel, data, applications, and projects.
- Based on the first level, the (2nd) *level of planning and control* describes the goals, metrics, and key performance indicators (KPIs) for implementing the strategy once it has been adopted, such as which methods (model development such as a KPI framework) are used to optimise it and in which lifecycle/journey phase the greatest potential is to be expected.
- How the strategy and target systems can be efficiently anchored in the organisation within the framework of *change management* is covered in the next (3rd) level.
- The (4th) *organisation and process level* describes the interaction between two or more business areas or departments (e.g. marketing and supply chain or similar) with one or more business partners.
- The (5th) *requirements engineering level* involves the determination of requirements for IT applications from the perspective of the strategy and processes.
- The (6th) *application level* details how processes are (supposed to be) supported by the information system, for instance functions or data of an information system are called up or used by another information system or user.

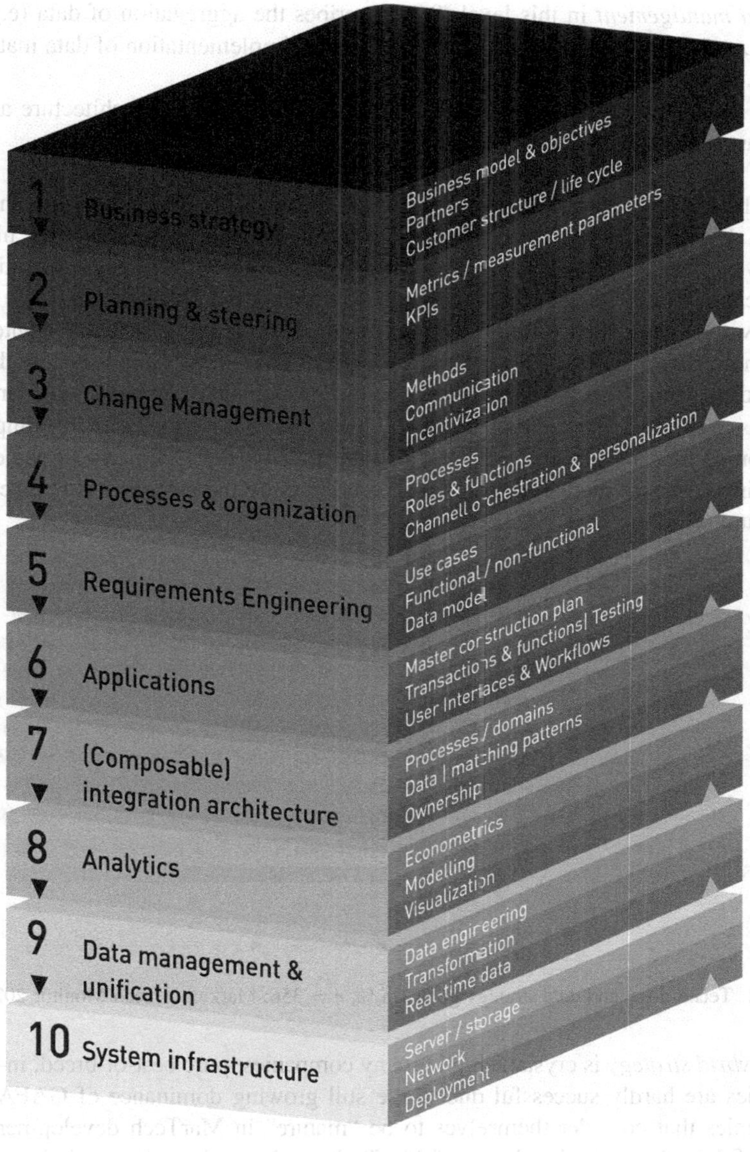

Fig. 2.1 MarTech or CustomerTech cube—levels for cascading the strategy down to the level of processes, applications, and data in data-driven marketing and sales (Marketing Tech Monitor 2024)

- The (7th) *integration level* establishes the connection between processes and data. Integration takes place between two or more systems (internal/external). The connection can be both synchronous (real-time) and asynchronous (batch).
- At the (8th) *analytics level*, the focus is on the visualisation and interpretation of data, for example based on econometric modelling (data science) or personalisation.

- *Data management* in this level (9th) describes the aggregation of data (e.g. via ETL operations and data fabrics) as well as the implementation of data matching (e.g. the creation of look-alike audiences).
- The (10th) *technical level* looks at the underlying technical architecture and its components such as network or deployment (e.g. cloud vs on premise).

At the top level (business strategy), the journey to data-driven customer interaction is driven by better customer service through personalisation (58%, highest priority), better insights along the customer journey (38%), and the integration of all touchpoints (34%) (Fig. 2.2). This puts customer retention at the top of the list—not new customer acquisition—which consequently requires scalable content in combination with data. The aggregation of various data sources allows the modelling of customer interaction along preferences and, consequently, the increase of long-tail sales as well as higher interaction rates. Personalisation creates trust: simplified decision-making by the user creates customer loyalty, the (subjectively perceived) switching costs are increased, and waste in addressing the customer is reduced to a minimum (Houlind et al., 2023).

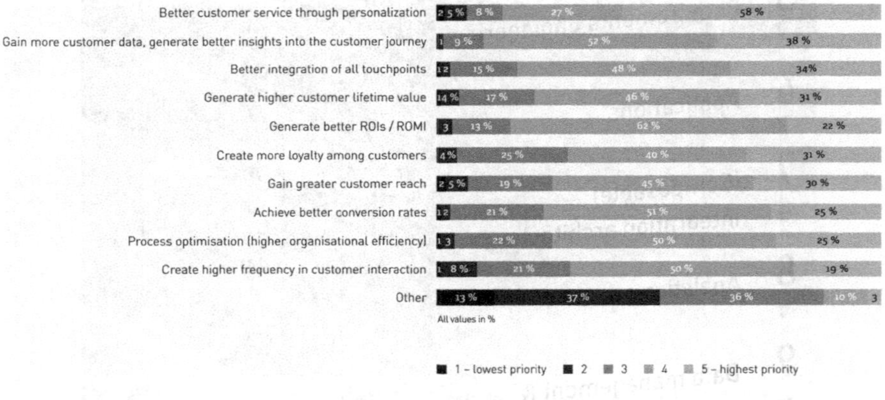

Fig. 2.2 Technology and data strategy goals (in %, $n = 356$; Marketing Tech Monitor 2023)

A *hybrid strategy* is crystallising in many companies: pure best-of-breed, in-house strategies are hardly successful due to the still growing dominance of GAFA data. Companies that consider themselves to be "mature" in MarTech development and successful in the operational use of MarTech tend to rely more on in-house and autonomy in core areas such as data infrastructure (e.g. via a CDP), the collection of own first-party data, and analytics on top (i.e. marketing mix modelling).

Regardless of whether you are a startup, a medium-sized company or a corporate group—anyone who does not vehemently collect party data will have a hard time with cross-platform, target-group-specific ad targeting in the coming years after the 3rd *party cookies have been banned.*—Carlos Yniguez (Managing Director Digital Unit, Bitburger Breweries).

The most important drivers for the development of a MarTech strategy and implementation are the combination of efficiency losses or increasing media inflation and the progressive fragmentation of touchpoints (78%), in combination with the elimination of third-party cookies (66%) as well as a lack of a customer experience or customer satisfaction (65%). Here, too, customer experience management proves to be the root cause, catalyst, and (innovation) driver of MarketingTech (Fig. 2.3).

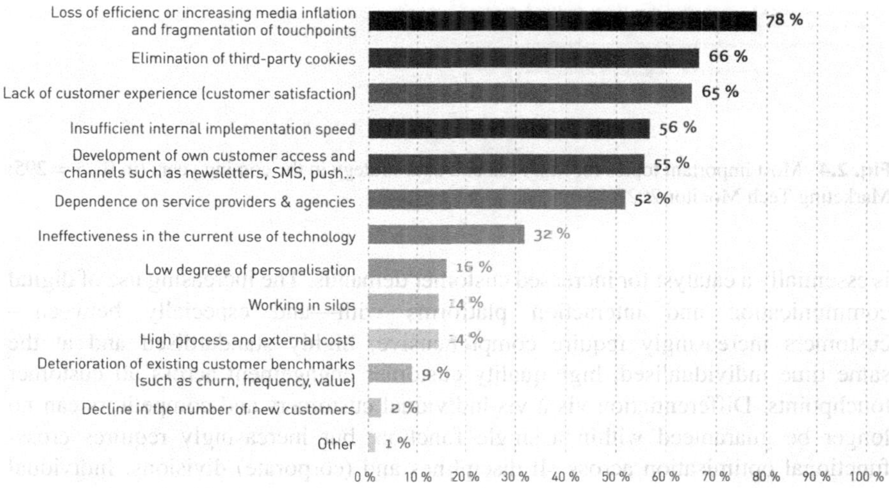

Fig. 2.3 Drivers of marketing technology and data strategy (in %, $n = 295$; Marketing Tech Monitor 2022)

While the use of MarTech in previous years was more focused on streamlining media buying processes and internal processes, the consolidation of the data landscape or data strategy (79%), the completion of the marketing technology landscape (66%), and the development of MarTech know-how (64%) are increasingly relegating these processes to second place (Fig. 2.4). The reason is trivial: an efficient user approach requires first-party data. Companies fall in one of two categories: either they use hardly any tools, or they use simply too many different tools that require a dedicated lifecycle management for planning the development of the entire application landscape.

> *The goal for us is to bring all the tools together … and to be able to take an end-to-end process perspective.*—Antonia Lepore (Head of Marketing, AXA Switzerland).

The overwhelming majority of respondents stated that *customer experience management* (CEM) will be a prominent focus of their work in the coming years (81%). In this context, analyses and projects prove that customer experience design

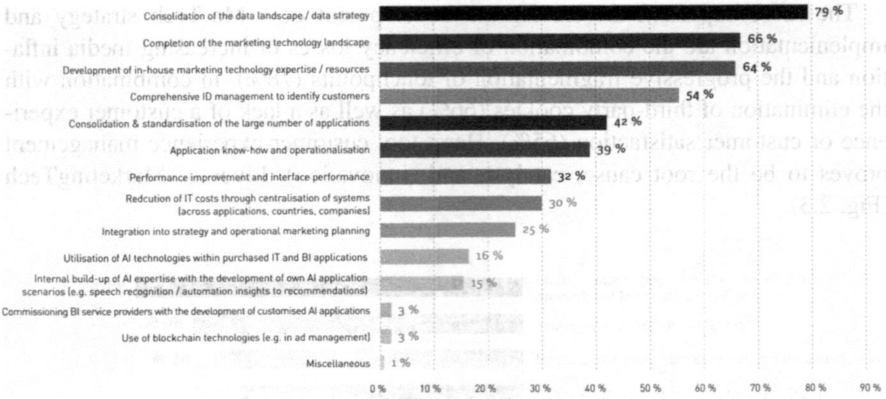

Fig. 2.4 Most important topics for MarTech and data strategy in the coming years (in %, $n = 295$; Marketing Tech Monitor 2022)

is essentially a catalyst for increased customer demands. The increasing use of digital communication and interaction platforms with—and especially between—customers increasingly require comprehensive, highly standardised and at the same time individualised, high-quality customer engagement across all customer touchpoints. Differentiation vis à vis individual customers and competitors can no longer be guaranteed within a single function, but increasingly requires cross-functional optimisation across all disciplines and (corporate) divisions. Individual topics must be addressed in dedicated projects, but these individual projects must contribute to an overall goal. The higher the share of services in the respective product/solution offering, the greater the focus on CEM . . . and the perceived risk if the transformation is not successful (Fig. 2.5).

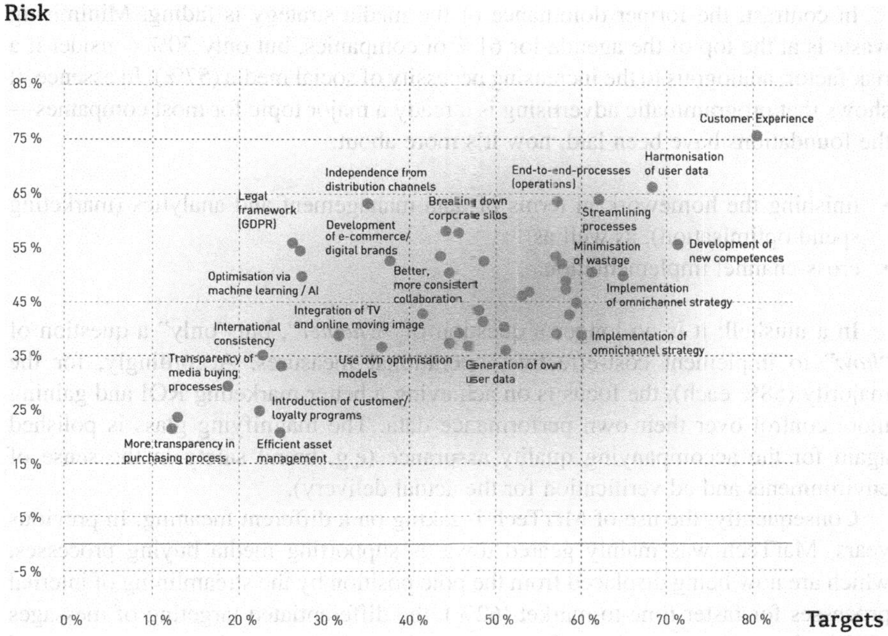

Fig. 2.5 Strategic prioritisation matrix of targets/objectives for the coming years and risks to a company's existence and competitiveness if the transformation process fails (in %, multiple answers, different number of cases; Marketing Tech Monitor 2021)

Therefore, the greatest strategic potential of risk lies in customer experience design and, for the majority, goes hand in hand with the further digitalisation of end-customer communication (60%) and differentiation into individual/micro-target groups (53%). The basis for customer centricity is the consolidation/harmonisation of user data (68% Fig. 2.6), followed by the generation of own (first-party) user data (60%). Risks are seen in securing the legal framework, in line with GDPR (56%). Alarmingly, the concept and the advantages of a cross-channel ID have not yet reached the desks and minds of most marketing decision-makers.

	Strategic Objectives	Risk Assessment	Delta
Consolidation and Harmonization of User Data	68 %	66 %	2 %
Generation of Own User Data	60 %	40 %	20 %
Development of a Cross Channel ID	47 %	52 %	-5 %
More Control on User Data	47 %	37 %	10 %
Securing juridical governance for a customer centric communication (GDPR)	26 %	56 %	-30 %
Implementation of loyalty program	21 %	25 %	-4 %
None of the above	7 %	16 %	-9 %

Fig. 2.6 Objectives around customer centricity in the coming years and risks for the company's existence and competitiveness if the transformation fails (in %, multiple answers, different number of cases (Marketing Tech Monitor 2022)

In contrast, the former dominance of the media strategy is fading. Minimising waste is at the top of the agenda for 61% of companies, but only 50% consider it a risk factor, analogous to the increasing necessity of social media (57%). In essence, it shows that programmatic advertising is already a major topic for most companies—the foundations have been laid, now it's more about:

- finishing the homework in terms of data management and analytics (marketing spend optimisation), as well as
- cross-channel implementation.

In a nutshell: it is no longer a question of "*whether*", but "only" a question of "*how*" to implement cost-effective, operational measures. Accordingly, for the majority (58% each), the focus is on achieving a better marketing ROI and gaining more control over their own performance data. The magnifying glass is polished again for the accompanying quality assurance (e.g. brand safety in the sense of environments and ad verification for the actual delivery).

Consequently, the use of MarTech is taking on a different meaning. In previous years, MarTech was mainly geared towards supporting media buying processes, which are now being displaced from the pole position by the streamlining of internal processes for faster time-to-market (62%), the differentiated targeting of messages (58%), better/faster options for optimisation (49%), or the automation and standardisation of processes within the framework of an emerging *Marketing Operations Management* function. This ranges from the campaign process and product development to the control of new product launches and internal projects such as the selection and implementation of a CDP or CRM system.

The analysis of the top five objectives and associated risks for the existence and competitiveness of a company underlines the importance of CEM, hand in hand with the development of new competences, the harmonisation of data, as well as the development of an efficient marketing operations function. The desire for competences in the environment of data-driven marketing and marketing tech still lags the articulated claim—even in the self-perception—of most marketing managers and Boards. This reveals an inherent contradiction between the importance of digital skills, on the one hand, and their own (actual) skills or concrete implementation, on the other. A further development and expansion of competences—not only paying lip service—appears to be imperative.

It is even more astonishing that managers themselves—as well as companies—make comparatively little effort to build up the necessary competences, for example through *training*. The topic is rarely addressed systematically and in a structured way in training courses. In some cases, training takes place, but then more likely on "trendy lifestyle" topics à la "digital life" and less on the basics and connections along the ten levels of the magic cube of data-driven marketing (the "MarTech cube"). Like the "chicken-and-egg problem": the exchange of experience requires experienced and competent discussion partners, which can hardly exist without the appropriate systematic teaching and internalisation of specific competences. Prominent role models such as a "digital leader" from *Amazon* et al. or even case studies from other companies are much less important than the public discussion about supposed "best practices" would suggest. These role models hardly help with the specific challenges of companies in reality. This applies more to:

- the success of competitors with a similar structure and similar market conditions,
- the successful testing of new applications and scenarios in one's own company and, above all,
- the example and conviction of the company's management.

In the opinion of the decision-makers, further postponement of the unanimously proclaimed need for training goes hand in hand with the danger of recklessly squandering existing competitive advantages.

This form of inconsistency runs like a common thread through the discussion about the development/expansion of data-driven marketing and the necessity of having to invest considerably in MarTech compared to the past. Three-fourths of the CMOs and marketing managers attest to a high degree of awareness of the risks of a failed transformation process in their company (74%), in contrast to a considerable lack of consistency in more advanced companies (44%, Fig. 2.7). The accompanying interviews show that about two-thirds of the companies perceive themselves to be partly in the "nirvana of tech despair" and "lost in the shuffle".

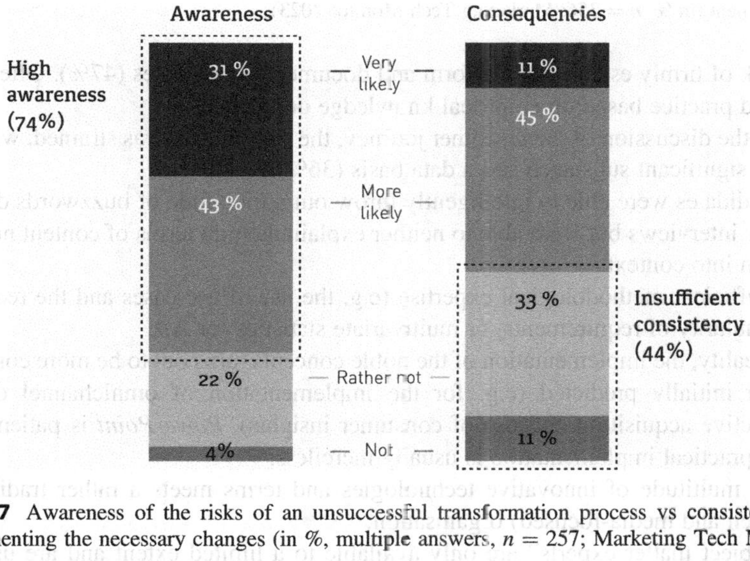

Fig. 2.7 Awareness of the risks of an unsuccessful transformation process vs consistency in implementing the necessary changes (in %, multiple answers, $n = 257$; Marketing Tech Monitor 2021)

The vision is willing, only the strategy for implementation and operationalisation are weak. The strategy is usually defined and (more or less) anchored in the organisation. However, the organisation, the IT applications in use and data management are hardly able to follow the *PowerPoint*-driven and often theory-soaked strategy concepts (Fig. 2.8). The reasons for this (as in previous years) are articulated in a *strategy and implementation gap*:

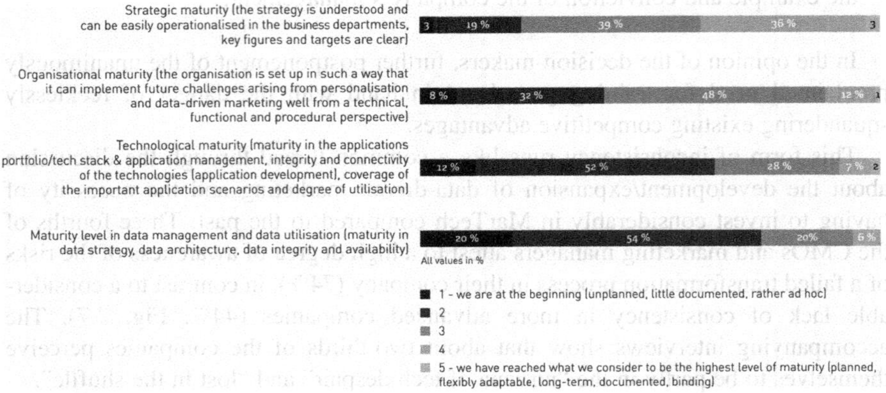

Fig. 2.8 Assessment of the maturity level across strategy, organisation, technology, and data management (in %, $n = 356$; Marketing Tech Monitor 2023)

- Lack of firmly established uniform and documented processes (47%). Often, the lived practice based on empirical knowledge dominates.
- For the discussion of the customer journey, the subjunctive was strained, without any significant substance and a data basis (36%).
- Candidates were able to intelligently throw out a multitude of buzzwords during their interviews but were able to neither explain them in terms of content nor put them into context.
- Insufficient methodological expertise (e.g. the use of use cases and the required granularity of requirements, or multivariate statistics for AI).
- In reality, the implementation of the noble concepts turns out to be more complex than initially predicted (e.g. for the implementation of omnichannel or the effective acquisition and use of consumer insights). *PowerPoint* is patient, but the practical implementation is usually merciless.
- The multitude of innovative technologies and terms meets a rather traditional (reach and media-focused) organisation.
- "Subject matter experts" are only available to a limited extent and are usually already overbooked for other projects. The consequence: time delays and insufficient depth in terms of content and concept. Accordingly, attempts are made to implement the projects step by step even without the necessary competences ... with all the difficulties and risks this entails.

- A lack of competences across the whole organisation is complained about, but not rectified with specific trainings. The need for training ranges from classic media topics to the basics of statistical analysis, buying classic and digital media, metrics, creating KPIs and assigning quality criteria per platform, frequency capping, basic analytics (e.g. *Google Analytics 4*), attribution, data management, audience building, or even marketing tech tools (incl. the project approach and setting).
- There are still a lot of hurdles as well as security issues (e.g. data security and GDPR).
- The availability of experienced project managers who can also say "no" in the case of escalating and overloading requirements and (tacit) extensions of a once approved scope.
- There is only rudimentary interaction between business and IT for further digitalisation. The tribal feuds that have been lovingly cultivated over the last few years are celebrated, in line with the movie "*All the way, [business and IT] boys*".
- Digital issues were outsourced to external agencies for cost/time reasons (with sometimes unclear legal data access and ownership).
- "*Failure by design*": Lamentations about a lack of competences go hand in hand with a lack of dedicated further education or training in the respective topics.
- The implementation of the noble concepts turns out to be more complex than initially predicted—for example, for the implementation of omnichannel, digitalisation in sales, or the effective acquisition and use of consumer insights.
- A multitude of (perceived) hurdles and uncertainties regarding data protection (e.g. GDPR) and security.

> *We try to find an intelligent mix between insourcing and outsourcing. We tend to outsource everything transactional, but we must develop strategic and conceptual topics in-house …*—Adriana Nuneva (CDO, Head of Marketing & Sales, CWS International).

According to *Machiavelli*, "*one change always causes another change*". In practice, difficulties usually arise in the interaction between IT, logistics/SCM, and the corporate culture. The consequence: Some omnichannel projects start out like *John Wayne* only to end up as *Monty Python*.

While the vast majority still consider themselves sufficiently prepared from the point of view of corporate goals and legal challenges (83%), the "island of bliss" is fading regarding marketing and communication strategies, data, or even technologies (Fig. 2.9). The majority puts a question mark on the existence of competencies both in marketing as a whole and in sub-topics such as data and technologies. Yesterday's defeat, as the "physics of power" teaches us, sometimes carries with it tomorrow's victory: The more companies deal with all the issues surrounding data-driven marketing and the digitalisation of customer interaction, the more critically competencies and previously announced strategies are questioned … and thus the foundation for the future is laid.

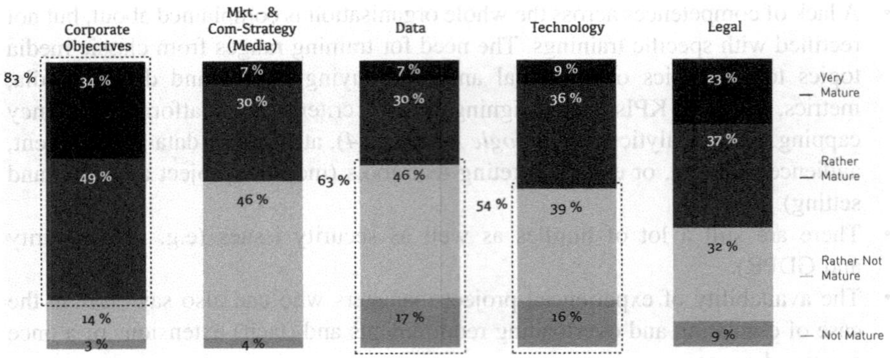

Fig. 2.9 Assessment of competences to meet challenges (in %, multiple answers, $n = 257$; Marketing Tech Monitor 2021)

In the leap from the initial phase (build-up) to the second phase (completion), the organisational *maturity level* records the greatest increase in most companies. In other words, after a (wild) first phase as a "software shopping queen", there is no way around the subsequent expansion of capabilities within the organisation. If the organisational maturity level is low, a disproportionate number of resources are consumed by (internal) processes and integration services. Only a higher organisational maturity level opens the door to serious customer centricity, beyond dealing with internal insufficiencies.

The goal is to turn every customer contact into a (personalised) data point—via anonymous website visitors to registration in the form of higher-value PII data (Fig. 2.10). The end of third-party cookies in 2025 (latest) will fundamentally change

	1st Party Data	2nd Party Data	3rd Party Data	ID-Networks / Supplement 3rd Party
Data types	**PII data =** personally identifiable information, e.g., e-mail, name, postal address, telephone number and purchase data	**PII data** from cooperations with card programs (e.g. Miles & More)		
	Personal but anonymous data, e.g., pseudonymous cookie ID, device ID, or advertising ID, IP address, other pseudonymous end user identifiers	**Personalised but anonymous data,** e.g., from cooperation with retailers (Retail Media)	**Personalised** but anonymous data from campaign tracking on external sites	**Personalised but anonymous data,** e.g., pseudonymous cookie ID or advertising ID, IP address, other pseudonymous end user identifiers
	Transactions and behavioural data	**Transaction data and behavioural data**	**Behavioural data**	
Data sources	POS, website, call centre (CDP/CRM)	Agencies, partners, DSPs, SSPs, ad servers	Professional data aggregators, third-party service providers such as credit agencies, publishers, social widget providers, Google marketing platforms, retargeting providers	ID networks such as ID+, NetID, ...
Acquisition	Own collection, expansion with customers via incentive systems	Contracts with partners, agencies	can be purchased / traded via DSPs	Networks offer ID matching (often via e-mail as identifier) plus possible data enrichment

Fig. 2.10 Data types and sources for developing a data strategy

the way advertising and content can be targeted, measured, and tracked—more and more first-party data strategies including contextual/probabilistic methods or ID solutions gain prominence.

Part of the MarTech strategy should be an (at least rough) *business case*. This is less a detailed analysis of all parameters and more a rough calculation of the extent to which the budgets set up at the beginning can be classified as sufficient for achieving the objectives, and what implications arise with regard to overall profitability. The informative value and validity of the business case depends largely on the quality and detail of the input variables such as the business model, the definition and delimitation of the relevant market, or the use of benchmarks for process changes. For the majority of MarTech projects, at least a basic business case is calculated (65%), followed by an investment in the future and competitiveness (26%). A rather abstract "future viability" usually opens the door to arbitrariness—both in a positive and a negative way.

Project experiences underline that even simple plausibility checks (e.g. with regard to average turnover per customer or relative market share) are often omitted during the development of the business case, as is the consideration of different conditions during a *sensitivity analysis*. For the estimation of cost–benefit effects, different scenarios can be evaluated in terms of a "best case", "worst case", and most probable case ("real case"), which allows an assessment of the economic risk.

> *A reliable ROI or CLV calculation helps—for this we only need to address offline media, including a reliable attribution*—Kirsten Nachtigall (Vice President Marketing, RTL Germany).

Realistically, the development and use of a business case, once it has been developed, often turns out to be rather questionable—and in view of a VUKA world, it can certainly hardly fulfil the self-imposed requirements, even if it may help to at least get a feeling for the magnitudes and mechanics of an envisaged project success:

- *Reality check*: Conceptually and theoretically correct assumptions certainly do not stand up to a pragmatic reality test. In the automotive sector, for example, extensive business cases for the introduction of a global CRM system were calculated down to the retail level—starting with the manufacturers' (OEM) strategy and going to the country organisations (wholesale/distribution) down to the level of the individual (mostly legally independent) car dealers. The focus of the benefits reported was on gaining additional time for the (potential) sale of new cars. On the dealership/retail level, this benefit, (formally correct and consistent) and certified by corporate financial accounting of the OEM, rather caused amusement among the dealers concerned in view of its unrealistic nature.
- *Wishful thinking*: The business case is usually needed for fundamental decisions at the management level. Since the actors involved will (or want to) subsequently take on project roles, the business case presents itself as an instrument for

checking the plausibility and approval of a project application. *Honni soit qui mal y pense.*

- *Paralysis by analysis*: The multitude of details leads to the interesting mechanics of a comprehensive business case getting lost in the sea of the most diverse hypotheses.
- *Self-fulfilling prophecy*: After the adoption of a (usually over-ambitious) business case, all possible efforts are made (against better judgement and experience) to achieve this business case and the associated milestones—sometimes against all reason. This means the project starts off with a heavy mortgage. Failure by design . . . again.

2.2 Meet Me at the Kissing (Touch) Point: Customer Journey Analysis Rediscovered

The customer journey analysis (outside-in) as the path of a potential customer from the first contact with a company, a product, or a service to the conclusion of a purchase and beyond as the foundation of MarTech is missing in most companies. Hence, the conceptual (process-oriented) basis for a successful implementation is not available.

Contrary to all the discussions and praise over the last few years, there is a lack of basic principles for the implementation of MarTech. Only just under 8% of company representatives state that they have defined their customer journey in both the macro- and micro-processes and have documented user models (Fig. 2.11). Across Europe,

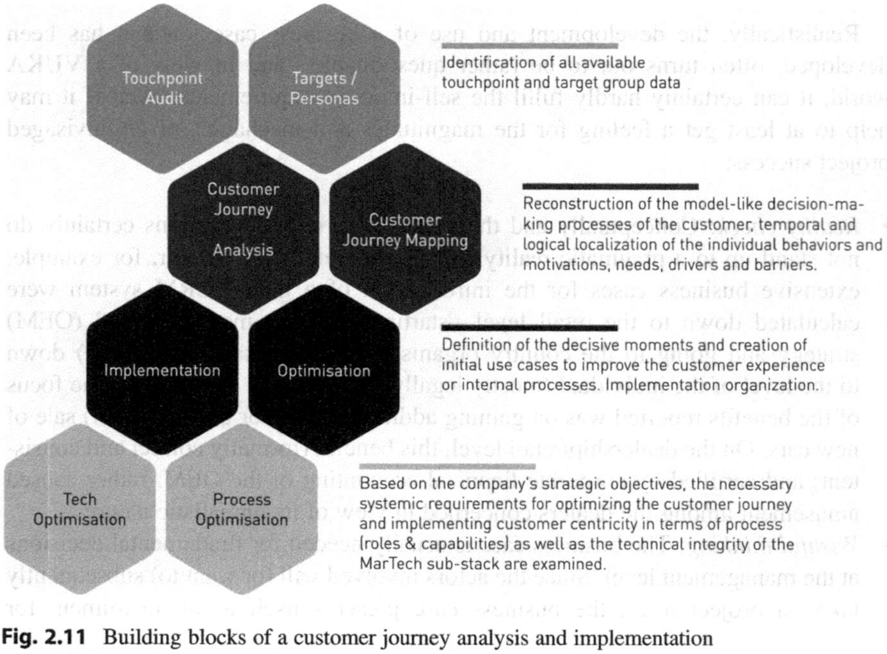

Fig. 2.11 Building blocks of a customer journey analysis and implementation

this adds up to merely ca. 25% (European Marketing Confederation, 2024). The *customer journey* as the path of a potential customer from the first contact with a company, a product, or a service to the conclusion of a purchase and beyond is missing as a conceptual basis, with the necessary granularity (outside–in) and flexibility.

> *Start with the customer journey. What does the customer's experience look like? What are the different types of touchpoints that they're experiencing with your business?* (Wood, 2022)

In most cases, the "Touchpoint Tinder" lacks a continuous description of all touchpoints that a potential customer passes through on their journey across all channels of interaction, until they perform a desired action such as a purchase or a recommendation. The customer journey analysis and map must be permanently developed further, in line with the underlying customer interactions. Fundamentals such as a data strategy that is widely recognised within the company and follows the corporate strategy retain a rather theoretical "wishful thinking": only 11% proclaim this for their own company (Fig. 2.12). In other words, conceptually, companies have deficits on all ends—from strategy and target pictures to the level of requirements management.

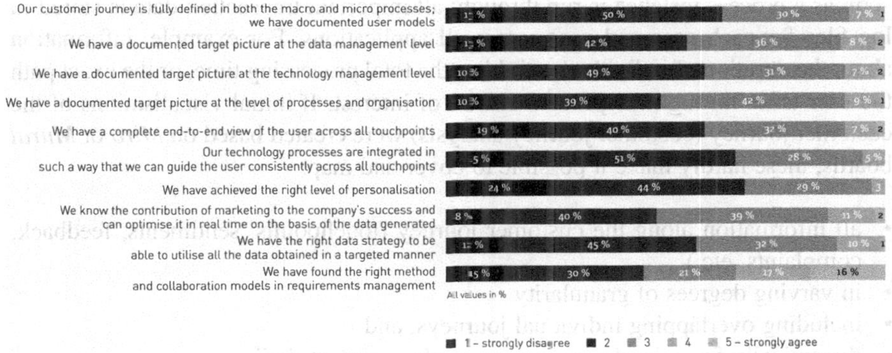

Fig. 2.12 MarTech readiness across target pictures and the customer journey (in %, $n = 356$; Marketing Tech Monitor 2023)

In each phase, the (potential) customer passes through various touchpoints until their journey ideally leads them to a purchase. In turn, this (in the best case) experience makes them a loyal customer through further, positive experiences. *Customer journey mapping* makes the complexity transparent by visualising the complete journey of the ideal, typical customer (persona) across all touchpoints (Fig. 2.13). Mapping helps to track, aggregate, analyse and, finally, evaluate singular customer experiences en masse. In this way, discrepancies between actual and

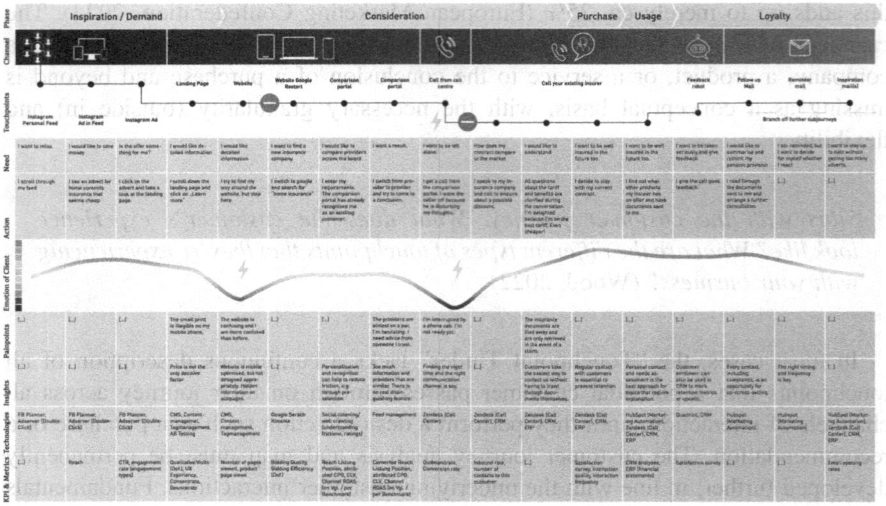

Fig. 2.13 Customer journey map (project example: insurance)

desired customer experiences and actions can be uncovered and improvements to be implemented can be pinpointed. User-related data can be supplemented by means of *process mining* via the systematic analysis and evaluation of business processes. As soon as a process instance is run through, all important transaction data is stored in log files for each case and user across all applications. For example, information about the duration of individual activities, the total processing time, or the exact path the user takes through the process can be of interest. If initial visualisations of the customer journey (customer journey analysis) were created based on *Miro* or *Mural* boards, these hardly make it possible to cover and map:

- all information along the customer journey (touchpoints, sentiments, feedback, complaints, etc.),
- in varying degrees of granularity,
- including overlapping individual journeys, and
- dynamically for a "customer journey under constant fire".

Turning water into wine for an exuberant customer journey: a complete end-to-end view of a user across all touchpoints is still lacking in almost 60% (top boxes) of companies today—accordingly, the integration of technology processes is also lagging in 66% of companies. For a better customer understanding and to uncover possible differences between actual and desired customer experiences, it can be helpful to work with different *customer journey maps* and test them against each other (Angrawe, 2020):

- *Current state*: Based on current data and the buyer persona. With the help of a map, the current actions, needs, and emotions of the persona during interaction are presented as a starting point for improvements to the overall customer experience.
- *Future state*: Presentation of different scenarios for the future customer experience, after the implementation of planned improvements.
- *Day In the Life Of (DILO)*: Combination of a customer's daily actions, needs, and emotions to identify potential pain points and tailor one's product/service offering accordingly.

The traceability of the digital customer journey is becoming increasingly difficult. This makes it more important to smartly link the available data points—online and offline.—Carlos Yniguez (Managing Director Digital Unit, Bitburger Breweries).

Customer journey mapping tools cover:

- experience mapping and visualisation tools (e.g. *Touchpoint* and *Visio*),
- customer experience software and voice-of-customer software (e.g. *Clarabridge*, *CX Omni*, *TheyDo*, and *SuiteCX*), or
- collaboration tools (e.g. *Asana*, *Mural*, and *Jive*).

and address a global software licensing market of around €10.4 billion annually with an average yearly growth rate of 17.7% (ReportLinker, 2022; Haije, 2021).
The topics and *challenges* of a customer journey analysis are as fundamental as they are trivial (Mixon & Horwitz, 2020):

- *Ignorance*: A customer journey analysis is not carried out because, based on years of experience in the market, the company is of the firm opinion that it already knows the customer and their needs or touchpoints very well . . . in particular by sales reps ("*We do know our customers!*").
- *Incompleteness*: Focus on purely increasing sales figures (inside-out), without considering the needs from the customer's point of view (outside-in).
- *Limitation to a few touchpoints* leads to a patchy customer experience journey.
- "*One-off*": Systematic monitoring and permanent implementation of this into regular processes are omitted. The customer journey study becomes "closet goods" . . . like many market research studies.
- *Lack of consistency*: No uniform value propositions across all touchpoints.

In addition to the tools level with the help of a customer journey map, there is a consistent lack of target pictures in relation to the use and activation of data, to the use of modern IT applications, or even to the structuring as building blocks of optimisation (Fig. 2.14). A lack of a conceptual foundation thus prevents an efficient personalisation (68%) or customer experience from the outset. As a result, a

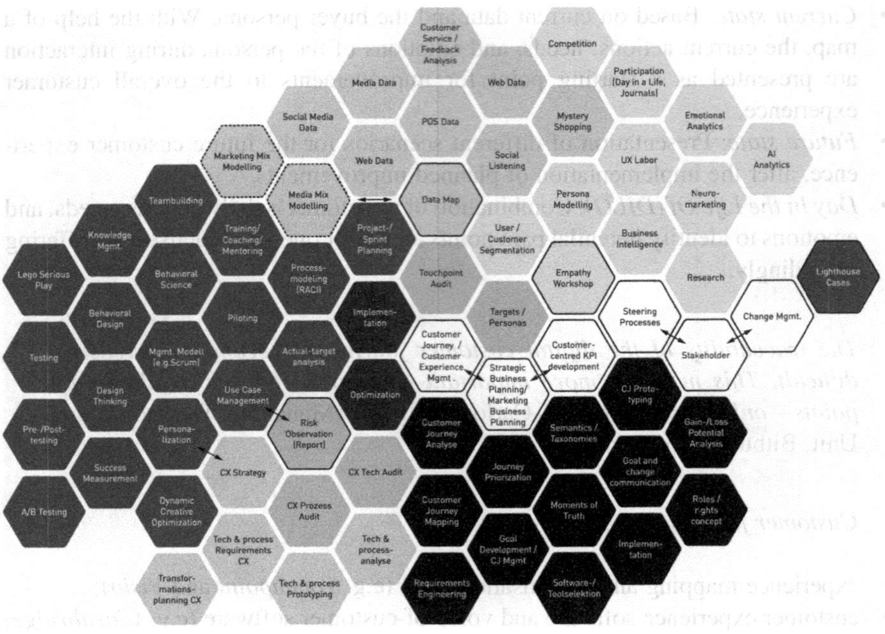

Fig. 2.14 Building blocks for customer journey optimisation

cascading of the strategy via capabilities, associated business objects and data down to the level of applications and architectures, from the customer's point of view, can hardly be achieved.

References

Angrawe, J. (2020). *The journey mapping playbook: A practical guide to preparing, facilitating and unlocking the value of customer journey mapping*.

Brearton, A. (2022, March). *Navigating the evolving MarTech landscape*. MarTech.

Brinker, S. (2021, September 15). *Keynote, marketing tech summit 2021*.

Brinker, S., & Riemersma, F. (2024, May). *MarTech for 2024*.

European Marketing Confederation. (2024, March). *European marketing agenda 2024*.

Haije, E. G. (2021, April). *Die 20 besten tools zum customer journey mapping*. Mopinion.

Houlind, R.; Riemersma, F.; Horsberg, A., & Andersson, M. (2023). *Hello $FirstName*.

Mixon, E., & Horwitz, L. (2020, June). *Customer journey mapping*. TechTarget.

ReportLinker. (2022, November). *Customer journey mapping software global market report 2022*.

Wood, C. (2022, December). *3 steps to building an effective MarTech stack*. MarTech.

Zylo. (2022, February). *2022 SaaS management index*.

Zylo. (2024, April). *2024 SaaS management index 2024*.

Let the MarTech Music Play ... Development Phases of the MarTech Universe

3

3.1 Bringing Order into Chaos ... A Fast-Growing Market Defines Its Own Structures

The analysis of maturity levels in data-driven customer interaction demonstrates that most companies are in the completion phase to expand capabilities and skills. The voyage into the MarTech universe starts in the build-up phase via *CMS and web analytics applications, followed by CRM as a "master record system". CDPs and iPaaS or integration tools are subsequently required for customer and application integration scenarios, while personalisation, attribution, and audience management tend to take the role of add-ons. In terms of usage value, CMS, CRM, and marketing automation have the most catching up to do in "fixing the basics".*

The universally invoked consolidation in the market with 14,106 applications (as of May 2024) is still a long-time coming, and categorisation is also becoming increasingly difficult, as many platforms bundle the most diverse functions in their own way and (albeit not entirely disinterestedly) label them differently (Brinker & Riemersma, 2024). The growth in the number of tools and providers seems to be immune (even without inoculation) to inflation worries and Covid and has grown about 18.5% just over a time period of 6 months. All in all, a growth of 9304% since 2011. Not surprisingly, GenAI is responsible for at least 73% of the increase—new AI-centric start-ups being in the long tail. And that is in addition to all the generative AI features that have been embedded into existing MarTech products since 2023. The other way around: the older and comparatively more "mature" a subcategory is in the market (e.g. AdTech), the more providers can be found here (Fig. 3.1).

Most of the newly created providers can be found in subject areas such as "content" and "social". The proliferation of applications, even functionally overlapping ones, will foreseeably continue to grow, differentiate, and "morph" between the categories (*atomisation* of the application landscape), which inevitably will lead to an increased need for integration and *aggregation* (aggregation). The consequence from the company/user perspective: they must fundamentally define

R. Strauss, *Data-Driven Customer Engagement*,
https://doi.org/10.1007/978-3-031-64295-1_3

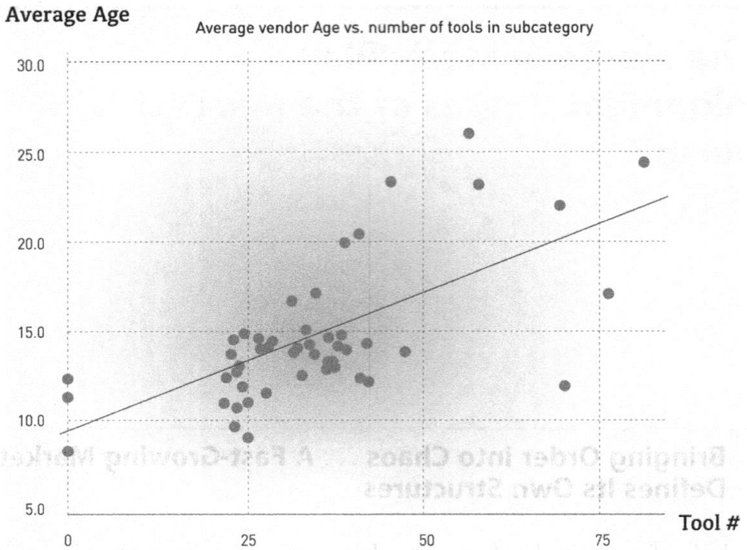

Fig. 3.1 Relationship between the number of IT applications available and the age of the application or vendor (Global MarTech vendor database, MarTechTribe.com, September 2023; Marketing Tech Monitor 2023)

the skeleton of the required processes and IT applications . . . which shall be robust and at the same time flexible for different (current/future) application scenarios.

There is no sign of Central Europe being "the late nation" according to the philosopher *Helmuth Plessner* . . . at least regarding MarTech. Contrary to intuitive expectations, the UK and Germany have a higher degree of maturity in the use of marketing technology than the USA, along the five levels of a *capability maturity model* across all benchmarks (Ilyas et al., 2023):

1. *Basic level (initial, unpredictable)*: There are no procedural models for processes or projects on the part of the company. The success or failure of a project is entirely up to the intuitive competence and skill of individuals. In crisis situations, all provisionally established structures are abandoned and replaced by ad hoc measures (provisional solutions, workarounds).
2. *Repeatable level (reactive)*: The experiences from previous projects are carefully evaluated and based on these, a procedure model for new projects is designed and declared binding. Project goals, time, and cost estimates are planned based on (realistic) experience. The costs, deadlines, and goals of the projects are systematically monitored. Projects and processes are largely stable. A basic quality assurance system is established.
3. *Defined level (proactive)*: Standard processes are fully documented and established throughout the company. These standard processes are an integral part of all trainings and the project culture. Projects/processes are always transparent and verifiable.

4. *Managed level (controlled)*: A quantified quality plan exists for both products and processes/projects. Productivity and quality are monitored through a dedicated data collection program. For this purpose, all incoming data is collected, analysed, and used for evaluation. Errors can be differentiated (statistically) in terms of causes and exceptional influences. Risk management for new processes is defined and firmly established. The predictability of process and project results is extremely high.
5. *Optimising level*: The whole organisation is in a permanent mode of improving all processes. The organisation has the tools and means to proactively identify strengths and weaknesses in the processes with the aim of avoiding errors. Best practice solutions are identified and disseminated, experience values (as "lessons learned") are collected and made available to all stakeholders. Consistent error analysis aims to prevent errors. The focus is on the reduction of errors and subsequent necessary improvement work, which lays the foundation for further differentiation of customer interaction and growth (also in terms of the number of IT applications used).

> *Fragile tech stacks break when new apps or data are added . . . antifragile [optimised] stacks gain value from new apps and data* (Taleb, 2014; Brinker, 2023).

According to *Forrester/Airtable*, larger companies use on average more than 367 different software tools. The consequence: the emergence of data silos and freely roaming processes that can hardly be integrated in a meaningful way (Forrester/Airtable, 2023). As a result, most companies (43%) are confronted with completing and expanding their own capabilities in the coming years (Fig. 3.2).

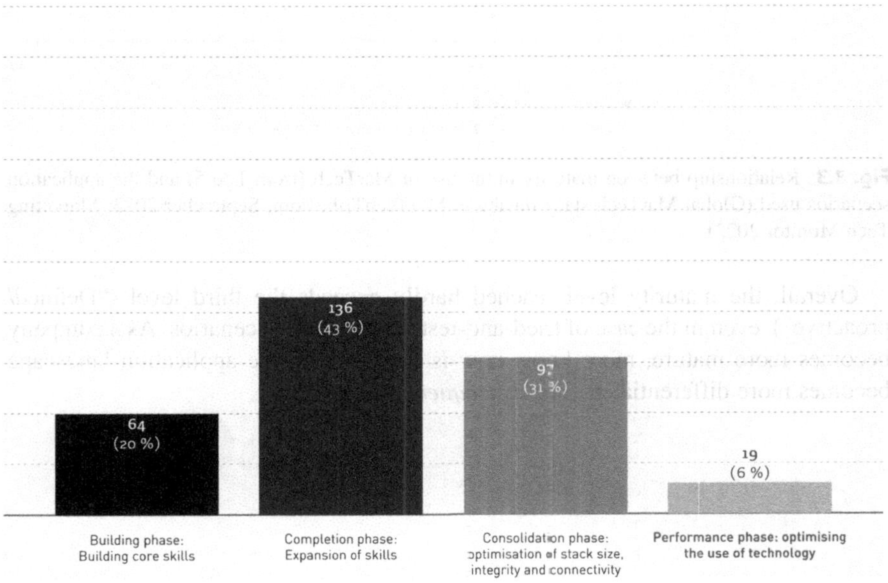

Fig. 3.2 Assessment of own maturity of the MarTech stack (in %, $n = 316$; Marketing Tech Monitor 2023)

Higher maturity levels (phase of performance) are reserved for a smaller selected group (6%), which, however, have shown to have a longer lead history over the last few years in all instances. Consolidation for optimising the stack, integrity, and connectivity is the focus for 31%, mostly as necessary clean-up work after actionist-based "shop-till-you-drop" shopping sprees in the "MarTech toy shop".

In most companies, the voyage into the MarTech universe starts in the *build-up phase* via CMS and web analytics applications, followed by marketing automation (MAP) and CRM as a "master record system". CDPs and iPaaS or integration tools are subsequently required for customer and application integration scenarios, while personalisation, attribution, and audience management tend to take the role of add-ons (Fig. 3.3). In terms of usage value, CMS, CRM, and marketing automation have the most catching up to do in "fixing the basics".

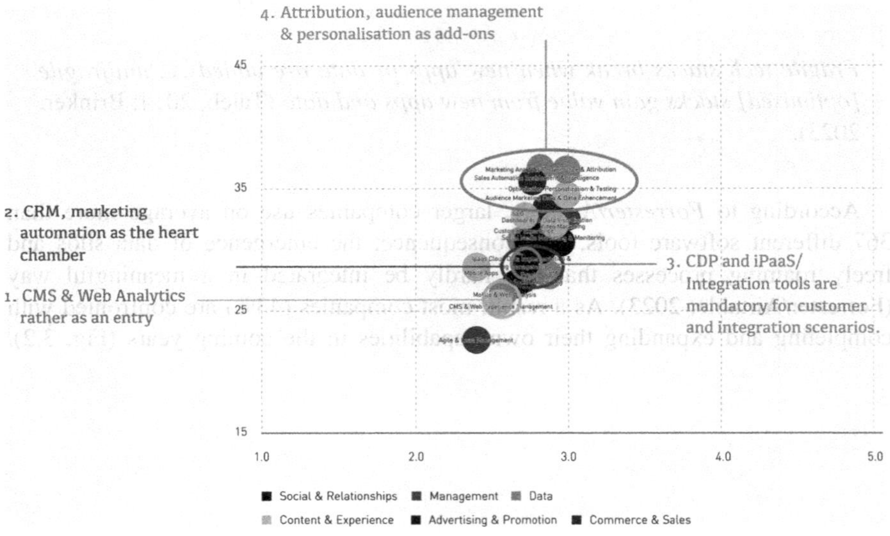

Fig. 3.3 Relationship between maturity in the use of MarTech (from 1 to 5) and the application scenarios used (Global MarTech stack database, MarTechTribe.com, September 2023; Marketing Tech Monitor 2023)

Overall, the maturity level reached hardly exceeds the third level ("Defined/ proactive"), even in the case of tried-and-tested application scenarios. As a company becomes more mature, more know-how is built up and the application landscape becomes more differentiated. The *consequence* (Fig. 3.4):

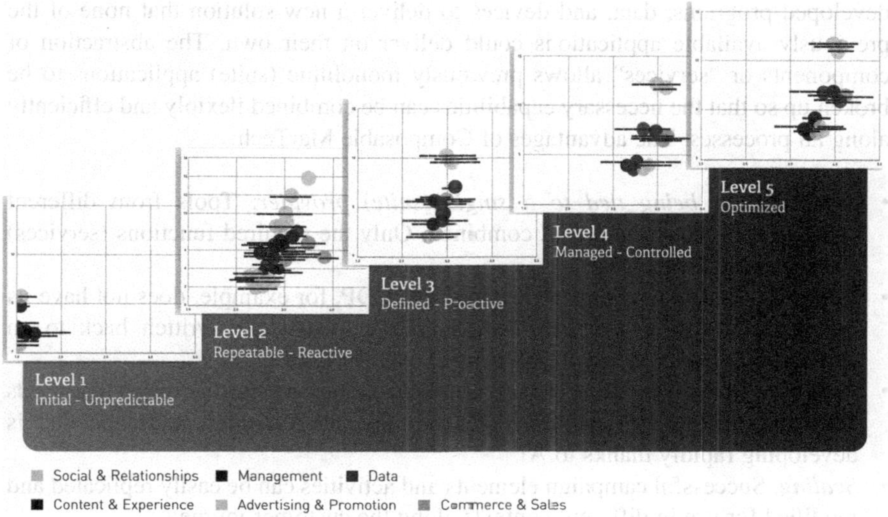

Fig. 3.4 Maturity level and application scenarios used in companies from almost 1200 MarTech stacks (Global MarTech stack database, MarTechTribe.com, September 2023; Marketing Tech Monitor 2023)

- Best-of-breed or best-of-feature solutions for specific application scenarios are used.
- AdTech leads the market with the highest maturity, closely followed by data and management solutions. Content and social (still) fall behind here, as content creation can hardly be scaled.
- Dedicated change management approaches are used.
- The number of complaints about the need to catch up in data management (à la CDPs) and marketing planning and steering (MRM) increases.
- There is a tendency towards "over-tooling", with escalating licence and operating costs, and the subsequent need for software lifecycle management (consolidation of the application landscape).

The higher the maturity level, the more likely it is to follow a strategy-driven and cascading approach to implementing data-driven marketing—with the aim to unite the multitude of soloists along the MarTech cube to create a choir across different levels and sing a common song.

Parallel to the AI wave and as a further turbo booster for achieving higher maturity levels, the paradigm of *composability* has gained popularity over the last two years . . . although the foundations date back to the 1960s with object-oriented programming or remote procedure calls, which in turn experienced a revival at the beginning of this century under the term modular, service-oriented architectures. Composability describes the idea of building and managing systems and tools as individual components that can be addressed or called up according to their business purpose. A composable application platform thus orchestrates independently developed programs, data, and devices to deliver a new solution that none of the previously available applications could deliver on their own. The abstraction of components or "services" allows previously monolithic (suite) applications to be broken up so that the necessary capabilities can be combined flexibly and efficiently along all processes. The advantages of Composable MarTech:

- *Avoidance of being tied to a single (suite) provider*: Tools from different providers can be selected and combined. Only the required functions (services) are called up in each case.
- *Complete data sovereignty*: A Composable CDP, for example, does not have its own customer data layer. Instead, data is activated and written back to an overarching data cloud, with full control over the CDP.
- *Flexibility*: The most suitable tools can be used flexibly for the respective needs along the customer journey in a technology and provider landscape that is developing rapidly thanks to AI.
- *Scaling*: Successful campaign elements and activities can be easily replicated and modified for use in different contexts along the customer journey.

3.2 The Maturity Assessment: MarTech Strategy Objectives and Maturity Levels

For most companies, the goal of MarTech is the automation and (plannable) optimisation of data/customer-driven marketing strategies and customer journeys, followed by higher efficiency in customer interaction, performance management, and marketing operations. In this customer-journey-driven transformation, few companies start from pole position (optimising technology use), but from the pit lane (completing capabilities). For the "rookies" (maturity phase: building central capabilities), bread-and-butter topics are on the agenda, such as the efficiency and effectiveness of marketing processes, the development of data strategies and the activation of data, as well as a customer experience design with the customer journey as a starting point. In other words, "down-to-earth" topics and "process-related homework" dominate, while more advanced topics such as ROI modelling are relegated to the back seat.

For most companies, the goal of MarketingTech is the automation and (plannable) optimisation of data/customer-driven marketing strategies and customer journeys (88%, top boxes), followed by higher efficiency in customer interaction, performance management, and marketing operations (Fig. 3.5). "*The purgatory of MarTech vanities*", loosely based on *Tom Woolfe*, is hotter than in previous years. While the customer journey has been widely discussed over the last 20 years or so in the context of "customer experience management" or "touchpoint analysis" (with a lot of subjunctives), it only now seems to be celebrating its breakthrough over the next coming years. The customer journey represents the central organising criterion as a "substantial basic architecture" and (ideally) ensures that work, customer, and

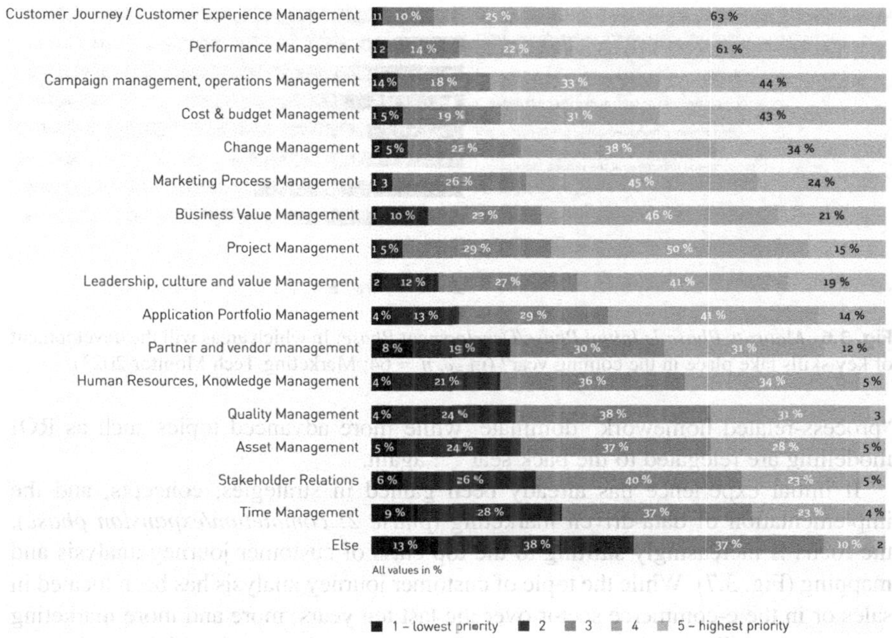

Fig. 3.5 Goals pursued with the technology and data strategy (in %, $n = 356$; Marketing Tech Monitor 2023)

data processes fit coherently into one another, in other words: consistency in goals and data, coherence in processes and data, and consistency in implementation.

The reasons for the increasing focus on the customer journey:

- The realisation that the use of data and IT applications to analyse and manage customer interactions is and can only be a means to an end, in other words an "enabler" for the implementation of a mass personalised and efficient customer approach. Put plainly: the IT application (the "enabler") has often become an end and objective in terms of perception and use, with all the associated challenges regarding implementation and the accompanying change management.
- The monstrance of the much-strained "customer experience" requires a conceptual and procedural substructure and backbone, with relevance from the customer's point of view.

In this customer-journey-driven transformation, few companies start from pole position (6%; optimising technology use), but from the pit lane (43%; completing capabilities). For the "rookies" in phase 1 (*maturity phase: building central capabilities*), bread-and-butter topics are on the agenda, such as the efficiency and effectiveness of marketing processes, the development of data strategies and the activation of data, as well as a customer experience design with the customer journey as a starting point (Fig. 3.6). In other words, "down-to-earth" topics and

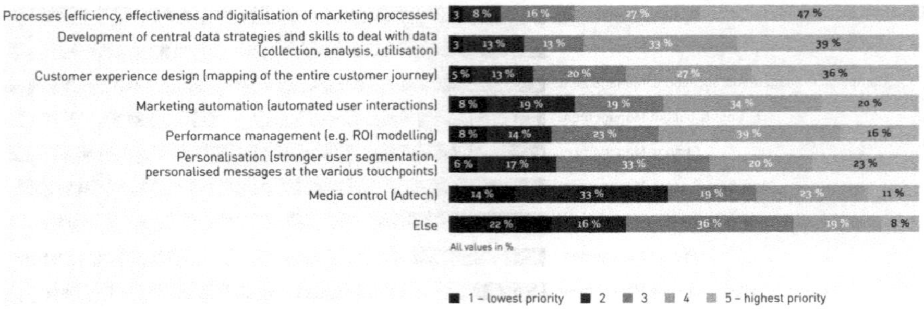

Fig. 3.6 *Maturity Phase 1: Initial Phase/Development Phase*: In which areas will the development of key skills take place in the coming year? (in %, $n = 64$; Marketing Tech Monitor 2023)

"process-related homework" dominate, while more advanced topics such as ROI modelling are relegated to the back seat . . . again.

If initial experience has already been gained in strategies, concepts, and the implementation of data-driven marketing (*phase 2: completion/expansion phase*), the focus is increasingly shifting to the top class of customer journey analysis and mapping (Fig. 3.7). While the topic of customer journey analysis has been located in sales or in the e-commerce sector over the last ten years, more and more marketing managers are discovering the methodology as a saviour and initial solution for achieving "customer centricity" and personalisation. In other words, the customer as the "object of desire" is leaving the field of theoretical *PowerPoint* orgies and moving into the centre of attention. At the same time, marketing management (e.g. in the form of MRM application scenarios) is receiving increased attention after many years in slumber. The reason is that the lofty projections of a Venetian marketing automation and ROI optimisation require a conceptual and procedural foundation in the sandbanks of data-driven customer interaction.

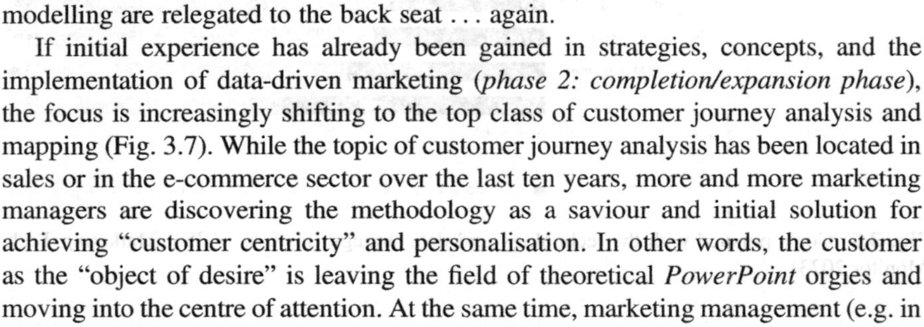

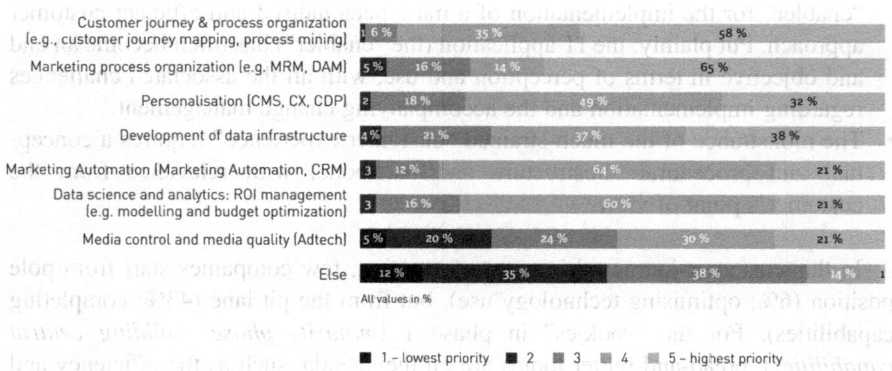

Fig. 3.7 *Maturity Phase 2: Completion/expansion phase*: In which areas will the completion/ expansion of key capabilities take place in the coming year? (in %, $n = 136$; Marketing Tech Monitor 2023)

As the build-up of know-how continues, the initial euphoria in phase 3, the *consolidation phase* gives way to the striving to reduce the complexity of (to simplify) one's own application landscape and to increase the integration possibilities (Fig. 3.8).

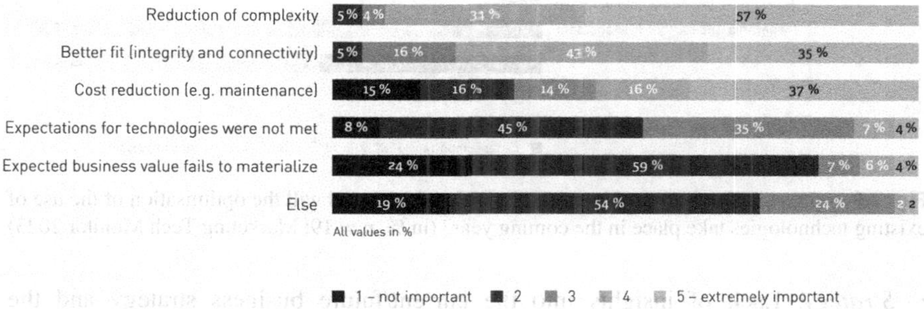

Fig. 3.8 *Maturity Phase 3: Phase of consolidation*: In which areas will consolidation take place in the coming year? (in %, $n = 97$; Marketing Tech Monitor 2023)

MarTech's razor: other things being equal, the simplest stack is best (Brinker, 2022).—Scott Brinker (Editor, chiefmartec.com / VP Platform Ecosystem, HubSpot).

Cost reductions through consolidation of the application landscape (lifecycle management) are only ranked first by 37%. The expectations of the technologies used and the targeted "business impact" were met in most cases, which is by no means a matter of course . . .

. . . yet the challenges associated with MarTech underutilisation, such as new business models and disrupted customer journeys, are making it difficult for marketers to demonstrate technology's value (Von Hoffman, 2022).

At the fourth and highest level of maturity (*performance phase*), the efforts are driven by adaptation to work processes and a better integration between different IT applications (Fig. 3.9). Working within the conflict zone between business processes (use cases) and the determination of detailed requirements for IT applications (requirements) often proves to be a *Jurassic Park*—there is a lack of know-how here in terms of:

- *Methodology*: Lack of equal understanding of the necessary granularity of use cases and detailed requirements.
- *Processes*: Insufficient (actual) knowledge about process flows.

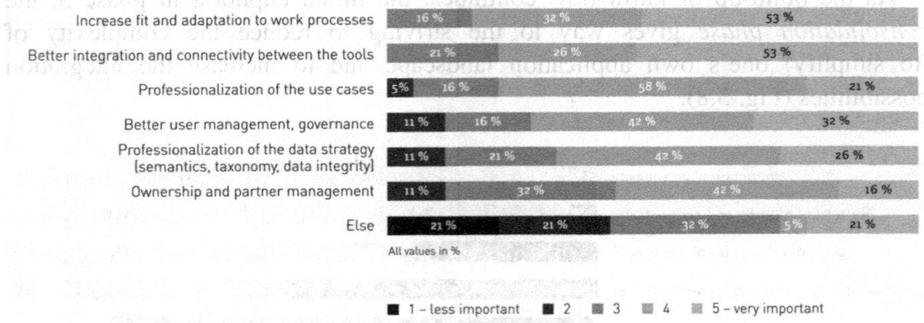

Fig. 3.9 *Maturity Phase 4: Performance phase*: In which areas will the optimisation of the use of existing technologies take place in the coming year? (in %, $n = 19$; Marketing Tech Monitor 2023)

- *Strategy*: Lack of insights into the current/future business strategy and the resulting consequences.
- *Technology*: To ensure better integration and connectivity between applications.
- *Professional data strategy*: A defined strategy to collect and activate all customer data points.

Across the different maturity levels on the way to data-driven marketing, the focus is on different questions and priorities:

- The higher the organisational maturity level, the more relevant are goals related to the company's success (e.g. the achievement of KPIs, reach, or customer loyalty).
- The lower the organisational maturity level, the more the focus is on structural/process-related goals (e.g. process optimisation, more frequent customer interaction or even customer service).
- With increasing maturity, all goals (e.g. personalisation, loyalty, and conversion rates) become more important. After a "strategic overload" with many simultaneously relevant and pursued goals, a "natural" focus on the most important goals takes place.
- The higher the maturity level, the more the goal is to acquire customer data along the customer journey and the focus on the frequency of customer interactions decreases.

The comparison of marketing tech application scenarios being used (along the dimensions of "employees", "processes", and "technologies") with turnover/employees makes it apparent, among other things, that "native/content advertising" processes and technologies, for example, have a positive influence on turnover/employees in the industry segment "consumer goods manufacturers" (positive correlation). "Collaboration" defies the logic of "a lot helps a lot" and cannot be solved with more tools or users (negative correlation) but requires standardised processes and objectives. This relationship is reversed for CRM. Standardised CRM processes and defined outputs have less influence on turnover/employees (and subsequently on profitability) in this industry segment, but the number of users (adoption) and tools used do. Within this industry segment, similarly structured companies (in terms of turnover/employees) show a higher maturity in individual application scenarios such as "video marketing".

3.3 Cherry Picking (Best-of-Breed) or "All-in-One" (Integrated Suite)?

For many companies, the current focus of the technology stack is still on established suites or walled garden providers. The interviews, workshops, and projects underline once again that it is comparatively (at least it appears to be) easier to start with a closed solution and learn the basic processes. For the future, only a few companies state that they will continue to rely on a full stack walled garden solution. The reasons for customised strategies from a user perspective: The more companies deal with the topic in the sense of a dedicated strategy for data-driven customer interaction, the more differentiated the requirements and longer-term development plans (master construction plan) are (i.e. *the imperative "depth in content)", the more they provide dedicated staff and budget for this purpose, the more they (painfully) experience that the full-bodied, chimerical promises and labels of ostensibly fully integrated full stack/suite offerings turn out to be a patchwork of (wildly) bought-in applications in reality, and the more individual strategies for building and expanding a technology stack are the order of the day.*

For the majority, the current focus of the technology stack is still on established suites or walled garden providers. The interviews, workshops, and projects underline once again that it is comparatively (and appears to be) easier to start with a closed solution and learn the basic processes. For the future, only a few companies state that they will continue to rely on a full stack walled garden solution. The reasons for *customised strategies* from a company's *user perspective*:

- the more companies deal with the topic in the sense of a dedicated MarketingTech strategy, the more differentiated the requirements and longer-term development plans (master construction plan) are (i.e. the imperative "depth in content)",
- the more they provide dedicated staff and budget for this purpose,
- the more they (painfully) experience that the full-bodied, chimerical promises and labels of ostensibly fully integrated full stack/suite offerings turn out to be a patchwork of (wildly) bought-in applications in reality, and
- the more individual strategies for building and expanding a technology stack are the order of the day.

After reaching a tipping point, the following applies: the more experience is available and the more the MarTech stack has reached a certain maturity, the fewer tools are subsequently used. The reason: after an initial wave of euphoria, the tools used are systematically phased out and cleaned up so as not to have to conduct costly

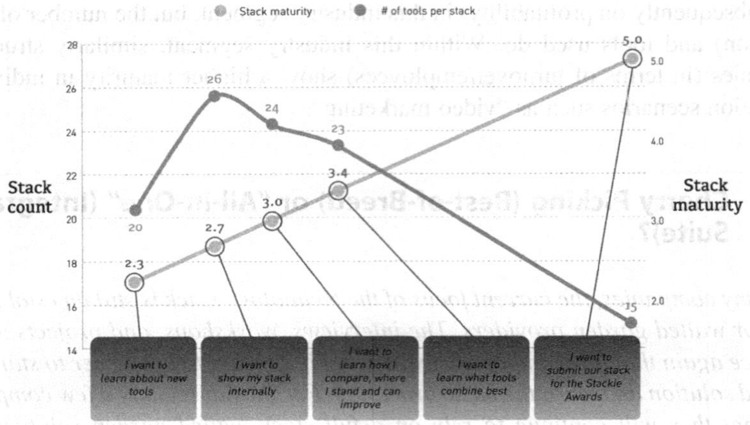

Fig. 3.10 Relationship between stack maturity and number of applications deployed (MarTechTribe, Marketing Tech Monitor 2023)

upgrades or maintain extensive integration scenarios. Thus, the development of the marketing tech stack follows the *Kübler-Ross Grief Cycle* over time (Fig. 3.10).

Even in companies' own perception, the degree of maturity still lags significantly behind expectations: only 1% of the companies say that their MarTech landscape has been optimised with foresight; for the majority (47%), the MarTech landscape is documented and comprehensible. After all, one-fifth of the companies have no overview. Their MarTech landscape is not documented and is viewed on an ad hoc basis. This phenomenon is not limited to smaller companies—even large companies state that they do not know and cannot understand which application landscapes exist in the different areas and markets or what is effectively used, including agency solutions.

A hybrid strategy is emerging in most companies. Purely best-of-breed, in-house strategies are hardly successful due to the rather strong dominance of GAFA data. Companies that consider themselves to be "mature" in MarTech, as well as successful in the operational use of MarTech, tend to rely more on in-house and autonomy in core areas such as data infrastructure (e.g. CDP), the collection of own party data, and analytics based on this data (e.g. attribution, marketing spend optimisation). AdTech for activation has (for most companies) mutated into a hygiene factor—these applications are mostly firmly established and run (comparatively) stable.

Against this background, the development around MarTech is being driven by at least *three overlapping effects*:

1. The development of the entire market for enterprise applications in the direction of "customer-built B2B" based on no-code applications.
2. The catching-up of marketing in comparison with sales and service ("marketing backlog").

3. The accelerating explosion of application scenarios ("explosion of apps") in marketing because of the above.

First, the market for enterprise applications has changed dramatically since the 1970s. While the first phase of on premise B2B was characterised by providers such as *SAP* (1972) or *Oracle* (1977), cloud-based platforms such as *Salesforce* have been taking off with subscription-based models since the early 2000s (Fig. 3.11). Over the last ten years, "product-led" companies such as *Slack* (2009) or *Dropbox* (2008) have dominated the market.

	On-prem B2B	Cloud-based B2B	Product-led B2B	Costumer-built B2B
Era	pre-2000s	2000s	2010s	2020s
Product	Complex, enterprise-buyer focused	Less complex, enterprise-admin focused	Simple, end-user focused	Building blocks (low barrier, high-ceilling)
Go-to-market strategy	Sales-led	Sales and product marketing-led	Product-led (bottoms-up adoption)	Customer-built adoption
Pricing model	Annual contract	Annual or subscription	Freemium	Freemium
Center of influence	Sales	Sales + Product Marketing	Growth product	Product + Success/Education
Core KPI	- Revenue (primary) - Sales efficiency	- Revenue (primary) - CAC/LTV (MQLs)	- User growth (primary) - User engagement	- User activation & product sophistication
Market size	Large enterprise only	Large SMBs, MM, enterprise	All knowledge workers	All knowledge workers + new software use cases

Fig. 3.11 Development path of enterprise applications since the mid-1970s (schematic, Marketing Tech Monitor 2021) (See also Peterson, D.: The rise of "customer-built growth", or how the "no code" design paradigm is revolutionizing enterprise software; in: Angular Ventures, October 21, 2021, for a similar approach)

Over the last few years, a further shift towards "*customer-built B2B*" has become apparent. A high degree of customisation of the immediate user experience, clearly definable use cases along concrete user requirements from "bottom up", coupled with an intuitive design and a wide variety of features (e.g. recommendations, collaboration) go hand in hand with a flexible product design and the possibility of independent (no/low-code) product expansion. Applications such as *Zapier, Airtable,* or *Miro* can be fully customised by the end user, coupled with a high degree of bottom-up self-services. Newer applications operate as *distributor APIs* and provide API-based bridges (as intermediaries) between old and new (transaction-based) business models, such as *Stripe* in banking or *Twilio* in telecommunications. *Twilio*, for example, integrates applications from service providers (e.g. *Uber*) based on APIs, with communication services from telecom providers (Fig. 3.12). The effort on the part of *Uber* only consists of the integration of *Twilio*, coordination and multiple interfaces to telecommunication providers are not required.

Second, there are signs of a race to catch up in digitalisation in marketing, compared to sales and service for example. While more classic CRM application scenarios in sales (e.g. pipeline opportunity management, mobile sales workplace) as well as in service (e.g. call centre, case management, request and complaint/service ticketing) have been largely established since the 1990s, the largest *backlog* of topics

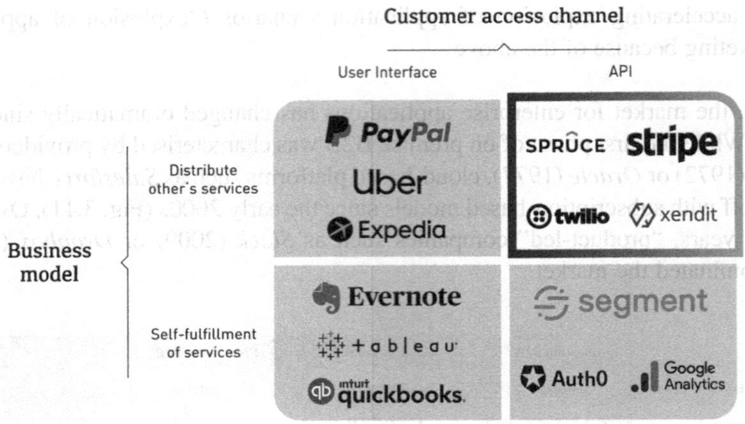

Fig. 3.12 Business models and customer access on the way to the distributor API model (Marketing Tech Monitor 2021) (See also Rowlands, J.: Distributor APIs: a massive product category hiding in plain sight, in: Medium, June 2021)

and associated market growth can still be found in all marketing-centric application fields.

> *Because marketing has historically kept itself isolated from sales and customer service due to the quite different way of thinking and very different cadences that these departments operated on. Sell now, service now and market over time, so to speak. Now that marketing is being given revenue objectives, it is being brought in as a critical partner to sales. This is forcing the alignment of goals and rules of engagement and service to marketing to the point that you are seeing technology alliances between companies like ServiceNow and Adobe (Digital Experience Cloud in particular) based on the use of marketing and service data, with the aim to improve each's single view of the customer. Things are changing. And marketing is now being forced to catch up.*—Paul Greenberg (Author of *CRM at the Speed of Light*).

The reason: while other business applications such as ERP (FI/CO), SCM, or HR (abstractly speaking) serve to produce (tangible) products or manage units, marketing applications ("only") manage customer preferences and produce or manage (intangible) messages.

> *We lost the first half in digitalisation in marketing and are behind in the second half.*—CMO, Insurance Group.

Third and lastly, the newly gained *customer-built B2B application* scenarios and higher degrees of freedom accelerate the development of applications in the field of

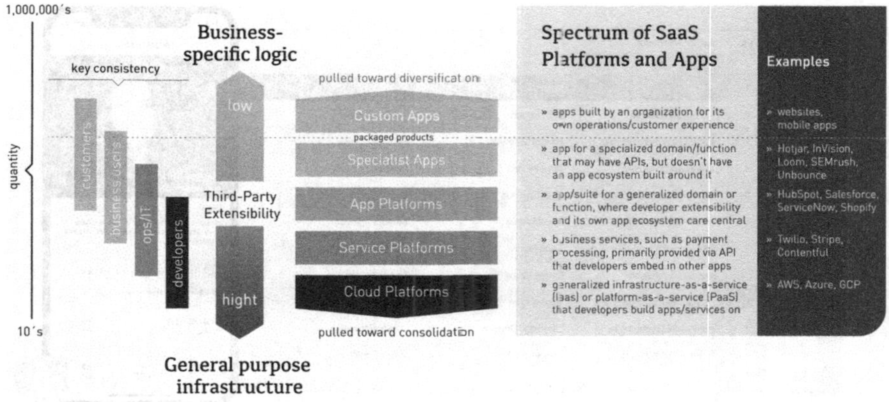

Fig. 3.13 Strategic development paths for platforms and apps in MarTech (according to *Brinker*, Marketing Tech Monitor 2022) (Brinker, S.: Platform dynamics driving MarTech app expansion and consolidation explained in one (relatively) simple model, in: Chiefmartec, May 2020)

MarTech (level 6) and are further spurred by the broad availability of a few cloud platforms such as *AWS* or *Azure* (level 10) (Fig. 3.13). These few consolidated cloud platforms, together with service platforms (e.g. generic payment processing) or application platforms (e.g. *Shopify* in e-commerce or *Atlassian/Jira*), provide the basis for highly specialised, enterprise-specific applications. For reasons of insufficient scalability in the long tail of the MarketingTech landscape, custom-app providers tend to move downwards (often as *packaged solutions*) in the direction of the platform, while platforms conversely try to integrate increasingly vertically and build their own business logics. This blurs the boundaries between the levels for most MarTech applications. IT service providers are picking up on this development and building at the specialist application level their own extensions for specific application scenarios, which in turn further blurs the boundaries between software and services (e.g. implementation). For the future, it is to be expected that platforms will tend to consolidate, while the number of apps based on them will continue to increase significantly (*explosion of apps*). Providers such as *Salesforce* or *HubSpot* offer nearly 10,000 partner apps on their respective marketplace, which according to their own information are also used by 91% of existing customers, resulting in more than ten million app downloads.

In addition to a few cloud and app platforms such as *HubSpot* or *Salesforce* (with their own ecosystems and marketplaces), custom apps will increasingly emerge at the top level, allowing the business department (as a "citizen developer") to build *no-code applications*. In *Glide*, for example, users can create mobile applications based on *Google Sheets* without coding (Fig. 3.14). The categories (rows) created in the spreadsheet appear directly in the menu of mobile applications such as city guides or mobile address books (Peterson, 2020).

The spectrum of no-code applications ranges from the database and spreadsheet-based generation of applications (as with *Glide*) to the creation of content or user

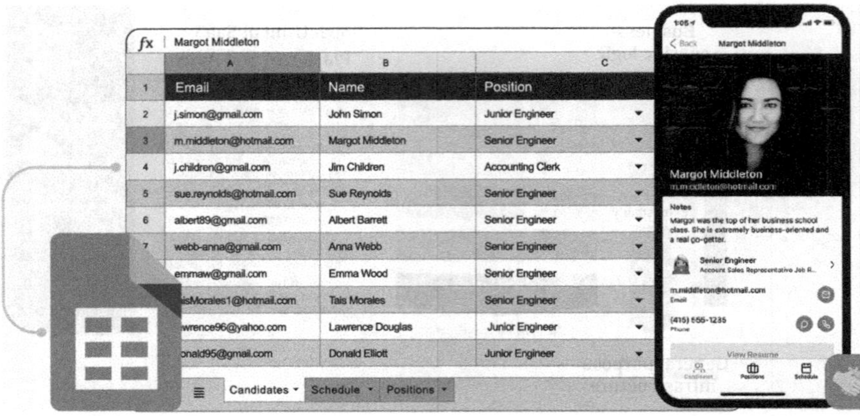

Fig. 3.14 Example of creating a mobile employee address book using the *Glide* app (with kind support and permission from Aloa.co; Marketing Tech Monitor 2022)

interface designs (as with *Jimdo*), to the generation of automation applications and workflows (as with *Zapier*, *automate.io* or *process.st*; Fig. 3.15). The advantages of democratising the creation of applications from within the business department are:

Provider	Functions	Pros	Cons
Bubble (www.bubble.io)	• Fast creation of web and mobile apps with significant functionality • Large ecosystem for templates and for finding existing solutions (MVPs)	• User-friendly and powerful • Integrates e-commerce, incl. payments • Large ecosystem • Web and mobile	• Complicated due to a enormous range of functions • No native mobile apps, no app store support
Glide (www.glideapps.com)	• Via *Google Sheets*, users can quickly convert data into an application • Simplicity and ease of use limit flexibility and customisation options	• Simple, data comes from Google Sheets • Integrated purchasing • Professional appearance • Template-based • Free trial version	• Layout limited, no drag and drop • Web application not native • Limited database functionality
Sharetribe (www.sharetribe.com)	• Easy creation of marketplaces • Integrated tools for availability and booking, payments, commissions, ratings and communication between seller and customer	• Fast/inexpensive creation of a marketplace of any size • Integration with *PayPal* and *Stripe* • Templates with easy visual customisation • Upgradeable to more powerful *Sharetribe Flex* with flexible customising	• Limited marketing functions • No shopping cart • No 3rd party plugins in *GO* version
Zapier (www.zapier.com)	• Data connection and workflow automation tool • Largest number of supported applications • Large/active community	• Integrated with large number of applications • Well documented • High number of useful templates and examples	• High costs • UI is not visually intuitive as with other providers • Handles multi-step tasks in a rather complex way

Fig. 3.15 Selection of no-code applications

- Agility: Via pre-built user interfaces and user experience features (e.g. forms, workflows, and dashboards), which can speed up the application creation process.
- Versatility: Increasing the scope of features and integration possibilities.
- Availability: (Forced) increase in the number of potential application developers from a business perspective.
- Increased productivity: More applications created in less time due to the elimination of long code lines; many features automate processes.
- Reduced costs: Quicker start-up with simultaneous cost reduction.

The basis is always a model-driven, explanation-centric approach, where the end user creates the design of an application through drag and drop or simple logics. Low-code platforms use a similar development model, but with a greater dependency or proportion of manual code to create the core architecture of an application.

> *Composable architectures, no-code development ('citizen development') and low-code applications dominate the evolution of most technology offerings. These are not long-term or even short-term road map capabilities. They are on the agenda right now or have already been built into the technology stack.*— Paul Greenberg (Author of *CRM at the Speed of Light*) (Greenberg, 2022).

Accordingly, the market research companies *Gartner* and *Forrester* predict that the market for low-code applications will grow to almost $187 billion by 2030 (Dilmegani, 2022). In this context, it is assumed that the development of no/low-code applications within business departments will account for a total of 65% of all application developments by 2024, especially around small and medium-sized application scenarios and projects. *Forrester* attests that half of all companies are already using a low-code platform, which was expected to reach the 80% mark already by the end of 2022, with an average growth of 22.7% by 2027 (Grandview Research, 2020; Taft, 2021). This indicates that, as part of the *democratisation of application development*, the business function will obtain the ability to build front-end applications to a limited extent in a self-service process . . . without the help of the IT organisation. This, in turn, will (inevitably) result in higher requirements for integration scenarios (with data and processes) as well as data protection and security.

Several overlapping effects are thus crystallising:

- From a strategy perspective, data-driven customer centricity and a focus on performance are causing a paradigm shift.
- KPI frameworks, which are often neglected, are experiencing a renaissance, as the aggregation of data only makes sense when used as the basis for a higher performance orientation and orchestration within the framework of comprehensive marketing operations.
- The new form of data, and a KPI-based marketing, requires a sustainable change process with all areas and employees impacted.

- Poorly documented processes and inadequate availability of the few, usually repeatedly overbooked "subject matter experts" lead to delays and insufficient depth of content within projects. At the same time, the effort required in all processes increases, as the different target groups are addressed in more detail.
- Instead of deriving requirements from the processes within the framework of requirements engineering and then selecting individual applications, this process is often reversed, which consequently might lead to the licensing of analytics applications . . . although the intended application scenario is MRM in the end.
- The explosion of applications (e.g. no-code) in specific application scenarios inevitably leads to integration challenges in terms of data and processes. This can be a native integration, or it can be performed via third-party applications such as *Zapier* for workflow automation, *Blendr.io* or *Automate.io*.
- The convergence of marketing and sales automation applications such as *HubSpot*, *Marketo,* or even *Act-On.*
- Although the lament of insufficient data aggregation has been extensively sung since the 1990s in the context of the multitude of publications in the field of CRM, neither the symptoms nor the causes have been eliminated. This is why the "data flagellant train" continues to make its rounds through the corporate corridors, and the pressure in this field is increasing exponentially.

In contrast to no-code applications, applications based on *open source* will not (be able to) become more widespread in MarketingTech in the foreseeable future, as most SaaS applications operate in a multi-tenant cloud. One exception to this is certainly *Mautic* as an open-source marketing automation project.

In the opposite direction to demand, MarTech applications from a *provider/ product perspective* are developing in the direction of a suite. Even singular best-of-breed offerings continue to "morph" organically or, through acquisitions and cooperation, inorganically in the direction of a full stack:

- E-Mail service providers have (smaller) databases and analytics capabilities.
- CDPs have analytics functions at the user level and will foreseeably expand in the direction of higher-value marketing analytics or even omnichannel campaign execution. *Bloomreach* or *ActionIQ* is moving in the direction of CRM, while *Tealium* focuses on end-to-end data integration (incl. analytics), or *Oracle CX Unity* propagates a multi-application scenario (incl. data management, analytics, and activation).
- *Habu* has expanded its data clean room to include analytics applications and dashboards, as well as integration with *Facebook* and the *Amazon Marketing Cloud.*
- *ActionIQ* released a new profile API in early 2023 that enables real-time access to external data, allowing the CDP to use data stored elsewhere without having to force-import it first. This kind of hybrid approach—storing part of the data in the CDP and reading in other data from external systems as needed—in turn, opens a wider range of application scenarios and architectures (ActionIQ, 2023).

- *Dynamic Yield*, as a personalisation platform, uses data from its owner *Mastercard* to create new ad targeting and personalised messaging at the individual level (Dynamic Yield, 2023).
- *Adobe* has added the *LiveRamp* app to their Exchange marketplace, making it easy for customers to apply *LiveRamp's RampID* to customer profiles in *Adobe Realtime CDP*. This, in turn, opens the door to audiences who also use *RampID* (Travis, 2023a).
- *Insider* as a cross-channel marketing platform consolidates customer profiles and provides a two-way exchange of data with other applications such as external CDPs (incl. *Segment*, *Tealium*, and *mParticle*) for CX control using a new integration hub (Cision, 2023a).
- *LiveRamp* and *Neustar/Transunion* have both launched identity resolution solutions for the *AWS Clean Rooms* service (Travis, 2023b).
- Data clean room (DCR) provider *Habu* has added native integration with *Google Cloud BigQuery*, making it easier for organisations to share data without exposing sensitive information. It shows the continued growth of data clean rooms and integration architectures with cloud databases (Dennen, 2023).
- *Lotame*, as a data-matching solution, has launched *Spherical* as a data platform with connectors for CDPs and data warehouses to make it easier for companies to connect their first-party data with other sources to enrich, model, and enable it for advertising (Lotame, 2023).
- *Twilio* launched *Segment Unify*, a real-time ID resolution solution that generates unified customer profiles within *Segment CDP* and exchanges them with external systems via a reverse ETL function. Integrating reverse ETL functions is an increasingly popular tactic for CDP vendors who otherwise face fierce and aggressive competition from stand-alone reverse ETL products (Twilio, 2023).
- The integration of *Qualtrics Experience ID* and *Twilio Segment* allows companies to create personalised customer experiences by combining operational data and customer experience data into a unified view (Qualtrics, 2023).
- DSPs (e.g. *OpenPath* from *The Trade Desk*) and SSPs (e.g. *Magnite*) are building direct relationships with publishers (as DSPs, e.g. *OpenPath*) and media agencies (as SSPs, e.g. *Magnite*) respectively, eroding the existing market model (in terms of features of the applications used, as well as roles in the market) (Shields, 2023).
- *Pinterest*, thanks to a partnership with *LiveRamp*, allows advertisers to upload their customer lists to the *LiveRamp* data clean room where they can be matched against the *Pinterest* membership file.
- *Hightouch* released the personalisation API at the end of 2022, which provides real-time access to cloud databases. However, data is first loaded into an intermediate "distributed, multi-regional data store" and only read in from the data warehouse with a time delay (Cision, 2023b).

Thus, a *dichotomy* in the (opposing) market development continues to crystallise:

- *Users*: With increasing experience and knowledge, tend to go in the direction of best-of-breed or use only those application scenarios from suite offerings (as a

service) that they need ("best-of-feature", *decomposition*). The focus is thus on the (process-related and IT-related) integration of a "patchwork quilt" or of "spaghetti architectures".
- *Software providers/vendors*: At the same time, try to cover as many parts of the marketing tech stack as possible to map continuous end-2-end process chains via a *vertical aggregation* of the most diverse application scenarios, with higher licence fees and a more difficult replacement of a deeply integrated IT application in many scenarios (Brinker & Riemersma, 2023).

One of the biggest challenges remains insufficient adoption of MarTech in many companies. According to *Gartner*, only 58% of marketing organisations use the full range of possibilities of their existing MarTech stack (Gartner, 2022). This figure rises even further for Central Europe. Up to 80% of the already introduced and licensed applications are only insufficiently used to date. Only (comparatively more trivial) application scenarios such as website analytics and reporting (interactive dashboards) are already being used in the best possible way. Most other applications have been selected and introduced at great expense, but so far pale in comparison with their technical/functional possibilities.

The main cause and driver for the user's urge to escape the GAFA sandstorm: complete data and process transparency as well as algorithms tailored to the specific strategies, processes, and requirements of the respective company. The performance of a tech stack in terms of process, function, and data integration largely depends on the interfaces between the individual components, which can (and should) be taken advantage of with *full stack providers*. The disadvantage of this: The insufficient adaptability to internal company processes and high complexity during operation. This means that the dependency on walled garden providers is gradually shifting towards individualised, company-specific MarTech strategies and thus the reduction of dependency on suite providers. In general, the more complex the on-going operation of a system is, the lower the willingness of companies to license and operate this area themselves in the future.

> *We need fewer large program packages; we rather look at focused, individual best-of-breed solutions.*—Dr. Nicolai Johannsen (VP Consumer Interactions, Otto)

Precarious is that especially complex and cost-intensive individual CRM applications (best-of-breed) and CRM platforms (suites) join (43%) the storeroom of not (sufficiently) used software. The accompanying interviews give indications of the causes in the MarketingTech strategy and implementation—for example, following a political/hierarchical decision, even higher-value CRM suites tend to be selected according to a "gut feeling", such as in line with the wish and preferences of the respective managing director or CEO. A substantive justification and validation has not taken place at all or only insufficiently—rather as a fig leaf for a rationalisation posthumously (Byrne & Gingras, 2017). Companies with a higher

	Best-of-Feature	Best-of-Insights	Best-of-Content
Value drivers	» Best-of-Feature (components, microservices)	» Best-of-Insight (moments of truth data points)	» Best-of-Content (evergreens, headless content, snackable content)
Unit	» Feature set	» Data point	» Digital asset
Democratization	» Democratization of martech	» Democratization of data	» Democratization of content
Skills	» Marketing Ops	» Data Ops	» Content Ops
Service	» Software as a Service	» Data as a Service	» Content as a Service
Tech trends	» Composable architecture, Platform Ecosystems, Low code/No code	» Headless CDPs & Public Clouds, reverse ETL, Tag Management	» Headless CMS & eCommerce, Messaging gateways, AI generated content
Best-of-Integration	» Workflow iPaaS	» Data iPaaS	» Content iPaaS?

Fig. 3.16 Paradigm shift in the use of IT applications to "best-of-feature", "best-of-insights", and "best-of-content" (MarTechTribe.com, Marketing Tech Monitor 2023)

"maturity" in the use of applications dissolve the rather tool-heavy discussion about "*best-of-suite*" or "*best-of-breed*" accordingly in a "*best-of-feature*", "*best-of-insights*", or "*best-of-content*" consideration (Fig. 3.16). The prerequisites for this:

- A broadly anchored know-how and common understanding of content and concepts across all ten levels of the *MarTech* cube.
- Well-defined use cases and requirements.
- Clear prioritisation of the most important scenarios and functionalities for usage.
- A point of orientation based on the customer journey, and the required personalisation of key touchpoints.

References

ActionIQ. (2023, March). *ActionIQ introduces profile api for real-time personalisation, connecting the data warehouse to the customer experience.*

Brinker, S. (2022, October 31). *When is a MarTech stack too complex?* Chiefmartec.

Brinker, S. (2023, February). *15 reflections on MarTech and more from 15 years of writing chiefmartec.com.* Chiefmartec.

Brinker, S., & Riemersma, F. (2023/2024). *Martech for 2024.*

Brinker, S.; Riemersma, F. (2024, May). *MarTech for 2024.*

Byrne, T., & Gingras, J. (2017). *The right way to select technology.*

Cision. (2023a, April). *Insider launches integration hub, WhatsApp Commerce, personalised search, and more than 20 new features to help businesses scale and future-proof their CX.*

Cision. (2023b, January). *Hightouch unveils personalisation API, combining the analytical power of the data warehouse with a real-time API.*

Dennen, S. (2023, April). *Habu announces partnership with google cloud to power privacy safe data collaboration and orchestration.* BusinessWire.

Dilmegani, C. (2022, March 7). *40 Low code/no-code statistics from reputable sources, updated.*

Dynamic Yield. (2023, March). *Dynamic yield launches element, bringing the power of mastercard to personalisation.*

Forrester/Airtable. (2023, March). *Software is fracturing your organisation.*

Gartner. (2022, September). *Disruptions derail progress in MarTech utilisation.*

Grandview Research. (2020, August). *Low-code application development platform market Sise, share & trends analysis report by component, by application, by deployment, by organisation, by region, and segment forecasts, 2020–2027.*

Greenberg, P. (2022, February). CRM watchlist 2022: And the winners are.... ZDNet.

Ilyas, M.; Khan, S. U.; Khan, H. U.; Rashid, N. (2023, February). *Software integration model: An assessment tool for global software development vendors.*

Lotame. (2023, January). *Lotame launches next-gen data platform spherical to extend data portability and interoperability.*

Peterson, D. (2020, August). *Why "no code operations" will be the next big job in tech.* Angular Ventures.

Qualtrics. (2023, March). *Qualtrics and Twilio raise the bar for customer experience with new integration and expanded partnership.*

Shields, R. (2023, April 3). *In a shrinking marketplace, Magnite explores media trading without DSPs.* Digiday.

Taft, D. K. (2021, March). *App dev focuses on low-code, Kubernetes development in 2021.* TechTarget.

Taleb, N. N. N. (2014). *Antifragile: Things that gain from disorder.*

Travis, C. (2023a, March). *LiveRamp and adobe real-time customer data platform enhance insights and activation with RampID.* BusinessWire.

Travis, C. (2023b, January). *LiveRamp announces identity resolution solution for AWS clean rooms.* BusinessWire.

Twilio. (2023, March). *Twilio supercharges customer profiles for data warehouse portability and extensibility.*

Von Hoffman, C. (2022, October). *Marketers making less use of MarTech's expanding capabilities.* MarTech.

4 I Go Where True (Money) Love Goes: Budgets and Market Potentials in MarTech

4.1 Growing Spendings for MarTech ... Despite Economical Uncertainties

More than 80% of companies expect budgets for MarTech to further increase in future. This means that the expectations of nearly doubled MarTech budgets have likewise increased significantly over the years. With regard to their own company, 31% are "bullish", even beyond the magic budget limit of the 15% to 20% share postulated in previous years. Only very few CMOs (2%) and digital marketing managers (4%) consider this spending volume to be "above average" compared to other market participants.

The budget share for MarTech (as a share of technology and system costs in the total marketing budget) is currently still at around 10% of the total marketing budget for more than 80% of companies in Central Europe. Despite all the prophecies of doom, inflation fears, and political risks, most companies expect the share of technology and system costs in the total marketing budget to continue to rise towards 15% to 20% over the next two to three years (32%, Fig. 4.1). This means that the

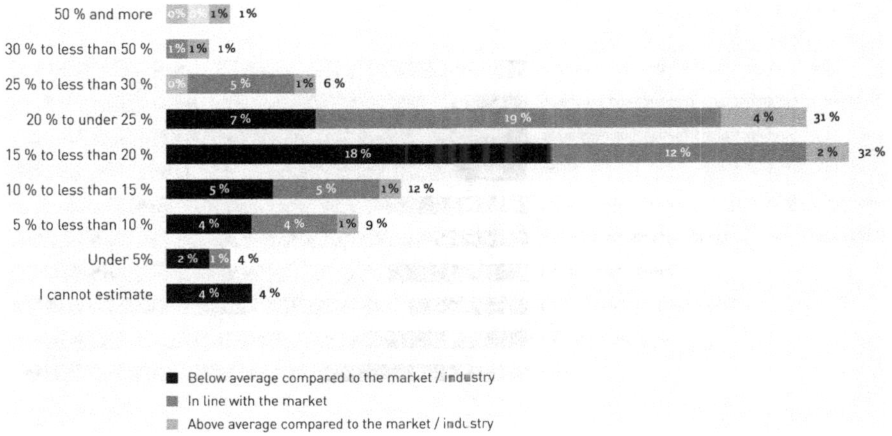

Fig. 4.1 Estimation of total marketing technology spend in the next 2 to 3 years (in %, $n = 356$; Marketing Tech Monitor 2023)

R. Strauss, *Data-Driven Customer Engagement*,
https://doi.org/10.1007/978-3-031-64295-1_4

expectations of nearly doubled MarTech budgets have likewise increased significantly. With regard to their own company, 31% are "bullish", even beyond the magic budget limit of the 15% to 20% share postulated in previous years. Only very few CMOs (2%) and digital marketing managers (4%) consider this spending volume to be "above average" compared to other market participants.

For more than 50% of the companies, this means a doubling of the budgets (measured as a share of the marketing budget) for all topics in MarTech. The comparison with the USA, UK, Norway, and Denmark with an average allocation of up to 26% of the marketing budget shows that this increase is "to catch up" with international MarTech budget benchmarks. As in previous years, it is remarkable that there are no significant differences between B2B and B2C, nor are there any serious differences between different industry segments. For more than 50% of the companies, a doubling of the budgets (measured as a share of the marketing budget) for all topics in MarTech is thus imminent.

The decision-making power over the necessary budgets shows: the responsibility for MarketingTech is not a role or an office that someone must hold—rather, it requires a "leader" who has an idea of where the journey should go and represents this vision in-house. In the words of former US President *Theodore Roosevelt*: "*Keep your eyes on the stars, and your feet on the ground*". In other words, for more than 40% of companies, the CMO or Head of Digital Marketing is not the master of the house, but only the "lodger in the bel étage".

The biggest growth is to be expected in the SME sector—here, more than 54% of the companies also want to further expand their expenditure in the area of MarTech in the coming years (Brinker, 2023a). The focus of all investments is on technology development/expansion, data management, and the further development of the strategy for data-driven customer interaction (Fig. 4.2). Relative losers in the competition of priorities are creation and production as well as the further expansion of personnel numbers and training, most of which will remain at the same level.

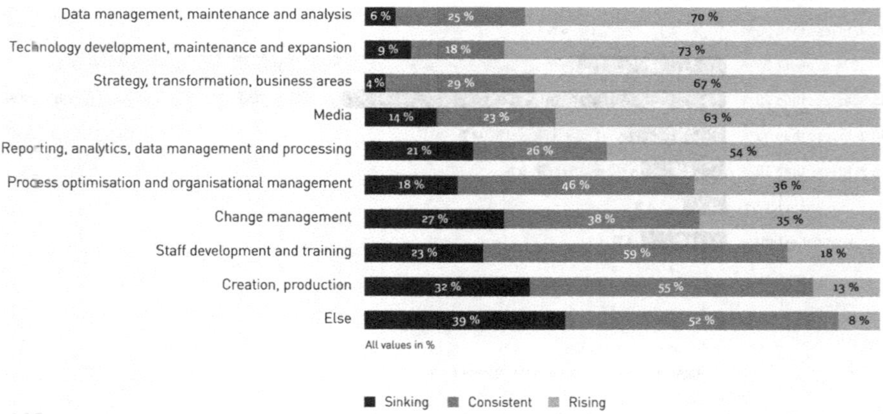

Fig. 4.2 Change in marketing budgets in the various investment areas in the coming year (in %, $n = 356$; Marketing Tech Monitor 2023)

Once again, it becomes apparent that the lower the function in the company (i.e. the closer to or the deeper in operations), the higher the assessment that larger investments are necessary—thus, technical experts tend to assume that higher investments are needed compared to the top management level, as do colleagues in IT. The possible reason is that at the lower levels in the hierarchy and in IT, there is more detailed knowledge about the (full) costs associated with a system introduction. As in previous years, "quick-win" or "fast-and-famous" strategies may have been an effective means of spreading happiness on all sides in the short term, but sustainable development and expansion requires greater commitment, higher budgets, and (also personal) time investment. The final decision regarding the investments required lies with the management and Board, followed by the marketing management function (e.g. the CMO). With an increasing organisational "flight altitude", the need to "pick up" these topic areas because of the required expenditures increases—so that going to the "Budget Canossa" does not end in the banishment to St Helena.

In the accompanying interviews, the marketing managers unanimously stated that they continue to see themselves caught in a quadrature of the circle (Fig. 4.3):

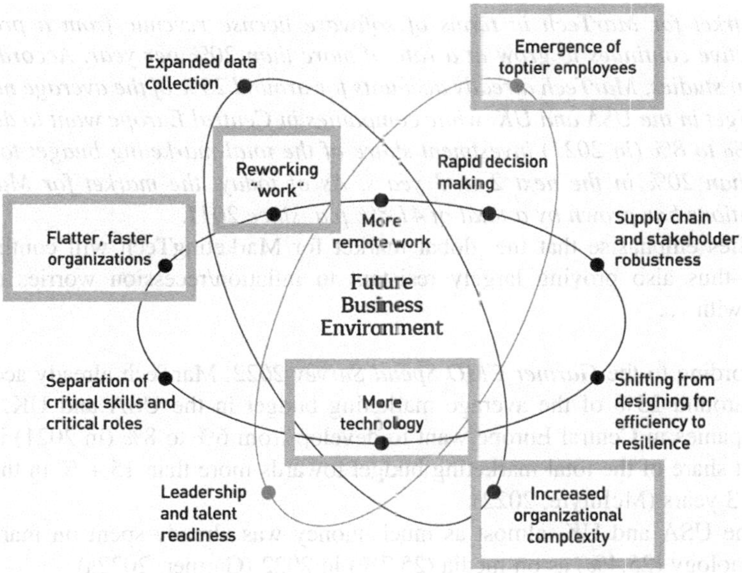

Fig. 4.3 The future post-Covid business and marketing environment (Marketing Tech Monitor 2021) (See also Brinker, S.: Marketing Superpowers: How AI & No-Code Transform Every Marketer into a Maker, adapted from Gartner, in: Chiefmartec, March 18, 2021)

- In addition to new competencies to be acquired (with at least the same headcount or even lower headcounts),
- the costs for MarTech must be covered out of the current marketing budget (as self-financing),
- the on-going projects for the implementation of data-driven marketing must continue to be implemented without endangering the on-going business even homoeopathically, and
- also compensate for the cost explosion due to inflation . . .,
- . . . although the majority (67%) are (still) relatively unimpressed by inflation, problems in the supply chains and the war in Eastern Europe (Von Hoffman, 2023).

The exciting question here loosely based on *John Maynard Keynes*: the secret to successful MarketingTech implementation lies in recognising what the average marketer thinks and what the average marketer is doing.

4.2 Market Potential of MarTech in 2024 and Beyond

The market for MarTech in terms of software license revenue from a provider perspective continues to grow at a rate of more than 20% per year. According to different studies, MarTech already accounts for around 25% of the average marketing budget in the USA and UK, while companies in Central Europe want to develop from 6% to 8% (in 2021) investment share of the total marketing budget towards more than 20% in the next 2 to 3 years. As of today, the market for MarTech applications has grown by a total of 41.8% p.a. since 2011.

Studies emphasise that the global market for MarketingTech will continue to boom—thus also proving largely resistant to inflation/recession worries (LXA, 2022), with . . .

- According to the *Gartner CMO Spend Survey 2022*, MarTech already accounts for around 25% of the average marketing budget in the USA and UK, while companies in Central Europe want to develop from 6% to 8% (in 2021) investment share of the total marketing budget towards more than 15 + % in the next 2 to 3 years (McIntyre, 2022).
- In the USA and UK, almost as much money was already spent on marketing technology (25.4%) as on media (25.7%) in 2022 (Gartner, 2022a).
- After the significant decline in global advertising spend of 8.8% in 2020 and a rapid recovery in 2021 (+19.3%) and 2022 (+8.0%), the Ad Spend Forecast assumes an increase in net advertising spend of $741 billion by the end of 2023. This corresponds to a forecast growth of only 3.8% in 2023 and beyond—but with a decreasing value of investments (inflation) and political uncertainties. Up to and including 2025, an average annual increase of 1.08% is expected in Germany and of 4.68% in Europe (Dentsu, 2022).

- The market for MarTech applications has grown by a total of 41.8% p.a. since 2011 (Brinker & Riemersma, 2024a).
- The *Online-Vermarkterkreis* (OVK) in Germany predicted net advertising investments of €5.4 billion for 2023 and following, with a plus of 4.6% (BVDW, 2023).
- 53% of CFOs say in the *Gartner* survey that they want to increase their marketing budget by at least 3% (Von Hoffmann, 2023).
- According to the latest CMO Survey, MarTech keeps taking larger bites out of marketing budgets: 17.3% last year, 19.9% this year, 23.5% next year, and 30.9% five years from now. This despite barely more than half (56.4%) of current tools being used and nearly half (48.8%) of the survey respondents reporting worse-than-expected results.[1]
- While more classic CRM application scenarios in sales and service have been largely established since the 1990s (e.g. pipeline opportunity management and call centre applications) and accordingly only grow by about 12% to 15% per year, the largest backlog of topics and associated market growth is found in all marketing-centric application fields (IDC, 2021). The result is a growth rate up to 10% compared to sales and service.
- Brands of all sizes are planning significant investments in MarTech—*IDC*, for example, expects most mid-sized companies (54%) to further increase their spending on modern marketing applications, while at the same time 31% want to reduce their MarTech stack in terms of the number of tools used (aggregation/consolidation) (IDC, 2023).
- *Chiefmartec* and *MarTechTribe's MarTech Supergraphic* analysis shows that the number of tools from a vendor perspective has grown by an average of more than 20% annually over the last years—a total of 9304% since 2011 (Brinker & Riemersma, 2024b).
- According to *Zion Market Research*, AI in marketing will have already reached an impressive USD 12.5 billion by 2022. Experts predict that this market will reach around USD 72.1 billion by 2030, with a CAGR of around 24.5% from 2023 to 2030 (Zion Market Research, 2024).
- The total global software licence revenue market across the "Application Development Software", "Enterprise Software", "Productivity Software", and "System Infrastructure Software" segments is expected to grow by an average of 5.72% annually from 2023 to 2027 (Gartner, 2023; Statista, 2023b). By comparison, the *GitHub* software marketplace has grown from three million users in 2013 to 100 million users in 2023 over the last 10 years (Sawers, 2023).
- Low-code development technologies are forecasted to continue growing at 19.6% annually between 2023 and 2024 (Gartner, 2022b).
- The lack of confidence in measuring ROI across most paid channels is driving the need for secure measurement capabilities in MarketingTech.[2]

[1] American Marketing Association & Duke University & Deloitte: CMO Survey Spring 2024.

[2] Nielsen Annual Marketing Report: Era of alignment, 2022.

- While one-third of companies in Central Europe plan to invest only 15% of their marketing budget in MarTech in the next 2 to 3 years, 4 out of 10 respondents say they plan to invest more than 20% of their marketing budget in MarTech in the future.

As before, the accompanying interviews underscore that it can be assumed this value will further approach the international average of 25% in the next 5 years. For the CDP segment alone, *Research & Markets* forecasts a sales volume of $10 billion in 2025 (MarTech Today, 2022). According to an analysis by the *CDP Institute*, 60 of the total 155 CDP providers are located in Europe, which in 2021 already accounted for approximately €500 million in software licence sales (CDP Institute, 2022). At the same time, the unmanageable scene of around 14,000 MarTech providers worldwide is becoming more and more differentiated. The number of acquisitions in the areas of MarTech, AdTech, and digital content increased by more than 200% in Q2 2021 compared to the previous year. Only due to the (political/economic) uncertainties that have arisen is the once-strong increase in company acquisitions declining for the first time in AdTech (−38%) and MarTech (−1%) in 2022/2023. Only acquisitions in "Digital Content" have been increasing (+30%) (Luma, 2022).

An additional driver of this development is the migration of former on premise to Software-as-a-Service offerings. Thus, between 75% and 90% of offerings feature SaaS deployment, with a projected growth of 76% according to *Gartner* … and rising. Therefore:

- The expenses for MarTech are (largely) immune to the fluctuations in the market environment, for example in relation to media spendings. The reasons:
  - Long-standing lead times and (strategic) decisions in most companies to continue to invest with high priority in the direction of digitalisation, data-driven marketing, and customer interaction (European Marketing Confederation (EMC), 2024).
  - The compulsion to combine (externally oriented) customer experience management with (internally focused) performance optimisation based on data.
  - The longer (pre-)duration of MarTech projects makes them largely immune to short-term fluctuations.
- Annual global spending on marketing automation tools is expected to reach $11.5 billion by 2027, with an annual growth rate of 17.7% (Statista, 2023a). *Forrester* estimated that the global marketing automation market will exceed $25 billion by 2023 (Forrester, 2018). *Gartner* expects the integration/automation market alone to grow to $32 billion by 2025, an increase of 50% in just 5 years (DiLemmo, 2022). The trend is confirmed in the overarching segment of "Communication Optimisation" (funnel management), including lead management, DXP, customer journey management, and DCO. Accordingly, this segment will grow by at least 11.4% (CAGR) up to 2026.
- Programmatic advertising investments continue to rise. In 2019, they already cracked the $106 billion mark worldwide (2021: $147 billion), and in 2022

already, according to *BVDW*, around 54% of digital advertising formats were already played out programmatically, a figure that is expected to rise to 70% by 2025 (BVDW, 2022). The exponential increase in available space (TV, DooH) in combination with the use of proprietary data by advertisers has emphatically fuelled the development over the last few years. In Central Europe, due to the already high market penetration, a more modest growth of 4.2% is expected for tools in programmatic media buying across DSPs, SSPs, ad servers and ad verification (CAGR, 2022–2026e), amounting to €171 million by 2026.

- The market for (comparatively simpler) web analytics applications, including tag management or on-site A/B testing, will grow by 11.7% per year until 2026. Globally, this market segment will continue to grow from $2.6 billion in 2018 to $10.7 billion in 2026 (19.3% CAGR, 2019–2026) (Allied Market Research, 2020). This development is supported by the further increasing importance of online shopping and "cookiegeddon adaptations" of the existing measurement landscape. The switch from *Universal Analytics* to *Google Analytics 4* will probably tend to have a minor impact on market development in this segment, as more than 70% of all websites have already implemented *Google Tracking* (Powderly, 2022).
- According to interviews with experts, the market for tools in marketing resource management (MRM) was already estimated at €845 million in 2021, which, however, includes overlapping sales around CRM and also services in the area of marketing mix modelling (analytics). By 2027, a market volume of $14 billion is estimated for MRM and DAM alone, with an average CAGR of almost 17%.[3] In Central Europe, around 50% of the companies surveyed state that they are in the tool selection process or want to use "marketing planning and steering solutions" in the future. Therefore, growth of around 17.7% (CAGR) can be expected in this segment up to 2026.

The market potential (revenue from software licence purchases/rentals) for MarTech will thus increase overall from €6 billion to €12.2 billion between 2022 and 2026e in Germany alone, with an average growth rate of 19.2% (CAGR; Fig. 4.4) (Brinker, 2023b). While higher growth was previously expected until 2025e, only to then slow down to a high plateau . . . AI is acting as a "turbo booster" in the direction of "real-time automation" and analytics, giving growth a further boost. Between 2021 and 2027, the market will grow by an average of 24.4% (CAGR). Expert estimates and project experience show that about three times this number must be estimated additionally for customising, system implementation, training, etc., so that the entire market (software licence purchases/rentals,

[3] Market Research Future: Marketing Resource Management Market Synopsis, February 2021 / Markets and Markets: Digital Asset Management Market with COVID-19 Impact Analysis, By Component (Solutions and Services), Business Function (HR, Sales & Marketing, and IT), Deployment Type, Organisation Sise, Vertical, and Region–Global Forecast to 2027; March 2022.

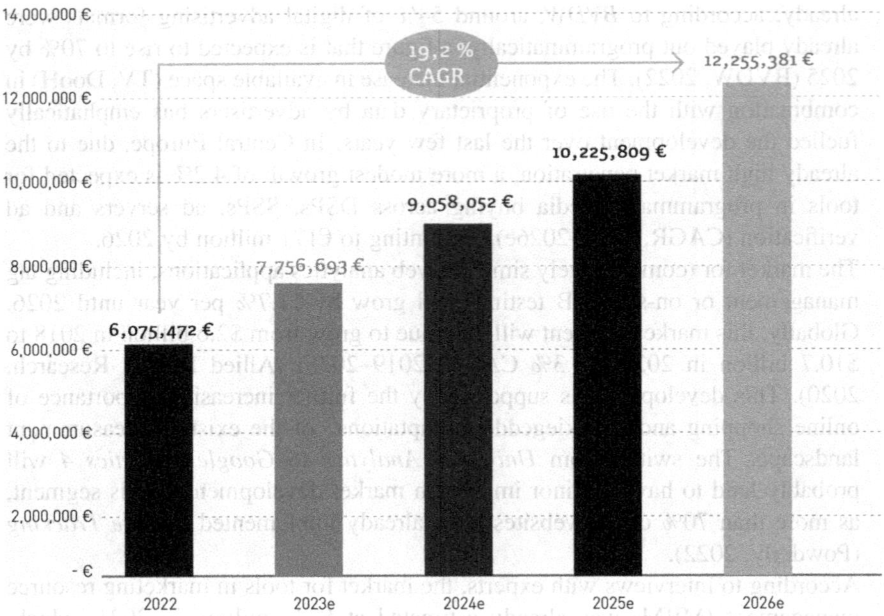

Fig. 4.4 Marketing tech spending in Germany from 2022 to 2026e (revenue from software licence purchases/rentals)

implementation, training, service, and support) for MarTech will account for a total market potential of more than €30 billion by 2026 in Germany alone.

The increasing technologisation and automation in marketing covers three areas:

- Automation and technologisation of media buying (AdTech with SSP, DSP, DCO, and ad verification) under changed legal conditions and new technical infrastructure, with comparatively minor further growth potential of 4.2% by 2026.[4]
- Technologisation of resources and processes (marketing planning and control) and optimisation of collaboration, "de-siloed" processes (incl. MRM, DAM, workflows, templates, and scenarios) with +17.7% CAGR.
- Further digitalisation of customer communication (CDPs, ID management, data clean rooms, personalisation and dynamic messaging, marketing automation, CRM stand-alone applications, next best offer management/NBO) across the entire customer journey, end-to-end communication with growth rates of around 20% up to 2026.

[4]MarketingTechLab Research April 2024, survey of experts; Verified Market Research: Global Ad Tech Software Market Sise By Product, By Application, By Geographic Scope And Forecast, March 2023.

- Marketing analytics and data science, for instance via own data science platform (e.g. *Hadoop Cluster*), interactive dashboards (reporting), digital or integrated attribution systems, online and offline attribution systems/UMIA, marketing spend optimisation or AI show growth potential of around 22.3% annually between 2022 and 2026e. By comparison, the global AI market in social media was already estimated at $815 million in 2020 and is expected to reach $3.7 billion by 2026 (28.8% CAGR).[5]

Across all company sizes and industry segments, two major topic areas have emerged simultaneously over the years:

- On the one hand, the more traditional *Marketing Mix Modelling* (MMM, marketing ROI, ROMI), econometric methods or *marketing math* have been experiencing a renaissance. The structural and methodological change will become more professional and automated thanks to AI and similar, with Causal AI.
- On the other hand, various fields of action of the company's internal performance are further consolidating in the form of a dedicated *Marketing Operations* function. The goal is the overarching control of budgets, processes, applications, data, reporting/performance optimisation, or even the further development of one's own organisation (competencies). In essence, it is about the role of a Chief Operating Officer (COO) in marketing.

The accompanying interviews show that, from a strategic point of view, marketing analytics, including the expansion stage of *Marketing Spend Optimisation* (in combination with predictive analytics and, in future, the use of Causal AI), is the focus of further marketing tech development. The strategic desire to control and optimise activities and budgets based on data and KPIs faces challenges such as:

- the previous use of "number clutter" in a wide variety of formats, media, and semantics (KPI definitions).
- the often (implicitly) articulated (unspecific) concern about giving an account of the previous use of funds and the results achieved ("accountability", perceived "vulnerability").
- the (comfortable) reporting established over years by the agencies commissioned versus an own culture for performance measurement and management.
- the unavailability of data platforms (in the building phase).
- the lack of tried-and-tested (multivariate) analysis methods in practice and
- a mediocre cooperation with the financial accounting department, which has now at least caught up with IT in terms of its importance as an interface.

[5]Mordor Intelligence: Künstliche Intelligenz (KI) im Social Media Markt–Wachstum, Trends, Auswirkungen von Covid-19 und Prognosen (2023–2028), March 2023.

#	According to net advertising investment	In € billion	According to MarTech spend in 2022 (incl. software licence purchases/rentals, customising, system implementation, training, service and support)	In € billion
1	UK	33.9	UK	22.1
2	Germany	26.9	Germany	17.4
3	France	14.9	France	7.0
4	Italy	8.0	Italy	3.0
5	Russia	6.8	Russia	2.8
6	Spain	5.8	Spain	2.2
7	Austria	4.3	Austria	1.7
8	Sweden	4.0	Sweden	1.6
9	Netherlands	4.0	Netherlands	1.6
10	Switzerland	3.5	Switzerland	1.4

Fig. 4.5 Development of marketing tech expenditure (incl. software licence purchases/rentals, customising, system implementation, training, service, and support) in the most important European markets (Marketing Tech Monitor 2022)

While gross advertising investment in Europe will grow by around 5%, MarTech (incl. Licences, training, implementation) will grow almost three times as fast (at 14.9% CAGR) by 2026e across the largest European markets (Fig. 4.5). Cumulative spending on MarketingTech in Europe (all markets) was estimated already at €46.2 billion in 2021, which corresponds to a share of around 15% of total global MarTech spending (software licence revenue in each case) (IAB Europe, 2021; S&P Global Market Intelligence, 2021; Dentsu, 2023). European growth is only lower than in other countries due to the comparatively high maturity of the UK market (23% of the marketing budget was spent on MarTech in 2021; only 7.1% CAGR between 2021 and 2026e). The other nine countries can expect MarTech investment growth rates of 18% to 25% until 2026.

References

Allied Market Research. (2020, February). *Web analytics market by deployment.*

Brinker, S. (2023a, March). *The future of MarTech apps is happening in SMB and the mid-market.* Here's why. Chiefmartec.

Brinker, S. (2023b, January). *2023 will be a chaotic year for MarTech, yet the start of a massive wave of growth.* Chiefmartec.

Brinker, S., & Riemersma, F. (2024a, May). *Martech for 2024*. p. 5.

Brinker, S., & Riemersma, F. (2024b, May). *MarTech for 2024*.

BVDW. (2022, September). *Trends im digitalen marketing: FOMA-Trendmonitor 2022.*

BVDW. (2023, February). *OVK-Webkonferenz zur Entwicklung des digitalen Werbemarktes.*

CDP Institute. (2022, January). *Customer data platform industry in EMEA.*

Dentsu. (2022, December). *Global Ad spend forecasts 2023*; IAB Europe 2022.

Dentsu. (2023). *Global Ad spend forecasts 2022*; Statista: Software revenue forecast worldwide 2023.

DiLemmo, L. (2022, March 20). *Why the business automation market is poised to explode*. MarTech.

European Marketing Confederation (EMC). (2024, March). *European marketing agenda 2024*.

Forrester. (2018, April). *Global marketing automation spending will reach $25 Billion By 2023*.

Gartner. (2022a). *Gartner's CMO spend and strategy survey: The state of marketing budget and strategy*, 2022.

Gartner. (2022b, December). *Gartner forecasts worldwide low-code development technologies market to grow 20% in 2023*.

Gartner. (2023, January 18). *Gartner forecasts worldwide IT spending to grow 2.4% in 2023*.

IAB Europe. (2021). *Adex benchmark 2020 study*.

IDC. (2021, August). *Europe CRM applications 2021–2025 forecast*.

IDC. (2023, March). *IDC forecasts double-digit revenue growth for SMB marketing campaign management software, White Paper*.

Luma. (2022). *2022 Full year market report, digital media & marketing M&A activity*.

LXA. (2022, November). *The state of MarTech 2022/23*.

MarTech Today. (2022). *Customer data platforms–a marketers guide*, 4th edition.

McIntyre, E. (2022, May). *Gartner CMO strategy and spend survey 2022*.

Powderly, H. (2022, March). *Most will stick with google analytics 4, but some are shopping for new platforms*. MarTech.

S&P Global Market Intelligence. (2021, February 10). *Digital ad spend in Europe resilient in face of pandemic*.

Sawers, P. (2023, January). *GitHub says it now has 100 M active users*. TechCrunch.

Statista. (2023a, March). *Marketing automation software market revenue worldwide in 2020 and 2027*.

Statista. (2023b). *Software revenue forecast worldwide*.

Von Hoffman, C. (2023, March). *MarTech spending continues strong despite rocky economy*. MarTech.

Von Hoffmann, C. (2023, March). *CFOs split on increasing or cutting marketing budgets*. MarTech.

Zion Market Research. (2024, January). *AI in marketing market trend, share, growth, size, analysis and forecast 2030*.

Data Readiness and Data Strategies . . . Without Data, You Are Just Another Person with an Opinion

5

5.1 In God We Trust, All Others Have to Bring Data . . . Data Readiness, Data Strategies, and Data Architectures

Contrary to the many discussions about "data-centricity", the systematic collection and use of data is rudimentary in most companies. The outcry for excellent data quality and the need to lay the foundation for data-driven marketing still often fade into darkness—only 20% of companies describe themselves as "data-ready". According to a Nielsen Annual Marketing Report, only 26% of global marketers have confidence in their audience data. Most companies thus still defy the theories postulated by all the saviours' ex cathedra *and have not yet formulated their own data strategy, do not have their own consistent data layer or any other technical infrastructure, still dream of standardised data sources and naming conventions for data mapping, do not yet manage to use data from different systems with full data integrity, which is why the lack of a key identifier for assigning the same entities is criticised—in order to be able to collect first-, second-, and third-party data under one user profile or ID. The logical consequence: for the next 2 to 3 years, the consolidation and harmonisation of user data* via *extract, transform, and load (ETL) processes (in data engineering) has top priority, followed by the automated target group definition and decision-making based on this (marketing analytics).*

Contrary to the many discussions about "data-centricity", the systematic collection and use of data is rudimentary in most companies. The outcry for excellent data quality and the need to lay the foundation for data-driven marketing still often fade into darkness—only 20% of companies describe themselves as "data-ready". According to a *Nielsen Annual Marketing Report*, only 26% of global marketers have confidence in their audience data (Nielsen Annual Marketing Report, 2022). The majority of companies thus still defy the theories postulated by all the saviours' ex cathedra and . . .

- . . . have not yet formulated their own data strategy.
- . . . do not have their own consistent data layer or any other technical infrastructure.

R. Strauss, *Data-Driven Customer Engagement*,
https://doi.org/10.1007/978-3-031-64295-1_5

- . . . still dream of standardised data sources and naming conventions for data mapping.
- . . . are weak in interpreting the data and deriving their own strategies.
- . . . have many data sources with partners (e.g. agencies), possibly with legal challenges.
- . . . do not yet manage to use data from different systems with full data integrity, which is why the lack of a key identifier for assigning the same entities is criticised—to be able to collect first-, second-, and third-party data under one user profile or ID.
- . . . repeatedly postpone the maintenance of master data due to the effort needed for this in day-to-day business.

The logical consequence: for the next 2 to 3 years, the consolidation and harmonisation of user data via extract, transform, and load (ETL) processes (in data engineering) has top priority, followed by the automated target group definition and decision-making based on this (marketing analytics; Fig. 5.1). There is already a lack of basics, such as an own data strategy, know-how for interpreting the data, key identifiers for assigning the same entities, the maintenance of master data, or even the dissolution of the black box of data sources at partners.

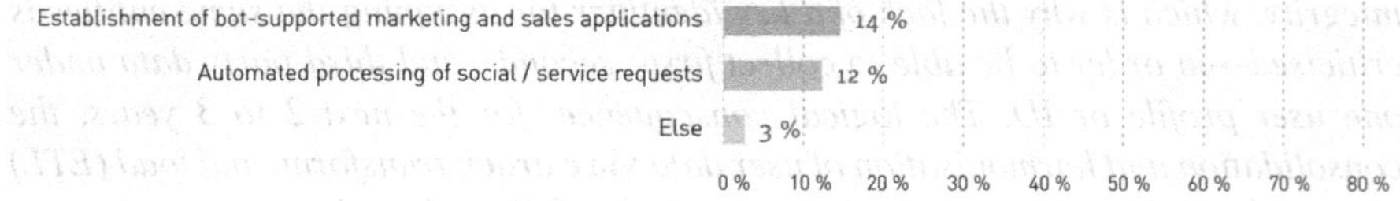

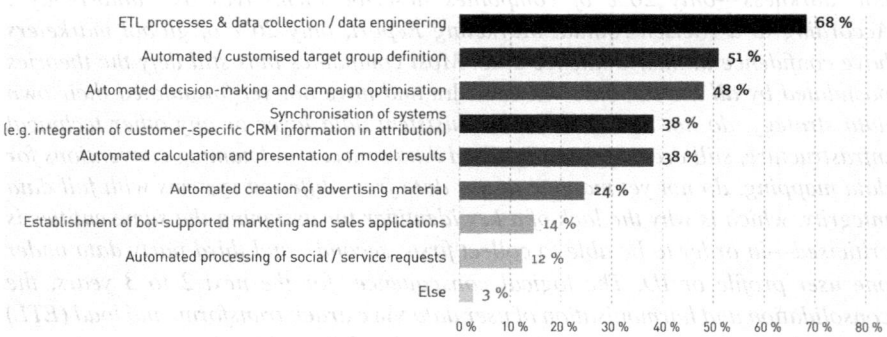

Fig. 5.1 Areas for higher levels of data automation in the coming years (in %, $n = 295$; Marketing Tech Monitor 2022)

In practical implementation, a data strategy always faces challenges at different levels (Fig. 5.2). Different definitions in terms of syntax and semantics (limitation/definition) are found in the most diverse repositories (separation/silos), which must be brought together via common layers and middleware architectures (aggregation). Otherwise, due to siloing, a sale in one functional area, for example, is something completely different than in another (silo bias), which is further reinforced by technologically predetermined distortions of the measured variables (technical recording, definition bias).

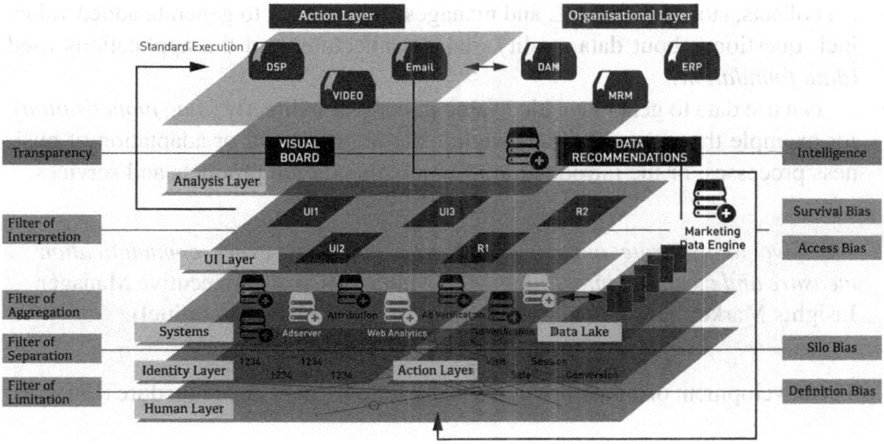

Fig. 5.2 Levels of data-driven marketing (schematic)

OTTO is developing its system landscape in online marketing along a value stream logic. The focus is on the question of what data is generated and used in the individual value stream elements. The aim is to be able to link all this data in the later, new system landscape. Data therefore form the foundation of the value stream, from planning and controlling, asset management and evaluation to control and optimisation—Stephan Huth (Head of Online Marketing Technology & Infrastructure, OTTO).

If the economic connection between channels and technologies is missing, access bias arises. Remuneration models with external service providers that are often geared towards individual performance create a "survival bias" through the interest-driven definition and reporting of results. Finally, the data must be made available at the highest level for interpretation and drawing conclusions (presentation, interpretation).

The foundation is the *data strategy*, which sets out a vision of how a company should manage and use data to deliver business value and develop a plan to achieve that vision (MIT CISR Data Board, 2018).

A data strategy is a highly dynamic process employed to support the acquisition, organisation, analysis, and delivery of data in support of business objectives.—Gartner, 2022.

A data strategy must therefore answer at least two questions, namely how a company . . .

- . . . collects, stores, processes, and manages data in order to generate added value, incl. questions about data quality, data architecture, and the applications used (*data foundation*).
- . . . can use data to generate added value directly or indirectly (*data monetisation*), for example through analytical insights, the improvement or adaptation of business processes, or the introduction of innovative digital products and services.

We have to generate our own 1st party data with every communication measure and customer interaction.—Dr Matthias Rasztar (Executive Manager Insights Marketing International, Dr August Oetker Nahrungsmittel).

The development of a data strategy usually follows an 8-step procedure (Fig. 5.3):

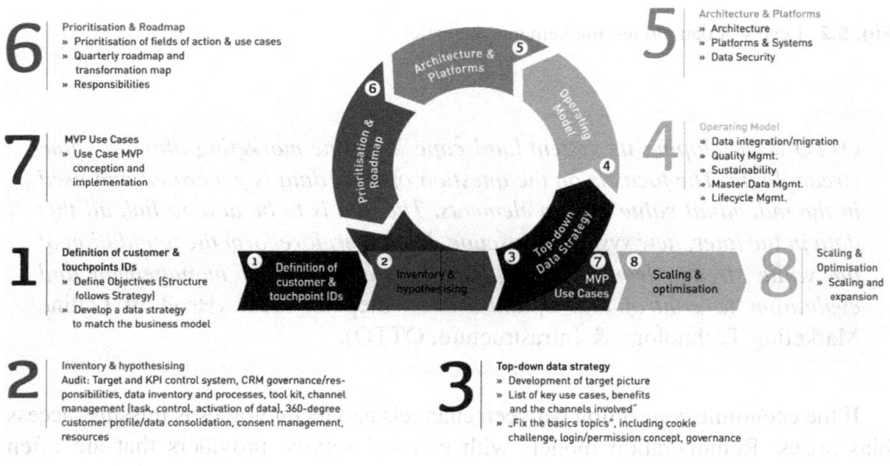

Fig. 5.3 Procedural model for developing a data strategy (Blokdyk, G.: Data Strategy A Complete Guide, Brendale 2021; Marr, B.: Data Strategy: How to Profit from a World of Big Data, Analytics and Artificial Intelligence, New York 2021

1. Starting with the *business strategy* (objective) and the desired monetisation of data. Analogous to the use of IT applications, the same applies: a data strategy is only the "inhibitor" of an overarching business strategy and the question of how insights can be generated from data-driven analytics that can subsequently be monetised (Bean, 2022).
2. This is followed by an *audit* of the existing target and control systems as well as data use (inventory), including existing consent. A holistic marketing and sales approach coupled with multi-faceted analytics requires an analysis of which application scenarios already exist today, which data inventory is already available today via the most diverse data types and sources, and which use cases will determine the business model in future.

3. From this, the *data strategy* as well as data governance rules are to be developed, along with a target picture as well as a prioritisation of the most important use cases for the future.
4. Then the operating model (*data foundation*) is defined, such as the required integration scenarios, quality management (data audits), or life cycle management (life cycle of data from creation to archiving). For this purpose, data guidelines and standards are to be defined in iterative cycles.
5. In addition to this more content-related/conceptual preparatory work, steps 4 and 5 lead to a *data architecture, platforms, and systems* (e.g. data fabric or CDP). The applications include necessary functionalities for data management (e.g. matching and stitching), while the data architecture outlines the conceptual data model and the storage/distribution of all data and data formats. Analyses by *Starburst* show that companies have an average of four to six data platforms—with an upward trend as the application scenarios used become more decentralised (Starburst, 2022). Against this background, data applications and architectures continue to gain momentum.

In step 5, there are different design options for data applications and architectures, from data lake to data mesh and data hubs to hybrid data architectures. In the simplest case as a *data lake*, both unstructured and structured data from various sources are organised in their raw format (Fig. 5.4). The raw data is only converted into another format, such as schema-on-read, when it is used. The flat structure allows exploratory analysis of the interrelationships between different data.

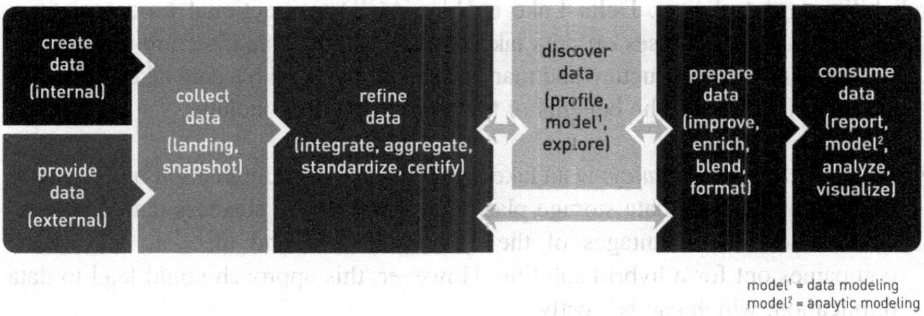

Fig. 5.4 Data lake or data hub architecture (schematic)

A *data hub* is a data-centric storage architecture that helps organisations consolidate and share data to enable analytics and AI workloads, among other things. A data hub can be viewed as a hub-and-spoke approach to storing and managing data. Data is physically moved and re-indexed in a new system. The advantages of data hubs (e.g. compared to data lakes) include the consolidation of data silos into a unified interface; the building of high-speed, high-throughput, and high-performance data pipelines; transparency and accessibility for all data; and a unified data storage management interface (Fig. 5.5). Data hubs are often built as joint projects between

Data Hub	Data Lake
Repository for different departments or companies	Centralized repository for companies
Saves semi structured data	Saves raw data and different formats
Data can be shared more easily	Data can be saved more easily
Data can be retrieved more easily	Data retrievals are more difficult
May cause issues with regard to data security	Too much data which needs to be pre-pared/enhanced may cause issues

Fig. 5.5 Differences between a data lake and a data hub

cooperating companies. These can use a data lake architecture or be organised decentral via blockchain.

A *data lakehouse* is a new, big-data storage architecture that combines the best features of both data warehouses and data lakes. A data lakehouse serves as a single repository for all data (structured, semi-structured, and unstructured) while enabling best-in-class machine learning, business intelligence, and streaming capabilities. Data lakehouses usually start as data lakes containing all data types. The data is then converted to the Delta Lake format (an open-source storage layer that brings reliability to data lakes). Delta Lake enables ACID transactional processes from traditional data warehouses on data lakes. Data lakehouse architecture combines a data warehouse's data structure and management features with a data lake's low-cost storage and flexibility. The benefits of this implementation include:

- *Reduced data redundancy*: Data lakehouses reduce data duplication by providing a single all-purpose data storage platform to cater to all business data demands. Because of the advantages of the data warehouse and the data lake, most companies opt for a hybrid solution. However, this approach could lead to data duplication, which can be costly.
- *Cost-effectiveness*: Data lakehouses implement the cost-effective storage features of data lakes by utilising low-cost object storage options. Additionally, data lakehouses eliminate the costs and time of maintaining multiple data storage systems by providing a single solution.
- *Support for a wider variety of workloads*: Data lakehouses provide direct access to some of the most widely used business intelligence (BI) tools (e.g. *Tableau*, *PowerBI*) to enable advanced analytics. Additionally, data lakehouses use open-data formats (e.g. *Parquet*) with APIs and machine learning libraries, incl. *Python/R*, making it straightforward for data scientists and machine learning engineers to utilise the data.

- *Ease of data versioning, governance, and security*: Data lakehouse architecture enforces schema and data integrity, making it easier to implement robust data security and governance mechanisms.

The main disadvantage of a data lakehouse is that it is still a relatively new and immature technology. As such, it is unclear whether it will live up to its promises. It may be years before data lakehouses can compete with mature big-data storage solutions. But with the current speed of modern innovation, it is difficult to predict whether a new data storage solution could eventually overtake it.

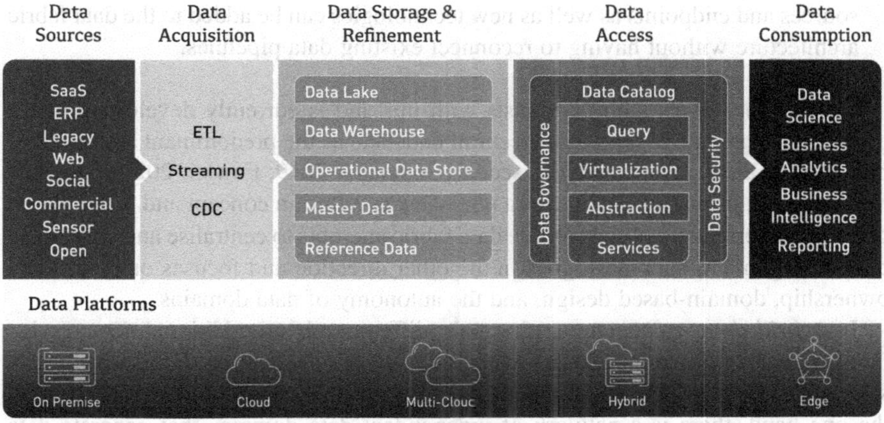

Fig. 5.6 Architecture of a data fabric (schematic)

Data fabric refers to a unified architecture consisting of services or technologies running on top of it and connecting different cloud and on-premise environments (Fig. 5.6) (Prukalpa, 2022; Wells, 2021). The focus is on maximising the value of the data, for example via . . .

- . . . a connection to virtually any data source through ready-made connectors and components, without programming.
- . . . functions for data import and data integration—both between data sources and between applications.
- . . . support for batch, real-time, and big-data application scenarios.
- . . . management of multiple environments, including on premise cloud, hybrid, and multi-cloud—both as a data source and as a data sink.
- . . . integrated data quality, data preparation, and data governance capabilities supported by augmented automation, incl. machine learning.
- . . . support for data exchange with internal and external stakeholders through API.

Accordingly, the *advantages of a data fabric* such as *Informatica* or *Talend* lie in:

- providing a single environment (without data silos) through which all data is captured and accessible, regardless of where it is stored.
- simple and unified data management, incl. data quality improvement, data integration, data governance, and data sharing and exchange; the use of multiple tools is not necessary, allowing faster access to (trusted) data.
- greater scalability, which ensures adaptation to growing data volumes, data sources, and applications.
- easier use of the cloud by supporting on premise, hybrid, and multi-cloud environments and faster migration between different environments.
- reduced dependency on legacy infrastructures and solutions; and, finally,
- the future proofing of the outlined data management infrastructure, as new data sources and endpoints as well as new technologies can be added to the data fabric architecture without having to reconnect existing data pipelines.

The *data mesh* paradigm contrasts with this and is currently developing into a promising candidate to replace the central data lake as the predominant architectural paradigm in the data and analytics sector (Dehghani, 2019; Fowler, 2020). The data mesh concept primarily establishes a new view as a design concept and is less based on technical problem-solving. While data fabric attempts to centralise and coordinate data management, data mesh goes in the other direction and focuses on distributed ownership, domain-based design, and the autonomy of data domains.

In *hybrid data architectures*, the main difference is an additional data service layer (Fig. 5.7) (Prukalpa, 2022; Wells, 2021). This decouples data use from data storage and closely links security and governance with the respective data access. On the one hand, there is a network of independent data domains that generate data

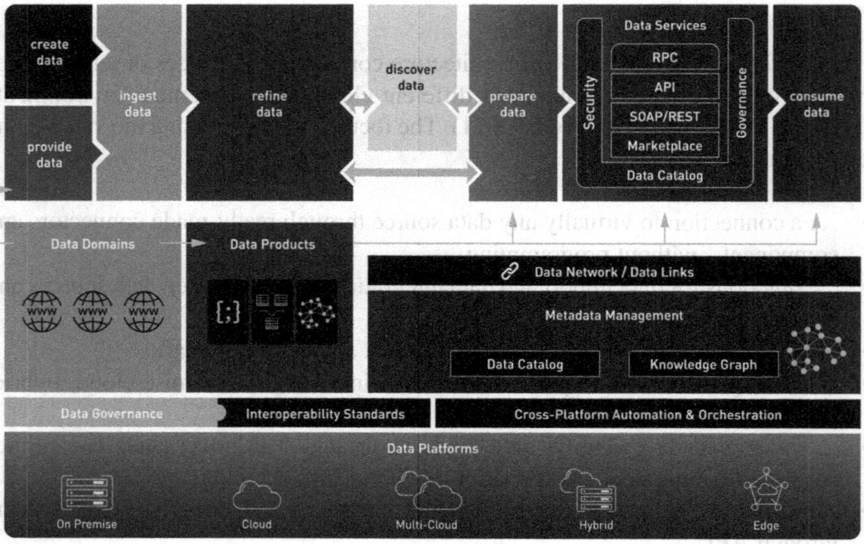

Fig. 5.7 Hybrid data architecture (schematic)

products themselves (e.g. legacy data warehouses). On the other hand, cross-platform automation and orchestration functions allow the bundling of the most diverse data sources.

The anchor point in most cases is on data warehouses (e.g. *Snowflake* or *Google BigQuery*). The goal is to establish a "single source of truth". But the challenge is that most of the time, the data warehouse itself presents itself as a monolithic data sink that is difficult to penetrate. Modern *Reverse ETL* concepts (e.g. *Census* and *Hightouch*) offer a remedy by transferring data from a central data warehouse to operative SaaS tools in marketing and sales (Myers, 2021). The most important application scenarios for reverse ETL can be found in the transfer of results from analysis tools into operative systems such as *HubSpot* or *Marketo*, in the automation of data pipelines or in the connection of a multitude of distributed data systems. The comparison with CDP applications shows:

- CDP is an application, reverse ETL is formally a process—which, however, has the potential to replace CDP application scenarios in the future.
- The scope of a CDP is purely limited to customer data.
- The target group for CDP is marketing and sales, for reverse ETL it is rather dedicated data specialists.
- CDP starts with data collection from raw customer data, reverse ETL with a data warehouse.

In any case (and in order not to fall into the trap of earlier EAI initiatives), it is advisable to start with smaller proofs of concepts (POCs) and the four to five most important use cases, as well as to use components such as DevOps to design all developments (e.g. variables, parameters) in a reusable way.

5.2 Data Management . . . May the Data Power Be with You!

The downer in data management: only just under 22% of companies consistently proclaim that they have already fully unified and aggregated available data. The consequence is that nearly two-thirds are planning investments in data management and AI. Looking at the development over the last few years, the trend towards having a unified data infrastructure will continue to strengthen in 2024 and beyond. The focus: optimising costs in data management and storage, focus on ROI and metrics in data management, the consolidation of data stacks, on premise connectors, active metadata replacing data catalogues, and building up skills . . . as data management technologies alone do not help.

The downer in data management: only just under 22% of companies consistently proclaim that they have already fully unified and aggregated available data (Marketing Tech Monitor, 2022; CCW Digital, Sprinklr, 2023). The consequence is that nearly two-thirds are planning investments in data management and AI. Looking at the development over the last few years, the trend towards having a unified data

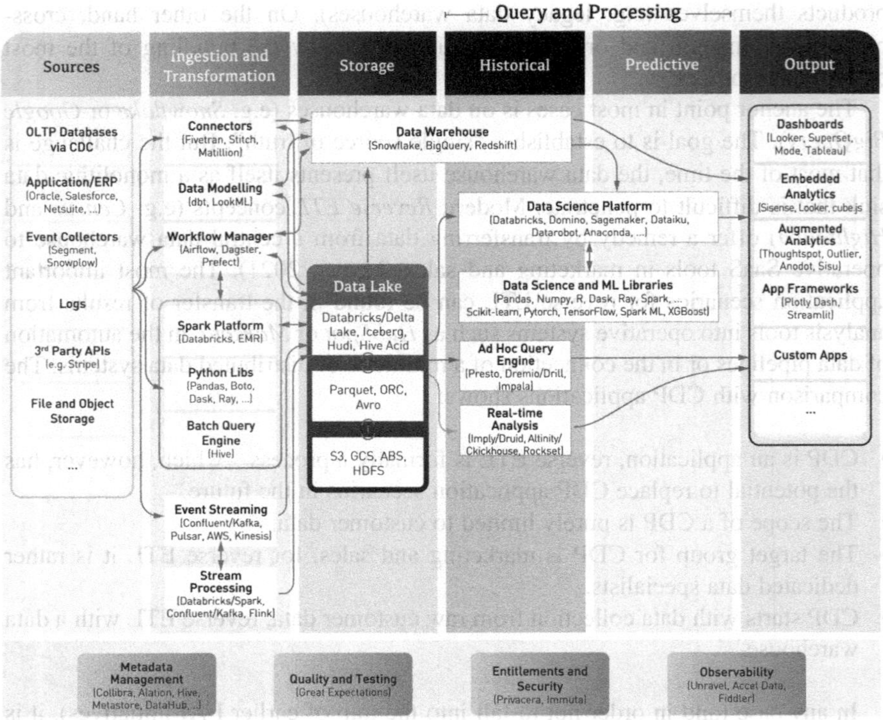

Fig. 5.8 Unified data infrastructure architecture (example, Marketing Tech Monitor 2023)

infrastructure will continue to strengthen in 2024 and beyond (Fig. 5.8), such as regarding the following:

- *Optimising costs in data management and storage*: Vendors such as *Snowflake* and *Databricks* are investing heavily in product optimisation. *Snowflake* has already introduced product improvements to speed up queries, reduce compute time, and lower costs. It now has a 10% average faster compute performance on *AWS*, a 10% to 40% faster performance for write-intensive data manipulation tasks, and 7% to 10% lower storage costs through better compression. Modern metadata platforms use popularity metrics to . . . .
  - . . . find unused data sets ("dark data") (e.g. via column-level lineage).
  - . . . see when data sets are not connected to data pipelines.
  - . . . perform redundancy analyses to delete duplicate data.

- *Focus on ROI and metrics in data management*: The focus here is increasingly on measuring ROI data and on data metrics, which is becoming "mainstream". (Proxy) metrics are proliferating, such as data usage metrics, page views, time required and acceptance of data products, satisfaction metrics (e.g. a d-NPS score for data users), and trust metrics (e.g. data downtime and quality indices).

- *Consolidation of data stacks*: Rather limited resources require focusing on what providers do best . . . rather than continuing to try to address every data problem with dedicated (new) platforms. Focus: interoperability, integration, consolidation, and the development of common standards. In 2022, *Fivetran* with the metadata API and *dbt* with a semantic layer launched more advanced integration scenarios. Newer applications such as *Lume AI* or *Numbers Station* AI automate data integration between applications using AI.
- *On premise connectors*: Vendors' search for new customers inevitably leads to support for legacy tools such as *Oracle* or *SAP*. For example, *Fivetran* acquired *HVR*, a tool for replicating ERP operational data, at the end of 2021.
- *Active metadata will replace data catalogues*: Enabling metadata is key to dozens of use cases related to visibility, cost management, quality, security, programmatic governance, or even data pipeline optimisation. With *Eventbridge*, for example, alerts are issued in the case of event-driven metadata automations (e.g. automatic tagging classifications). *Trident AI* uses the power of *ChatGPT-3* to automatically generate descriptions and READMEs for new datasets based on previous metadata. Via a *GitHub* integration, a list of affected datasets is automatically generated for each *GitHub* pull request.
- *Data management technologies alone do not help*: A formerly purely technical data management is complemented by core processes along all customer interactions. The visualisation and mapping of the most important use cases provide the "connectors" between the levels and the basis for a (technical) solution design (Fig. 5.9).
- *Data contracts*: They will establish themselves as an internal agreement between data producers and consumers, including governance rules. Data producers commit to produce data that adheres to predefined rules (e.g. data schemas, SLAs for accuracy or completeness) and to adhere to guidelines for the use and manipulation of all data. Responsibility (data governance) is assigned to the data producers (source). Dedicated tools are also available for this purpose, such as:
  - *yaml* files in the semantic layer of *dbt*, where data analysts can define their own metrics while building a *dbt* model.
  - *Open Lineage* from *Airflow*, which generates metadata about queries and executes datasets as DAGs; or
  - *Atlan's GitHub* extension, which creates a list of downstream assets affected by a request.
- *Semantic layers will gradually become established*: The semantic layer is the layer in a data architecture that uses semantics (words) that the business user also understands. Instead of raw tables with column names, semantic layers and data schemas are built, for example with column names like "customer". Semantic layers hide complex codes from business users while keeping it documented and accessible to data teams. Data producers can now define metrics in *dbt*, for example, and data consumers can query these metrics in downstream tools. Regardless of which BI tool they use, data analysts and business users can call up ad hoc statistics and be confident that the answers provided are correct. This process becomes easier as more tools are integrated into the semantic layer.

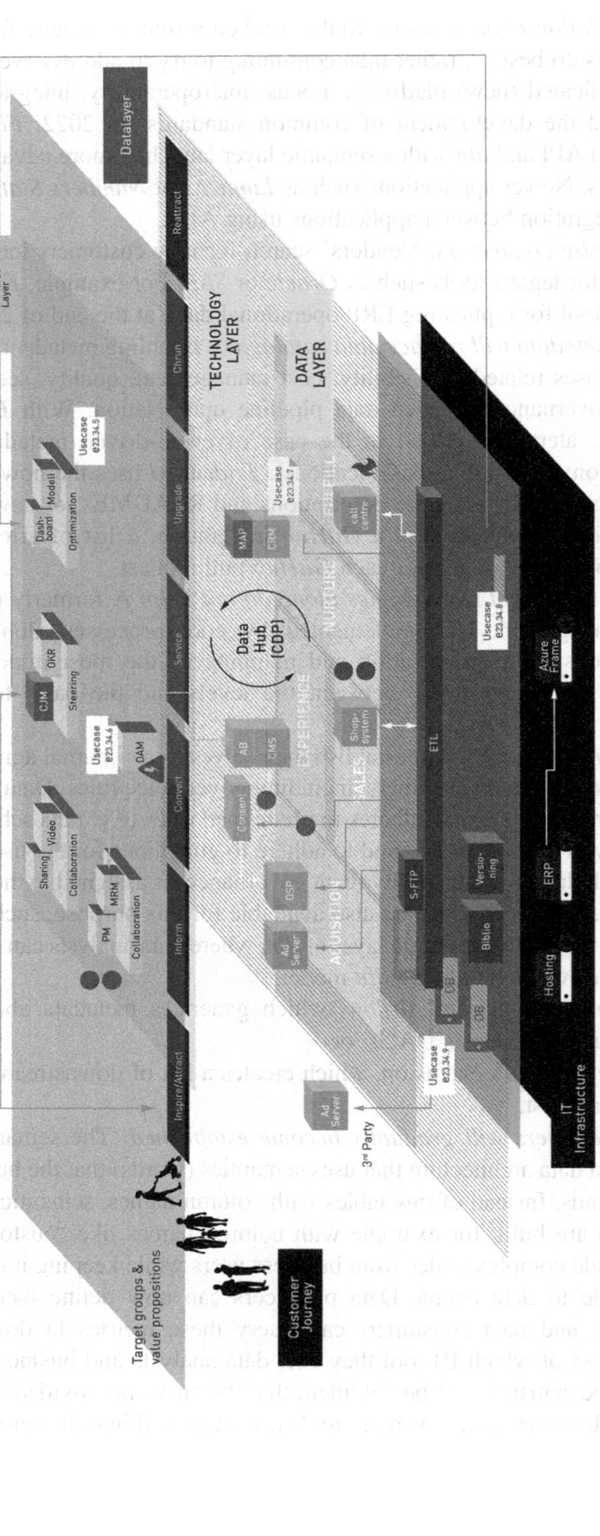

Fig. 5.9 Levels of infrastructure, data, applications, and processes (project example: FMCG manufacturer)

- *Data activation complements CDPs*: In 2022, some reverse ETL vendors tried to reposition this tool category under the label "data activation". In part, this was also an inevitable consequence of modern data stacks that, like *Snowflake* and *Hightouch*, have the same data and functionality as many CDPs. Modern data stacks generate data in specialised SaaS products, route it into storage systems like *Snowflake*, where it is combined with other data and transformed in an API layer. The result is the customisability and ease of use of a CDP combined with the power of modern cloud computing solutions.
- *Data mesh architectures are going live*: In 2024, data mesh architectures are increasingly emerging, including reference architectures and implementation tools such as:
  - metadata platforms that integrate into developer workflows (e.g. APIs from *Atlan* and integration from *GitHub*).
  - data quality and validation tools (e.g. *Great Expectations* and *Monte Carlo*), and
  - using *Git*-like processes for data producers to integrate testing, metadata management, documentation, etc. (like *dbt*).
- *"Data reliability"*: "Data monitoring/observability" and "data quality" will merge into one category: "data reliability". Existing providers will continue to grow organically/inorganically (e.g. the acquisition of *Databand* by *IBM* in July 2022), comparatively newer providers will become mainstream (e.g. *Kensu* and *Monte Carlo*), and increasingly new tools will enter the market (e.g. *Metadata Metrics* by *BigEye*). In parallel, the number of open-source tools will continue to increase.

The further development in the direction of unified data infrastructures ensures that the foundation of the "MarTech philharmonic" continues to set.

5.3 Ways Out of "CookieGeddon"

With the announcement of Google to close down third-party cookies latest in 2025, all companies are looking for alternatives to track and measure online customer interaction. The alternatives stretch from first-party data, ID networks, cohort targeting, contextual or semantic targeting, down to modelling approaches and data pushes based on first-party data. Data Clean Rooms provide a secure environment for data exchange. Server-Side Tracking allows the continuation of tracking, while still being conforming with GDPR.

5.3.1 In Search of the Sacred Cookie Substitute

Latest in spring 2025, Google announced to shut down third-party cookies in Chrome, which would decrease reach in the market for addressing customers of up to 75%. Alternatives stretch from first-party data, ID networks, cohort targeting, contextual or semantic targeting, down to modelling approaches and data pushes based on first-party data. Currently, the majority focuses on first-party data.

With the argument of data protection, cross-domain tracking is to be prevented in the future. However, the proposed procedure and the legal framework defined in accordance with the GDPR and ePrivacy Directive tend to privilege companies with a high login rate, and thus existing personalised first-party data—which, in turn, is mainly the case with GAFA. The irony of history: overall, the already existing dependencies and oligopolies in the data/advertising market are further cemented. The GDPR and the ePrivacy Directive have thus turned the hunter's fence of the walled garden into a man-high Roman palisade fence. According to *Albert Camus*, the eternal contradiction between grand GDPR promises and meagre deeds could be summed up as: "*The absurd only makes sense insofar as one does not resign oneself to it*". As a counterstrategy for, among other things, the restriction on the use of third-party cookies, alternatives are therefore being discussed, such as:

- *First-party data (cookies)*: The collection of own data is and remains of central importance. The prerequisite for the collection of first-party data is that the respective domain (e.g. websites, content platforms, or apps) belongs to the company itself. The only limitation is that first-party data cannot always answer the question about which interests other users (might) have.
- *Cohort targeting*: First-party data of the publisher is used with the help of which the demand side can book previously coordinated cohort audiences with publishers. This can be done via pre-targeted deals, via curation on the SSP side or via data marketplace audience booking in the DSP.
- *ID networks*: Use of ID networks such as *netID*, *Utiq*, *Unified ID 2.0*, or *LiveRamp*, whereby none of the networks will probably suffice on its own due to a lack of critical mass and market penetration, but all will (must) adapt to the fact that DSPs/SSPs will (must) map several ID networks. Instead of cookies, IDs are used that are responsible for matching the data from the systems and platforms involved. The user's login on the publisher website is always the first point of contact to generate an ID, usually based on the E-Mail address that the publisher shares with the respective provider. Publishers and advertisers can continue to use the previous audience targeting throughout the entire programmatic journey, provided that the demand side actively supports the respective ID system. At the same time, first-party data from advertisers can also be applied. However, this "*ID+*" (e.g. from *Zeotap*) is:
  - publisher- or network/association-specific (i.e. it can only be read by the respective publisher) or
  - user-specific (i.e. it is only created for the respective E-Mail address specified. The transmission of the E-Mail address without consent is again critical from a data protection perspective, which means an opt-in should be available here as well).

  Applications such as *Zeotap* generate an ID, per SSP and DSP with which they are integrated, that can then be read by the individual market participants (Priebe, 2021). When a user logs onto a partner's website (publisher or e-commerce platform), the E-Mail address is transmitted in encrypted form to the service provider (assuming the user's explicit consent)—who converts it into an *"ID+"* identifier (or "token") and then plays it back. Targeting segments are filled with this *"ID+"*, which belong to a specific audience. The service provider assigns the sourced data from data partners to different segments based on socio-demographic data, interests, purchase intentions, or app use. These are made available for targeting on its own platform or in marketplaces where the solution is integrated. Customers or agencies are then able to activate them via DSPs. This allows any market participant who supports the service provider's infrastructure to link their user data to the identity solution—it simply creates a link between an ID and an attribute. The emergence of *data partnerships* will add further fuel to this model (as with *AdForm* and *The Trade Desk*).

- *Contextual or semantic targeting*: The environment will experience a renaissance. A comparatively easier implementation is offset by disadvantages, such as the fact that offers with multilayered content are difficult to capture or can only be used across marketers to a limited extent, which in turn limits their reach. Contextual targeting is an alternative strategy, especially from the publisher's point of view, to still be able to offer sufficient target-group-relevant reach with less data.
- *Modelling approaches and data pushes based on first-party data*: Using media mix modelling and digital attribution (at the individual segment level), offline channels can also be integrated. Customer-specific scorings (e.g. purchase probabilities or churn prediction) are calculated and included in the shopping platforms for improved tracking. Based on a game-theoretical approach, causalities can be derived from turnover and budget use in different categories and an attribution can be modelled.

For the future, from today's perspective, it is to be expected that only a fraction of the inventory can be addressed via IDs, but the majority will remain anonymous. According to *Max Weber*, *"the trained ruthlessness of the gaze into the realities of life"* is increasing and with it, inevitably, the pressure towards marketing mix modelling and the collection of own first-party data.

5.3.2 Data Clean Rooms . . . the Switzerland of Secure Data

Data clean rooms (DCRs) offer two or more parties the opportunity to connect their data using the independent platform of a third party (technology provider), with the aim to make analyses and targeting segments (audiences) usable in a privacy-compliant manner. The uploaded data goes through an encryption process, so that it can be compared anonymously, and is available for analyses and activation (retargeting). Incoming data is encrypted and processed in such a way that it can be used across the board without the partners involved being able to see the respective source data of other partners. With user consent, users can be tracked down to the POS level (e.g. *for customer journey analysis and attribution), but only at the first-*

	Independent Vendors			Data Warehouses	Walled Gardens & Publishers	
Type	Pure Play DCR	Identity and Data Provider with DCR	CDP with DCR	Data Warehouse DCR	Walled Garden DCR	Publisher
Vendor Examples	InfoSum Habu Decentriq Optable	Liveramp Merkury Neustar	Adobe BlueConic	Databricks Snowflake Google (upcoming)	Amazon Facebook Google	Disney NBCU Roku
Cookieless ID	No	Yes	No	No	No	Sometimes
ID Agnostic	Yes	No	Yes	Yes	No	No
No-Code UI	Yes	No	Yes	No	No	Sometimes

Fig. 5.10 The market for data clean rooms (DCR; Marketing Tech Monitor 2021) (For a similar approach, see Delval, S.: Demystifying the Data Clean Room Market, in: ActionIQ, April 2023)

party level and by one of the DCR partners. A second DCR partner can contribute its own data for pattern recognition. Machine learning is used to draw conclusions about anonymous web traffic.

Data clean rooms (DCRs) offer two or more parties the opportunity to connect their data using the independent platform of a third party (technology provider), with the aim to make analyses and targeting segments (audiences) usable in a privacy-compliant manner. The uploaded data goes through an encryption process, so that it can be compared anonymously, and is available for analyses and activation (retargeting; Fig. 5.10). Incoming data is encrypted and processed in such a way that it can be used across the board without the partners involved being able to see the respective source data of other partners. With user consent, users can be tracked down to the POS level (e.g. for customer journey analysis and attribution), but only at the first-party level and by one of the DCR partners. A second DCR partner can contribute its own data for pattern recognition. Machine learning is used to draw conclusions about anonymous web traffic. With the help of *cross-ID graphs*, companies can track customers across different touchpoints. These graphs are either person-based on identifiers or probability-based on impression or behavioural data.

The *advantages* for the data partners involved:

- GDPR compliant: Compliance with the privacy of a user, because only the supplying first party (owner) can track activities granularly on an event and profile basis, provided consent is given.
- Profile extension: Use of data and extension of profiling, without the need for third-party tracking or granular disclosure of user data.

Several concepts of DCRs are to be distinguished here:

- Walled gardens and publishers (e.g. *Google Ads Data Hub*, *Facebook*, and *Amazon Marketing Cloud*).
- Dedicated (pure play) DCR providers (e.g. *Infosum*, *LiveRamp*, and *Decentriq*).
- Data-as-a-Service or data warehouse providers (e.g. *Snowflake*).

The *differences* are mainly in the use of cookies, agnostic IDs, and no-code user interfaces:

- Cookie-less ID: Alternative identity solutions of third-party cookies provided by vendors.
- ID agnostic: Ability of a DCR to work with any identity chosen by the collaborating parties involved, as opposed to forced use of one or a few specific identities.
- No-code user interface: Allows business users to use the system to collaborate with other data providers without relying on data development or data analysis teams.

DCRs of the walled gardens offer the advantage of being able to draw from a large data pool and open direct activation in the respective (closed) ecosystem. The disadvantage is that the dependency on the respective GAFA provider is further cemented. Free DCRs, however, offer the advantage of being able to combine different data sets for targeting via data partnerships. The prerequisites for this are in any case (Sluis, 2022):

- the stringent organisation of incoming data, incl. consistent campaign taxonomies with logical categories for gaining subsequent insights;
- enough customer information with more than 1000 users to gain valid insights, as DCRs work based on aggregated cohorts;
- technical understanding (e.g. for SQL queries); and
- an experienced data science team to validate and draw further conclusions (Fig. 5.11).

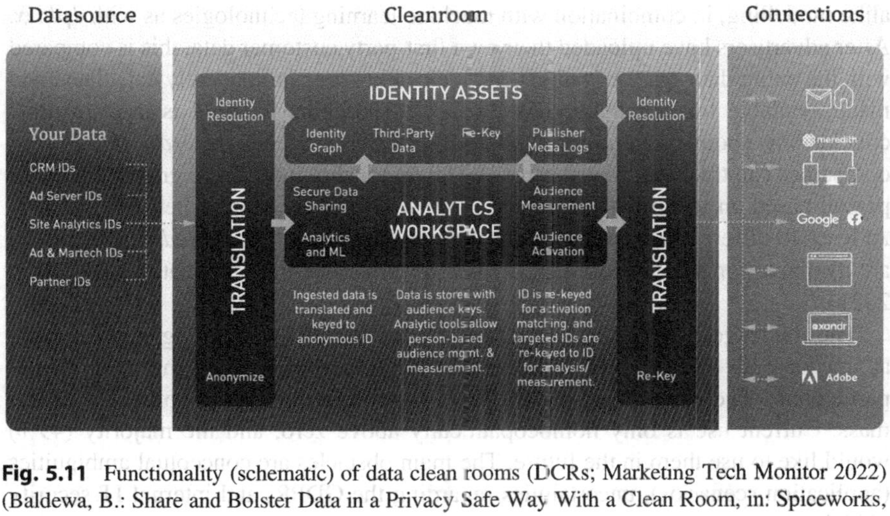

Fig. 5.11 Functionality (schematic) of data clean rooms (DCRs; Marketing Tech Monitor 2022) (Baldewa, B.: Share and Bolster Data in a Privacy Safe Way With a Clean Room, in: Spiceworks, July 2021)

The disadvantage is that the accumulated data in reporting and ad targeting is not nearly as accurate as data based on IDs. If first-party and transactional data is not shared with connected collaborative partners, this reduces the performance and usefulness of a DCR. For most companies, it is necessary to manually aggregate results from different DCRs (e.g. *Facebook* or *Google*), under the complication of a lack of standards. This will gradually increase the market power of the walled gardens—for example, *Google Ads Data Hub* is already the most widely used DCR. Since the DCRs lack compatibility among themselves, new data silos are to be expected. The consequence is that the hunter's fence of walled gardens further continues to evolve into man-high Roman palisade fences, again.

A further development of DCR envisages the processing of data in completely separate, individual databases. DCR specialists such as *Decentriq* do not have access to the input data (unlike *Infosum* and *LiveRamp*) but process it by converting it into mathematical representations and comparing it only on a highly aggregated, statistical basis. The result is personalisable categories that are made available to participants according to their respective eligibility. The data always remains the property of the respective parties involved, including the consent to be obtained (Kopnarski, 2021).

How the creation of a data partnership between advertisers and publishers (e.g. in the retail media sector) works varies greatly depending on the business model and the provider of a DCR. Often, the data is uploaded once by an advertiser, who then selects the publishers with whom he would like to enter an exchange. In return, both parties give each other explicit permission to carry out data reconciliation with each other. Consequently, DCRs do not have to be set up anew for each new process but can be used directly—provided mutual permission is granted. As a result, advertisers and publishers can evaluate, segment, and activate data in an aggregated, statistical form.

Based on the availability of the data, there is, for example, the possibility of look-alike modelling, in combination with machine learning technologies as with *1plusx*. After advertisers have uploaded their own first-party customer data, this is compared with the entire data space of publishers, look-alikes are automatically calculated and made available for activation (Disney, 2022). Machine learning is used to draw conclusions about anonymous web traffic. With the help of *cross-ID graphs*, companies can track customers across different touchpoints. These graphs are either person-based on identifiers or probability-based on impression or behavioural data. At least 40 different platforms such as *Arthur*, *Determined AI*, or *Red Hat Openshift* are available for the development of such machine learning applications (Dawson, 2021).

The challenge is to achieve critical mass in the market by involving brands as well as media and data partners to create a neutral platform for multiple market participants. The current use of DCRs is still far from the boiling point of a critical mass. Current use is only homoeopathically above zero, and the majority (49%) would like to use them in the future. The main obstacles are conceptual ambiguities (application scenarios), uncertainties regarding the GDPR, and internal IT security guidelines.

Via direct integrators, measurements within a DCR can also take place for walled garden providers by matching *Meta* or *Google* users with pre-formed panel lists using encrypted E-Mail addresses. In this way, a contact with corresponding campaigns on the platforms is verifiable and—as soon as the hash is decrypted—the contact can be enriched with further information from the provider's own data.

5.3.3 Careless (Data) Whisper: From Client to Server-Side Tracking

In server-side tracking, a so-called tunnel or proxy is used to load analytics indirectly and/or to send tracking events to Analytics. An advantage of server-side tracking with tag manager and a first-party tunnel for analytics is that the final tracking can be the same for all end devices and platforms (e.g. apps, websites). The advantages of this tracking approach are fewer tracking scripts in the browser, no uncontrolled reloading of third-party scripts, and faster loading times. In addition, the tracking proxy can be used as a privacy firewall and anonymise all data before further distribution. However, in terms of data protection law, this configuration must be evaluated in the same way as client-side tracking (consent). Furthermore, the proxy tunnel might also be used to partially disguise the call of analytics.

With traditional *client-side tracking* based on JavaScript, data is sent directly from the user's browser (client) to the tracking server. This form of tracking has the advantage that it takes place on the user's device and allows direct access to user-specific data such as cookies, URL parameters, user agent, referrer, and IP address. Location data (via IP address) can be used for personalisation, among other things. Client-side tags are executed in the browser via tag management systems, such as *Google Tag Manager* or *Tealium*, to be able to use comprehensive contextual data to personalise the user experience, serve ads, and deliver dynamic content to visitors. Tags or tracking pixels thus enable the connection to web analytics software or advertising networks (Fig. 5.12). The process (Jasarevic, 2020; Dr. DSGVO, 2021):

- The user calls up the website, and the browser then requests the page from the server.
- The server responds and sends the requested page to the browser (client side).
- The browser reads the page and finds that a *Google Tag Manager* is included in the header area, which requests a script from the tag management server (1).
- The tag management server responds and transmits (2) the script with all tracking codes that have been defined in the *Tag Manager*.
- As soon as the user performs actions (e.g. clicks) on the website, the container—from the user's client-side browser—sends data (3) to the website analytics application. The *Tag Manager* loads, for example, *Google Analytics* (4).
- Analytics on the website sends tracking data to a dedicated *Google Analytics* database (5).

Loading the *Google Tag Manager* therefore requires two data transfers: (1) a request to the Tag Manager and (2) the subsequent response to this request, then to

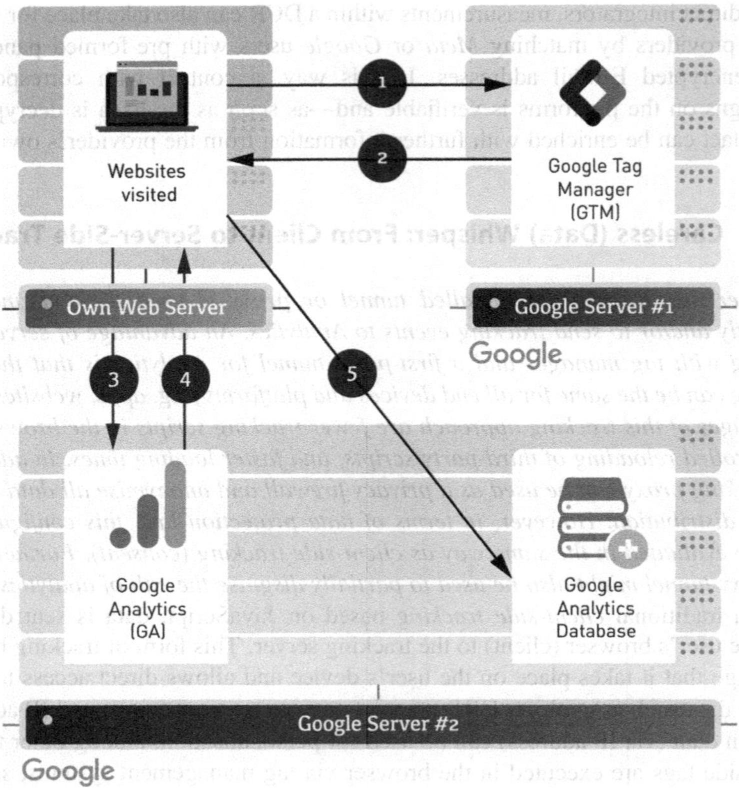

Fig. 5.12 Sequence of traditional client-side tracking (schematic)

the *Google Analytics* component. This results in a total of four data transfers for the retrieval of the *Google Tag Manager* and *Analytics*. The last data transfer is the logging of a user action in *Analytics*. One advantage lies in a comparatively simple implementation: providers provide a code snippet that is simply copied and pasted onto the website. The server, on which the website currently being visited is operated, is legitimate in terms of data protection law. Other servers (third party), however, collect data or pass it on without the (explicit) consent of the user. The downside is that new browser technologies and data protection regulations are shaking up this construct. Due to consent banners, browser-side restrictions (e.g. ITP and ETP), ad blockers and operating systems (iOS 14), 20% to 50% of the tracking data is often missing—this means that even online, no seamless customer journey can be mapped.

In server-side tracking, a so-called tunnel or proxy is used to load analytics indirectly and/or to send tracking events to Analytics. An advantage of *server-side tracking with tag manager and a first-party tunnel for analytics* is that the final tracking can be the same for all end devices and platforms (e.g. apps, websites) (Fig. 5.13):

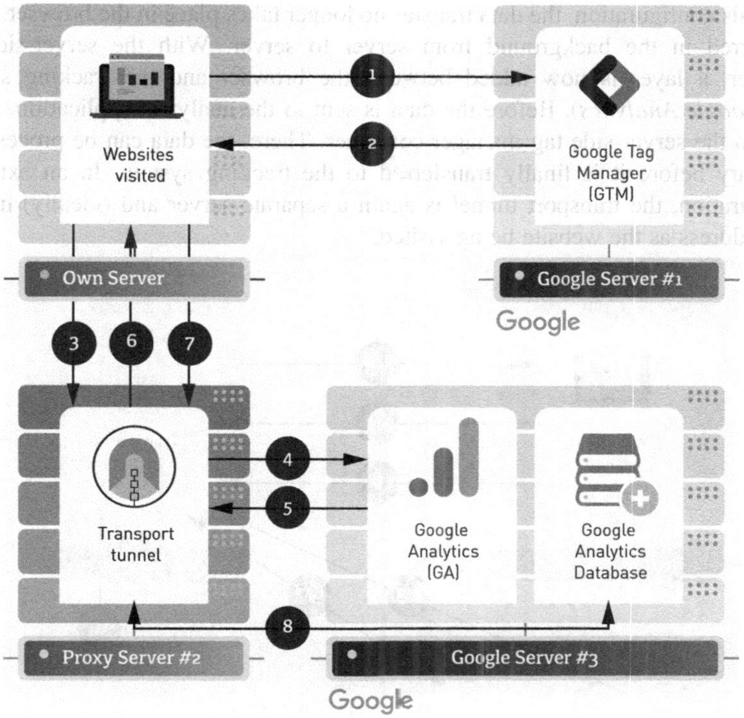

Fig. 5.13 Server-side tracking with the Tag Manager and a first-party tunnel for Analytics (schematic)

- The browser reads the page and finds that the tag manager is embedded in the header area, which requests a script from the tag management server (1).
- The tag management server responds and transmits (2) the script with all tracking codes that have been defined in the user interface of the tag manager.
- Indirectly (3), via a proxy transport tunnel, analytics is loaded (6).
- This, in turn, passes the request via the transport tunnel to an analytics system (4/5).
- Finally, data is sent via analytics to the tracking system via the tunnel/proxy (8).

The advantages of this tracking approach are fewer tracking scripts in the browser, no uncontrolled reloading of third-party scripts, and faster loading times. In addition, the tracking proxy can be used as a privacy firewall and anonymise all data before further distribution. However, in terms of data protection law, this configuration must be evaluated in the same way as client-side tracking (consent). In addition, the proxy tunnel might also be used to partially disguise the call of analytics.

In this configuration, the data transfer no longer takes place in the browser, but is transferred in the background from server to server. With the server-side tag manager, a layer is now added between the browser and the tracking service (e.g. *Google Analytics*). Before the data is sent to the analytics application, it first lands in the server-side tag manager container. There, the data can be processed if necessary before it is finally transferred to the tracking system. In an extended configuration, the transport tunnel is again a separate server and (ideally) has the same address as the website being visited.

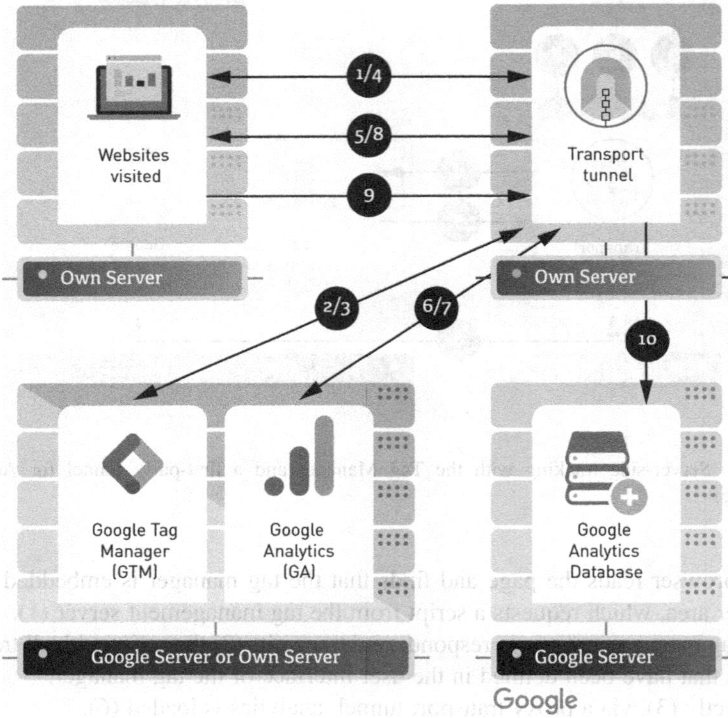

Fig. 5.14 Server-side tracking with a first-party proxy for all data transfers (schematic)

In the third scenario, *server-side tracking with a first-party proxy for all data transfers*, all data transfers are handled via a separate proxy server. Tracking takes place independently of the client (depending on the browser version) and allows a higher accuracy in data collection, as no HTTP tracking request can be lost, nor can ad blockers prevent the request (Fig. 5.14). The browser therefore plays no role and cannot block tracking:

- The website retrieves the *Google Tag Manager* from its own server (1).
- The tag manager is loaded from a separate server (2/3).
- Similarly, *Google Analytics* is retrieved via the proxy (5/8).

- The results are made available to the tunnel (9).
- From the tunnel, they are sent to analytics (6).

A central proxy system collects all data and then passes it on to third-party providers. Additional solutions such as a tag management system or content delivery networks are not needed. From a data protection perspective, server-side tracking makes it possible to send fewer personal data about the website visitor to *Google* and other providers. Tracking is not based on cookies and can be better mapped across devices and applications. The disadvantage is that browser interactions which do not trigger access to the web server (e.g. mouse tracking or dynamically changing the display) are not recorded. However, the implementation is initially more costly for the operator of a website.

Analogous to data clean rooms, penetration in the market is still comparatively low—only just under 9% of companies state that they already use server-side tracking in 2023, with a cumulative 64% indicating potential for the future.

Previous solutions do not change anything in terms of compliance with data protection requirements (consent with explicit opt-in). Exceptions to the strict consent requirement—"unconditional necessity" according to Section 5, paragraph 3, page 2e of the Privacy Directive (II.1.a.) or the appeal to downstream processing in server-side tracking (user cannot be mapped thanks to pseudonymisation and twin servers)—are not applicable to third-party services even if recognised interpretation methods are exhausted, considering case law. Providers such as *Jentis* offer ways out by generating synthetic client IDs (without IP address), which can be transferred to third-party providers as part of a consent-free downstream processing phase and, in the specific individual case, within a "predominantly legitimate" interest pursuant to Section 6, paragraph 1 of the GDPR. In addition, sufficient safeguards must be implemented in this case, which can currently be assessed with reasonable argument as "supplementary measures" within the meaning of the European Court of Justic ruling from 16 July 2020 in the "*Schrems II*" case. However, the survey of data protection experts also shows differences in legal interpretations.

5.4 Customer Data Platforms: Data Love Unlimited

The complexity of implementation and a lack of integration are the main obstacles to the meaningful use of data. CDPs *try to precisely overcome this weakness by serving as a "bridge" between the different forms of data collection and data types. CDPs (primarily) work with personalised first-party data, which is aggregated as PII and cookie information as consistently as possible on a user profile, and then collected directly from the user, before using various key identifiers (in addition to anonymous IDs,* e.g. *personal identifiers such as E-Mail or postal addresses) for data synchronisation.*

The hype around customer data platforms (CDPs) is likely to continue unabated in the coming years—for the same reason as before: the complexity of implementation and a lack of integration are the main obstacles to the meaningful use of data.

CDPs try to precisely overcome this weakness by serving as a "bridge" between the different forms of data collection and data types (Fig. 5.15).

Solution	Known Data	Unknown Data	Semi- and Unstructured Data	Ultra-Granular Flexible Data from Multiple Sources (Single Customer View)	Realtime Ingestion/ Access	Out-of-the-Box Analytics Capabilities	Marketer Independence from IT	Available to All Outside-Solutions
CDP	yes	yes	yes	yes	yes	yes	yes	yes
Data Warehouse	yes	yes	yes	yes	no	no	no	yes
CRM	yes	no	no	no	no	no	yes	no
DMP	no	yes	no	no	yes	yes	yes	yes
Marketing Automation Platform	yes	no	no	no	no	no	yes	yes

Fig. 5.15 Differences between CDPs and other MarTech applications (Marketing Tech Monitor 2023) (For a similar approach, see MarTech: Customer Data Platforms: A Marketers Guide; sixth edition, 2022, p. 11)

CDPs (primarily) work with personalised first-party data, which is aggregated as PII and cookie information as consistently as possible on a user profile, and then collected directly from the user, before using various key identifiers (in addition to anonymous IDs, e.g. personal identifiers such as E-Mail or postal addresses) for data synchronisation (Fig. 5.16). Cookie data is anonymised or pseudonymised. The result is a cross-platform, individualised user profile. *Data stitching* combines data sets from different sources and devices to gain a comprehensive insight into customer behaviour and the customer journey (across devices). In *data matching*, the same "units" within a CDP are probabilistically or deterministically matched.

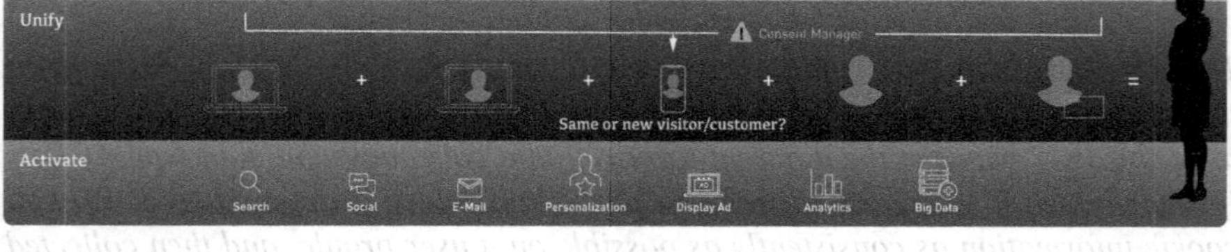

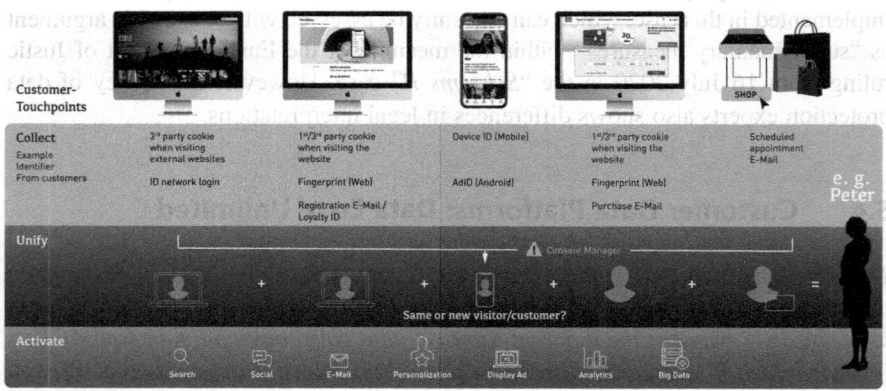

Fig. 5.16 Data aggregation and activation via a CDP (schematic)

Using individual identifiers between personalised first-party CRM data and anonymised first- /third-party cookie data (DMP), CDPs thus bridge across different data types, such as (Fig. 5.17):

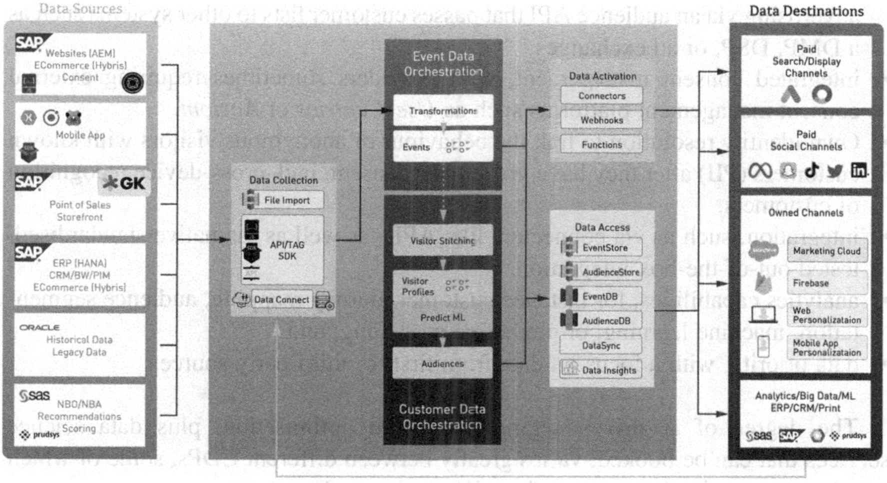

Fig. 5.17 Functional building blocks and architecture of a CDP (schematic; Marketing Tech Monitor 2023)

- *Events*: Behavioural data resulting from user actions such as website, app, or browser sessions.
- *Customer attributes*: Names, addresses, contact details, birthdays, etc.; as well as predictions based on machine learning and purchase probabilities with modern CDPs.
- *Transaction data*: Purchases, returns, and other information from e-commerce or POS/ERP systems.
- *Campaign metrics*: Engagement, reach, impressions, and other campaign-related numbers.
- *Customer service data*: Live chat data, number and duration of interactions, service tickets and frequency, NPS scores, and other personalised data from CRM systems.

While most CDPs have features such as identity resolution, offline/online data, analytics, or even out-of-the-box third party or API-based integration, *differences* are evident in the details, such as:

- persistent storage of customer data over a longer period.
- real-time data updates, in response to changes.
- options to load and export data to the CDP or share data with other services.
- ability to personalise and activate across channels, share segments with other MarTech applications (e.g. marketing automation tools), ESPs or web content management systems for dynamic interactions, and product/content recommendations (campaign capability); ideally, a CDP supports digital

advertising via an audience API that passes customer lists to other systems such as a DMP, DSP, or ad exchanges.
- integrated consent management, with providers sometimes requiring external consent management platforms such as *UserCentrics* or *Acxiom*.
- Own identity resolution to link the behaviour of anonymous visitors with known customers (PII) after they have given their consent, incl. cross-device recognition of customers.
- integration, such as via connectors like APIs, as well as via native standardised/ tested out-of-the-box integration.
- analytics capabilities, for instance customer journey mapping, audience segmentation, machine learning, or predictive modelling; and
- data priority, with a focus on data from first- or third-party sources.

The degree of AI-driven segmentation and optimisation, plus data science services that can be booked, varies greatly between different CDPs, some of which are already perceived in extracts from BI platforms (Fig. 5.18).

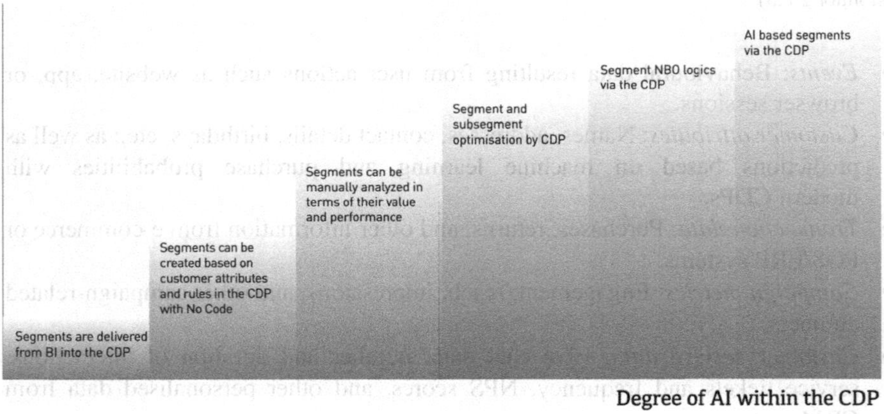

Fig. 5.18 Degree of implementation of artificial intelligence in a CDP

The inflationary use of the term CDP means that, according to the *Customer Data Platform Institute*, applications should only be called *Real CDP* if they fulfil criteria such as: the collection of data from any source, the collection of all details of this data, an indefinite and persistent data storage, the uniform creation of profiles of identified persons, and the sharing of data with any connected system. Accordingly, CDPs differentiate further through the data collection, data unifying, and data activation phases of the marketing tech stack (Fig. 5.19):
- *Data CDP*: A CDP that collects customer data from different source systems, links these customer IDs, and stores the results in a database that is accessible to external systems. In practice, this application segment (e.g. *Twilio Segment* or *Tealium*) also extracts target group segments and transfers them to external systems. The applications are often started as tag management or web analytics

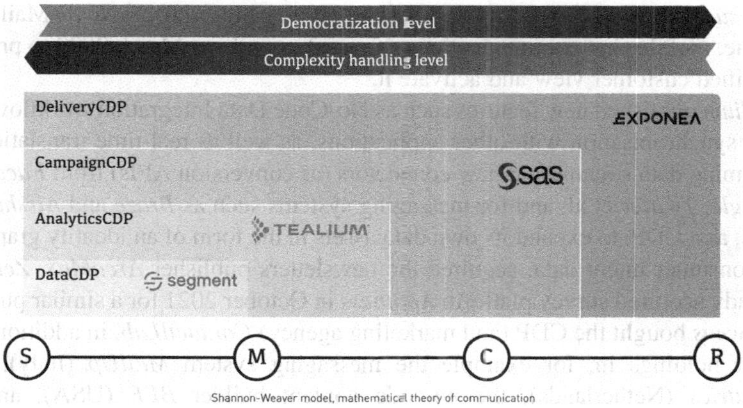

Fig. 5.19 Complexity and democratisation levels of CDPs (according to MarTechTribe; Marketing Tech Monitor 2021)

applications. Use cases include merging customer data from multiple data sources (e.g. websites, ERP and CRM) or performing data cleansing and standardising the different data formats during import

- *Analytics CDP*: In addition to data aggregation, there are analytical use cases ranging from simple customer segmentation to machine learning, predictive modelling, and journey mapping. Applications such as *Appier*, *Neustar/Transunion*, *Treasure Data*, *Oracle,* or more recently *Tealium* automate the distribution of data to other systems around marketing automation. Use cases can be found, for example, in the analysis of the conversion of a campaign (e.g. responses such as orders) or in the creation of exact customer profiles, segments, or personas for targeted addressing via E-Mail or on the website.
- *Campaign/Engagement CDP*: Beyond data aggregation, these applications (e.g. *CrossEngage*, *SAS*, *ActionIQ*, or *Dun & Bradstreet*) also provide activation, such as personalised messaging, outbound marketing campaigns, real-time interactions, or product or content recommendations, to orchestrate customer management across channels. Examples of use cases include creating a look-alike match or even sending web visitors to a DMP for retargeting.
- *Delivery CDP*: Aggregation of data, analytics, customer interactions, and delivery of personalised messages via E-Mail, the website, mobile app, CRM, a display ad, or various combinations. Examples include *Adobe Real-Time CDP*, *Zeta*, or *Bloomreach Engagement*. Applications in this environment often started as campaign management systems and have subsequently added CDP functionalities.

As before, the application scenario for most CDPs changes over time, directly or via partner solutions. For example:

- *Treasure Data*, as a CDP, announced a partnership with *Sinch* (E-Mail, text, phone, mobile chat communications services) as early as March 2022 to produce a unified customer view and activate it.
- *Tealium* published new features such as No-Code Data Integration workflows and data synchronisation with other applications, as well as real-time translations of incoming data streams and new connectors (as conversion APIs) from *Facebook*, *Google*, *Twitter* et al. and for messaging systems such as *Braze* and *Airship*.
- *Zeta*, as a CDP, to expand its own data assets in the form of an identity graph and of consumer intent data, acquired the newsletters publisher *ArcaMax*. *Zeta* had already acquired survey platform *Apptness* in October 2021 for a similar purpose.
- *Growens* bought the CDP (and marketing agency) *ContactlLab*, in addition to its other holdings in, for example the messaging system *MailUp* (Italy), *CDP Datatrics* (Netherlands), the no-code content builder *BEE* (USA), and the E-Mail provider *Acumbamail* (Spain).
- The CDP *Optimove* has further expanded its campaign capabilities by acquiring the mobile messaging platform *Kumulos*. This acquisition adds push notifications, in-app and web messaging, and geofencing. *Optimove* had already added an E-Mail engine with the acquisition of *PowerInBox* in 2018.
- *Treasure Data* has further expanded its product portfolio with a new omnichannel journey orchestration tool (Journey Orchestration). This includes, among other things, a no-code journey builder as well as the possibility of aligning customer journeys with phases in the life cycle or specific events, up to and including journey dashboards.
- *Treasure Data* also integrates *Acxiom*'s Identity solution into its CDP to improve data collection and identification and make data accessible everywhere. Both technologies essentially allow companies to build their own identity graph to get a more granular view of users and their cross-channel customer journey.

The wild fabrication about aggregated data is increasingly translating into demand on the corporate side: more than 77% of marketing decision-makers indicate that they are planning to introduce a CDP in the future or are already in the selection phase, regardless of B2C or B2B application scenarios (Fig. 5.20). According to a global *Twilio* survey, more than a third of Gen Z and millennials will buy from another brand if the interaction is not personalised in real time (Twilio, 2024). Almost 20% of companies will have replaced their existing CDP for this purpose in 2023 already, making CDPs one of the applications with the greatest "swap potential". Accordingly, the augurs expect the CDP market to triple by 2028 . . . the utilisation of existing infrastructure, better cross-channel data control, modularity, and interoperability will open up further market potential for the coming years.

The perfidious thing about the introduction and use of CDPs across all clusters is that the selection still turns out to be comparatively simple—the live operation, however, extremely complex due to the multilayered and rather complex possibilities of use. Despite all the glorification and hype that CDPs have experienced recently, they nevertheless must face a harsh reality:

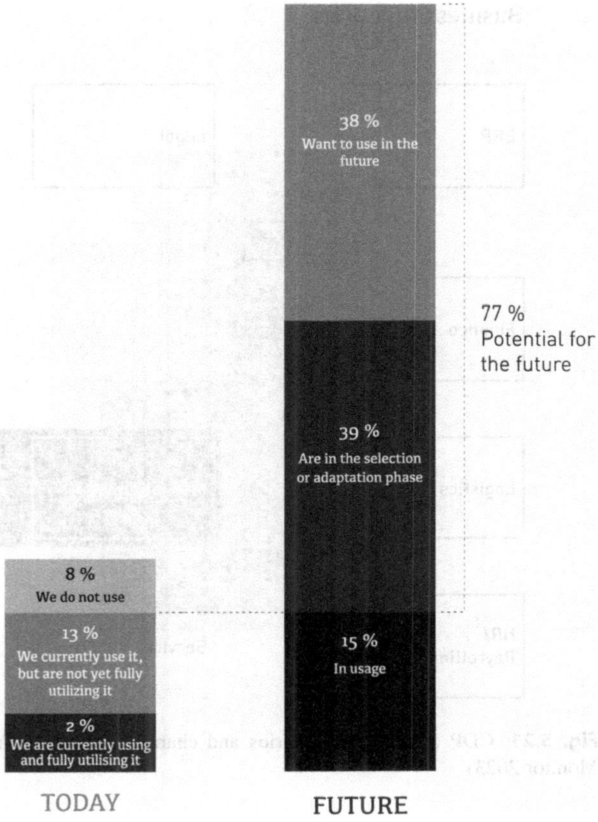

Fig. 5.20 CDP use already implemented and plans for the future (in %, $n = 295$; Marketing Tech Monitor 2022)

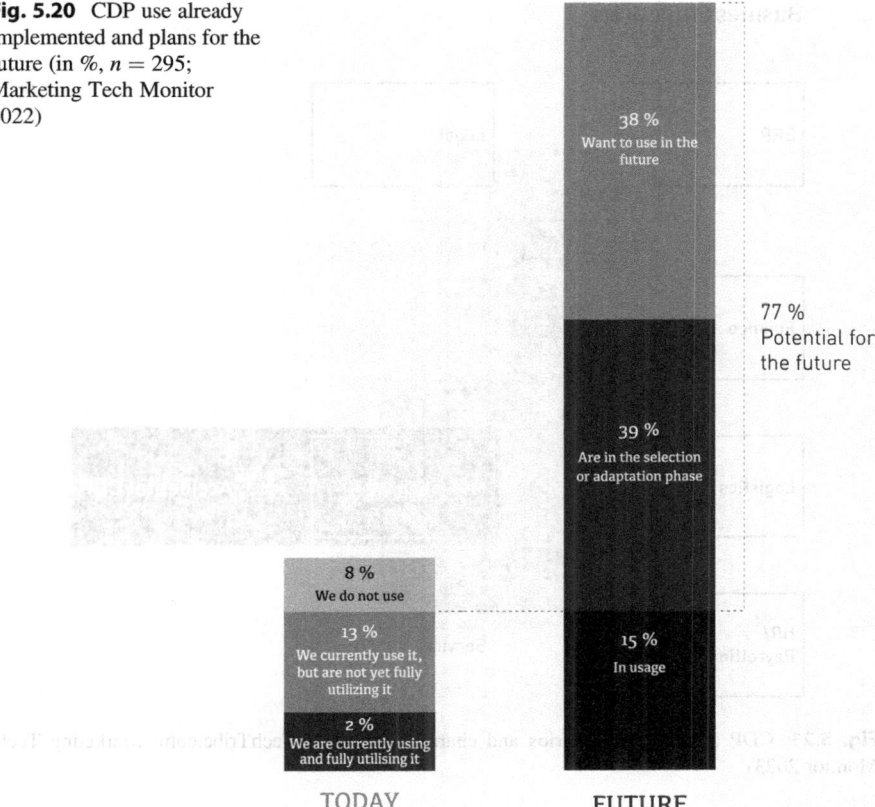

- Technologically, CDP measurements on the web today are still largely based on cookies, a discontinued model. The development of the ID network market and its integration into CDPs will thus be decisive for the success of all providers in the future.
- At the same time, painstakingly created 360-degree customer profiles from a multitude of data sources face a rather disappointing number of activation options in the "reality check".

Across the application scenarios and based upon their origin and coverage of application scenarios, CDPs can be broken down as (Fig. 5.21):

- *Accidental CDPs*: Applications that were originally designed for a different application area, such as marketing automation.
- *Data* CDPs: Collecting customer data from source systems or tracking/tagging systems (e.g. *Segment*)
- *Analytical CDPs*: Analytical applications aimed at customer segmentation and audience building (e.g. *mParticle*).

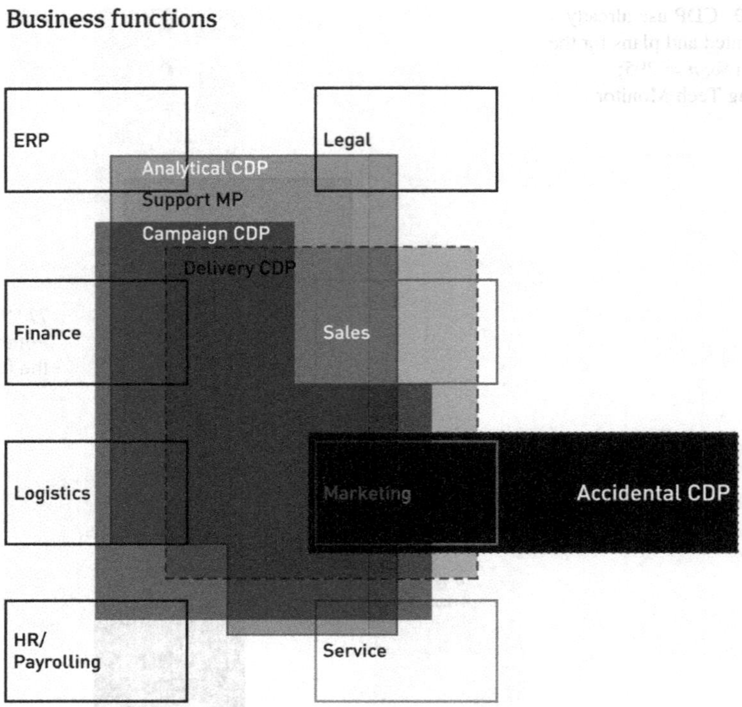

Fig. 5.21 CDP application scenarios and characteristics (MarTechTribe.com; Marketing Tech Monitor 2023)

- *Campaign CDPs*: Customer interactions through data activation and analytics (e.g. *SAS*).
- *Delivery CDPs*: Delivery of cross-channel messages based on customer interactions (e.g. *Bloomreach*).

A "CDP connector race" has been observed in the market for about 2 years now. Analogous to the emergence of portal applications at the beginning of the 2000s, CDPs advertise native interfaces to a variety of other applications (Byrne, 2023). Depending on the extent of CDP use (and different patterns are emerging here), the use of a CDP can fail due to potholes in data management—which is why it is imperative to fit a CDP into an overarching data architecture.

The key to success is to find out how much development effort is required for a true "real-time" integration, for example in the context of a proof of concept (POC). The challenge in most architectures is decoupling the content layer from the data layer. In essence, the success of an implementation is determined by the functions (Fig. 5.22). Although "Behavioural Reporting", "Custom Reports", "Omnichannel Personalisation", and "Segment/Persona Profiles with Interaction Timelines" are held in the highest esteem, they also have the greatest functional deficits.

"Most liked"	"Most used"	"Most missed"
Behavioural Reporting	Multichannel/Omnichannel Data Collection	Data Quality Monitoring
Real-time Data Collection	Behavioural Reporting	Predictive Content
GDPR, CCPA or HIPAA Compliance	Custom Event Tracking	Omnichannel Personalisation
Custom Reports	Real-time Data Collection	Integrated and Incoming Events
Multichannel/Omnichannel Data Collection	Consent Management	Behavioural Reporting
Consent Management	Channel Reporting	Data-driven Segmentation
	Custom Reports	Segmentation Based on Journey Stage
		Channel Reporting
		Behavioural Segmentation
		Segment / Persona Profiles with Interaction Timelines

Fig. 5.22 Analysis and evaluation of the most important CDP application scenarios (Top 10) (MarTechTribe: Global MarTech Requirements Database, April 2023, G2 Tool Evaluation, March 2023)

5.5 Cross-Channel ID Management: Is the 360-Degree View of the Customer Finally Coming?

The advent of the post-cookie era has led to a feverish search for technical solutions that can compensate for the gradual loss of reach. The so-called device graphs are one approach, but their probabilistic approach can neither compensate for the 1:1 targeting demanded by the market, nor can they be implemented due to mechanisms such as frequency caps. The goal of login data alliances: to create an antipole in Central Europe to the US-dominated walled gardens, which in recent years have established a quasi-standard for authentication on the net with their social login. From a business perspective, the advantages of login alliances are obvious: the digital identities of individual users are protected so that sensitive data does (must) not leave the EU legal area. However, so far only a few companies claim to already be working with a data alliance. The much-vaunted noble desire for "platform-agnostic" methods apparently still ends at one's own front door and consequently lacks critical mass in adoption.

The advent of the post-cookie era has led to a feverish search for technical solutions that can compensate for the gradual loss of reach. The so-called device graphs are one approach, but their probabilistic approach can neither compensate for the 1:1 targeting demanded by the market nor can they be implemented due to mechanisms such as frequency caps. The goal of login data alliances such as *Verimi*, *netID,* and *Utiq*: to create an antipole in Central Europe to the US-dominated walled gardens, which in recent years have established a quasi-standard for authentication on the net with their social login. From a business perspective, the advantages of login alliances are obvious: the digital identities of individual users are protected so that sensitive data does (must) not leave the EU legal area. However, so far only a few companies claim to already be working with a data alliance. The much-vaunted noble desire for "platform-agnostic" methods apparently still ends at one's own front door.

Motivated by this, other providers have recently entered the market, such as *LiveRamp* and *Zeotap*. The criteria for assessing the respective solutions range from the uniqueness and stability of the ID, cross-device support, availability along the entire digital exploitation chain and conformity with data protection to the level of distribution in the market (penetration). To ensure the uniqueness of the ID, all providers use either an E-Mail address or a telephone number to generate the ID (Fig. 5.23). Data protection requirements are secured in each case using different encryption methods. The challenge with this approach is that not all publishers and advertisers have sufficient E-Mail addresses, including consent, from their users.

	Prebid	LiveRamp	ZEOTAP	Unified iD	BritePool	neustar fabrick ID	ID5	netID	G	
Cross-Device	✗	✓	✓	✓	✓	✓	✓	✓		✓
Support AdTech	✓	✓	✓	✓	✓	✓	✓	✓	✓	✓
Conforming with GDPR	In consideration	In consideration	✓	In consideration	In consideration	In consideration	✗	✓	tbd	In consideration
Certification	✗	✗	ePrivacy Seal	✗	✗	✗	✗	Tech Certification	✗	✗
ID Stability	✓	Until Opt-Out	Until Opt-Out	Until Opt-Out	Until Opt-Out	Until Opt-Out	Until Opt-Out	✓	Topics for 3 weeks	Until Opt-Out
ID Basis	Shared ID (not Cross Domain)	E-Mail oder Phone Number	E-Mail oder Phone Number	E-Mail oder Phone Number not proprietary, incl. SSO-light optional	E-Mail	E-Mail oder Phone Number	E-Mail, Soft Signals, probabilistic & determininistic, Fingerprinting (not optional)	E-Mail/NetID Account required (Membership)	Provision of topics in the browser	E-Mail, Community incl. SSO
Reach	N/A	10–15 % in DE	5–10 %	0 %	N/A	N/A	5–10 %	ca. 50 - 60 % Internet user in DE	All Chrome user (ca. 70%)	Only UK
Market Coverage Media Agencies	Shared ID	low	low	low	N/A	N/A	low	low	high	Only UK

Fig. 5.23 Overview of different ID providers (Marketing Tech Monitor 2021)

The most important functions on the part of ID providers (Parker, 2022; MarTech, 2021):

- Onboarding of data (including online/offline matching).
- Availability of a proprietary identity graph.
- Establishing/securing ownership of first-party data on the client side.
- Persistent person/household IDs.
- Compliance with all data protection regulations.
- APIs for third-party system integration.

Some of the vendors further differentiate their ID platforms via advanced features such as:

- the establishment of confidence scoring,
- private (first-party data) and/or second-party data identity graphs, and
- pre-built connectors to other MarTech platforms.

In the programmatic environment, not all ID solutions are supported yet, although DSP providers are gradually adapting to this. The fact that DSP providers do not want to offer the matching of their own IDs (cookies) with the IDs of dedicated ID providers currently appears problematic. Thus, all ID solutions always remain in their own domain—resulting in a new walled garden. Nevertheless, the potential for the future seems immense: 76% of the companies want to use an ID solution in the future (Fig. 5.24). "Glory Days" for ID providers.

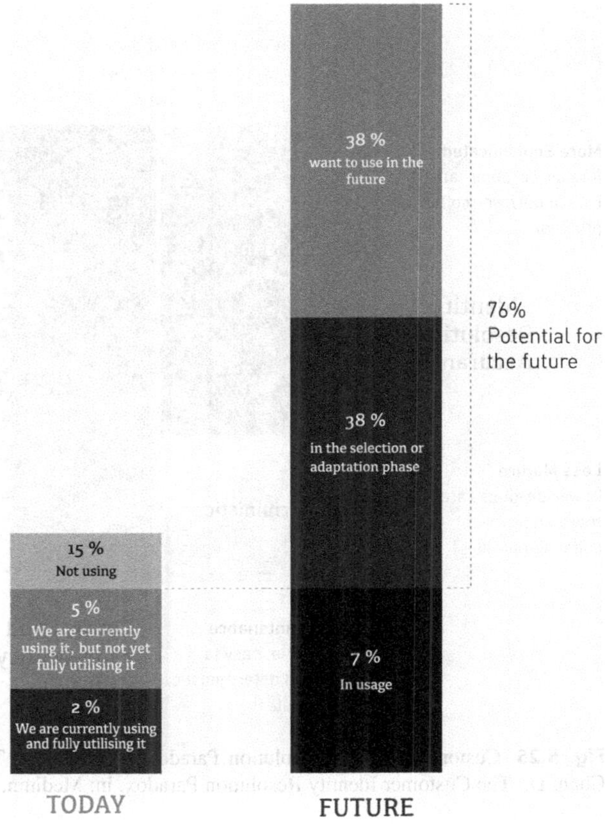

Fig. 5.24 Technology use already implemented and plans for the future in the area of ID management (in %, $n = 295$; Marketing Tech Monitor 2022)

Device graphs are one approach, but due to their (mostly) probabilistic approach, they can neither compensate for the 1:1 response demanded by the market nor can they be implemented, mostly due to mechanisms such as frequency caps:

- *Deterministic approaches* are convincing due to their simplicity and transparency or traceability. However, the simplification of the IDR logic ensures the assigned identities are less accurate, for example because Jochen Mueller and Jo Mueller are one and the same ("under collapse") or Jochen Mueller jmueller@E-Mail.com and Janine Mueller jamueller@E-Mail.com are actually two different people ("over collapse").

• *Probabilistic approaches* aggregate those identities that have higher statistical assignment rates. This often makes the advanced logic of the identity resolution solution difficult to understand and manage (black box).

Some advanced IDR solutions attempt to balance algorithmic/probabilistic features with deterministic features. The challenge with this is that the most used confidence values result in a probabilistic approach (*Customer Identity Resolution Paradox*; Fig. 5.25).

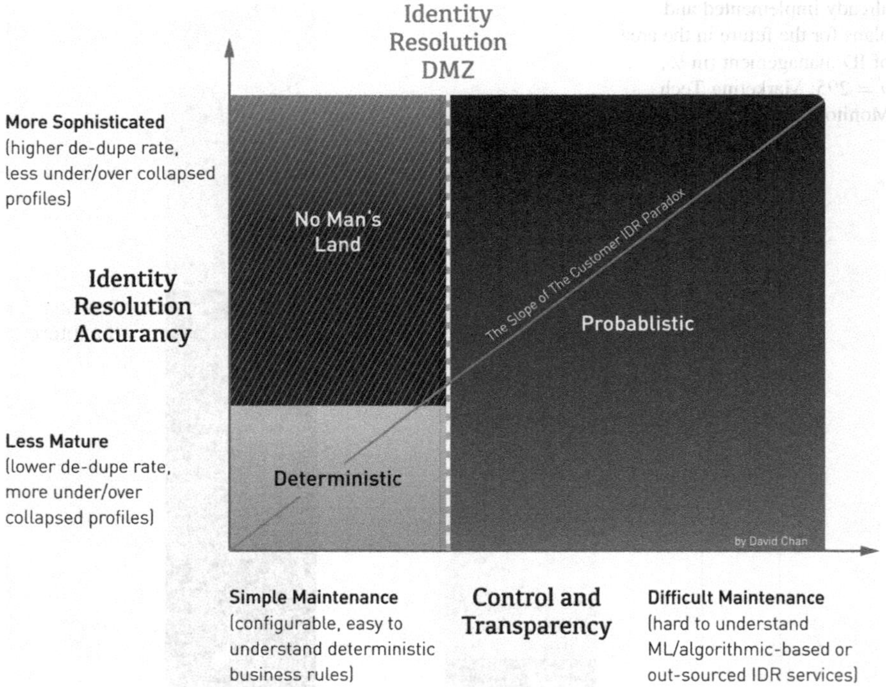

Fig. 5.25 Customer Identity Resolution Paradoxon (Marketing Tech Monitor 2023) (See also Chan, D.: The Customer Identity Resolution Paradox, in: Medium, August 2022)

All ID vendors work with execution systems, so market penetration is dictated by the adoption of CX and DSP applications, which is why no vendor has yet been able to achieve a sufficiently large market coverage and make any corresponding efforts:

• *Xandr* (now *Microsoft Advertising Network*), as a large international provider with a DSP, SSP, and Curate solution, is basically open to all ID systems and is focusing on *Unified ID 2.0*, *RampID*, and *netID* in 2022, which was rolled out more widely by the end of 2022.
• *The Trade Desk*, as one of the largest DSP providers in the international market, has itself launched *Unified ID*, which is now starting the development of a European version, called EUID, with *LiveRamp* and some other European

providers. While *Trade Desk* takes care of the technology itself, *LiveRamp* helps with their *Authenticated Traffic Solution* (*ATS*). *ATS* offers market participants a first-party authentication option to identify users using *LiveRamp's* ID graph and link them to data in the next step. As part of the collaboration, AdTech companies will also be able to bid on *LiveRamp's* own *Ramp ID* via *The Trade Desk* in Europe. Both IDs, *EUID* and *Ramp-ID*, should eventually become interoperable.
- *LiveRamp* has entered in parallel a partnership with *Adobe*. As both companies announced in early 2022, *LiveRamp's* identifier solution *Ramp-ID* will be supported across channels by *Adobe Advertising Cloud*. This includes desktop display, desktop video, mobile web, mobile in-app, smart TV (CTV), native and audio. The goal is to enable identity-based targeting and measurement without third-party cookies.
- *Active Agent/Adition* has already integrated *ID5* and *netID*, but is basically taking the approach of wanting to integrate every ID.
- *Adform* has already integrated several other ID networks such as *Unified ID 2.0*, *LiveRamp*, *ID*, *PreBid*, *netID*, *PubCommon ID*, *ID+* (*Zeotap*), *BritePool*, *Epsilon* and *Neustar/Transunion*. At the same time, they have launched *ID Fusion*, which virtually generates an (internal) overarching super-ID and integrates other ID providers.
- *Transunion/Neustar* has already launched *Fabrick* at the end of 2021 to generate critical mass—an ecosystem for publishers and other platforms to establish a network of identities in an infrastructure that enables messages to be sent to the (anonymous) identities in real time and on a large scale.

There is no free lunch: ID providers are remunerated via a CPM or via a CPM in addition to the CPMs of the media spends. In addition to deterministic methods for matching IDs, probabilistic methods are also used, with a much higher degree of inaccuracy. Therefore, before using comprehensive, DSP-specific ID solutions or cross-device or household graphs, it is advisable to question which methods are used for matching in each case, including the costs induced by this. The costs are foreseeably either reflected in the inventory prices on the publisher side or increase AdTech costs (via the DSPs) on the part of the advertising companies.

The criteria for assessing the respective solutions range from the uniqueness and stability of the ID, cross-device support, availability along the entire digital exploitation chain and conformity with data protection to the level of distribution in the market (penetration). To ensure the uniqueness of the ID, all providers use either an E-Mail address or a telephone number to generate the ID. Data protection requirements are secured in each case via different encryption methods. The challenge with this approach is that not all publishers and advertisers have sufficient E-Mail addresses, including consent from their users, for example for data exchange within the ecosystem of retail media (Fig. 5.26).

New movement came into the market at the beginning of 2023 with the announcement of the telecom providers *Deutsche Telekom*, *Orange*, *Telefónica*, and *Vodafone*. Together, they have received approval from the EU Commission for antitrust law for the application to establish the joint venture *Utiq*. The objective

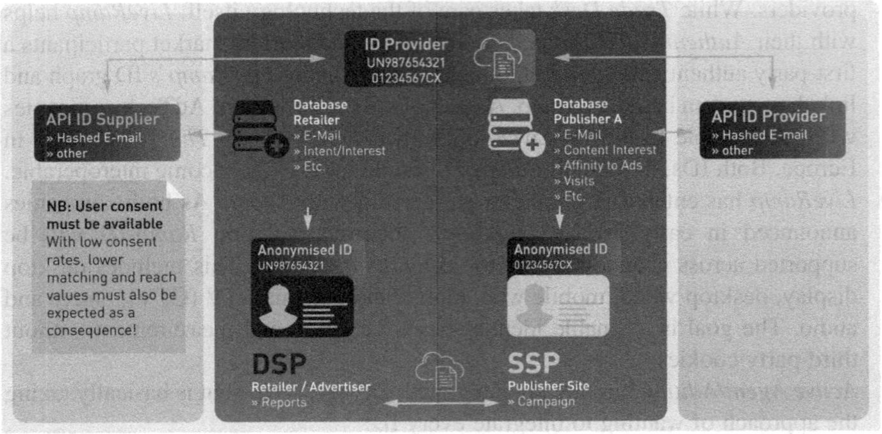

Fig. 5.26 Transfer of anonymised IDs within the context of retail media (project example)

of the cooperation is to establish a cross-operator targeting solution for digital advertising on mobile devices with a large reach as a "privacy-friendly, digital identification solution". The companies plan to generate a "secure, pseudonymised token", with the user's ID being provided by the participating network operator. This will enable advertisers and publishers to recognise mobile users without revealing personal data. With the help of the generated ID, personalised advertising can be displayed, specifically as "delivery of online display advertising" and "website/app optimisation" on an opt-in basis by first obtaining consent through a pop-up. In a separate privacy centre, users are to be allowed to view and revoke their consents.

The underlying technology is based on the *Vodafone* project *Trustpid*. In the *Trustpid* procedure, the telecommunications providers give access to a network-based infrastructure for the service. They create a pseudonym (if the user actively agrees) by processing the user's IP address. On this basis, further pseudonymous tokens are created, which are then managed by *Trustpid*. Beyond that, the network operators or *Trustpid* do not pass on any customer data (e.g. demographic or network data). It is Alice in ID Wonderland—other ID solutions can only dream of the operators' enormous reach (which extends across the whole of Europe). However, the advertiser data is not matched across the board. Advertisers' data remains in their respective silos and each advertiser addresses its target group based on its own opt-in registered touchpoints (Lomas, 2023). The data can therefore not be enriched, analogous to the targeting solutions from US providers. In addition, *Trustpid* generates a new token every 90 days, which means that the link to the previously collected data is lost (Lepitak, 2023).

After the green light from the EU, the biggest challenge for the success of the project is probably obtaining user consent. *Apple's App Tracking Transparency* (ATT) has shown that even with full transparency towards mobile users, the consent rates are initially rather low. The user as the "object of desire" refuses to accept the sophisticated technical concepts and targeting variants. The telcos as senders could also seem rather "scary" to some users—after all, the whole range of personal data is available here thanks to an official (mobile phone) contract.

In reality, the much-vaunted noble desire for "platform-agnostic" methods still ends at one's own front door: only a few companies say they are already working with a data alliance. Most company representatives are rather cautiously optimistic about the future success of data alliances—technology providers with their own data platforms continue to receive the most encouragement. The irony of the story: at the same time, the majority of precisely these technology providers have a US provenance, which again counteracts the intended data protection. The follow-up questions in the interviews underline this. There is a noble desire for a counterpool to the US-dominated platforms, but the actual own commitment rather exposes this desire as a fig leaf discussion. At the same time, the ID providers face a chicken-and-egg problem due to a *lack of critical mass*: if only a few companies join them, it is all the less attractive for private users to consult their services. Also, media agencies might be reluctant to support the use of unified IDs since a unified ID would

- ... directly provide transparency on the effective media reach ... instead of the "reported or fine-tuned media reach".
- ... would detect which traffic is human (with an ID) or bot traffic ... reducing ad fraud to a minimum.
- ... indirectly open transparency also for fee structures and kickbacks on the side of the media agencies.

5.6 Blockchain and NFTs in Web3: Goodbye Centralised Data Management and GAFA?!

The blockchain as a distributed ledger technology is basically nothing more than a decentralised protocol for transactions between parties that transparently records every change on the part of all participants. Decentralised in this context indicates that the protocol—figuratively speaking as a huge database—is not located on a server at one company but is distributed across many computers. Whereas it used to be a ledger that was responsible for managing all the details of a transaction, it is now replaced by a transparent, decentralised database.

The blockchain as a distributed ledger technology is basically nothing more than a decentralised protocol for transactions between parties that transparently records every change on the part of all participants. Decentralised in this context indicates that the protocol—figuratively speaking as a huge database—is not located on a server at one company (as is the case with *Facebook*) but is distributed across many computers. Whereas it used to be a ledger that was responsible for managing all the details of a transaction, it is now replaced by a transparent, decentralised database. Every piece of information captured by the system is verifiable. The need for a central authority to vouch for the authenticity of the data is eliminated. The blockchain is thus a neutral system of information processing that belongs to no one and can hardly be manipulated due to the redundancy of the distributed data storage.

Transactions can be any kind of information. The parties are the participants who take part in a blockchain-based solution and follow the respective rules of the blockchain. It enables transactions directly between the participants without the involvement of an (otherwise fee-based) intermediary. This also prevents frictions such as dominant monopolies and walled gardens. Transparency in the blockchain arises from the fact that the journal (ledger) is constantly controlled by a network of the so-called *miners* or validators. These miners verify the deposited information block by block and share it in the network, in which every participant has access to the same blockchain. They are paid for their work (i.e. the provision of computing power for the proof-of-work process), for example via tokens.

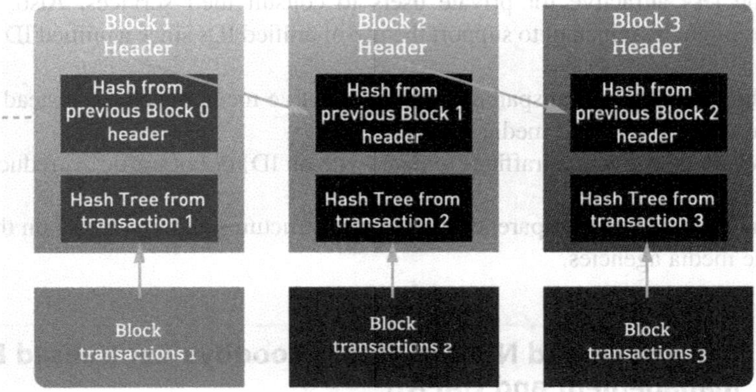

Fig. 5.27 Example of a simplified blockchain

In the simplest application example for bitcoins, a blockchain consists of a series of data blocks in which one or more transactions are combined and provided with a checksum—in other words, they are combined in pairs to form a hash tree (Fig. 5.27). The contents of a block (transactions in the ledger) are hashed to assign a unique numeric value. The definition of hash is the processing of the content of a file to assign a unique numeric value to the content. Using the numeric value, search algorithms can identify the contents of a file. The root of the tree is then stored in the associated header. The entire header is then also hashed, and this value is stored in the following header (Ali et al., 2019).

This ensures that no transaction can be changed without also changing the associated header and all subsequent blocks. The sequential storage of data in a blockchain means that it cannot be subsequently changed without damaging the integrity of the entire system, making the manipulation of data virtually impossible. The decentralised consensus mechanism replaces the need for a trustworthy (third) instance to confirm the integrity of transactions. New blocks are created via a consensus process and then appended to the blockchain.

The blockchain as a distributed ledger technology therefore is basically nothing more than a decentralised protocol for transactions between parties that transparently

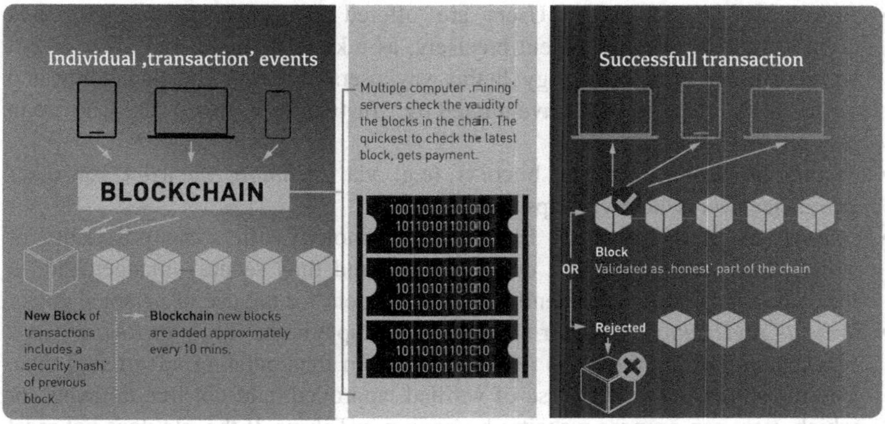

Fig. 5.28 Blockchain process (schematic, Marketing Tech Monitor 2022)

records every change on the part of all participants. Whereas it used to be a ledger that was responsible for managing all the details of a transaction, it has now been replaced by a transparent, decentralised database (Fig. 5.28). Every piece of information captured by the system is verifiable.

> *The Blockchain will permanently revolutionise the way we advertise and shape customer interaction.*—Tim Alexander (Global CMO, Deutsche Bank).

From the point of view of marketing and sales, blockchain thus has the potential to revolutionise existing structures in the long term, such as (Wood, 2022; Scherf, 2019):

- *Product creation and liability*: The blockchain can ensure that the path of individual raw materials through the supply chain, up to the finished product, remains traceable, for example in the case of luxury goods (i.e. batch tracing). To obtain this information, customers only need to scan a QR code via their smartphone.
- *Monetisation of original content*: Authors and content producers can distribute their content via the blockchain and get paid for it immediately. The system thus tends to offer creatives better conditions in direct sales. In the music industry and the management of rights, a blockchain-based music service presents itself as a public (decentralised) music shop in which record contracts are no longer necessary; artists manage the rights to their own music themselves and set the conditions for the use of the music, so that fans and artists interact directly with each other. The distribution process as in the *Decent Network* does not require external third parties; artists can easily control and manage copyrights and prices themselves.

- *Prevention of fake news*: Users are offered an economic incentive (via cryptocurrency) to rank content precisely, as a kind of "audit trail" for content based on blockchain technology. In this way, users can better understand how and where news originated and have it rated by "trustworthy" other users, who are in turn remunerated for this.
- *Mobile payment*: Spending bitcoins (e.g. via *Lightning Network*) or other currencies everywhere via apps.
- *Anonymised customer data*: Blockchain technology offers the possibility of storing transaction data in a decentralised—and thus secure—manner and, at the same time, using it efficiently, as does consent for the use of personal data.
- *Website registration*: Another application example is the *adChain Registry* as a blockchain-based protocol to prevent bots from manipulating advertising data. The registry acts as a database of verified, approved, and bot-free domains for which users can propose websites by paying *adTokens*. If the site does not meet the standards, the user loses his deposited *adTokens*. In essence, advertisers pay for registered websites on the *adChain* as a certification authority.
- *Securing advertising data in direct business between advertisers and publishers*: *AdHash*, for example, is an advertising platform that enables publishers and advertisers to place ads, manage campaigns, and collect performance data on-site, on their own servers—without intermediaries. By using a blockchain, unique IDs are implemented for each ad, securing the ad placement process so that it can be transparently verified at any time who is advertising what, why, and where. In addition to reducing complexity, the trust problem is solved by a direct transaction channel between advertisers and publishers. All decisions are stored via the platform in a publicly verifiable journal. The value chain, in which many service providers participate, is reduced at its core to an ad server. Smart contracts are concluded that take effect precisely when a predefined event occurs (e.g. a website is visited by certain users). Blockchain-based campaigns for *Chris Hadfield* (author of "*Apollo Murders*"), for example, show a 4.3 times higher engagement, 1.6 times more visitors, and a cost-per-click reduced by a factor of 4.3 via contextual targeting.
- *Increasing the efficiency of online advertising*: Advertisements are only booked, delivered, and billed when an identified user visits a page, and this is stored in the control platform. Advertisers can also define in the platform which environments and pages are desired and which are not. Issues such as ad fraud or brand safety are thus a thing of the past. Similarly, other irregularities are prevented, such as:
  - *Below-the-fold ad playback*: Although the user could not see the ad playback, excessively high CPMs are shown in combination with unusually short time-to-click periods. These can then be analysed in the form of a heat map.
  - *Prevention of ad reloads*: An analysis of the time-to-click and time-on-page distributions shows that header bidding wrappers as intermediaries (due to pre-bid-based CPM) ensure both parameters do not gradually decrease linearly—rather, via ad reloads across all ad exchanges as fraudulent behaviour, the ads are reported multiple times in the tracking.

- *Auditing processes*: Advertisers who want to track in detail how the respective budgets have been used receive this information directly from the advertising platform connected to the blockchain in an automated way.
- *Avoidance of advertising reactance*: The platform stores what kind of advertising someone individually finds useful and acceptable. In other words, an opt-in system that makes "hard" opt-outs à la ad blockers unnecessary.

Web3 envisages a decentralised, immutable version of the global network based on blockchains—free of intermediaries and equipped with the same cryptographic verifiability as cryptocurrencies, *non-fungible tokens* (NFTs) and DApps, a new type of decentralised application based on a distributed ledger. NFTs as "non-replaceable tokens" represent digital certificates that clarify the authenticity of a digital file on the blockchain and are simultaneously its rights of use. NFTs are managed via smart contracts. These computer protocols map the NFT contracts and verify the settlement on the technical side. The NFTs can be bought and sold with smart contracts via suitable trading platforms. The respective transaction is executed based on the blockchain. In the process, both buyers and sellers must be identified via their respective crypto wallets (Fig. 5.29).

This digital ownership certificate therefore clearly proves who the owner of an original digital file is. This file can be a photo, a video, or an audio recording. It is clearly stored in the blockchain that the original file belongs to a user who created the NFT or purchased it on a marketplace. NFTs therefore also have the potential to be individualised and to serve as a space for advertising—in other words, to replace the much-discussed cookies with a uniform, blockchain-based ID. The self-sovereign identity (SSID) approach allows users to decide which companies or services use the

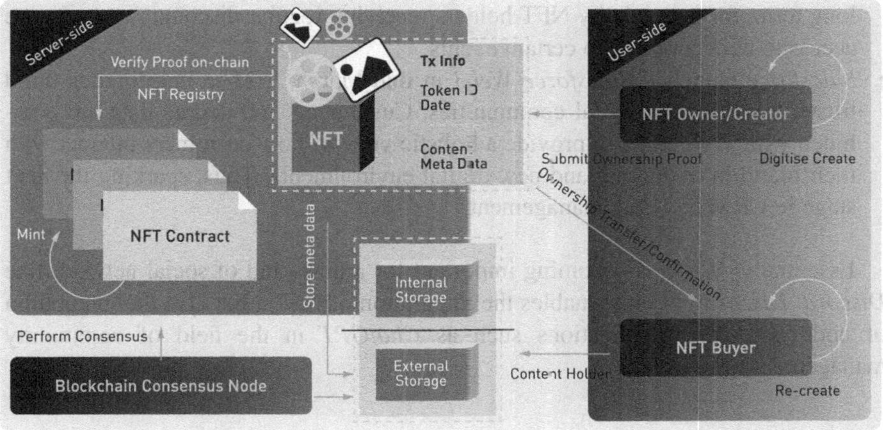

Fig. 5.29 Standard use and workflows for NFTs (Marketing Tech Monitor 2022) (Bhujel, S.; Rahulamathavan, Y.: A Survey: Security, Transparency, and Scalability Issues of NFT's and Its Marketplaces, in: Sensors, Vol. 22 (2022), No. 8833)

data and which do not. The user has the option to separate their wallet, and thus their SSID, from a company at any time. However, this comes with risks:

- Long-term storage/security of digital objects: NFT is merely the proof of authenticity for the respective digital object. The latter is not stored in the blockchain (unlike the NFT). Long-term storage of the digital asset on normal web servers is not low risk, whereas NFT depends on the security of the stored asset.
- High resource consumption by the blockchain (e.g. electricity, hardware).
- Risk of money laundering and price bubbles.

Companies can "reward" fans and followers with NFTs, for example like a loyalty program. Against this backdrop:

- *Mattel* develops digital versions of the popular *Hot Wheels* toy cars and sells them through its own marketplace. The NFTs here are animations in which legendary *Hot Wheels* vehicles are assembled in detail from individual parts.
- *Nike* secured a patent for its *Crytpokicks* back in 2019. The idea: sneaker fans not only buy a shoe, but also receive a unique NFT with a digital image of the sneaker. *Nike* can thus prove the authenticity of its shoes and offer customers a unique product that can last long beyond the physical product and whose value increases over time.
- *Adidas* launched a cooperation with the blockchain game "*The Sandbox*" at the end of 2021, in which they jointly created the "*Adiverse*", a digital world that makes the brand accessible to game players and in which they can also purchase digital goods such as clothing for their avatar in the form of NFTs. At the same time, Adidas is launching its own proof of attendance protocol (POAP) collection of NFTs that attendees of real or virtual events receive for showing up. These tokens primarily offer the possibility to bind customers with first-party data in the long term, for example by NFT holders receiving regular discounts or exclusive access to collections or to certain events.
- *Salesforce* launched *Salesforce Web3* in mid-March 2023 to help brands build trusted, sustainable digital communities. Customers' 360-degree data are combined with Web3 data to provide a holistic view of how customers interact with their brand in traditional and new digital environments. Thus, sparking the next stage in CRM and data management.

Essentially, Web3 is becoming important for a new kind of social network like *Discord*. *Discord* not only enables the integration of NFTs, but also the integration of code and other applications such as *ChatGPT* in the field of community management.

References

Ali, M. S., Vecchio, M., Pincheira, M., Dolui, K., Antonelli, F., & Rehmani, M. H. (2019). Applications of Blockchain in the internet of things: A comprehensive study. *IEEE Communications Surveys & Tutorials, 21*(2).

Bean, R. (2022, February). *Why becoming a data-driven organisation is so hard*. Harvard Business Review.

Byrne, T. (2023, March). *The CDP connector myth*. MarTech.

CCW Digital, Sprinklr. (2023, March). *Outsmarting adversity: How brands can future-proof contact centers in a possible economic downturn*.

Dawson, R. (2021, December). *How do you evaluate MLOps platforms?* MLOps Community.

Dehghani, Z. (2019, May). *How to move beyond a monolithic data lake to a distributed data mesh*.

Disney. (2022, March). *Disney's proprietary clean room data solution sets its sights on measurement & activation*.

Dr. DSGVO. (2021, May 17). *Serverseitiges Tracking: Unterschied zum Client Side Tracking und Datenschutzaspekte*.

Fowler, M. (2020, December). *Data mesh principles and logical architecture*.

Jasarevic, D. (2020, September 5). *Google tag manager: So funktioniert das serverseitige Tagging*. t3n.

Kopnarski, N. (2021, September 24). *Können Data Clean Rooms die personalisierte Werbung retten?* ADZINE.

Lepitak, S. (2023, February 10). *Marketing power set to shift as EU telecom giants get green light for joint platform*. Adweek.

Lomas, N. (2023, January). *European carriers file to create joint venture for opt-in ad targeting of mobile users*. TechCrunch.

Marketing Tech Monitor. (2022).

MarTech. (2021, December). *Enterprise identity resolution platforms*.

MIT CISR Data Board. (2018).

Myers, A. (2021, February). *Reverse ETL—A primer*. Memory Leak.

Nielsen Annual Marketing Report. (2022).

Parker, P. (2022, January). *23 questions to ask identity resolution vendors during a demo*. MarTech.

Priebe, A. (2021, April 1). *Im Maschinenraum der Werbe-IDs*. ADZINE.

Prukalpa. (2022, January 11). *The future of the modern data stack in 2022*. Towards Data Science.

Scherf, J. (2019). *Zukunftsmärkte, Nachhaltigkeit, Transformation/Blockchain im Marketing: Daten, Transparenz, Nachhaltigkeit—Potenziale und Bedingungen der Blockchain-Technologie für das Marketing von Unternehmen*.

Sluis, S. (2022, October). *Google unveils PAIR for clean-room-style activation*. AdExchanger.

Starburst. (2022, March). *The 2022 state of data & what's next*.

Twilio. (2024, April). *2024 State of customer engagement report*.

Wells, D. (2021 June). *Data architecture: Complex vs. complicated*. Eckerson Group.

Wood, C. (2022, January). *How marketers will use blockchain technology and NFTs in 2022 for identity, branding and engagement*. MarTech.

Online Data Protection According to GDPR: Or: What Is Actually (Still) Allowed? (Dr Simon Menke)

6

The area of online data protection is characterised by a multitude of different legal points of view. In addition, the existing legal situation is in part extremely complicated and permanently in flux, among other things because some important legal questions from the area have not yet been (finally) clarified by the courts. The following contains a data protection classification of topics that are particularly relevant for the practice of online marketing:

6.1 Online Tracking

Online tracking has been the subject of extensive discussions on data protection law for quite some time. These discussions initially revolved primarily around the question of whether consent must be obtained in principle for online tracking to be carried out. Furthermore, the exact requirements for obtaining consent for online tracking were and are still being discussed, insofar as such consent must be obtained. In addition, individual browser providers have switched to blocking third-party cookies. In this context, *Google* has announced that "*Chrome*" will prevent cross-website tracking in the future ("*Privacy Sandbox Project*"). Furthermore, *Apple* has made specifications regarding obtaining consent for the use of the *IDFA* as an app identifier. These changes have consequences for individualised online marketing at the "user level", which is still widespread today. How the changes described will play out in practice remains to be seen. What is certain, however, is that further (new) discussions on data protection law will arise with them.

6.2 Basic Consent Requirement

Regarding the collection of tracking data, the relevant EU regulation can be found in Section 5, paragraph 3 of the *ePrivacy Directive*. According to this, the storage of data on end devices (e.g. by setting cookies) as well as the retrieval of data from end

R. Strauss, *Data-Driven Customer Engagement*,
https://doi.org/10.1007/978-3-031-64295-1_6

devices ("access") generally requires the consent of the user. The basic idea behind this requirement is that the integrity of end devices is worth protecting. In the view of the European legislator, the integrity of terminal equipment is worth protecting to such an extent that the basic consent requirement also applies if the data processed by accessing the respective terminal equipment is anonymous. The provision in Section 5, paragraph 3 of the ePrivacy Directive is also technology neutral. This means that it applies not only to the setting of cookies, but also to the use of other technologies such as "browser fingerprinting". After decisions of the ECJ and the BGH, the German legislator explicitly implemented the previously discussed requirements in Section 25 of the German Telecommunications Telemedia Data Protection Act (*TTDSG*) on 1 December 2021 with a delay of several years. The provision in Section 25 of the TTDSG, and thus the basic consent requirement, incidentally, refers exclusively to access to the respective terminal device. The further processing of tracking data is assessed according to the General Data Protection Regulation (GDPR). Any consent required for further processing can be obtained together with the consent pursuant to Section 25 of the TTDSG. The requirements standardised in the GDPR regarding obtaining consent apply to the consent pursuant to Section 25 of the TTDSG.

6.3 Exceptions to the Consent Requirement

It is not necessary to obtain consent if, among other things, access to the terminal device is "*absolutely necessary*" for the operator of the website to be able to make it available to the user. In this context, in the absence of a legal definition, it has not been conclusively clarified what is meant by "absolutely necessary". However, there is broad agreement that the assessment of the issue discussed here must be based on the respective subpage or the respective "feature" of a website. The user also has no right to demand that a website operator design his website in such a way that it does not contain any "features", for example for which the setting of a cookie is necessary. To the extent that this is technically possible, a cookie may only be set in such cases if the respective user makes use of the "feature".

It is certain that the so-called "*technically necessary*" cookies fall under the exception to the consent requirement discussed here. The setting of such cookies is, for example, necessary for maintaining a login. It is also recognised that, among other things, the setting of cookies for the purpose of implementing legal requirements does not require consent. A typical application for this is the setting of a "zero cookie" for the purpose of implementing the revocation of a granted tracking opt-in. The question of whether the collection of tracking data for the purpose of carrying outreach measurement (in particular the analysis of the number of views of individual sub-pages) is possible without obtaining consent is frequently discussed in practice. In this regard, a reasonable and pragmatic position was taken by the French data protection authority (CNIL). According to this position, the setting of cookies for the purpose of analysing aggregated tracking data, for example, is possible without consent if the user is informed of this and granted a right to object in this regard. However, it remains to be seen whether this view, which is not shared by all data protection authorities, will stand up to judicial review. In practice, cookies are also often set for billing purposes. This is the case, among other things, in affiliate marketing, to enable the settlement of a CPC and/or a CPO remuneration. The choice of how website operators finance the operation of their website is exclusively up to them, insofar as the method of financing is in line with the existing legal requirements. In this context, it should be noted that there is no legal requirement that prohibits website operators from integrating (non-individualised) advertisements into their website. It is also the sole responsibility of the advertiser and the publisher to decide which type of remuneration they agree upon. The fact that the debtor of the service to be remunerated must be able to prove that a claim for remuneration has arisen corresponds to the general principles of civil law. Insofar as the setting of cookies is necessary for such proof, this must also be "absolutely necessary" by law.

6.4 Design of the Banner Text

In practice, data protection advisors are often asked what exact information the text on the content banner (on the "first layer") must contain. There is no explicit legal regulation in this regard. However, it is recognised that the complete content of consent declarations can be made available to the user by means of a transparent link. The complete content of the consent text can then be viewed on the "second layer". Such a procedure is basically also in the interest of the users since banner text that is too detailed often scares them off and the content is not taken note of. Users who wish to read the exact information before giving the requested consent have the possibility to retrieve it by means of a click. In addition to the content of the consent form, the user must also be provided with further information to ensure sufficient transparency as well as to ensure fair processing of the data. To comply with the legal requirements, the following information should be reproduced on the "first layer":

- "Designation" of the data controller (website operator) collecting the consent.
- the number of partners to whom data are transmitted based on consent and who further process them as data controllers based on consent.
- The purposes of the data processing operations.
- The fact that "profiling" is conducted, where this is the case.
- An indication that the consent given can be permanently revoked on the "second layer".

In the opinion at least of the German data protection authorities, it must also be pointed out that data is transferred to the so-called unsafe third countries (e.g. USA), if this is the case.

6.5 "Nudging"/"Cookie Walls"

Regarding the legal assessment of obtaining consent for the implementation of online tracking measures, there is an intensive discussion about "nudging". In this context, "nudging" is understood to mean the design of opt-in banners in such a way that they entice online users to give their consent. Some argue that the required voluntary consent is only given if the possibility to agree to tracking measures and the possibility to refuse this consent are designed on an equal footing. To fulfil this requirement, two buttons of the same size, next to each other and in a neutral colour would be necessary. This view was expressed by the *German Federal Council*, among others, in its statement on the draft of the TTDSG. In connection with the topic discussed here, however, it must be considered that website operators have a legitimate interest in obtaining consent for the purpose of collecting online tracking data. Often, website operators heavily rely on obtaining such consent. This applies, for example, in cases where the respective website has no relevant "organic reach", and sufficient frequency can only be achieved using certain online marketing tools. Insofar as practice shows that users are mostly "annoyed" by the display of content banners, and therefore often give consent without sufficient knowledge of the information provided on the respective data processing, this circumstance cannot be blamed on the website operators. A law is only good if it achieves the desired effect in practice. Since this is not the case—as in the subject area discussed here—it cannot be the task of the market participants (here the website operators) to compensate for the "deficiency" emanating from the law by an excessive implementation of the legal requirements. Against this background, it was correct for the German government to reject the aforementioned proposal of advisory and supervisory boards.

However, it should also be noted that in practice, there are designs of "consent banners" for which it is questionable whether they meet the legal requirements. For example, "cookie walls" are sometimes used—in other words, cookie banners that make the viewing of content dependent on the user's consent to be tracked. Insofar as, in such a case, the "cookie wall" is provided with a conspicuous "agree" button, but the user can only refuse to give consent if, for example, they have to call up the data protection information linked in the "wall" and search extensively for the possibility of refusal in this, the consent given is very unlikely to be effective due to the lack of "voluntariness" (this was also the case, for example, in a recent decision of the LG München I in Germany).

Furthermore, it should be noted that the European legislator has standardised a ban on the use of "dark patterns" in the recently passed Digital Services Act (DSA). *Dark patterns* are design patterns that induce users to behave in a certain way that is contrary to their interests and thereby exploit the design power unilaterally in the interest of their users. According to the widely held view, this also influences the design of consent banners, with the consequence that there must basically be an equal possibility of consent and rejection. However, the requirement in the DSA only applies to "online platforms" and thus not to simple online shops, among others.

6.6 Payment with Data/Pure Models

Also of considerable relevance for practice is the question of whether the so-called "prohibition of tying" can be relevant in cases where data subjects (e.g. online users) receive a consideration of economic value for giving consent (e.g. free access to editorial content of a news magazine), but in return must consent to the use of their data for certain purposes. In the case of this "tying", the required voluntariness of consent is missing ("paying with data").

The possibility of "payment with data" has been recognised by the European legislator in the "*Digital Content Directive*". However, this directive also states that the existing data protection regulations must be complied with. Against this background, on the one hand, a provision should be inserted in the terms of use, which the data subjects must accept, to the effect that the data subject must give consent to the intended use of data in return for the possibility of using the service with an economic value. On the other hand, for reasons of caution, the data controller should obtain the user's consent, which the user is contractually obliged to grant, in compliance with the legal requirements. To avoid the existence of "tying" in violation of data protection, the data subject should also be given the option of using the service without consent to data use—but then for an appropriate fee. In addition, the data subject must have the possibility to revoke the consent given. If consent is revoked, however, the possibility of using the service free of charge also regularly ceases to exist. A "trend" towards such a procedure can be observed on websites with editorial/journalistic content (*pure models*). The possibility of a data-protection-compliant design of pure models was only recently recognised by the German data protection authorities.

6.7 Evidence of Consent Given/IAB Framework (TCF 2.0)

Website operators must be able to prove the extent of consent as well as the fact that such consent has been granted. The use of the so-called *IAB Framework* has gradually become established in practice to provide such proof within the AdTech chain. The reason that the use of the *IAB Framework* has become increasingly established in practice is that marketers of online advertising inventory, among others, presuppose the use of the framework as mandatory for cooperation. This approach is a consequence of far-reaching reviews of online tracking measures by the German data protection authorities.

Insofar as a website operator wishes to integrate the *IAB Framework*, they must, in addition to the specifications for technical integration, also consider the specifications of the IAB with regard to the way in which consent is obtained for the implementation of online tracking measures. This means that the website operator must use a "*Consent Management Platform*" (CMP). Such CMPs, by means of which banner solutions are usually mapped, are offered on the market by service providers (e.g. *OneTrust* or *Usercentrics*). However, it is also possible for website operators to develop their own CMP solution, which is then checked by the *IAB* regarding compliance with the *IAB's* specifications. These specifications concern, among other things, the consent/notice text to be integrated into the banner solutions. It should be noted, however, that there is no legal certainty about compliance with the *IAB's* specifications, as they do not have the status of law. This is often misjudged in practice.

Furthermore, the *IAB Framework* has been criticised by the European data protection authorities. However, this criticism does not imply that the *IAB Framework* is illegal per se. Rather, it is questionable who is responsible for the individual data processing operations and whether, regarding certain processing operations, a so-called "joint responsibility", which is subject to explicit requirements from the GDPR (including the conclusion of "*joint controller agreements*", joint and several liability) exists. This legal question was submitted to the ECJ for an answer, and the decision is currently awaited.

6.8 Privacy Sandbox Project

Google's announcement to make the relevant changes to *Chrome*, the most widely used browser in Europe, has caused unrest in the advertising market. *Google* wants—according to its own statements—to stop cross-website tracking to reinforce the privacy of users. In many places, the "death" of third-party cookies, which are currently used (frequently) to recognise users on the websites of publishers and thus to display individualised advertising based on data that was previously collected on the advertisers' own websites, is being predicted. What is to be supported from the point of view of data protection—viewed in isolation—privileges, however, among others, are market participants who, since a login is required for the use of their services, can identify the users even without the use of third-party cookies. To what extent such "privileging" is lawful is a question of antitrust law.

According to the information currently available in the "privacy sandbox", advertisers will be able to "write" information into the Chrome browser used when their website is accessed by the respective user. This information can then be used by the website operator for the purpose of targeting individualised advertising on third-party sites. Such "writing" of information into the browser is likely to fall under the scope of the provision in Section 25 of the TTDSG in Germany and thus again be subject to consent.

Even after the introduction of the "privacy sandbox", the collection of tracking data based on the use of first-party cookies will still be technically possible. The tracking data collected using first-party cookies can be used for the following measures, among others:

- individualisation of one's own website based on interest clusters.
- adaptation of the search hit display based on the evaluation of user behaviour by online shops.
- optimisation of the display of advertisements on online marketplaces (sponsored products), and

- Use of information on click behaviour to optimise suggestions of comparable content by streaming platforms.

With regard to the fact that first-party cookie tracking will also be possible after the introduction of the privacy sandbox, it should be noted that individual large platform ecosystems can make optimal use of this, since they can, for example, in contrast to original online shops, collect data via their own services and these services often also have advertising space with a high reach at the same time. When carrying out online tracking using first-party cookies, the requirements from Section 25 of the TTDSG (basic consent requirement) must also be observed. The law does not differentiate between first- and third-party tracking at this point.

6.9 Privacy Information Management Systems (PIMS)

PIMS are systems that allow online users to manage consent. The previous federal government in Germany included the promotion of the establishment of PIMS on the market in its data strategy. Consequently, the German legislator included a regulation on PIMS in the TTDSG (Section 26). This first clarifies that it is possible for consent under Section 25 of the TTDSG to be administered by such systems/services (Section 26, paragraph 1). In addition, Section 26, paragraph 1 of the TTDSG sets out requirements that the operators of PIMS must fulfil to be granted recognition by an independent body, which is still to be designated by means of a statutory instrument. Essential requirements in this context are that

- the operators of the PIMS have no economic interest of their own in the consent granted and the data managed and must be independent of companies that have such an interest, and
- that PIMS operators do not process the data and consent for purposes other than administration.

A central element of the provision in Section 26 of the TTDSG for practice is the requirement that "software for retrieving and displaying information from the internet" (e.g. browsers) must comply with opt-in settings made by users in PIMS and consider the integration of recognised PIMS. This requirement is intended to cushion the existing market power of browser providers to some extent. However, website operators must also comply with the settings made.

The legal ordinance that will regulate the exact details of the PIMS has not yet been finalised. However, it will be important for advertisers and publishers that it cannot be interpreted to mean that the PIMS can be designed in practice in such a way that all tracking is fundamentally prevented from the outset. Incidentally, such a design would also not implement the legislator's intention to create an alternative with the regulation on PIMS that considers the interests of consumers and companies.

6.10 Real-Time Bidding Methods

In the field of online marketing, real-time bidding procedures have been increasingly used in recent years. Within the framework of these procedures, online advertising spaces are auctioned in real time. The advertisers have the possibility, for example, to submit bids for the display of individualised online ads on advertising spaces of third parties (to users for whom they have information such as affinities).

The use of real-time bidding procedures is criticised in many places from a data protection point of view. This is mainly because many technical service providers (e.g. DMPs, DSPs, and SSPs) are usually involved and the processes are not easy for website users to understand. Particularly due to the substantial number of technical service providers, it is regularly claimed about real-time bidding procedures that their use is fundamentally accompanied by a loss of control over the processed data. A detailed data protection law discussion of this complex topic would "go beyond" the scope of this publication. Despite this circumstance, the following tips can be given, by means of which the use of real-time bidding procedures can be secured (to a certain extent) in terms of data protection law:

- The number of service providers used should be reduced to a minimum (in practice, there are companies that have "built" the "AdTech stack" entirely themselves).
- If an external DMP is used, contractual provisions should be made with it that stipulate that the DMP service provider may process the data (segments) exclusively for the purposes and on the instructions of the DMP user.
- The DMP should be designed in such a way that it enables the use of a K-anonymity procedure (a certain number X [at least 10] of users must be assigned the same segment combinations).
- The ID lists stored in an external DSP should not be assigned clear identifiers (e.g. "sports affinity").

Since the use of real-time bidding methods is the subject of fierce public criticism, the collection of raw data and its processing for the purpose of segmentation, as well as the use of the segments for the purpose of targeting individualised advertising, should also be secured by obtaining legally compliant consent (via a consent banner).

6.11 Use of "Alternative Identifiers"

As it will no longer be possible to use third-party cookies for the recognition of users on third-party websites, the use of "alternative identifiers" will be required in the future for the recognition. Such an "alternative identifier" can be hashed values of E-Mail addresses. Hashing, by which the E-Mail address is converted into another value, represents data processing that is not subject to the provisions of the TTDSG, but to those of the GDPR. As a result, "hashing" does not generally require consent, as the GDPR also includes other legal bases such as the processing of data based on a balancing of interests. In this regard, however, it should be noted that in many cases, the further processing of tracking data also requires consent under the GDPR. This is often the case, for example, when exceptionally large profiles are created. Insofar as the hash values of the E-Mail addresses are (also) processed within the scope of the further processing of tracking data requiring consent, consent must also be obtained for these. Consent for the "hashing" of the E-Mail addresses can be obtained via the consent banner used on the website. In this context, the use of the E-Mail addresses for the purpose of "hashing" as well as for the purpose of recognising the user on third-party sites must be transparently pointed out in the declaration of consent. Incidentally, hashing does not usually result in anonymisation (e.g. of the E-Mail address). This is especially true if the hash value is "synchronised" with other personal data (e.g. an *IDFA*).

6.12 Audience Matching Tools

In practice, online marketing tools are offered for use whose mode of operation is based on determining online users to whom a company wishes to advertise by matching E-Mail addresses or hash values of E-Mail addresses collected by both the advertiser and the tool provider. The ability to use such marketing tools is likely to become more relevant to many advertisers in the future, simply due to the blocking of third-party cookies. The functionality of audience matching tools is regularly designed in such a way that the user of the tool (e.g. advertiser) compiles a list of data, usually collected by themself, which they assign to people they want to advertise to or not. The list created by the advertiser is compared with data collected by the tool provider. The tool providers may be, for example, operators of social media platforms or other platform operators who, when creating a user account for the respective platform, request the E-Mail address of the user who creates the account. The result of the matching is a list of data of users that both the advertiser and the tool provider "know" ("audience"). The tool provider then has the possibility, among other things, to serve the advertisements intended by the advertiser on a website operated by him (e.g. social media platform) to the users who are part of this "audience". In addition, it is possible that the tool provider creates look-alike audiences based on further data about online users (which the tool provider collects themself).

It is questionable whether such tools can be used on the legal basis of the balancing of interests and thus without obtaining consent. Regarding this question, there is case law on the "old" law (BDSG 2009), according to which obtaining consent is required. Even if the substantive reasoning of the court is not exclusively convincing, for reasons of caution it must be expected that other courts—now based on the requirements from the GDPR—will also come to the same conclusion. The basis for the argument that audience matching tools can be used based on the legal basis of the balancing of interests would be (significantly) improved if the matching was not carried out by the tool provider itself, but by a neutral third party (trusted third party). In practice, however, this is unfortunately only the case with very few tools.

Further detailed explanations—also on other topics of online data protection—can be found in: Menke, S.: *Handbuch Kundendatenschutz*; Erich Schmidt Verlag, 2022.

Measurement and KPI Optimisation . . . Oldie, But Goldie

7

7.1 Master Yoda Is Back: The Revival of Marketing Planning and Steering

The schizophrenic situation: while marketing planning and steering gains high attention, while the actual quality of the planning is in their own perspective rather bad. The overwhelming majority (approx. three quarters) of marketing managers and executives are of the opinion that content-related, high-quality, and professional planning must become increasingly important in view of the explosion of customer touchpoints—however, they would not grant themselves a place on the winners' rostrum for the quality and consistency of their own planning. Research shows that most marketing managers and executives are very aware of the importance of professional planning and control (aspiration), but in (cruel) reality only about one-third can meet this aspiration in their own opinion.

Marketing is increasingly confronted with the obligation to prove that its budgets and expenditures also produce objectively verifiable and measurable results. If one asks marketing managers about the most important reason for the prevailing uncertainty regarding the effectiveness and efficiency of marketing strategies as well as tactics, the answer usually crystallises to be a *lack of or inadequate marketing planning* (Strauß, 2008). This is often . . .

- . . . . insufficiently synchronised with the corporate strategy and planning as a whole.
- . . . . too limited to the planning of tactics and measures, neglecting content planning on a topic and program level.
- . . . . only an adaptation of the planning from the previous year, with only minor modifications in terms of content and timing ("binder-of-the-shelf syndrome").
- . . . . not backed up by a target system/metrics derived from the strategy, which cascades down to the level of individual measures and channels (KPI framework).
- . . . . hardly coordinated with other areas (e.g. sales, trade marketing, foreign branches, etc.) by agreeing on precise operationalised metrics for the objectives.

R. Strauss, *Data-Driven Customer Engagement*,
https://doi.org/10.1007/978-3-031-64295-1_7

- . . . . not sufficiently detailed to efficiently map the multitude and specificities of channels, individual measures, targets, metrics, and budgets. . .

. . . which is why "marketing planning and steering" is becoming increasingly important as a field of action for all marketing managers. The overwhelming majority (approx. three quarters) of marketing managers and executives are of the opinion that content-related, high-quality, and professional planning must become increasingly important in view of the explosion of customer touchpoints—however, they would not grant themselves a place on the winners' rostrum for the quality and consistency of their own planning. Research shows that most marketing managers and executives are very aware of the importance of professional planning and control (aspiration), but in (cruel) reality only about one-third can meet this aspiration in their own opinion (Fig. 7.1).

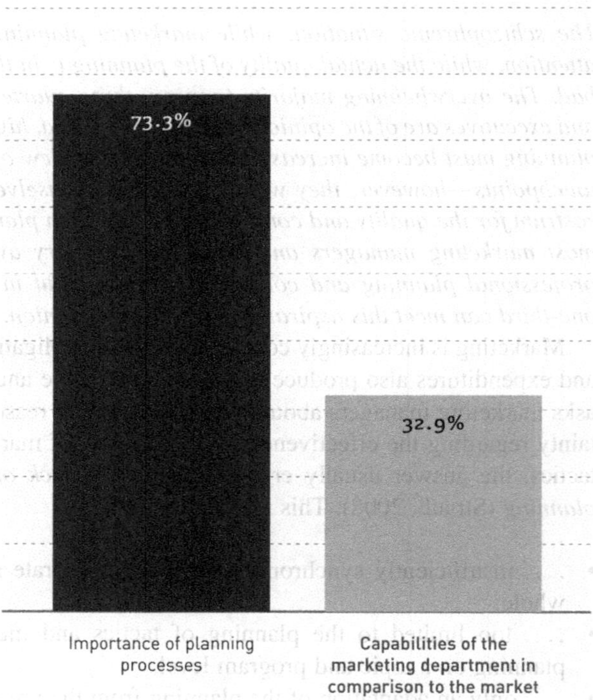

Fig. 7.1 Integrated planning and steering systems in corporate reality (Marketing Tech Monitor 2022)

Applications in the field of marketing resource management (MRM) (e.g. *Marmind*, *Uptempo*, *SAS 360 Plan*, or *Aprimo*) or digital asset management (DAM) for centralised and media-neutral storage, administration, and output of multimedia components (i.e. text, images, graphics, audio, and video), as well as ready-made communication media (e.g. advertisements and TV commercials), should provide a remedy. Project examples show that the use of such applications can reduce campaign creation by over 70%, the time required for the creation of communication media by over 60%, agency costs by over 25%, and the total advertising expenditure by 5% to 10% through consolidation. The focus is on cascading through strategic prioritisation, goals, KPIs, and content at a program level to the campaign architecture and individual measure level (Fig. 7.2).

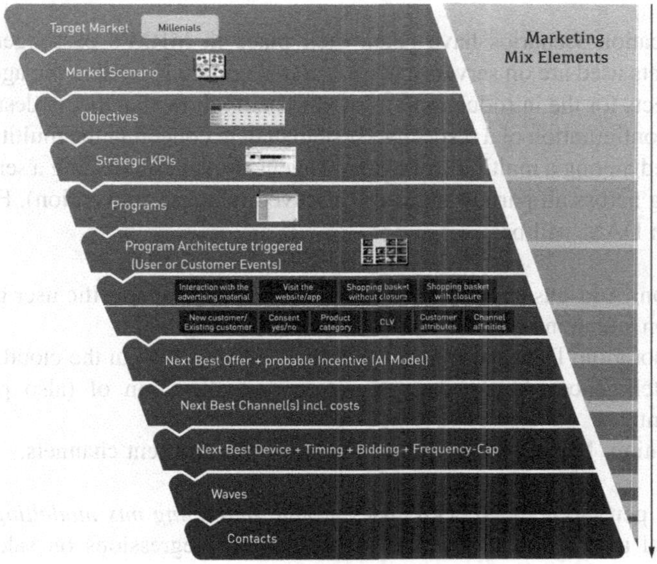

Fig. 7.2 Overview of the structure and levels of marketing planning (Strauß, R. E.: Marketing Planning by Design, London/New York 2008)

In addition to more push-driven campaigns, the trend is increasingly moving towards *triggered campaigns*—in other words, the action of a customer (e.g. shopping basket filled, login, visit to the website, purchase of a certain product) triggers a campaign. In line with the program architecture (actions of different target groups, e.g. interaction with an advertising medium, website visit without shopping basket, website visit with shopping basket, shopping basket sent), a next best offer is launched on the basis of artificial intelligence and the associated incentives, an AI model provides next best channel(s) and, if applicable, device/timing/next best bidding as well as frequency cap, until contacts are generated.

Nearly 55% of the companies complain that they would already be using an application if it could remain as it is in 8% of all cases. A total of 15% of the companies are already looking for newer and more contemporary solutions, which means that a considerable number of tenders and bids can be expected over the next few years. The accompanying interviews show that …

- … in some cases, even simple calendar functionalities in reporting or BI tools are interpreted as MRM.

- . . . the term and the application scenarios that fall under it are not clear and self-explanatory—for example, even most marketing managers in the consumer goods sector state that they cannot really explain which application scenarios fall under the term "marketing resource management".
- . . . the management of budgets in the cost centre in ERP FI/CO is used synonymously with MRM.

DAM application scenarios have taken their place in MRM's passenger seat. Most of the assets used are on servers and *SharePoints* or are located at the agencies in charge. Projects for the introduction of DAM systems show that the hardest work lies less in the configuration of a respective system than in collecting the multitude of assets distributed among a multitude of external agencies and establishing a sensible, uniform tagging across all parties and users involved (naming convention). For the future, trends in DAM will be:

- Simplification: Add-ons and tools that increase usability for specific user groups or application situations or limit it in a cost-efficient way.
- Smart collaboration: Data sharing and real-time collaboration in the cloud.
- Artificial intelligence: Automatic recognition and allocation of (also partial) image content.
- Individualisation: Management of dynamic assets for different channels.

The greatest pent-up demand crystallises around *marketing mix modelling*. The use of statistical analysis methods such as multivariate regressions on sales and marketing time-series data (e.g. to estimate the effects of different tactics on sales and to make predictions about the use of individual measures) is slowly awakening from its slumber: 60% of companies state that they are either in the selection or adoption phase or want to use this in the future. The marketing operations wave is thus *ante portas*.

The analysis of functions used shows that in practice, "Processing Functions" in planning or budget management still dominate (Fig. 7.3). While "Campaign Planning" or "Budget Allocation" are held in the highest esteem, they clearly fall behind in adoption, like "Managing Campaign Calendar".

"Most liked"	"Most used"	"Most missed"
Campaign Planning	Desktop Application	Managing Campaign Calendar
Campaign Management	Invoice Approval Management	Campaign Resource Management
Desktop Application	Managing Campaign Calendar	Campaign Management
Asset Viewing Roles/Rights	Asset Viewing Roles/Rights	Budget Allocation
Budget Allocation	Budget Allocation	Managing Production Calendar
Brand Asset Management	Cost Location Management	Budget Monitoring
Managing Campaign Calendar	Budget Re-allocation	Link-sharing with External Users
Campaign Creation Wizard/Templates	Managing of Supplier Financials	Assigning of (Approval) Tasks
Managing Production Calendar	Budget Monitoring	Task and Approval Workflows
Campaign Creation	Link-sharing with External Users	Brand Asset Management

Fig. 7.3 Analysis and evaluation of the most important MRM application scenarios (Top 10) (MarTechTribe: Global MarTech Requirements Database; April 2023/G2: Tool Evaluation; March 2023)

7.2 Measure It or Forget It . . . from Strategy to Targets to Metrics (KPIS)

Often, marketing organisations suffer due to a lack of clearly defined goals, metrics, and target values as well as systems for measuring the achievement of goals are missing. Even if reports are produced, they arrive with a delay of up to 2 months at the level of the actors involved and show high inaccuracies. Support for fine-grained activity and process control in real time can therefore hardly be expected. Planning and steering suffer from the "paralysis-by-analysis" syndrome. The supposedly simple applicability of arbitrary metrics, KPIs and "fancy" target system methodologies à la OKR should not obscure the fact that the initial determination of the KPI systems and their interdependencies in a KPI driver tree is associated with greater expenses—such as the question of which target should be measured with which KPI and how these can be correctly determined.

The quantitative survey, workshops, and accompanying interviews underline the fact that companies often have *inadequate procedures for planning and steering* (Fig. 7.4) (CMO Community, 2023; Hartnett et al., 2021; Strauß, 2008):

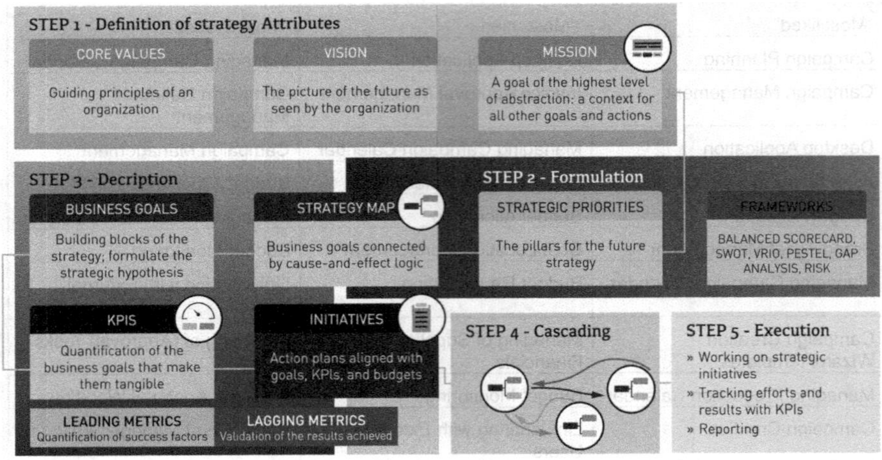

Fig. 7.4 Determination of goals, priorities, metrics, KPIs, and target values (Marketing Tech Monitor 2022)

- Clearly defined goals, metrics, and target values as well as systems for measuring the achievement of goals are missing—a systematic cost–benefit calculation for marketing programs and activities is consequently absent.
- Even if reports are produced, they arrive with a delay of up to 2 months at the level of the actors involved and show high inaccuracies. Support for fine-grained activity and process control in real time can therefore hardly be expected.
- Planning and steering suffer from the "paralysis-by-analysis shock": up to 20 metrics and (supposed) KPIs are defined, but without a synopsis (i.e. evaluation) or resulting recommendations for action ("metrics that matter"). The collection and tracking of up to 20—theoretically certainly sensible in themselves—different KPIs usually leads to the fact that after an initial phase of euphoria, the tracking is either soon discontinued altogether due to the high complexity and the usually low actual explanatory contribution or a "natural focus" on a few selected KPIs takes place. In other words, conceptual over-engineering gives way to everyday pragmatism.
- Most of the working time is consumed by operations, while analysis and evaluation following all activities must take a back seat in comparison. The result: the resulting dashboards are at best taken note of in the organisation, without any implications as to whether the direction of the strategy and the activities based on it are effective.
- Even companies that already pose on the catwalk as proud owners of a KPI framework complain about an insufficient "fit" in terms of strategy, measures/activities, and channels used—but at the same time, they shy away from the associated internal effort and a more comprehensive conceptual (internal) discussion.

While dealing with different touchpoints alongside customer journeys, it is vital for a company to conclude its customer experience management by defining the ambitions that it wants to pursue. These ambitions must cover the company's 'North Star' or set of key performance indicators (KPIs) for its activities as well as define a distinctive customer experience strategy (Schögel & Herhausen, 2023).

- In some cases, theoretically abstract KPI logics are developed, but these are insufficiently operationalised and anchored in the organisation (change management).
- The metrics used were conceptually derived from the strategy on the drawing board, but never explored in data science (e.g. via factor analysis) with the help of real data for actual correlations and causalities.
- Syntax beats semantics: KPIs are defined differently in terms of content, such as a "lead".
- The KPI euphoria suffers a shipwreck at the latest when the data is available: often there is no aggregation and standardisation of all data (data engineering). Lack of data access, inadequate aggregation via a naming convention and heterogeneous, distributed data structures and platforms prove to be road-bumpers on the way to KPI heaven. This means that both conceptual and data-side prerequisites are missing right from the start (Kambuj, 2021).
- Often, individual KPIs are used, but there are no end-to-end considerations along meshed value chains, which makes a data-based decision hardly possible, as the connections between the silos remain rather nebulous. In some cases, roles are set up for "marketing steering and planning" without sufficient networking (with sales, controlling, IT, etc.).
- Attribution problem as a psychological factor: if "things go well", it was one's own success, and if things go badly or wrong, it was "the circumstances".
- Insufficient holistic thinking and leadership vs optimisation of own bonus.
- Fragmented customer journeys make valid root cause analyses difficult.
- Or the reporting of results has been outsourced to external service providers (agencies), who (understandably) also like to shine in reporting as a "self-fulfilling prophecy" with success stories.

The challenge is the interplay between brand and performance . . . in other words: what impact does a strong brand have on subsequent conversion?—Benedikt Schaumann (Head of Consumer Communication Services, Nestlé Deutschland).

The supposedly simple applicability of arbitrary metrics, KPIs, and "fancy" target system methodologies à la OKR should not obscure the fact that the initial determination of the KPI systems and their interdependencies in a *KPI driver tree* is associated with greater expenses—such as the question of which target should be measured with which KPI and how these can be correctly determined (Fig. 7.5).

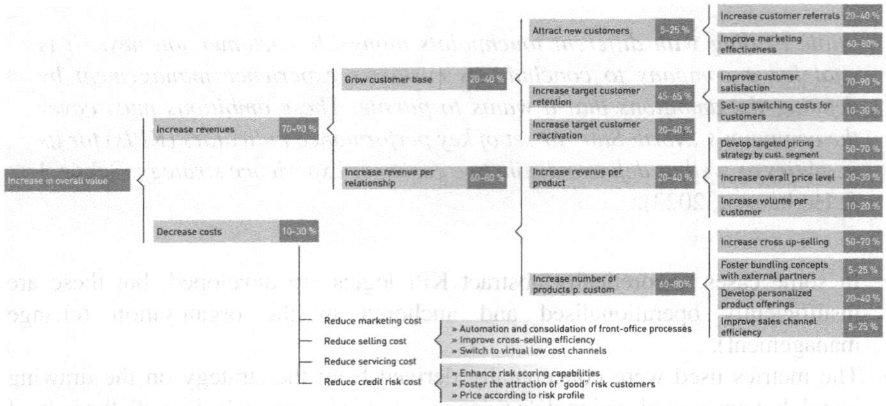

Fig. 7.5 Example of a KPI driver tree (project example) (Strauß, R. E.: Marketing Planning by Design, London/New York 2008)

As a result, most companies tend to give themselves a poor report card in terms of a KPI framework for measuring and steering all activities towards measurable business goals, with clear causalities to investments, derived from the company's strategic goals. Only just over 13% would apply for a "KPI award". The KPIs must be developed specifically for each company to break down the respective visions and strategies to the level of quantifiable metrics for all activities. Cause-and-effect chains between the different perspectives allow the analysis of causal relationships.

With the help of the cascading KPI performance framework, we can stringently manage our digital programs across the individual funnel stages.—Dr Matthias Rasztar (Executive Manager Insights Marketing International, Dr August Oetker Nahrungsmittel).

The crucial distinction is between:

- company frameworks (focus on NPS, EBIT, ROMI),
- digital acceleration KPIs (e.g. e-commerce share, CLV, digital breakthrough), and
- turnaround KPIs (e.g. "Key battlefield growth of x brands and x customers", "Growth core SKUs", "Assortment mix", "Innovation index", or "Roll-out of digital initiatives").

The best way to develop your own KPI framework is to start simple, along the funnel, and then get more and more granular towards marketing KPIs.—Adriana Nuneva (CMO/CDO, CWS International).

Several approaches are available for building an overarching and cascading governance, such as balanced scorecard, OKR, MBO, OGSM, constraints analysis, or Hoshin Kanri (Fig. 7.6).

Method	Description	Advantages / Disadvantages
Balanced Scorecard (BSC)	• Financial performance indicators (e.g.turnover, EBIT) with customer (e.g. NPS), internal process (e.g. lead times) and learning/development perspectives (e.g. training, satisfaction) • Anticipatory performance indicators take the place of financial (ex post) results figures. • The focus is on the vision, which is to be operationalised through concrete strategies and activities down to the level of key performance indicators for individual activities.	+ Visual image of the strategy derivation/ vivid basis for discussion + Transparent cause-and-effect relationships + Explanation of cascading and alignment – Unidirectional alignment from bottom to top – Strategy maps are difficult to maintain. – High complexity in implementation
Objectives, goals, strategies, measurements (OGSM)	• Basis for strategic planning, its implementation, and the subsequent monitoring of the success of goals/KPIs • Makes the core goals of a company visible and guarantees that all activities are aligned with the KPIs. • Quantitative goals are the numerical KPIs that define whether the qualitative objectives have been achieved. • Strategies are initiatives undertaken to achieve the goals. • Strategies are decisions that can be differentiated between "where to play" (e.g. product categories, distribution channels), "how to win" (e.g differentiation or cost leadership) and"capabilities" (e.g. processes or IT). • Measures provide the measurable implementation for the respective strategy to track responsibilities and timelines.	+ Clear definition and derivation of objectives, core strategies and initiatives as well as responsibilities and timings + Concise, one-page format allows for quick action. – Unclear terminology (e.g. goals vs objectives, strategies defined as simple action plans) – No agreement on what should be quantified through measurement: level of strategy, goals, or objectives. – Early vs late indicators: like Hoshin Kanri, OGSM makes no distinction between early and late indicators.
Hoshin Kanri	• Strategy description tool by providing an overview of top-level strategic priorities and their link to specific improvement goals (via performance indicators) and targets. • Focus on continuous improvement (Plan – Do – Check – Act cycle) • Importance of strategy alignment and discussion ("catch ball") • Proposal to track performance of an individual	+ Fine-grained planning, less implementation – Rigid implementation necessary – Requires long-term commitment, patience, and continued support from senior management. – Relatively static; breakthrough targets must be consistent over a five-year period.
Objectives and key results (OKR)	• Lightweight goal-setting framework • Agile tool for strategy implementation • Framework suggests focusing on a few key objectives ("objectives") and tracking their implementation with several lagging indicators ("key results"). • OKR process consists of four steps, ending with a review of results. • The recommended process cycle time is one quarter.	+ Company goals operationalised and linked to the work context of teams/employees. + Transparency and communication within the company + Acceleration of internal coordination processes + Promotion of intrinsic motivation, incl. resource planning + Easy to understand and implement. + Focusing, as no more than four objectives per company and per team + High speed of reaction to changes in the marketplace. + Self-organisation and readiness for action required and encouraged. – Use as a "control instrument" leads to rejections. – Requires commitment and time capacities (especially OKR master) – Requires open corporate culture and desire for more agility

Fig. 7.6 Instruments of strategic planning and controlling (Marketing Tech Monitor 2022)

A rather lightweight and agile variant for translating the framework into a process for consistent control of the implementation is thus found in the use of the *OKR methodology*. The ultimate goal is to give an organisation a common direction and, at the same time, allow maximum autonomy of the acting teams. This makes the OKR method particularly suitable for

- when staff involvement and responsibility is to be strengthened,
- a higher degree of focus is required (i.e. orientation towards a few important goals instead of doing everything "a little bit"),
- cooperation is to be promoted, departmental boundaries and silo thinking are to be overcome, conflicts of goals are to be avoided, or other, and
- interactions and dependencies are to be made transparent.

OKR helps us to set the framework—this sets the framework for the cooperation . . . but: this also requires the respective leader to let go.—Tobias Lorenz (Head of Marketing, E.ON).

OKRs are a top-down and bottom-up instrument—in other words, the sub-goals and key results are not only cascaded, but there is always feedback between the levels. For this purpose, the OKR method uses a simple syntax: a qualitative objective is formulated that stands for itself and calls for action. So: "*We will [objective] as measured by [set of key results].*" (Doerr, 2018) An objective is a directional goal with an emotional and motivating function for teams and employees (Fig. 7.7). Two to five quantitative metrics (key results) are linked to this objective, which allow a clear and unambiguous evaluation. Thus, the key results are the success drivers of the objective. The key results are the yardstick for assessing

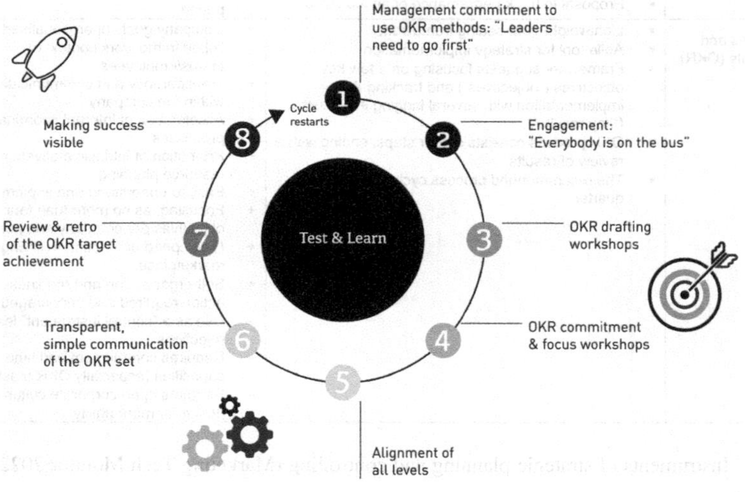

Fig. 7.7 OKR cycle (example: Deutsche Telekom; Marketing Tech Monitor 2021)

how close one has already come to achieving a goal: "No number, no key results". OKRs, however, focus on the effect or the result (outcome). Ideally, the outcome is always linked to the customer or the recipient of a service. Thus, a KPI can be a key result, but never an objective.

The biggest challenge is focus. Monitoring and discussing progress weekly at all levels leads to a disproportionate effort unless everything is automated. Project examples show that a monthly review seems appropriate, including team and organisational goals (collaboration) as part of the OKRs (Fig. 7.8).

Type	Time required	Purpose	Key
Daily check-in	5 mins	Daily activities and notes	Don't sit Admin only Never cancel
Weekly Tactical	45–90 mins	Planning Problem-solving Next week's activities	Set the agenda with the team, at the meeting Postpone strategic discussions
Monthly Strategic	2–4 hours	Mini-strategic review Brainstorm and reflect Longer term planning	1-2 topic Prepare and research Agenda in advance Bring ideas Create debate – good conflict
Quarterly Review	1–2 days	Date review Trends Team development Strategic	Limit the socialising Don't over structure and overburden the agenda Create opportunities to critique and create

Fig. 7.8 Formats for the organisational anchoring of a KPI framework (Lencioni, P. M.: Death by Meeting: A Leadership Fable ... About Solving the Most Painful Problem in Business, San Francisco 2004)

7.3 From Data Dusk Till Dawn: Data Science and Marketing Analytics Ante Portas

Successes—as well as failures—must be systematically tracked, made transparent and available in a feedback loop for further activities or planning. Additionally collected data along the customer journey, together with more advanced (multivariate) modelling techniques, allow the measurement of multi- and omni-channel effects (attribution) and, subsequently, the cross-channel optimisation in an overall marketing mix modelling, including "what-if" scenarios, an optimised activity calendar, and DIY simulation tools. The interviews and feedback from marketing managers and board members show that a higher degree of automation, the use of artificial intelligence and (econometric) prediction models can be expected in the future as part of marketing spend optimisation.

The explosion of touchpoints and new interaction channels (e.g. *TikTok*), hyper-fragmented media investments, the digitalisation of classic channels, non-linear customer journeys, but also the increased possibilities of real-time processing of large amounts of data and the automation of analyses continue to fuel data science in marketing (e.g. speed, automation, standardisation). While the data science flagellant bandwagon used to bemoan the low interest in marketing mix modelling and analytics, the need is growing by leaps and bounds with the implementation of data-driven marketing—especially about one's own evaluation competence. At the same time, a paradigm shift is taking place: while purely digital attribution was still allowed to celebrate wild champagne parties in recent years, integrated offline/online models (UMIA) are increasingly being nominated for the Oscar.

Back in 2010, it could be proven that in economically turbulent times (e.g. Covid, recession) the most successful companies strike a balance between selective cost-cutting and investment in future growth (Gulati et al., 2010). As the analysis of POS data shows, consumer demand does not simply disappear in times of economic difficulty, but rather actually increases in many categories. So instead of a knee-jerk reaction of "yes" or "no" to decisions about cutting marketing or advertising budgets, a better approach is to continually re-evaluate which channels and touchpoints are most efficient through *marketing mix modelling* and reallocate budgets accordingly on an on-going (aggregated) basis (Runge et al., 2023). The goal is to forecast the impact of (future) advertising campaigns, optimise the media mix (short/long term), and reallocate marketing budgets to maximise the respective target metric.

More and more touchpoints with an ever-increasing richness of functionality have led to an unprecedented growth of heterogeneous marketing data in syntax and semantics. As a result, a deeper analysis casts the fairy tale of the "seamless customer journey" as sheer wishful thinking—this presents itself at best as a string of individual snapshots from the analytics instant camera. And is further fuelled by the fact that usually several "agency chefs" (are supposed to) cook the "analytics candlelight dinner" together for companies.

In a modelling without long-term effects, media moves little at first. Only when the long-term effects on the brand are considered can the full impact be seen.—Dimitri Herber (Head of Media & Digital Marketing, Warsteiner Brewery Haus Cramer).

In the practical process model, the collection and consolidation of all data available from various (online/offline) sources is the first step (phase 1, Fig. 7.9). The diversity of the supplied data in terms of syntax and semantics usually ensures consolidation that requires considerable effort and leads to considerable data losses and incompatibilities during the matching at the beginning; or the in-house media agency does not necessarily appreciate the collection of data and the accompanying

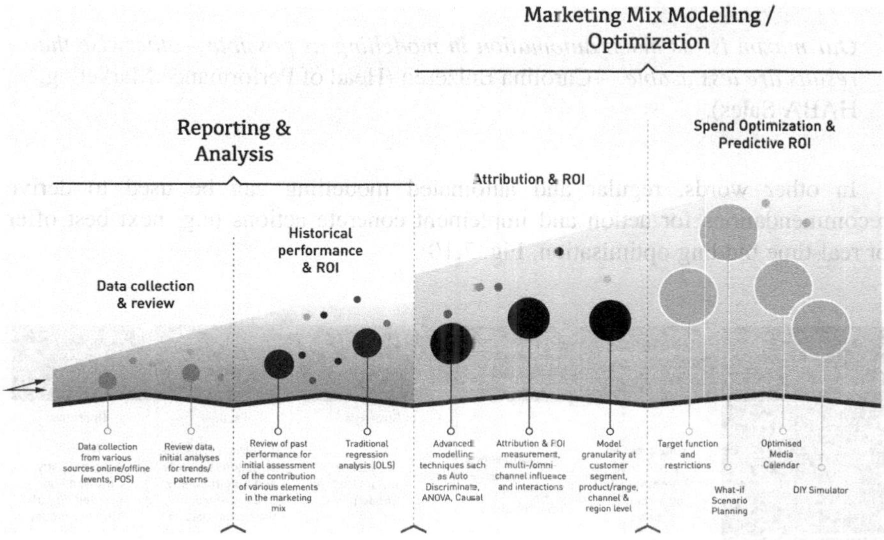

Fig. 7.9 Build-up of digital marketing phases, up to marketing mix modelling (Marketing Tech Monitor 2020)

transparency by giving "standing ovations". Based on the consolidated data, initial estimates for the contribution of various elements in the marketing mix can be made (phase 2).

In most cases, the analysis of the historical performance and the marketing ROI ensure the metrics and key figures used must at least be subjected to a critical analysis—if not fundamentally redefined. The simple applicability of any metrics should not obscure the fact that the initial determination of the metrics systems is, in turn, associated with greater expenditure—especially due to the question of which metric should be used to measure which goal and how these can be correctly determined ("metrics that matter"). Subsequently, successes—as well as failures—must be systematically tracked, made transparent and available in a feedback loop for further activities or planning. Additionally collected data along the customer journey, together with more advanced (multivariate) modelling techniques, allow the measurement of multi- and omni-channel effects (attribution, phase 3) and, subsequently, the cross-channel optimisation in an overall marketing mix modelling, including "what-if" scenarios, an optimised activity calendar, and DIY simulation tools (phase 4).

The interviews and feedback from marketing managers and board members show that a higher degree of *automation*, the use of artificial intelligence and (econometric) prediction models can be expected in the future as part of marketing spend optimisation.

Our maxim is: as much automation in modelling as possible—otherwise the results are less usable.—Carolina Balzereit (Head of Performance Marketing, HABA Sales).

In other words, regular and automated modelling can be used to derive recommendations for action and implement concrete actions (e.g. next best offer or real-time bidding optimisation, Fig. 7.10).

Layer	1 Data preparation and data cleansing	2 Visualisation and descriptive data analysis	3 Modelling	4 Recommendations	5 Direct Actions
Decision Layer			Strategic	Tactical	Operative
Description	Data pipeline performed automatically on a regular basis	Visualisations created automatically on a regular basis	Regularly automated modelling	Recommendations for action regularly and automatically derived from the model results	Actions automatically derived and executed directly from the model
Potential Use Cases	» Databases (PostgresSQL, MongoDB, Hadoop) » File-Server (SFTP) » Excel	» Dashboard (Power BI, Tableau) » UI (intern/extern) Excel	Methods: » Regression » Forecast » Clustering » Trend Analysis Modells: » Brand Value Model » Market Pricing & Competitor Response	» Marketing Mix Modelling » Promotion Response Modelling » Attribution Modelling	» Real-Time Advertising » Direct Consumer Response Models » Automated segmentation of creatives via view monitoring » Real Time Bidding Optimization » Next Best Offer

Complexity of automation

Fig. 7.10 Degree of automation around data science and marketing analytics (Marketing Tech Monitor 2022)

Data science and modelling usually pursue a relatively simple purpose: to enable decision-making through simplifications, for example via "what-if" scenarios. However, here, too, we have to say goodbye to lofty theoretical ambitions. The desire and will to use scenario planning tools is high, the "modelling meat" is weak—only 16% of companies use them (Fig. 7.11). With the emergence of highly standardised "fast-food models" (especially from media agencies or most recently from *Google*), the initial effort for first analyses is reduced to a minimum, even though generalist and unspecific modelling can hardly focus on the strategic corporate and marketing goals—for example, regarding the fundamental question of which KPI can or should be optimised.

At the same time, the need for tactical decision scenarios has grown significantly. In milliseconds, programmatic purchasing, and the insertion of advertising messages for specific target groups, can be determined with the help of automatically generated creative assets or content. The velocity, volume, and entropy of data are

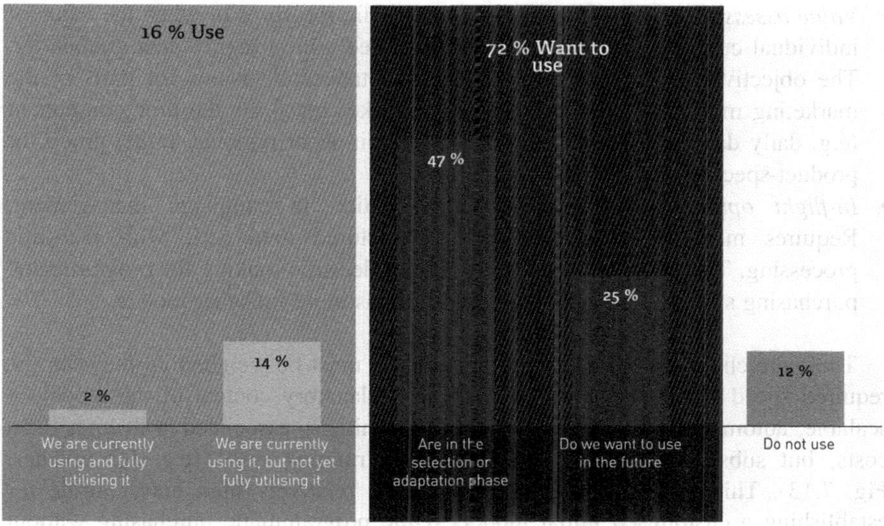

Fig. 7.11 Current technology use of scenario planning: already implemented and planned for the future (in %, $n = 295$; Marketing Tech Monitor 2022)

increasing. Tailored modelling is therefore emerging alongside fast-food modelling and automation, resulting in three types of marketing models (Fig. 7.12):

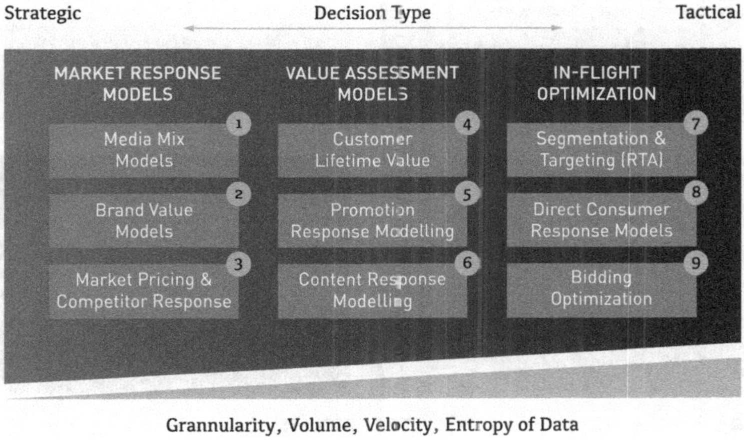

Fig. 7.12 Categorisation of marketing model types (Marketing Tech Monitor 2022)

- *Market response*: Typically for strategic questions. Usually does not require too high granularity or dimensionality of data. Many of the data sets needed for this model are available in standardised monthly routines.

- *Value assessment*: For the evaluation of specific measures or when the value of individual customer groups is to be determined with a higher data granularity. The objective of this model is to generate static conclusions for parts of the marketing mix. The increase in dimension takes place via the time component (e.g. daily data), but usually requires the addition of regional, target-group, or product-specific hierarchies.
- *In-flight optimisation*: (Permanent) application in campaign management. Requires many semi-structured or unstructured data sets, with real-time processing. This model serves as a basis for decision-making for programmatic purchasing systems and is, in turn, also used as input for other models.

Thus, the choice of the degree of automation must be weighed up between the required speed of result generation and the explanatory content of the model. A scalable, automated, and customised model is initially associated with high fixed costs, but subsequently with rather marginal running costs (e.g. for updates, Fig. 7.13). This means that there is initially a relatively high entry hurdle for establishing a customised initial model. While programmatic purchasing without algorithmic optimisation is inconceivable, the establishment of permanent modelling for decision-making support has become rather rare.

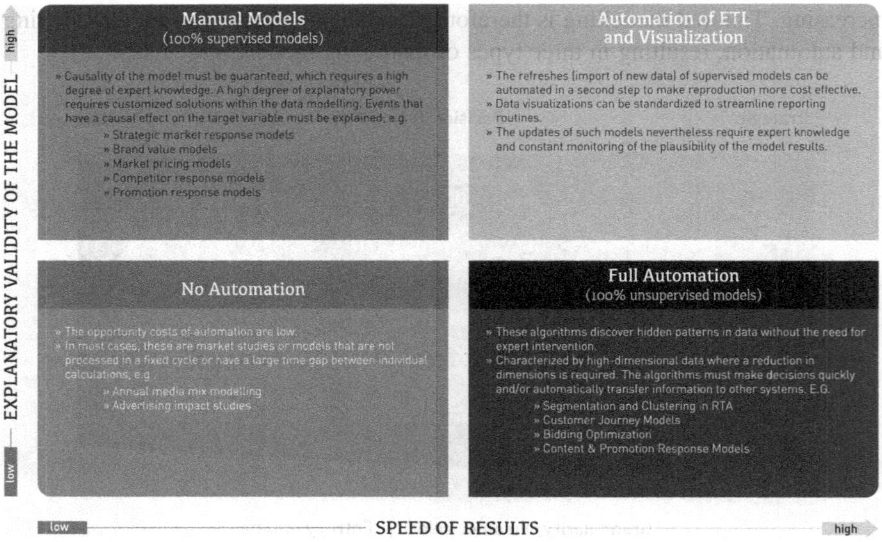

Fig. 7.13 Decision matrix for the degree of model automation (Marketing Tech Monitor 2022)

The process model always starts with the collection and consolidation of all data available from various (online/offline) sources. The diversity of the supplied data in terms of syntax and semantics usually ensures consolidation that requires considerable effort and leads to considerable data losses and incompatibilities in the matching process right from the start. Building on the consolidated data, initial estimates can be derived for the contribution of various elements in the marketing mix. The field of tension: easy, intuitively catchy user interfaces, on the one hand, and maximally robust and powerful data infrastructures "in the engine room", on the other. Data collection along the customer journey, together with more advanced (multivariate) modelling techniques, allows the measurement of multi- and omni-channel effects (attribution) and subsequently cross-channel optimisation in an overall marketing mix modelling, including "what-if" scenarios, an optimised activity calendar, or even DIY simulation tools. The interviews and feedback from marketing managers and board members show that a higher degree of automation, the use of artificial intelligence and (econometric) prediction models can be expected in the future as part of marketing spend optimisation. In a project example in the consumer goods sector, 360 models, including price elasticities at the SKU level and for product ranges, were determined. This makes marketing a holistic management tool for the company. The creation of dashboards remains an on-going topic, as the conceptual background must come together with all the data—especially regarding the cooperation between marketing and sales (Fig. 7.14).

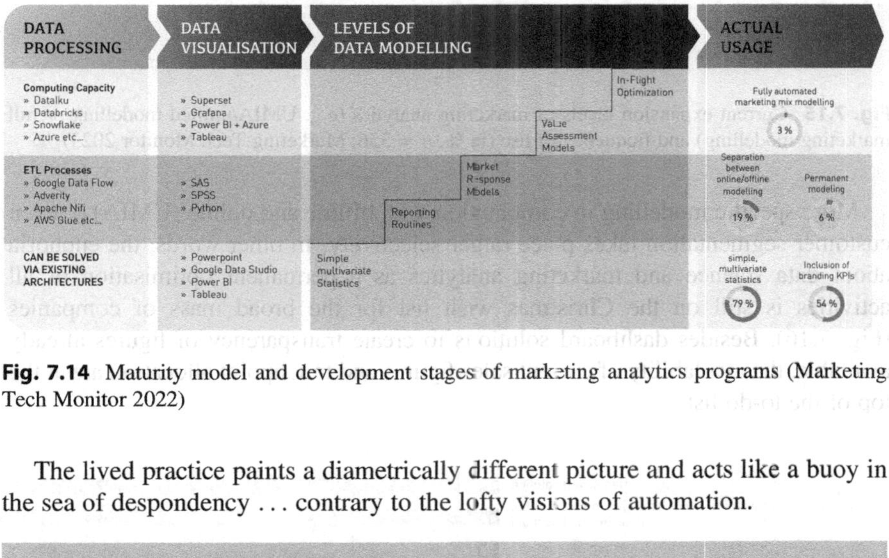

Fig. 7.14 Maturity model and development stages of marketing analytics programs (Marketing Tech Monitor 2022)

The lived practice paints a diametrically different picture and acts like a buoy in the sea of despondency . . . contrary to the lofty visions of automation.

> *Ideally, modelling should not be carried out only once a year or even less frequently to leverage all optimisation potential; 'always-on' would of course be best.*—Thorsten Müller (Director Data Driven Marketing & Media DACH/ Nordics, RECKITT).

A systematic approach to marketing mix modelling is still in its infancy. Even simple (descriptive) analyses are carried out monthly at most, while 62% of companies carry out higher-quality marketing mix modelling on an annual basis (Fig. 7.15).

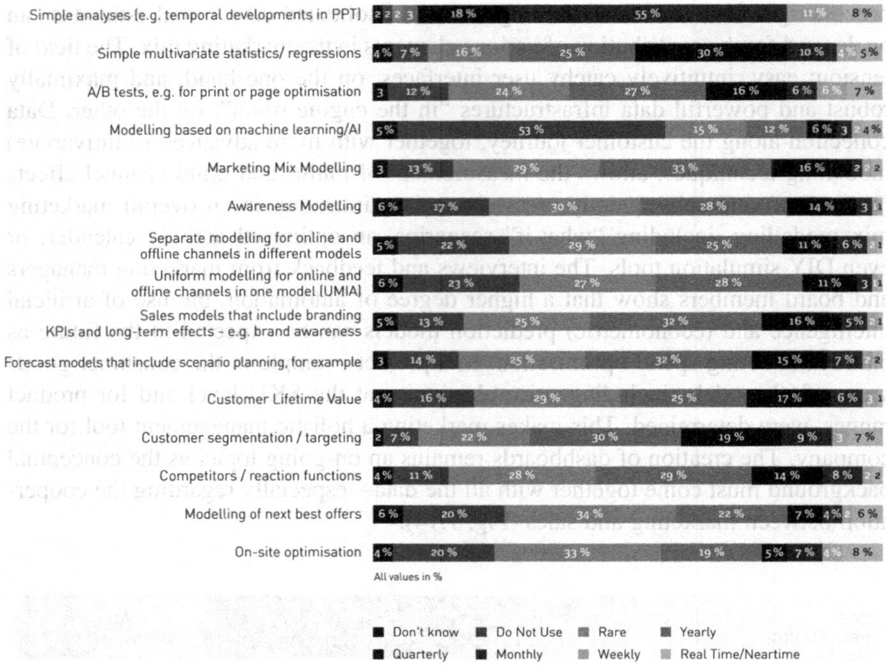

Fig. 7.15 Current expansion levels of marketing analytics (e.g. UMIA/unified modelling or full marketing modelling) and frequency of use (in %, $n = 356$; Marketing Tech Monitor 2023)

More specific modelling in combination with offline and online (UMIA) or even customer segmentation takes place rather selectively. In other words, the euphoria about data science and marketing analytics as a permanent optimisation of all activities is still on the Christmas wish list for the broad mass of companies (Fig. 7.16). Besides dashboard solutions to create transparency of figures already available, the availability of current sales figures and touchpoint allocation are at the top of the to-do list.

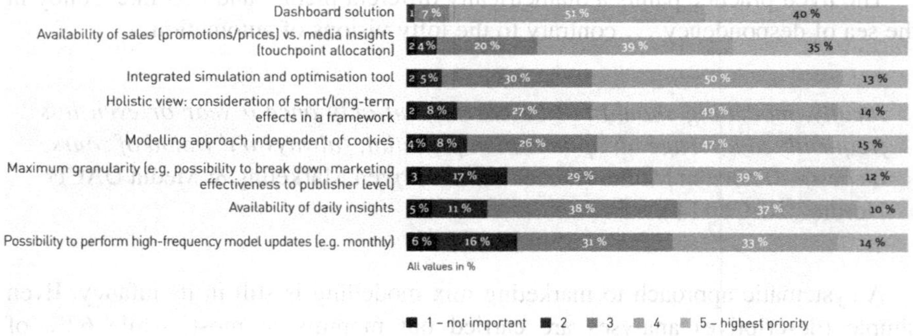

Fig. 7.16 Most important features in marketing optimisation programs (in %, $n = 356$; Marketing Tech Monitor 2023)

While simple modelling is basically still a manageable complexity, the biggest problems arise in obtaining all the data (e.g. from media agencies) and standardising it (e.g. from different TV broadcast formats). Projects show that up to three quarters of the effort is required for the procurement of data, and only just under a quarter for the actual modelling and the determination of recommendations for action.

Modelling results that are not accessible to all staff involved are not sufficiently used for optimisation.—Renata Dadic (Head of Media and Website Management, Deutsche Bank).

Accordingly, the focus is mostly on controlling all marketing activities, followed by optimising media budgets by channel or distribution channel (Fig. 7.17). Other models, such as optimising prices or capacity utilisation (e.g. in the tourism sector), occur comparatively little, even though the data once collected could also serve such models. For innovative companies, AI (machine learning) offers the opportunity to fill the "gap" caused by time delays in data delivery: real-time metrics derived from key performance indicators (e.g. store visits, searches, or views) fill the data gaps in the regression analyses used with forecast data.

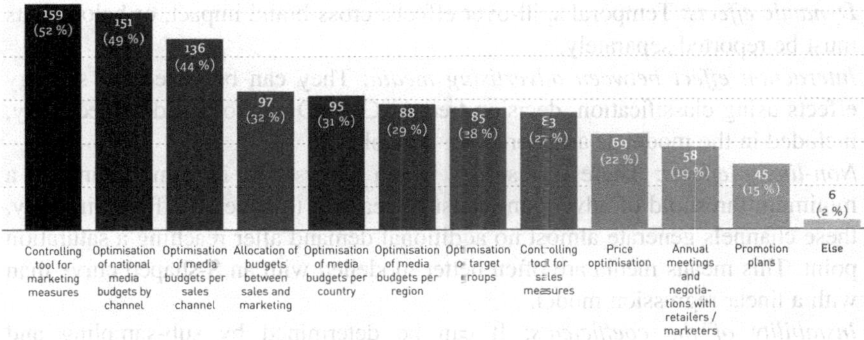

Fig. 7.17 Most important objectives for the use of modelling/statistical models and evaluations in marketing and sales (in %, multiple responses, $n = 356$; Marketing Tech Monitor 2023)

The *challenges* of implementing and using marketing mix modelling and the use of higher-order analytics are as complex as they have been known for many years:

- *Availability of data*: Beyond the optimisation of web tracking, data (especially offline data) is not available initially. Higher (company-internal) transparency and optimisation tends to be met with reluctance by the media agencies involved (due to self-interest). Based on studies (e.g. *Best-for-Planning*), they often come to different conclusions than data-driven recommendations.

> *"The data situation does not allow for meaningful marketing mix modelling, as there is no robust data for the hospitality sector."*—Felix Jahnen (Head of Digital Transformation, Jägermeister)

- *Multicollinearity*: When two or more explanatory variables have an extraordinarily strong correlation with each other. With increasing multicollinearity, for example in regression analysis, the estimation of the regression coefficients is imprecise, and the model interpretation is no longer clear (the aggregation of variables is necessary to describe the background factors, for example with the help of a factor analysis).
- *Lack of standards in measurement*: In other words, lack of a consensus on how the effectiveness of marketing interventions should be measured—as ROMI or ROAS or based on incremental revenue from the campaign/activity.
- *Lack of transparency of the models*: Providers are reluctant to answer requests for details of the models. Without the ability to check the model themselves, companies can neither validate nor confirm the accuracy of the models. If necessary, this can be compensated for by withholding selected data and ex-post validation with the results from the modelling (*hold-out sampling*).
- *Measurement of advertising content*: Commercials can show the same GRP number but appeal to customers very differently.
- *Dynamic effects*: Temporal spill-over effects, cross-brand impact, or halo effects must be reported separately.
- *Interaction effect between advertising media*: They can be tested for synergy effects using classification, decision tree, or CHAID methods and, if necessary, included in the model as an interaction variable.
- *Non-linear effects*: There is research which shows that in some channels, a minimum threshold of advertising must be reached to have an effect. Similarly, these channels generate almost no additional demand after reaching a saturation point. This means media are often better modelled with an S-shaped curve than with a linear regression model.
- *Instability of the coefficients*: It can be determined by sub-sampling and estimating the coefficients in different sub-samples.
- *Lack of integration/use of the results in practice*: The analyses and modelling carried out are not taken up in the on-going planning process, which results in a "modelling for the trash bin", with the results of the modelling being "cupboard goods".

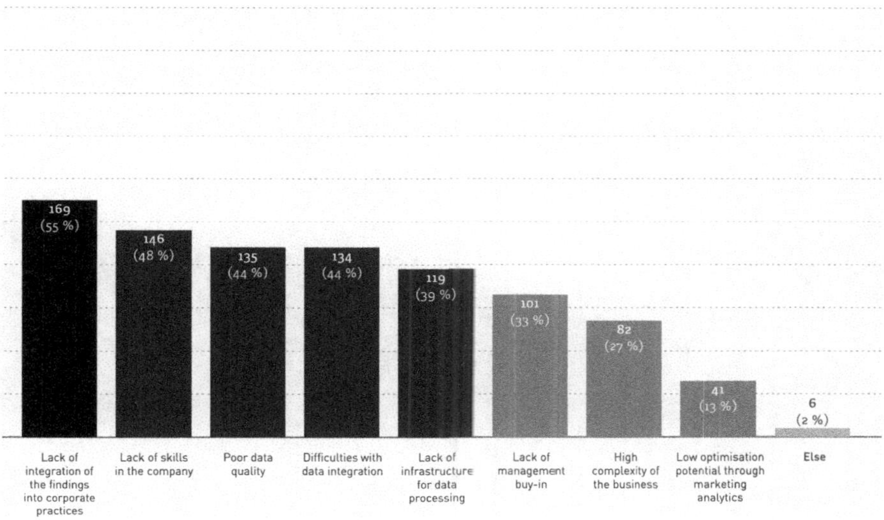

Fig. 7.18 Main barriers to the adoption and use of modelling and marketing analytics (in %, multiple responses, $n = 356$; Marketing Tech Monitor 2023)

The Achilles' heel in most companies lies in integration into business practices and processes (55%), seconded by insufficient know-how (48%) and insufficient data quality (44%, Fig. 7.18). At the same time, a supposedly low usefulness due to only insufficient optimisation potential falls away as an argument (13%).

References

CMO Community. (2023, Oktober).

Doerr, J. (2018). Measure what matters: OKRs: The simple idea that drives 10x growth.

Gulati, R., Nohria, N., & Wohlgezogen, F. (2010, March). *Roaring out of recession*. Harvard Business Review.

Hartnett, N., Gelzinis, J., Beal, V., Kennedy, R., & Sharp, B. (2021, June). When brands go dark. *Journal of Advertising Research*.

Kambuj, A. (2021, April). *The 7 Traits of a Modern Metrics Stack*. Falkon.

Runge, J., Patter, H., & Skokan, I. (2023, March). *A new gold standard for digital Ad measurement?* Harvard Business Review.

Schögel, M., & Herhausen, D. (2023). *The customer experience navigator*. p. 33.

Strauß, R. E. (2008). *Marketing planning by design*.

Pandora's AI Box: The AI Tsunami Is Rolling In

8

8.1 AI Foundations ... Stairway to AI Heaven

AI has been jumping from "zero to hero" since the advent of ChatGPT in 2023. The challenge: new phrases and terms need to be explained, e.g. *strong* vs. *weak AI, foundations models, machine learning, or deep learning.*

Since the beginning of 2023, the discussion about generative AI has given a considerable boost to discussions about artificial intelligence (AI). However, the drama starts at the beginning: different ideas meet novel terms. Artificial intelligence stands as an umbrella term for all applications in which machines perform human-like intelligence. This includes machine learning, natural language processing (NLP), and deep learning. What is new is not so much the perception/input of data as the learning and understanding. What genuine AI systems have in common is that they are trained in the processing component and can thus learn and achieve better results than conventional methods, based on rigid, clearly defined, and hard-coded sets of rules. The catchiest examples of this are speech, text, and image recognition. AI systems not only recognise letters in an image (syntax), but they also know what the word "complaint" means (semantics).

Strong AI describes the point at which IT systems can think and act in a human-like (or superior) way (Russel, 2012). This process is also used to train the automatic description (labelling) of images. Humans add descriptions (tags) to images, for example, and the algorithm learns to classify new images itself based on examples. Applications such as ChatGPT are classified as *weak AI* for solving predefined tasks. Examples are systems that can recognise images or convert spoken language into text. Machine learning is often equated with AI, but strictly speaking this is one tool among many in AI (Fig. 8.1). *Machine learning* (ML) subsumes all processes in which computer algorithms learn from data, for example to recognise patterns or to show desired behaviour, without each individual case being explicitly programmed.

In *supervised learning*, a learning algorithm tries to find a hypothesis that makes predictions which are as accurate as possible based on statistical forecasts. The results of the learning process can be compared with the known, correct results—

R. Strauss, *Data-Driven Customer Engagement*,
https://doi.org/10.1007/978-3-031-64295-1_8

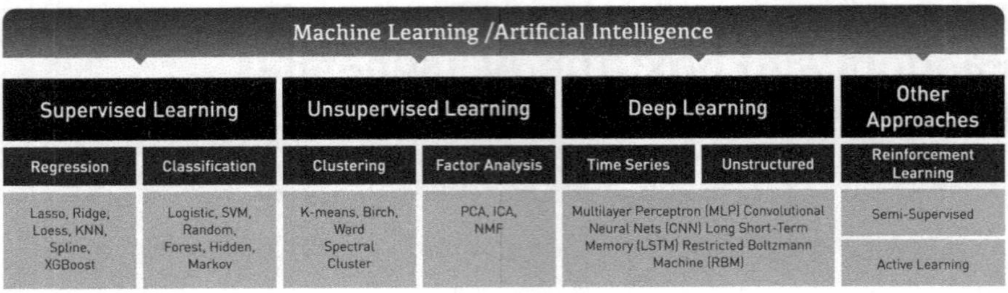

Fig. 8.1 Classification of the different forms of artificial intelligence (AI)

in other words, "supervised". The membership of new, unknown data is estimated based on the trained model. In *unsupervised learning*, there are no known target values or environmental rewards at the beginning. Rather, the exploratory data analysis attempts to recognise patterns in the input data that deviate from a structureless noise. An *artificial neural network*, for example, is guided by the similarity to the input values and adapts the weights accordingly. There are diverse types of neural networks designed for specific purposes. Perceptrons, the earliest form, paved the way for multilayer perceptrons (MLPs) and convolutional neural networks (CNNs), which are extensively used in image recognition. Recurrent neural networks (RNNs) excel in making predictions for time-series data, while autoencoders focus on creating abstract representations from input data.

Deep learning focuses on more complex application scenarios, for example, because of artificial neural networks that have numerous intermediate layers (hidden layers) between the input layer and the output layer and thus have an extensive inner structure. The topology of a network (the assignment of connections to nodes) is designed depending on the task at hand. The construction of a network is followed by the training phase, in which the network "learns" by modifying the weights of the neurons. This enables neural networks to capture complicated non-linear functions via a "learning" algorithm: using iterative/recursive loops, an attempt is made to determine all parameters of a function from existing input and desired output values. Unlike traditional machine learning, deep learning excels in processing unstructured data, automating feature extraction, and performing tasks with minimal human intervention. It includes supervised, unsupervised, semi-supervised, self-supervised, and reinforcement learning. *Deep neural networks* refine predictions using layers of interconnected nodes and utilise forward propagation and back propagation for training. Diverse types of neural networks, such as CNNs for image processing, RNNs for sequential data, and transformers for text generation, are tailored to specific tasks. In contrast to machine learning, in *cognitive learning* the learning algorithms are not predetermined. Put simply, these systems form hypotheses on structures and statements from the recognised patterns in the data sets (exploratory), which are then validated with probabilities and hypotheses in a wide variety of application scenarios.

Natural Language Processing (NLP) allows computers to comprehend, generate, and manipulate both written and spoken human language. This technology is the foundation for virtual assistants like *Siri*, *Cortana*, *Google Assistant*, and *Alexa*, as well as AI applications like *ChatGPT*, *Claude*, and *BART*. It plays a vital role in various applications, from web search to sentiment analysis. Recent advancements in NLP, driven by machine learning, especially deep learning, have enabled to uncover complex language patterns from extensive datasets (Fig. 8.2). At the core of NLP are machine learning models, with deep learning leading the way. Techniques like pre-trained foundation models such as LLMs and transfer learning allow for adaptability to new tasks with minimal training data. API providers like *OpenAI* have developed pre-trained LLM models tailored to various applications, further accelerating development. Preprocessing techniques like tokenisation, bag-of-words models, and stop word removal are crucial in NLP. While part-of-speech tagging and syntactic parsing have their place, modern deep learning-based models have less reliance on them.

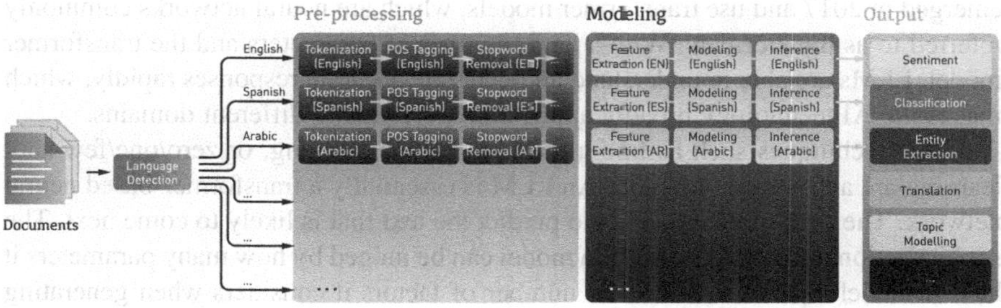

Fig. 8.2 Classical NLP approach (See also Thanaki, J.: Python Natural Language Processing, New York 2017)

Reinforcement learning relies on the strategy of natural learning and stands for a series of machine learning methods in which an agent independently learns a strategy to maximise the rewards it receives. In this process, the agent is not shown which action is best in which situation, but receives a reward at certain points in time, which can also be negative. Based on these rewards, the agent approximates a utility function that describes the value of a certain state or action. *Deep reinforcement learning* (DRL) combines artificial neural networks and reinforcement learning, advancing AI's understanding of the visual world. It allows agents to learn tasks with specific goals, such as playing video games from pixel data or controlling real-world robots using camera input. DRL addresses the challenge of linking immediate actions with delayed outcomes, akin to human decision-making. Its progress in uncertain, dynamic environments signifies a step towards practical AI solutions. Learning here can be compared to a kind of conditioning, in which the system is "rewarded" if it has reacted correctly and "punished" if the result does not correspond to the expectation. Simplified, the learning process, called agent, is in an environment that has a distinct finite set of states and actions. At any given time, the agent determines the state of the environment and reacts to it with one of the actions available. The environment reacts to the action and "rewards" or "punishes" the agent's action. The agent takes this reaction from the environment and adjusts its behaviour in future decisions. A "reward" thereby reinforces the execution of the action, and a "punishment" leads to a change in future decisions of the agent when choosing an action. The system or agent is in a *Markov decision process* in which the environment, state, and actions are fixed. It makes the agent figure out how to get to a maximum "reward".

Large Language Models, like the transformer networks, are the backbone of modern AI. A large language model (LLM) is a type of AI algorithm that uses deep learning techniques and massively large data sets to understand, summarise, generate, and predict new content. For helping them learn the complexity and linkages of language, LLMs are pre-trained on a vast amount of data (Vaswani et al., 2017). The term Generative AI also is closely connected with LLMs, which are, in fact, a type of Generative AI that has been specifically architected to help generate text-based content. Parameters are a machine learning term for the variables present in the model on which it was trained that can be used to infer latest content. Modern LLMs emerged in 2017 and use transformer models, which are neural networks commonly referred to as transformers. With a large number of parameters and the transformer model, LLMs are able to understand and generate accurate responses rapidly, which makes the AI technology broadly applicable across many different domains.

Using techniques such as fine-tuning, in-context learning, or zero/one/few-shot learning are at the core of LLMs. An LLM is essentially a transformer-based neural network. The goal of the model is to predict the text that is likely to come next. The sophistication and performance of a model can be judged by how many parameters it has. A model's parameters are the number of factors it considers when generating output. LLMs can be applied to a variety of use cases and industries, including healthcare, retail and tech, for, among others, text summarisation, text generation, sentiment analysis, content creation, chatbots, conversational AI, named entity recognition, speech recognition and synthesis, or recommendation systems (e.g. within CRM) (Simon, 2021). Once the model is pre-trained, it can be trained further with task-specific, new data to fine-tune it for specific use cases. In the context of *ChatGPT*, for example, LLM capabilities are limited to the textual training data they are trained with, which means they are limited in their knowledge of the world. The models learn the relationships within the training data, and these may include false information, biases, or toxic language.

Some LLMs are referred to as *foundation models*. A foundation model is so large and impactful that it serves as the foundation for further optimisations and specific use cases. These models consist of multiple layers, including self-attention and feed-forward layers, enabling them to understand context and meaning in sequential data.

At the foundational layer, an LLM needs to be trained on a large volume—sometimes referred to as a corpus—of data that is typically petabytes in size. The training can take multiple steps, usually

- starting with an unsupervised learning approach. In that approach, the model is trained on unstructured data and unlabelled data. The benefit of training on un-labelled data is that there is often vastly more data available. At this stage, the model begins to derive relationships between different words and concepts.

- The next step for some LLMs is training and fine-tuning with a form of self-supervised learning. Here, some data labelling has occurred, assisting the model to identify different concepts more accurately.
- Next, the LLM undertakes deep learning as it goes through the transformer neural network process. The transformer model architecture enables the LLM to understand and recognise the relationships and connections between words and concepts using a self-attention mechanism. That mechanism can assign a score, commonly referred to as a weight, to a given item (called a token) to determine the relationship.
- Once an LLM has been trained, a base exists on which the AI can be used for practical purposes. By querying the LLM with a prompt, the AI model inference can generate a response, which could be an answer to a question, newly generated text, summarised text, or a sentiment analysis report (Fig. 8.3).

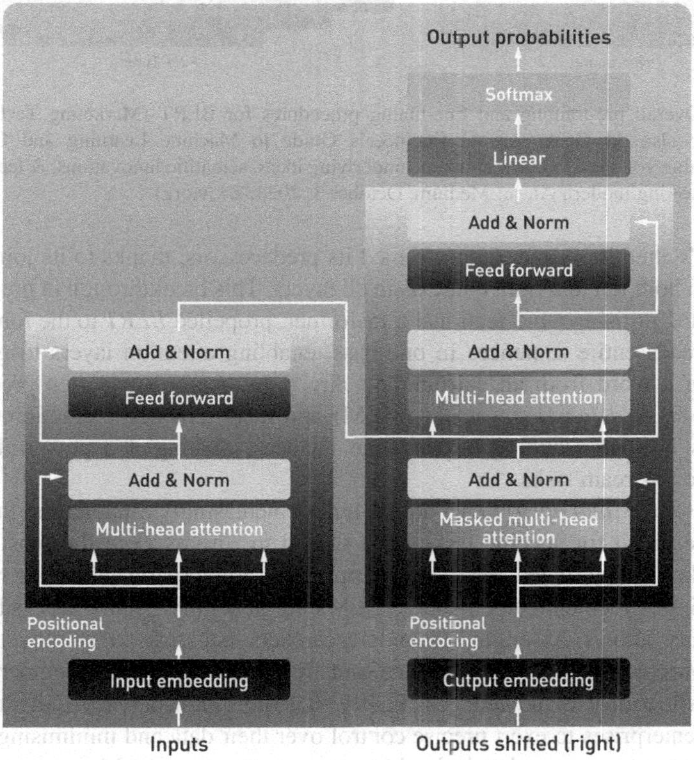

Fig. 8.3 Transformer model architecture of large language models

Bidirectional encoder representations from transformers (*BERT*) revolutionised natural language processing. Unlike earlier models like *Glove*, which had fixed word embeddings regardless of context, *BERT* harnessed bidirectional transformers, allowing it to consider both left and right contexts simultaneously (Fig. 8.4). This provided a more nuanced understanding of word meanings. In comparison, *embeddings from language models* (*ELMo*), unique and context-dependent, concatenated left-to-right and right-to-left information, missing out on the full contextual picture.

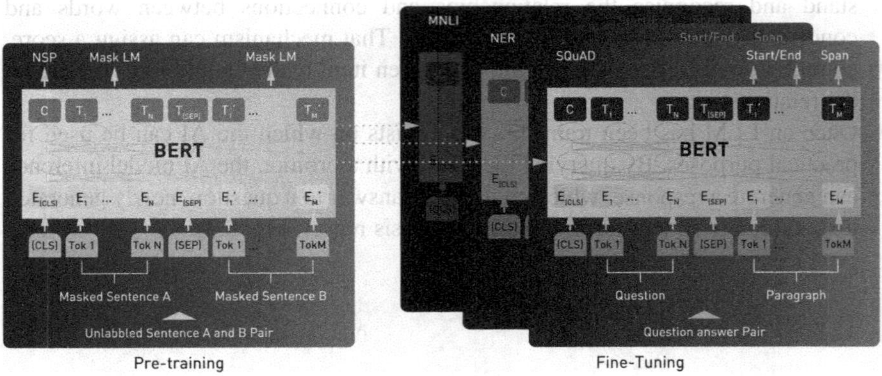

Fig. 8.4 Overall pre-training and fine-tuning procedures for BERT (Marketing Tech Monitor 2024) (See also AI Geek: An AI Engineer's Guide to Machine Learning and Generative AI. Everything you need to know about the underlying ideas, scientific innovations, & technologies that are powering modern AI, in: Medium, October 3, 2023; arxiv.org)

BERT's attention layers outperformed its predecessors, thanks to its joint conditioning on both left and right contexts in all layers. This breakthrough in pre-training architecture, utilising a bidirectional transformer, propelled *BERT* to the forefront of NLP. It reads entire sentences in one pass, enabling attention layers to grasp the context of a word from all surrounding directions. *BERT's* two-step pre-training process—*masked language model* (MLM) and next sentence prediction—further fine-tunes its understanding of language nuances, making it a powerful tool in various downstream tasks.

Open-source (and open) LLMs are becoming increasingly capable, and fine-tuned models designed for specific tasks have started to surpass even the most capable models like *GPT-4*. In contrast to their proprietary counterparts, which are restricted by licensing agreements, open-source LLMs are generally openly accessible. This accessibility allows AI engineers and researchers not only to employ them for various purposes but also to enhance and distribute them. This democratisation brings forth a host of advantages. Firstly, it fosters transparency and flexibility, enabling enterprises to exert precise control over their data and minimising the risk of unauthorised access or data leaks. Moreover, open-source LLMs are considerably more cost-effective in the long run, as they do not incur licensing fees. Additionally, they allow for customisation and fine-tuning to suit specific organisational needs, a task that would be both cumbersome and costly with proprietary models. The open-source model ecosystem empowers a diverse community to contribute, resulting in cutting-edge solutions.

LLMs generate responses by randomly sampling words based in part on probabilities. Their "language" consists of numbers that map to tokens (OpenAI & Jones, 2024).

However, it is essential to acknowledge and address potential risks, including issues of bias, misinformation, consent, and security. Through education and robust AI governance, these challenges can be mitigated, ensuring the responsible and effective use of open-source LLMs in a variety of domains (Fig. 8.5). The landscape of open-source LLMs is evolving rapidly, and models like *Llama-2* and *Mistral* are emerging as the preferred choices for many AI researchers and engineers.

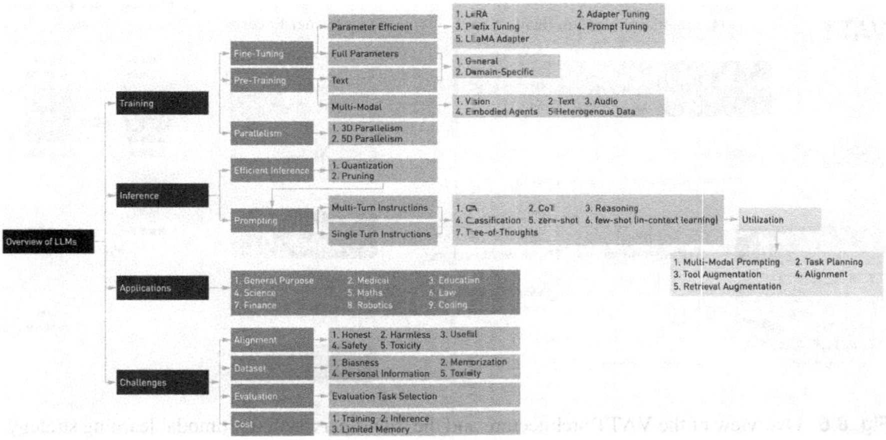

Fig. 8.5 A broader overview of LLMs, dividing LLMs into four branches: Training, Inference, Applications, and Challenges (Marketing Tech Monitor 2024) (See also for a detailed description AI Geek: An AI Engineer's Guide to Machine Learning and Generative AI. Everything you need to know about the underlying ideas, scientific innovations, & technologies that are powering modern AI, in: Medium, October 2023 / arxiv.org)

For successful prompt engineering for AI applications, two crucial factors of LLMs must be considered: Temperature and Top P:

- *Temperature* influences text randomness, with lower values favouring conservative predictions and higher values fostering creativity. Adjusting temperature is key to tailoring output for specific tasks. For fact-based questions, a lower temperature is suitable for prioritising accuracy. Conversely, creative tasks, like poetry generation, benefit from higher temperatures for imaginative results.
- In contrast, *Top P* controls response determinism. A lower value narrows token choices for more precise but potentially less diverse output, while a higher value encourages diversity by considering a wider token range. A lower Top P is ideal for accuracy-driven tasks and should be increased for more diverse responses.

Video-audio-text transformer (*VATT*) is a groundbreaking framework for unsupervised multimodal representation learning (Fig. 8.6). By leveraging convolution-free transformer architectures, *VATT* processes raw signals like video, audio, and text to extract rich, joint embeddings. This versatility proves invaluable across various downstream tasks, from video action recognition to text-to-video retrieval. *VATT's* architecture combines elements from BERT and ViT, with a focus on preserving modality-specific processing. Through unsupervised learning and noisy contrastive estimation, *VATT* creates a common space for meaningful representations, revolutionising applications in speech recognition, image captioning, and video retrieval. *VATT's* capacity to unify modalities promises a paradigm shift in multimodal AI.

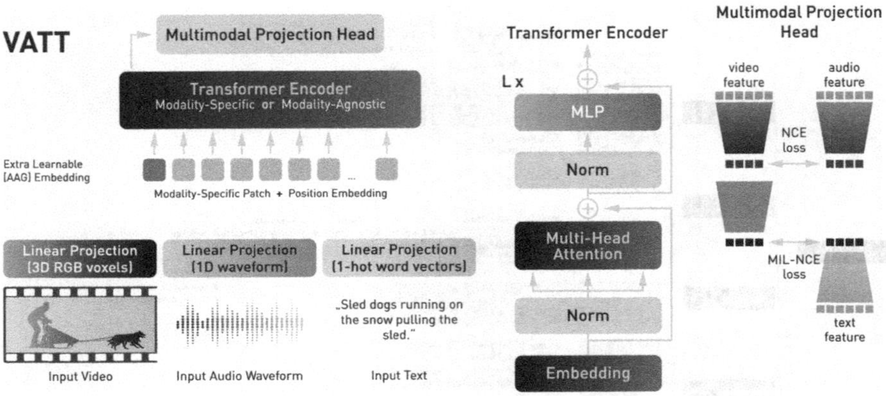

Fig. 8.6 Overview of the VATT architecture and the self-supervised, multimodal learning strategy (Marketing Tech Monitor 2024) (See also AI Geek: An AI Engineer's Guide to Machine Learning and Generative AI. Everything you need to know about the underlying ideas, scientific innovations, & technologies that are powering modern AI, in: Medium, October 3, 2023 for a detailed description)

With *ChatGPT* as an application around LLMs and supervised/reinforcement learning, the deployment and use of AI has slowly left the embryonic stage—the contours of future use are already emerging on the ultrasound machine. This has led to a boom in development and investment in newer *application scenarios*, which stretch from creative development to price optimisation and customer experience management (Fig. 8.7).

Generative pre-trained transformers (*GPT*) represent a monumental leap in AI, underpinned by the transformer architecture. Therefore, from zero to hero: the speech application *ChatGPT* has proven to be a "gamechanger" for the assessment of AI since early 2023. These models, including the renowned *GPT-3* and 4, empower applications like *ChatGPT* to craft remarkably human-like text and content, revolutionising sectors from marketing to education. *GPT's* impact is profound, streamlining tasks from language translation to content creation at an unprecedented pace. With applications spanning social media content creation, code

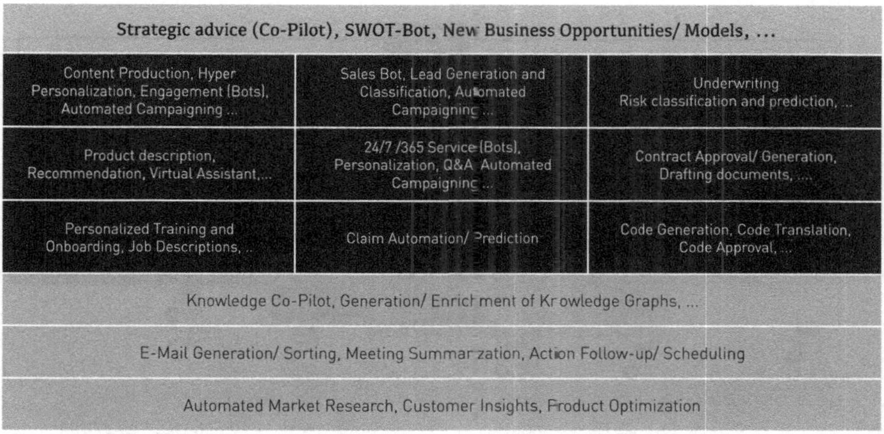
Strategic advice (Co-Pilot), SWOT-Bot, New Business Opportunities/ Models, ...
Content Production, Hyper Personalization, Engagement (Bots), Automated Campaigning ...
Sales Bot, Lead Generation and Classification, Automated Campaigning ...
Underwriting Risk classification and prediction, ...
Product description, Recommendation, Virtual Assistant,...
24/7 /365 Service (Bots), Personalization, Q&A Automated Campaigning ...
Contract Approval/ Generation, Drafting documents, ...
Personalized Training and Onboarding, Job Descriptions, ..
Claim Automation/ Prediction
Code Generation, Code Translation, Code Approval, ...
Knowledge Co-Pilot, Generation/ Enrichment of Knowledge Graphs, ...
E-Mail Generation/ Sorting, Meeting Summarization, Action Follow-up/ Scheduling
Automated Market Research, Customer Insights, Product Optimization

Fig. 8.7 Scenarios for the use of Gen AI in marketing (adapted from Gentsch, Marketing Tech Monitor 2024)

generation, data analysis, and interactive voice assistants, *GPT's* versatility is striking. Its functioning relies on neural-network-based language prediction, utilising the transformer architecture's self-attention mechanisms. By processing vast data sets, *GPT-3* already, with its 175 billion parameters, attains a level of proficiency and fluency that marks a paradigm shift in AI capabilities. To train *GPT*, the model is fed a large text data set and then asked to predict the next word in a sequence based on the previous words (Brown et al., 2020).

ChatGPT shows that AI will have an even stronger role in optimising marketing in the future, whether through AI-powered content creation, marketing automation or scoring customers. Companies need to build analytics and data science talent and to develop AI capabilities now to keep playing the game.— Dr Martino Saracino (Head of Marketing Insights and Analytics, Digital Accelerator, QIAGEN).

The model is then evaluated for its ability to accurately predict the next word and its parameters are adjusted accordingly to gradually improve its performance. This process is repeated until the model has reached a satisfactory level of performance (Fig. 8.8).

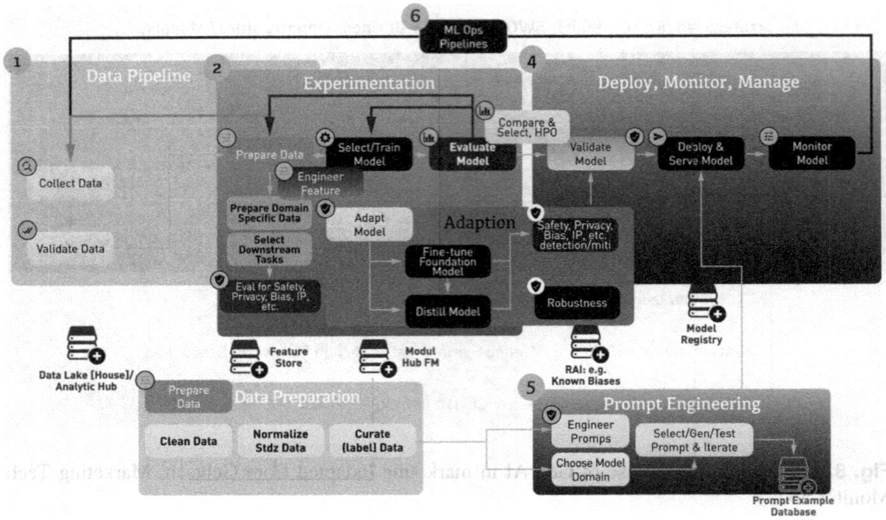

Fig. 8.8 Generative AI cycle (schematic, Marketing Tech Monitor 2023) (See also Kannal, A.: GenAI Applications Reference Architecture—Part 1, in: Medium, December 4, 2023; Arsanjani, A.: The Generative AI Life-cycle, in: Medium, March 2023 for a detailed description)

As use increases, data volume grows, and with human-generated text, the system is trained as "weak AI" (unsupervised), although contextualisation and creativity skills are (currently) still lacking. Thus, the system learns to produce text that sounds natural and appealing in a conversational context, by independently recognising patterns and structures in the data (syntax) (Wolfram, 2023). As a result, multimodal applications are currently exploding, as is their use in software development. In addition to *ChatGPT*, providers are available in a wide variety of segments, in areas such as:

- search and audio (e.g. *Symbl.ai*, *balto*, *Elise*, or *PolyAI*),
- text, chat, and translation (e.g. *DeepL*, *grammarly*, *copy.ai*),
- video (e.g. *Veed.io*, *videoverse* or *Rephrase.AI*),
- BI (e.g. *Persado* or *unbounce*), or
- coding (with *replit* or *warp*).

At a very high level, the workflow can be divided into three stages (Fig. 8.9) (Arsanjani, 2023; Bornstein & Radovanovic, 2023; Kannal, 2023):

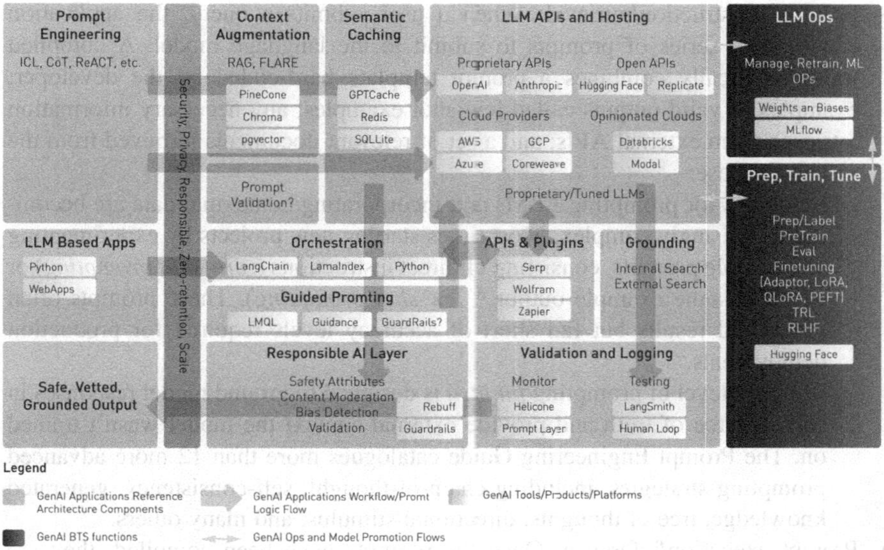

Fig. 8.9 GenAI applications reference architecture (Draft, Marketing Tech Monitor 2024) (See also Arsanjani, A.: Generative AI Lifecycle Patterns. in: Medium, September 18, 2023; Bornstein, M.; Radovanovic, R.: Emerging Architectures for LLM Applications, in: Andreessen Horowitz, June 20, 2023; Kannal, A.: GenAI Applications Reference Architecture—Part 1, in: Medium, December 4, 2023)

- Data preprocessing/embedding: This stage involves storing private data (legal documents, in our example) to be retrieved later. Typically, the documents are broken into chunks, passed through an embedding model, then stored in a specialised database called a vector database:
  - Contextual data for LLM apps includes text documents, PDFs, and even structured formats like CSV or SQL tables. Data-loading and transformation solutions for this data vary widely across developers we spoke with. Most use traditional ETL tools like *Databricks* or *Airflow*. Some also use document loaders built into orchestration frameworks like *LangChain* and *LlamaIndex*.
  - The most important piece of the preprocessing pipeline, from a systems standpoint, is the *vector database*. It's responsible for efficiently storing, comparing, and retrieving up to billions of embeddings (such as *Pinecone*). There's a huge range of vector databases available, such as
    - Open-source systems like *Weaviate*, *Vespa*, and *Qdrant*.
    - Local vector management libraries like *Chroma* and *Faiss*.
    - OLTP extensions like *pgvector*.

- Prompt construction/retrieval: When a user submits a query, the application constructs a series of prompts to submit to the language model. A compiled prompt typically combines a prompt template hard-coded by the developer; examples of valid outputs called few-shot examples; any necessary information retrieved from external APIs; and a set of relevant documents retrieved from the vector database:
  - Strategies for prompting LLMs and incorporating contextual data are becoming increasingly complex. Most times starting new projects by experimenting with simple prompts, consisting of direct instructions (*zero-shot prompting*) or possibly some example outputs (*few-shot prompting*). These prompts often give good results but fall short of accuracy levels required for production deployments.
  - The next level of prompting *jiu jitsu* is designed to ground model responses in some source of truth and provide external context the model wasn't trained on. The Prompt Engineering Guide catalogues more than 12 more advanced prompting strategies, including chain-of-thought, self-consistency, generated knowledge, tree of thoughts, directional stimulus, and many others.
- Prompt execution/inference: Once the prompts have been compiled, they are submitted to a pre-trained LLM for inference—including both proprietary model APIs and open-source or self-trained models. Some developers also add operational systems like logging, caching, and validation at this stage.

8.2 AI . . . Between Hype and Hope

As of May 2024, the focus of use is accordingly on conversational AI (e.g. *chatbots in service) and content creation* (e.g. *for social media). Strategic objectives of AI providers such as OpenAI are (1.) the further development of their own solution, for example in the direction of multimodal speech, text and image models based on larger data volumes and parameters, (2.) providing plug-in functionalities as "embedded AI" in other IT solutions to achieve higher market penetration (scaling) and to generate critical mass effects, and (3.) accelerate the development and expansion of their own ecosystem* via *investments.*

Although, according to the *European Marketing Agenda 2023*, no company has placed the topic of "artificial intelligence" at the top of their hit parade at the beginning of 2023, the majority are already familiarising themselves with the topic or have already launched initial pilots (Fig. 8.10) (European Marketing Confederation, 2023; Hesel et al., 2022). Beyond the hype, estimates expect an increase in labour productivity of up to 35% (Noy & Zhang, 2023). Thus, for about 80% of the workforce, at least 10% of their work tasks are affected by *GPT* models, and for 19% of workers at least 50% of their tasks are fully replaceable (Manning et al., 2023).

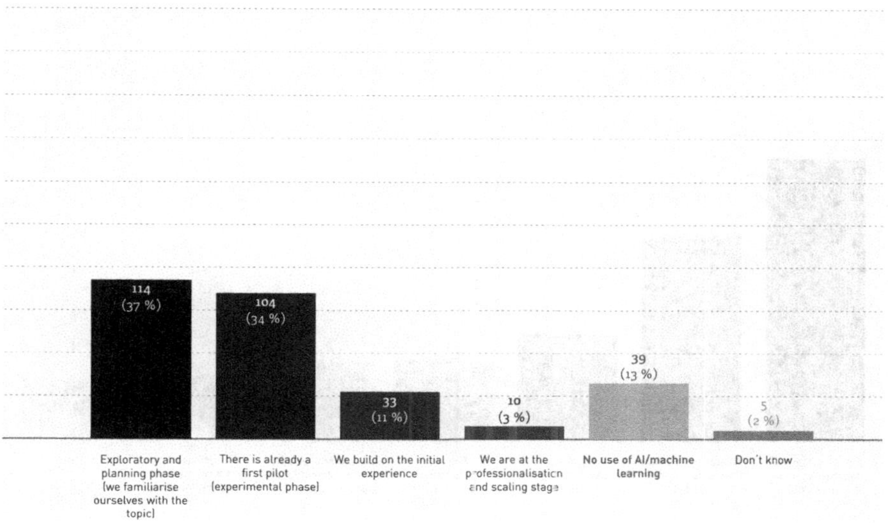

Fig. 8.10 Intensity of engagement with and use of artificial intelligence in marketing, sales, and service (in %, $n = 305$; Marketing Tech Monitor 2023)

The myriad of possible application scenarios ranges from digital voice assistants (e.g. *Google Assistant*), big data analytics (e.g. for pattern recognition in user behaviour), the classification of websites and advertising content according to relevance, hyper-targeting and (content) personalisation, chatbots in customer service, next best action or offer in marketing automation or even personalised content or content creation. From the point of view of marketing and sales, AI application scenarios thus offer (within limits) the option for:

- *Zero-shot response generation*: The generation of responses to unprecedented requests, without any fine-tuning or additional training.
- *Contextual understanding*: Applications such as *ChatGPT* can maintain a consistent understanding of the context of a conversation, which enables it to generate responses that are or appear relevant and on-topic.
- *Personalisation*: *ChatGPT* can be tuned to specific data sets or specific targets, for example, so that it can deliver personalised responses tailored to specific audiences or use cases.

The current focus of use is accordingly on conversational AI (e.g. chatbots in service) and content creation (e.g. for social media; Fig. 8.11).

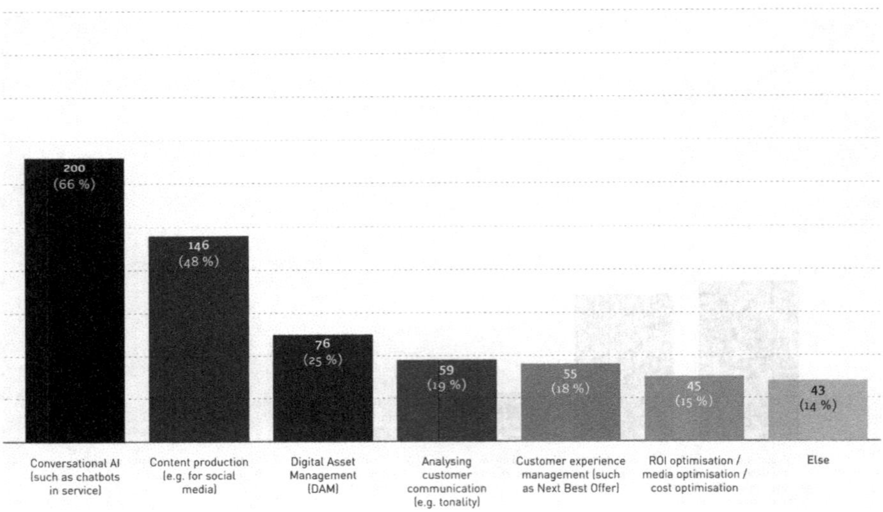

Fig. 8.11 Application scenarios used for AI (in %, multiple responses, n = 356; Marketing Tech Monitor 2023)

In the foreseeable future, AI application scenarios will become an integral part of other applications in the fields of CRM, social media management, or DAM, e.g.:

- In March 2023, *HubSpot* introduced *ChatSpot,* a new generative AI functionality in the pilot phase. The new app combines technologies from *HubSpot's* own CRM with *ChatGPT, DALL-E 2,* and *Google Docs* applications such as *Google Sheets* and *Google Slides. ChatSpot* generates E-Mails and other messages with contextual information from each customer's account. *ChatUX* is designed to make it easier for users to use CRM via general language input (Wood, 2023a).
- Social media management provider *Sprout Social* acquired AI-based sentiment analysis company *Repustate* in early 2023 (SproutSocial, 2023).
- *Adobe* launched *Firefly* in early March 2023 as a generative AI-based tool for the development of creative assets.
- *Intercom's Fin* uses *OpenAI GPT-4* and *Intercom's* proprietary machine learning technology to provide trusted answers to support customer questions. More difficult questions are routed to support staff via workflow.
- *Instreamatic* generates spoken ads that match the context of the listener. Location, time of day, current activity, and other variables are used as input for an automatically generated ad script that is read aloud by an automatically generated voice in a podcast, game, or other medium (GlobalNewsWire, 2023).
- Digital customer experience analytics platform *Glassbox* has announced that it will integrate *ChatGPT* for digital experiences. Users will be able to ask questions in their native language and have *ChatGPT* respond.
- *Course5 Intelligence* has integrated *OpenAI's GPT* models into *Course5 Compete*, its (proprietary) AI-powered marketplace. The goal: to improve product assortment (turnover rate) and recommendations via matching.

- *DeepSights* from *Market Logic Software* is an AI assistant trained to answer questions about market research and consumer intelligence. It has been specifically trained to understand the context of questions dealing with market research results, embedded in standard applications such as *Microsoft Teams*.
- *Optiwise.ai* has integrated *ChatGPT* into the optimisation of *Walmart's* marketplace. Using the knowledge base, *ChatGPT* generates content (optimised product detail pages) that enables sellers to improve visibility, engagement, and conversions.
- *Salsify PXM OpenAI Accelerator* is part of the *Commerce Experience Platform*. This uses generative AI to accelerate the creation of product content across the product catalogue.
- *Baidu's MediaGo AI* integration automatically optimises the delivery mode, ad delivery strategy, and algorithm based on different scenarios as data feeds change. It predicts user behaviour by analysing historical and real-time data for precise ad delivery.
- *ChannelMix AI* analyses real-time data from multiple channels, including TV, social media, E-Mail marketing, search marketing, direct mail and more, to create scenarios that predict the optimal media mix and budget.
- Similarly, *Horizon* has launched *Neon*, an AI platform for e-commerce that allows media investments to be planned and optimised for revenue outcomes (Cision, 2023a).
- London-based *causaLens* and pioneer of causal AI has announced the launch of *decisionOS*, the first operating system to use AI-based cause-and-effect reasoning for all aspects of decision-making in an enterprise (Ortega, 2023).
- *Google* has been offering API access to generative AI models since March 2023, allowing developers to embed them directly into their own products (Yang & Gokturk, 2023). At the same time, trial versions of AI-based functions for image generation, text creation and categorisation in *Gmail*, *Docs*, *Sheets* and other productivity tools will be offered. *Google* plans to launch the *Bard* chatbot as a nucleus for further AI applications.
- *Reply.io* as an E-Mail engine has launched *Jason AI*, an add-on that uses *ChatGPT's* API along with *Reply.io's* natural language processing (NLP) to generate, personalise, and optimise E-Mails. *Jason AI* uses NLP algorithms and *ChatGPT's* language model to identify keywords and phrases, to identify the intent of E-Mails and to generate suggested responses.
- *Blaze* uses AI for software development: via an OpenAI API, users can enter descriptions that are translated into code (Miller, 2023).
- At the end of April 2023, *Amazon Web Services* announced a series of services that will allow developers to create AI chatbots and other tools based on pre-trained models from *Anthropic*, *AI21*, *Stability AI* and *Amazon's* own *Titan* family, such as foundation models like *Amazon Bedrock*.
- *SOCi*, as a marketing platform for distributed brands and commerce organisations, uses *ChatGPT's* natural language model for intelligent responses to online reviews in real time for multi-location commerce organisations (Steele, 2023).

- *Mailchimp's* E-Mail content generator aims to provide generative AI to small and medium-sized businesses. Personalised E-Mail content can be generated in natural language, tailored to brand, tone of voice and objectives.
- *Zeta Marketing Cloud* announced several AI-based enhancements in Q2/2023, including omnichannel forecasting, improved propensity scoring, and no-code data warehouse connectivity (BusinessWire, 2023).
- *Microsoft Dynamics 365* added AI-based *Microsoft AI Copilot* as a *Power Platform* in March 2023 (powered by *Azure OpenAI Service* with *GPT*), such as customer segment search in CDP and E-Mail drafting (Von Hoffmann, 2023a; Lardinois, 2023). In *Power Apps*, the main low-code tool in *Power Platform*, users can now enter phrases such as "*Create a time and expense app so my employees can submit their time and expense reports*" and *Copilot* will create that app. In addition to creating user interfaces and integrating with different data sources, *Copilot* can also help analyse and visualise data (e.g. "*What are the most common reasons why an inspection fails*?"). *Microsoft Bing* has already been enhanced with an AI platform, which subsequently raises the question of copyright protection in the search sector.
- *Grammarly* announced *GrammarlyGO* in early March 2023. *GrammarlyGO* is a generative AI content creation tool for businesses and individuals which aims to generate relevant copy that matches personal voice as well as brand style and context for professional use cases (Wood, 2023b).
- *Typeface* translates brand attributes via generative AI as part of the automated creation of personalised content in social media (Cision, 2023b).

Strategic objectives of AI providers such as *OpenAI* (OpenAI, 2023a; Von Hoffmann, 2023b):

- Further development of their own solution, for example in the direction of multimodal speech, text, and image models based on larger data volumes and parameters.
- Provision of plug-in functionalities as "embedded AI" in other IT solutions to achieve higher market penetration (scaling) and to generate critical mass effects, for example around CRM or social media. To this end, the costs of the *ChatGPT API*, for example, were reduced by 90%. At the beginning of March 2023, plug-ins were made available for *Klarna*, *Slack*, *Shopify*, *Wolfram*, and *Expedia*. Plug-ins open the integration of multilayered data from a wide range of platforms and application contexts ... beyond pure training data.
- Further acceleration of the development and expansion of their own ecosystem via investments (Fig. 8.12).

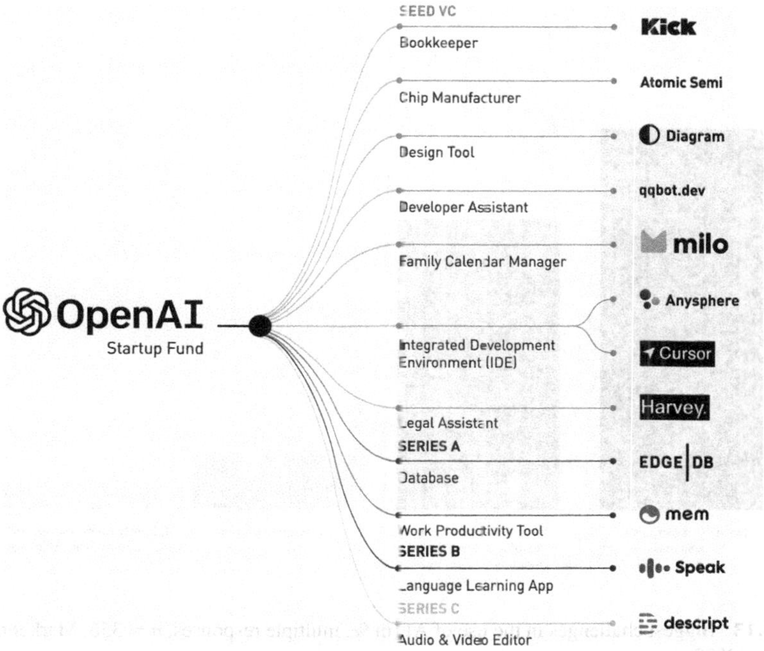

Fig. 8.12 OpenAI investment strategy for building a generative AI ecosystem (as of August 2023) (See also: CB Insights: Analyzing OpenAI's investment strategy: How the ChatGPT maker is building a generative AI ecosystem, February 2023)

With the launch of *GPT-4* in early March 2023, multimodal, augmented language models can be realised using 100 trillion parameters, capable of processing and understanding different languages/media (sentiments) (OpenAI, 2023b). The modalities can be visual, acoustic, or textual (multilingual) and include, for example, images, videos, audio recordings, text documents, or other forms of data with industry-specific context. In the medium term, it is expected that such *large language models* (LLMs) in AI will also lead to a greater uptake of in-house development of further MarTech applications (Peterson, 2023).

The challenge of this is that while technologies develop exponentially (quickly), business organisations manage at best a logarithmic (slow) change. Following *Goethe*, most organisations assume the earth is shaped by the power of leisure ... in the sense that "*soft water breaks the stone*". However, the technological or intellectual counterpart in the form of modern MarketingTech and AI dictates the speed of evolution, beyond all leisure, in the best style of an impetuous *Alexander von Humboldt* on his own "big expedition". In practice, *Goethe's* leisureliness has so far ensured the full-bodied promises of salvation mostly fail because of trivial basics, such as insufficient in-house know-how or still insufficiently aggregated or available data (Fig. 8.13).

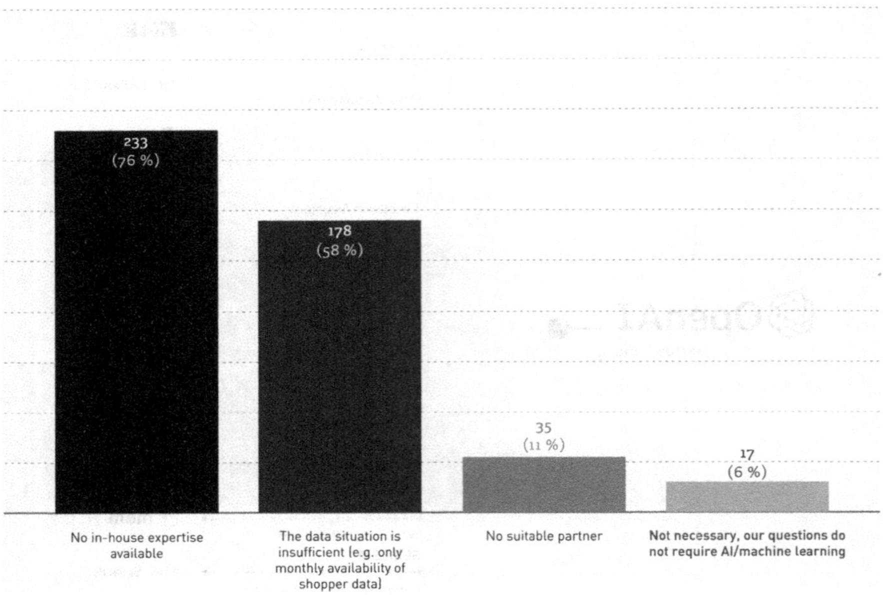

Fig. 8.13 Biggest challenges in the use of AI (in %, multiple responses, $n = 356$; Marketing Tech Monitor 2023)

The next wave of AI in marketing and sales is already *ante portas* with *Causal AI*. The fundamental problem with existing AI models is that the model learns from training data and, in this case, the data to answer counterfactual questions is not observed and measured. The other approach to consider is to conduct randomised control trials (also referred to as A/B testing). Therefore, causality is not a novel concept—such trials have been the gold standard for measuring the impact of interventions for a long time. However, there are practical challenges in using them (Hurwitz & Thompson, 2023):

- Ensuring random assignment between the control and treatment group is not always feasible, and systematic differences between groups bias the results.
- Randomised controlled trials are expensive and time-consuming.
- Ethical issues arise in conducting random trials in many situations—is it ethical to expose people to potentially harmful treatments?

The problem with this approach, however, is that the greater the number or complexity of interventions, the harder it is to select look-alike and mimic control groups. Causal graphical models (probabilistic graphical models which encode assumptions about the data-generating process), however, solve this problem. One of the most popular causal graphical models is a *Bayesian network*. It looks like a spider's web or network of connections that reveal the effect of each variable on others (Fig. 8.14).

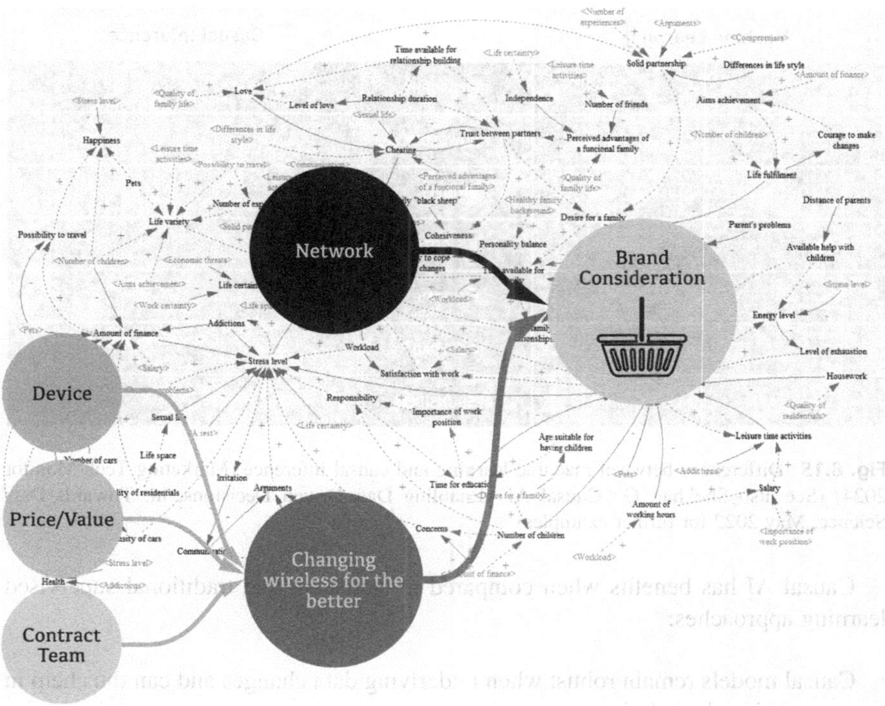

Fig. 8.14 Example of a Bayesian network showing how various factors impact sales (project example in Telco)

The above questions are all causal questions and, unlike many conventional machine learning tasks, cannot be answered using only passively observed data and traditional machine learning algorithms. New approaches to machine learning based on principles of causal reasoning provide a promising path forward. Causal inference bridges the gap between prediction plus decision-making and allows researchers and program designers to simulate an intervention and infer causality by relying on data already available (Fig. 8.15).

Machine Learning		Casual Inference
Confirmation	PHILOSOPHY	Revelation
Correlations	KNOWLEDGE	Causality
Supervides/Unsupervides	MODELS	Meta Learning, Inverse Propensity Weighting
Predictions	INSIGHTS	Decisions, Interventions, Counterfactuals
Operational/Tactical	OUTCOME	Strategic & Value Generation
Historical Observed Data	WORLOAD	Interventional, Observational, Domain
Limited Explainability	RESPONSIBLE	Fair and free from Bias

Fig. 8.15 Differences between machine learning and causal inference (Marketing Tech Monitor 2024) (See also Shekhar, G.: Causal AI—Enabling Data-Driven Decisions, in: Towards Data Science, May 2022 for further examples)

Causal AI has benefits when compared to statistical and traditional supervised learning approaches:

- Causal models remain robust when underlying data changes and can thus help in generalising the solution to unseen data.
- Causal AI helps measure the impact of an intervention and is a very good tool for decision-making.
- Causal models also allow us to respond to situations we have not seen before and enable the solution to plan for unforeseen counterfactual situation.
- Causal models also allow humans to generalise previously gained knowledge to unseen and different challenges.

Causal inference enables estimating the causal effect of an intervention based on outcome from real-world observational data, holding all other variables constant. For instance, the impact of an intervention in addressing target groups with different campaigns. The target group base was divided into two treatment groups: Group 1, those who received the campaign, and Group 2, employees who did not receive any communication. A causal effect estimate requires computing the difference between the outcome when the target group receives the impulse and the situation when they do not, keeping other variables constant. We need to be aware that only one of the outcomes is possible—in other words, either a target group received the communication or not. The unobserved outcome is a counterfactual one. Causal inference methods employ various assumptions to let us estimate the unobservable counterfactual outcome.

Some of the factors that make the causal inference problem challenging are (Hurwitz & Thompson, 2023):

- *Confounders*: A confounder is a variable that influences both the treatment and outcome. Fundamentally, if something other than the treatment differs between the treated and control groups, we cannot conclusively say that any difference observed in the outcome is due solely to the treatment.
- *Selection bias*: When the distribution of the observed group is not representative of the group, we are interested in computing the causal effect. If we directly train the causal model on the data without handling selection bias, the trained model works poorly in estimating the outcomes for the units in the other group.
- *Measuring treatment effect*: The treatment effect can be measured at the population (average treatment effect), treated group, sub-group (conditional average treatment effect [CATE]), and individual levels (individual treatment effect [ITE]).

There are two fundamental approaches to causal inference:

- *Potential outcomes framework*: Compares the outcome of an individual who was not exposed to the campaign and has received communication. So, for each target group member who was exposed to the campaign, the Causal AI algorithms will find an individual in the data set who was not exposed to the communication but who is identical in other significant respects such as age, experience, hierarchy, department, demographics, etc. The limitation of this approach is that the approach can test the impact of only one intervention at a time.
- *Causal graph model*: This approach helps us map the different causal paths to an outcome of interest and shows how different variables relate to each other. One widely used method is the structural equation model, in which we specify the variables that may interact and how they might do so—the model then analyses the data to reveal whether they do. The limitation of this model is that it tests only the linkages between the specified variables. Another causal graph method is the causal Bayesian network, which estimates the relationships between all variables in a data set.

Causal inference consists of a family of methods, and at its core are two types of estimation methods and algorithms:

- *Estimation methods under un-confoundedness*: The assumption made here is that we are measuring all confounding variables in observed data. If that is not the case, then the results will have some bias in them. Matching methods and re-weighting methods are two of the commonly used methods for estimation. The key theme implemented is to create a "pseudo-population" to address the challenge due to different distributions of the treated and control groups. This is being accomplished through finding the closest match using distance metrics (matching methods), weighting the samples (inverse propensity weighting). Apart from the above, the other methods for estimation include meta learners, forest-based estimators (non-linear models), etc.

- *Estimation methods for quasi-experiments*: In quasi-experiments, pre-existing groups have received different treatments and there is a lack of randomness in the creation of the groups. Commonly used approaches include simple natural experiments, instrumental variables (IV), and regression-discontinuity models.

Machine learning methods as mentioned above, as well as the linear regression, also help isolate the causal effect and confounders. Machine learning methods are particularly useful when capturing non-linear relationships, and in some cases, such as with variational learning, they estimate or approximate the distribution of confounding variables that are not directly observed in the study (e.g. as used by *Netflix* using double ML, Fig. 8.16).

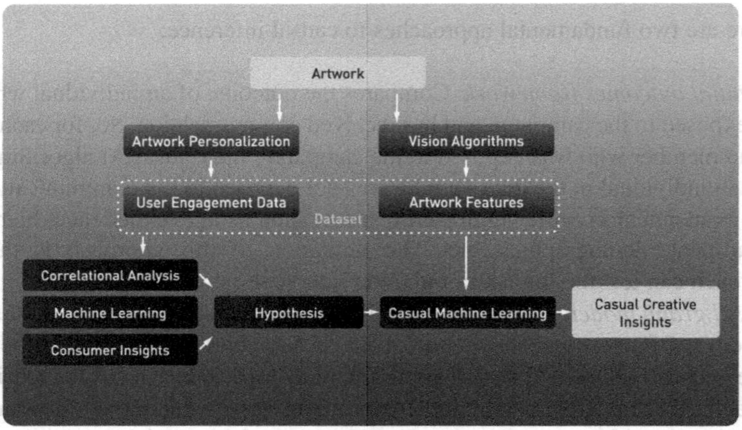

Fig. 8.16 The causal ML framework of *Netflix* (Marketing Tech Monitor 2024) (See also Netflix Technology Blog: Causal Machine Learning for Creative Insights, January 2023 for a detailed schematic description)

Netflix represents the success of an artwork with the take rate: the probability of an average user to watch the promoted title after seeing its promotional artwork, adjusted for the popularity of the title. Every show on the *Netflix* platform has multiple promotional artwork assets. Using *Netflix's* Artwork Personalisation, these assets are served to hundreds of millions of members every day. To power this recommendation system, user engagement patterns are taken into consideration and analysed whether these engagements with artwork resulted in a successful title selection. With the capability to annotate a given image, an artwork asset in this case, a series of computer vision algorithms is used to gather objective image metadata, latent representation of the image, as well as some of the contextual metadata that a given image contains. This process allows the data set to consist of both the image features and user data, all to understand which image components lead to successful user engagement—using machine learning algorithms, consumer insights, and correlational analysis for discovering high-level associations between image features and an artwork's success. These statistically significant associations become the hypotheses for the next step.

Building on a specific hypothesis, it can be tested by deploying causal machine learning algorithms. This framework reduces the experimental effort to uncover causal relationships, while considering confounding among the high-level variables (i.e. the variables that may influence both the treatment/intervention and outcome). For example, the presence of a face in an artwork causally improves the asset performance, especially images with an expressive facial emotion that is in line with the tone of the title. The differences between pictures are not only the presence of a face. There are many other variances, like the difference in background, text placement, font size, and face size. Causal machine learning makes it possible to understand an artwork's performance based on the causal impact of its treatment.

To make sure our hypothesis matches the causal framework, it is important we go over the identification assumptions:

- *Consistency*: The treatment component is sufficiently well-defined. Machine learning algorithms may predict whether the artwork contains a face. That is why the first assumption is that the face detection algorithm is mostly accurate (~92% average precision).
- *Positivity/probabilistic assignment*: Every unit (artwork) has some chance of getting treated. The propensity score—as the probability of receiving the treatment based on certain baseline characteristics—of having a face for samples with different covariates. If a certain subset of artwork (e.g. artwork from a certain genre) has close to a 0 or 1 propensity score for having a face, these samples are discarded from the analysis.
- *Individualistic assignment/stable unit treatment value assumption (SUTVA)*: The potential outcomes of a unit do not depend on the treatments assigned to others. Creatives make the decision to create artwork with or without faces based on considerations limited to the title of interest itself. This decision is not dependent on whether other assets have a face on them or not.
- *Conditional exchangeability (un-confoundedness)*: There are no unmeasured confounders. This assumption is (by definition) not testable. Given a data set, it is not known if there has been an unobserved confounder. However, we can test the sensitivity of our conclusions towards the violation of this assumption in various ways.

After having established the hypothesis to be a causal inference problem, the focus is on the causal machine learning application. Predictive machine learning (ML) models distil patterns and associations to predict outcomes but are limited with regard to explaining cause-and-effect relationships, as their model structure does not reflect causality (the relationship between cause and effect). Causal ML helps to estimate treatment effects from observational data, where it is challenging to conduct clean randomisations. Back-to-back publications on causal ML—such as double ML, causal forests, causal neural networks and many more—showcased a tool set for investigating treatment effects, via combining domain knowledge with ML in the learning system. Unlike predictive ML models, causal ML explicitly controls for confounders, by modelling both treatment of interest as a function of confounders (i.e. propensity scores) and the impact of confounders on the outcome of interest. In doing so, causal ML isolates the causal impact of treatment on outcome. Moreover, the estimation steps of causal ML are carefully set up to achieve better error bounds for the estimated treatment effects, another consideration often overlooked in predictive ML. Compared to more traditional causal inference methods anchored on linear models, causal ML leverages the latest ML techniques to not only better control for confounders (when propensity or outcome models are hard to capture by linear models) but also to more flexibly estimate treatment effects (when treatment effect heterogeneity is non-linear).

Lately, *OpenAI* eases the development of custom generative AI models to let companies build tailored versions of *ChatGPT*, now a common third party add-on, and promised a GPT Store to help developers sell the tailored versions. *OpenAI* also snuck in a promise to defend enterprise customers and developers against copyright claims, matching protections from other major generative AI developers.

References

Arsanjani, A. (2023, September 18). *Generative AI lifecycle patterns*. Medium.

Bornstein, M., & Radovanovic, R. (2023, June 20). *Emerging architectures for LLM applications*. Andreessen Horowitz.

Brown, T.B., Mann, B., & Ryder, N. et al. (2020, July). *Language models are few-shot learners*.

BusinessWire. (2023, March). *The zeta marketing platform unveils new capabilities that empower marketers to drive more predictable outcomes*.

Cision. (2023a, January). *Horizon media's night market launches Neon; an eCommerce predictive AI platform to plan and optimise media investments to revenue outcomes*.

Cision. (2023b, February). *Typeface emerges from stealth with a generative AI application for enterprise content creation and $65 million in funding*.

European Marketing Confederation. (2023/2024, March). European Marketing Agenda 2023/2024.

GlobalNewsWire. (2023, March). *Instreamatic launches contextual audio ads to better engage audiences with real-time, dynamically-created, hyper-relevant generative AI* ads.

Hesel, N., Buder, F., & Unfried, M. (2022, November). The next frontier in intelligent augmentation: Human-machine collaboration in strategic marketing decision-making. *NIM Marketing Intelligence Review, 14*(2).

Hurwitz, J. S., & Thompson, J. K. (2023). *Causal artificial intelligence: The next step in effective business AI*.

Kannal, A. (2023, December 4). *GenAI applications reference architecture—Part 1*. Medium.

Lardinois, F. (2023, March). *Microsoft's new power platform AI Copilot will build your apps for you*. TechCrunch.

Manning, S., Mishkin, P., Rock, D., & Eloundou, T. (2023, March). *GPTs are GPTs: An early look at the labor market impact, potential of large language models*. University of Pennsylvania.

Miller, R. (2023, January). *Blaze makes coding more accessible with AI-driven, no code app builder*. TechCrunch.

Noy, S., & Zhang, W. (2023, March 2). *Experimental evidence on the productivity effects of generative artificial intelligence*. MIT.

OpenAI. (2023a, March 1). *Introducing ChatGPT and Whisper APIs*.

OpenAI. (2023b, March). *GPT-4 technical report*.

OpenAI, & Jones, S. (2024, February 28). *OpenAI explains why GPT understands nothing*. blog.metamirror.io.

Ortega, A. (2023, January). *Causalens launches the first operating system for decision-making—powered by Causal AI*. BusinessWire.

Peterson, D. (2023, April). *LLMs and the future of customer-built software design*. Medium.

Russel, S. (2012). *Norvig, P.: Künstliche Intelligenz, Ein moderner Ansatz*.

Simon, J. (2021, October 26). *Large language models: A new moore's law?*. Hugging Face—The AI community building the future. https://huggingface.co/blog/large-language-models

SproutSocial. (2023, January). *Sprout social acquires repustate*.

Steele, J. (2023, March). *SOCi Raises $120 M, accelerates vision of redefining marketing software*. Cision.

Vaswani, A., Shazeer, N., Parmar, N., Uszkoreit, J., Jones, L., Gomez, A. N., Kaiser, L., & Polosukhin, I. (2017, December, 6). *Attention is all you need*; arXiv.org. https://arxiv.org/abs/1706.03762

Von Hoffmann, V. (2023a, March). *Microsoft unveils AI "copilots" for sales, CRM, and customer support*. MarTech.

Von Hoffmann, V. (2023b, March). *OpenAI unveils ChatGPT API at very low prices*. MarTech.

Wolfram, S. (2023, February 14). *What is ChatGPT doing … and why does it work?* Medium.

Wood, C. (2023a, March). *HubSpot debuts ChatSpot generative AI tool*. MarTech.

Wood, C. (2023b, March). *Grammarly introduces generative AI tool GrammarlyGO*. MarTech.

Yang, J., & Gokturk, B. (2023, March 14). *Google cloud brings generative AI to developers, businesses, and governments*. Google Cloud.

CRM Meets Customer Experience: Moments of Truth for the Customer

9

9.1 CRM and Customer Experience … You'll Never Walk Alone

Even while CRM has been widely discussed over the last 25–30 years, implementations are still lagging: in many cases, CRM is used for the (internal) management of the system of record, less for steering the customer interaction. Despite all the CRM and Customer Experience euphoria, reality paints a different picture: only 15% of the companies say that they are already leveraging the possibilities of their CRM system, while two-thirds of the companies have a CRM system but are not yet tapping into its full potential.

CRM as the basis of a more comprehensive customer experience management has been discussed as a (technology-neutral) marketing and sales concept since the mid-1990s. In the final analysis, CRM means increasing customer loyalty and facilitating the acquisition of new customers while at the same time improving customer profitability with existing customers. Traditional approaches from the areas of marketing and sales thus form the basis, and these are supplemented by technologies such as data analytics or applications for sales support (sales force automation). While more classic CRM application scenarios in sales (e.g. pipeline opportunity management, mobile sales workplace) as well as in service (e.g. call centre, case management, request and complaint/service ticketing) have been largely established since the 1990s, CRM has experienced a true revival in recent years due to:

- The need to link online and offline and strive for an integrated omnichannel approach; to link the traditional offline business model with digital media across all touchpoints.

R. Strauss, *Data-Driven Customer Engagement*,
https://doi.org/10.1007/978-3-031-64295-1_9

"We need to rethink CRM—the decline of 3rd party cookies and increased customer expectations are fuelling a reload for comprehensive end-to-end processes ... including standardisation. Specialised processes prevent us from becoming simpler"—Rolf Kreuzer (CTO, Migros FM, Switzerland)

- The need to differentiate from the competition of increasingly homogeneous product and service offerings and increasing market transparency. Increasingly smaller (perceived) quality differences are leading to interchangeable products and services that make it difficult to differentiate from the competition. In addition to legal binding options (e.g. contract terms and associated switching barriers), it is necessary to build and expand customer loyalty via unique, mass personalised customer experiences.

However, when managing the customer experience, every interaction counts, as each one elicits and experience for the customer, which accumulate into their overall experience. Customer experience management needs to consider all interactions with a customer throughout the entire customer journey (Schögel & Herhausen, 2023).

- The loss of customer data due to regulation (e.g. ePrivacy Directive), browser-based exclusion, or ad blockers, which ensure interaction based on personalised first-party data is experiencing a revival and
- The linking of functional properties of the product with experience-creating, emotionally shaped elements. Tectonic shifts in the structure of consumers' needs and values are contributing to the fact that individual expectations and wishes are becoming increasingly important—accumulated in the "moment of truth".

At RTL+, we currently have 2.7 million paying customers—here we will continue to work on personalised data and contact routes—Kirsten Nachtigall (Vice President Marketing, RTL)

In this vein, CRM application scenarios are the top priority for 67% of the companies, to secure customer loyalty and systematic market cultivation as a "single source of truth" across all customer interactions.

CRM will cease to be the centre of the universe (Alfonso, 2021).

The spectrum of alternative CRM applications extends across (Fig. 9.1):

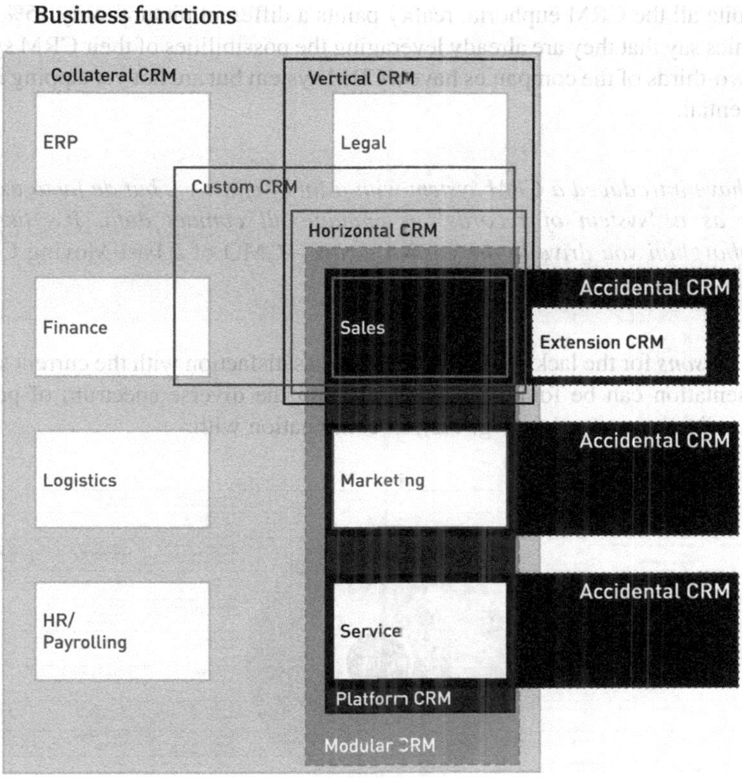

Fig. 9.1 CRM application areas and characteristics (MarTechTribe.com, April 2023; Marketing Tech Monitor 2023)

- *Accidental CRM*: Applications originally designed for a different application area, such as sales (e.g. *Outlook*, *Lotus Notes*, *Airtable*, *Trello*), marketing (e.g. *MailChimp*), or service (e.g. *Kapture.cx*, *Genesys*, *Alure*).
- *Extension CRM*: CRM as an add-on on a host system (e.g. *Copper/Spreadsheet*, *Trypigeon.co/Gmail*, *CRMmble/Trello*).
- *Custom-built CRM*: Own developments like in sales (mostly in the B2C environment).
- *Collateral CRM*: As an add-on to ERP suites (e.g. *NetSuite*, *SAP*, *Alure*).
- *Vertical CRM*: Industry-specific, for instance due to legal requirements such as in the pharmaceutical sector (e.g. *Veeva*, *SimpleChurchCRM.com*, *Backbase.com*).
- *Horizontal CRM*: Stand-alone CRM applications in a delimited functional area such as call centre or pipeline management in sales (e.g. *Pipedrive*, *Close*).
- *Platform CRM*: As a (unified) software package across sales, marketing, and service (e.g. *Vtiger*, *BuddyCRM*).
- *Modular CRM*: As one of several software modules (e.g. *HubSpot*, *Salesforce*).

Despite all the CRM euphoria, reality paints a different picture: only 15% of the companies say that they are already leveraging the possibilities of their CRM system, while two-thirds of the companies have a CRM system but are not yet tapping into its full potential.

> *We have introduced a CRM system with a lot of effort ... but de facto use it only as a 'system of records' to manage all contact data. It's like a Lamborghini you drive to the garden centre*—CMO of a Fast Moving Consumer Goods company

The *reasons* for the lack of CRM or for the dissatisfaction with the current state of implementation can be found not least (also) in the diverse spectrum of possible CRM application scenarios (Fig. 9.2), in combination with:

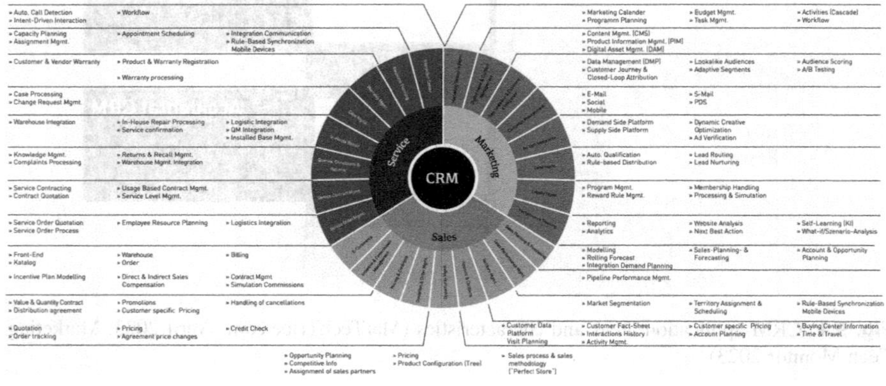

Fig. 9.2 Overview of CRM application scenarios (Strauß, 2019)

- *Processes*: They are unclear or not (sufficiently) documented, especially across different divisions and markets.
- *Subject matter experts*: A profound understanding of processes is missing or is only located with individual employees ("go-to persons"), who in most cases are already overbooked with other projects.
- *Requirements*: Working in the conflicting area between business processes (use cases) and the determination of detailed requirements for IT applications (requirements) is still uncharted territory—resulting in inadequately defined business requirements.
- *Overload*: With requirements during the project and the constant discussion of what is "in scope" and what is or must be "out of scope".
- *Lack of experienced project managers*: Those who have already introduced CRM applications several times and have enough authority to say "no" when the complexity gets out of hand. Projects often start in a "youth-in-research" mode

. . . with gradually decreasing euphoria and a "quiet quitting" of subject matter experts over time.

- *Management support*: This goes hand in hand with insufficient support from top management.
- *Insufficient change management*: As a systematic and lived accompaniment of the change process for the realignment of all customer interfaces . . . beyond atmospheric *PowerPoint* platitudes.
- *Conflicting goals*: Short-term turnover/sales targets are diametrically opposed to longer-term customer management and the requirements of day-to-day business.
- *Insufficient functional coverage*: 55% of companies, for example, state that their CRM system cannot be adapted to their specific needs, 75% complain about the insufficient consolidation of customer data as a basic requirement, and 81% consequently complain about a lack of relevant, personalised messaging (SugarCRM, 2022).

> *CRM means for us to have finally one single source of truth, with marketing automation on top*—Jonas Richter (Head of Digital Marketing Platforms, EMEA, Olympus)

The (by definition) cross-functional nature of CRM:

- Lead management via marketing (contact) to pipeline (opportunity) and purchase completion.
- From marketing planning, segmentation, and multichannel campaign management to reporting.
- The creation of a centralised customer master record with attributes from all customer interactions.
- Including a pretty complex IT technical integration of:
  - merchandise management (checking article availability, e-commerce, or financial accounting/billing), or
  - the integration of the stationary POS/retailer and loyalty management programs, or
  - trade promotion management between suppliers (Fast Moving Consumer Goods companies) and retailers.

Consequently, this often makes it difficult to "encapsulate" smaller application scenarios (i.e. to functionally delimit them—such as for MRM). This means that complexity is (unfortunately) an inherent part of the CRM DNA.

I think that CRM has taken broader ground in companies—it is seen as a must-have technology system that is used for supporting sales, marketing, and customer service operations. That's led to a $50+ billion US industry. However, what it hasn't done is become simple to use—especially as it scales up to the enterprise-sized companies—nor has it fulfilled the promise that many of the early thought leaders hoped it would, which was to be more than just an operational technology system. That said, the value that companies receive from CRM systems is fairly evident if it is done right. But even with that value, adoption problems remain because it can be a complex system with a lot of moving parts. For example, looking at the sales component of CRM (salesforce automation). On the one hand, the basic functions like opportunity management, contact management and pipeline management are always there. But there are also many additional capabilities that cover things like sales and marketing alignment, compensation planning, sales onboarding. There are similar additions in marketing and customer service applications too. So, on the one hand we are seeing wide implementation and a continued double digit growth market in CRM, and on the other hand still facing lingering adoption problems as the solutions and platforms grow richer and richer—Paul Greenberg (Author of *CRM at the Speed of Light*)

If one analyses the development since the 1990s, CRM has gradually no longer been allowed to sail into the sunset with *Kate Blanchet* in its arms on the bow railing of the *Titanic* but is collectively banished to the diaspora of the engine room:

- *Positioning*: In the perception as well as in the operative projects, CRM was often reduced purely to an IT application—directly connected with a certain provider. In other words, it has not been possible to put the underlying customer engagement concept and the economic objective in the foreground, but rather to drape the IT application scenario in the shop window of perception. The IT application, the "enabler", became an end in the perception ... with all the associated challenges in implementation and change management.
- *Creative renaming*: The creative renaming of IT applications on the part of the providers is more likely to cause further confusion. For example, the interview partners on the customer side consistently state that they can hardly understand the conceptual difference between CRM and "Experience Platforms".

- *Differentiation in terms of content*: The lack of differentiation in terms of content is thus compensated for by creative renaming. Thus, no one on the side of the providers asked could explain the differences between CRM and customer experience management in terms of content/concept.

The analysis of the used and desired CRM application scenarios shows: simple application scenarios predominate, but even these are not sufficiently used (insufficient adoption, Fig. 9.3). While marketing automation is often put on the "most missed" list, basic functions such as "Lead Assignment/Distribution", "Lead Scoring", or "Behavioural Segmentation" tend to receive lower approval rates ("most missed"). The use of CRM is often reduced to the management of the "System of Record" and simpler application scenarios.

Over the last 4 to 5 years, the CRM view is gradually being displaced by a more comprehensive *Customer Experience Management* (CEM). CEM (i.e. experience design) focuses on creating high-quality and consistent interactions with the customer across all touchpoints and throughout the life cycle of a customer or product (Fluckinger, 2020; Sheehan, 2019; Priestley, 2019).

"Most liked"	"Most used"	"Most missed"
E-Mail Marketing	E-Mail Marketing	Text Message
Message Personalisation	Landing Page/Form Editor	Sales Collaboration
Landing Page / Form Editor	Message Personalisation	Integration of Messages Outside of CRM Against Contact
Case Management	Case Management	Marketing Automation
Online Support	Campaign Templates	Mobile
Campaign Templates	Dynamic Lists	Landing Page / Form Editor
Call Centre	Online Support	Sales Forecasting
E-Mail Editor	Call Centre	Offer Effectiveness
Text Message	E-Mail Editor	Custom Pipelines
Dynamic Lists		CMS Integration

Fig. 9.3 Analysis and evaluation of the most important CRM application scenarios (Top 10) (MarTechTribe, 2023a; G2, 2023)

> *In the modern world, the physical and digital experiences a customer has—from the initial interaction to the chat with customer service—have become crucial (Webber & Trinidad, 2023).*

The key to customer loyalty is to provide the customer with the best-possible experience ("moments of truth") at all times. The customer experience is significantly shaped by the perceived quality as well as the "experience flow"—in other words, the extent to which services and products are presented as high quality, tailored to the user's needs (relevant) and in a natural sequence in terms of perceived attributes and presentations. The focus is on the desire for diverse, but consistent, and high-quality dialogue opportunities between customers and companies. In other words: optimal customer satisfaction with optimal utilisation of the customer's potential ("share of wallet"). The life cycle of a customer experience thus encompasses all customer relationships at all levels—from brand awareness before purchase to replacement or disposal of products and solutions (Carlzon, 1989; Jaffe, 2010; Webb, 2011). The overwhelming majority of senior executives in marketing across Europe have identified customer experience management as a prominent focus since 2020.

The more "loyalty-traditional" industries such as transport companies and brand manufacturers like *Apple* serve as models. The higher the share of services in the respective product/solution offering, the more customer experience management becomes the focus of attention. The challenges for a more comprehensive customer experience approach are certainly complex, but in most cases can be traced back to five factors: (Daniels, 2020; Priestley, 2019)

1. *Other organisational units involved*: Customer experience design extends far beyond the functional boundaries of individual business units.
2. *Change management*: Project experience shows that, in addition to inadequate processes and systems, the biggest hurdles to implementing systematic customer experience management can be found in changing employee behaviour. As a result, such a change process to realign all customer interfaces not only requires considerable effort, but usually extends over a longer period.
3. *Insufficient measurability*: The success of a high-quality and brand-compliant orchestration of all customer interactions can only, in the rarest of cases, be directly tracked in metrics, let alone directly proven in terms of its indirect sales impact.
4. *Conflicting goals*: Short-term revenue/sales goals are diametrically opposed to the longer-term customer experience.
5. *Insufficiently integrated processes and systems*: Poorly integrated, overarching processes and supporting IT systems render the claim of consistent high-quality customer interaction moot. What still proves to be an inconvenience, but still a tried-and-tested procedure, with low customer volumes, regularly fails in the high-volume B2C environment.
6. *Insufficient data quality*: In contrast to the many discussions about customer centricity, the systematic collection and use of customer data as the basis for an overarching customer experience design only takes place to a rudimentary extent in most companies. Both the passive collection of data by recording all sales interactions and the active collection of customer data (through direct questioning) are either hardly used systematically and in an integrated way or

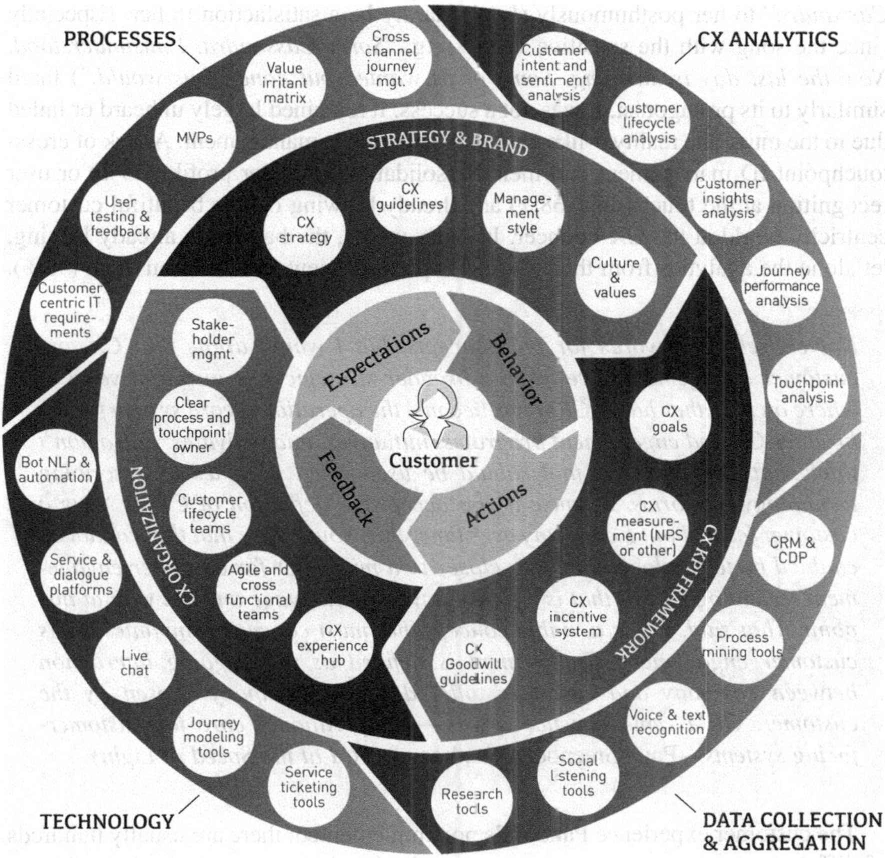

Fig. 9.4 Dimensions of customer experience management

there is "overkill" due to the excessive use of surveys. The cry for excellent data quality goes unheard in most cases.

The term "customer centricity" thus often seems to have escaped from the wind tunnel of a public relations (PR) factory (Fig. 9.4).

Thus, the unanimous opinion in the "*House of Cards* of the customer experience" is about efficient implementation, rather than further conceptual penetration of the topic. Like *Cassandra* in the streets of *Troy*, even companies (e.g. insurance companies) that have been working intensively on this topic for a long time and prophesy a glorious future for it report that they would nevertheless classify themselves as "still far from the goal". The challenges mean that implementation usually takes years, usually with only minor, interim successes. The fate of the customer experience thus appears to be open now—that of *Cassandra* is well known. She was stabbed to death. The fact that the pop group *ABBA* dedicated the song "*Sorry*

Cassandra" to her posthumously should hardly be a satisfaction to her. Especially since the song with the sensitive verses (e.g. "*Sorry Cassandra, I misunderstood. Now the last day is dawning. Some of us wanted but none of us would.*") fared similarly to its protagonist. It was not a success. It remained largely unheard or failed due to the mundane reality—like customer experience management. A lack of cross-touchpoint ID management and their consolidation in a user profile (69%) or user recognition at the touchpoint (68%) are already blowing off the beautiful customer centricity world at the CX bouncer. In other words, the basics are already lacking, let alone the analytics from the customer's point of view that build on them (48%).

Not entirely new words for old concepts, but I would argue that CX and customer engagement have taken a broader strategic role in recent years—where on the other hand, CRM has become the operational core system for the broader CX and engagement programs, initiatives, and activities. I also don't think that CX is a term that should be used when it comes to describing technology platforms, because if you accept the definition of CX as 'how a customer feels about a company over time' then you realise that that cannot be enabled by technology. So CX is closer to a misnomer for customer engagement technologies, but that is a fight I have tried to wage and not won at this point. That said, CX is a viable concept that must concern companies, as is customer engagement. Engagement is defined as the ongoing interaction between company and customer, offered by the company chosen by the customer. CRM remains what it was—an operational core for customer-facing systems—Paul Greenberg (Author of *CRM at the Speed of Light*)

The customer experience Pandora's box implemented: there are usually hundreds of different customer processes at an organisational and process level, in simpler omnichannel product segments (e.g. retail or consumer goods manufacturers) and in more complex segments such as insurance companies and energy suppliers as well as in the mobile phone sector. Case studies and projects usually reveal have two different entry points in this respect: in an ideal world, comprehensive transparency is created about ACTUAL processes, customer satisfaction and drivers/KPIs along all processes. A small piquant side effect: the organisation may be paralysed for months by collecting and collating data, without having made a single customer happier or being able to show concrete successes of any kind. Therefore, in most cases, a (second) more pragmatic approach seems advisable: to start with the analysis of key touchpoints alongside the customer journey, supporting processes, and concrete pain points from the customer's point of view, which have a demonstrable impact on satisfaction and business development.

The reality today is still far from *Fast & Furious*: only 15% of companies have a holistic customer experience strategy in place (Harvard Business Review, 2023).

It's not just about the transactional value, but also about having an uplifting experience which contributes to us having an affinity for an organisation—Shiv Singh (CMO & Customer Experience Officer, LendingTree) (Wood, 2022)

While CRM takes a more instrumental and processual approach (inside-out), CX management focuses on customer perception as a superordinate concept (outside-in) (Fig. 9.5).

Customer Relationship Management (CRM)	Customer Experience Management (CX)
Includes all strategies, concepts and application scenarios to actively design and analyse all customer interactions and data throughout the entire customer life cycle.	A customer's perception after interacting with a company, brand, product or service.
Improves customer relationships across marketing, sales and service; supports customer retention and sales growth.	Collection of all processes that organise, track and control interactions with a customer over the entire customer lifecycle
Aggregates data across all customer interactions and channels, including websites, call centres, live chats, mail, marketing assets and social media.	CX extends the vision of an optimised customer journey via simple conversions and sales to all areas of the company and channels
Provides all employees with direct customer contact with detailed information about the customer such as contact details, purchase history, preferences or complaints.	Requires a 360-degree view of the customer, using integrated, up-to-date data on all customer interactions and analysis points to serve customers with a higher degree of personalisation.
Consolidates customer data and documents into one database so that users in the department have easy access to a 360-degree view of the customer.	Critical steps of a successful CX strategy include understanding customer needs, developing a customer vision, developing emotional customer loyalty and gathering all types of customer feedback.
Additional functionalities include artificial intelligence, analytics, geolocation, mobile sales workstations, workflow automation, lead management and HR integration (such as shift planning).	Leading CRM/CX providers focus on creating a personalised customer experience.
Inside-Out: Marketing, Sales, Customer Service, Online	Outside-In: Design, Voice-of-Customer, Customer Journey, Personas, Customer Insight, Culture

Fig. 9.5 Differentiation between customer relationship management (CRM) and customer experience (CX, Marketing Tech Monitor 2023) (See also Fluckinger, 2020; Amsler, 2019; Gartner, 2020)

In this context, the discussions during workshops and projects prove that customer experience essentially represents a catalyst for increased customer requirements. The increasing use of digital communication and interaction platforms with, and especially between, customers increasingly require comprehensive, highly standardised yet individualised (personalised) customer management across all customer interfaces. Most companies are branded by "spaghetti landscapes" of individual IT solutions with significant challenges in process and application integration (Forrester, 2022a).

> *Customers want power over the use of their personal data but expect highly relevant messages from companies. Companies need to develop better strategies to collect customer data more agilely, enrich real-time customer profiles in CRM and use them along all sales and marketing channels for personalised customer approaches*—Dr Martino Saracino (Head of Marketing Insights and Analytics, Digital Accelerator, QIAGEN)

Case studies and project experiences prove that four pillars usually must be established in parallel:

- *CX/customer satisfaction circles*: Receive input from the CX/customer satisfaction cockpit, or satisfaction results or KPIs from BI models. In a cross-functional composition, such as by experts from BI (analytics), (own/external) trade, offer, customer care, marketing/CRM or digital product management, pragmatic procedural/organisational measures to improve satisfaction are discussed and decided along a CX map (Fig. 9.6).

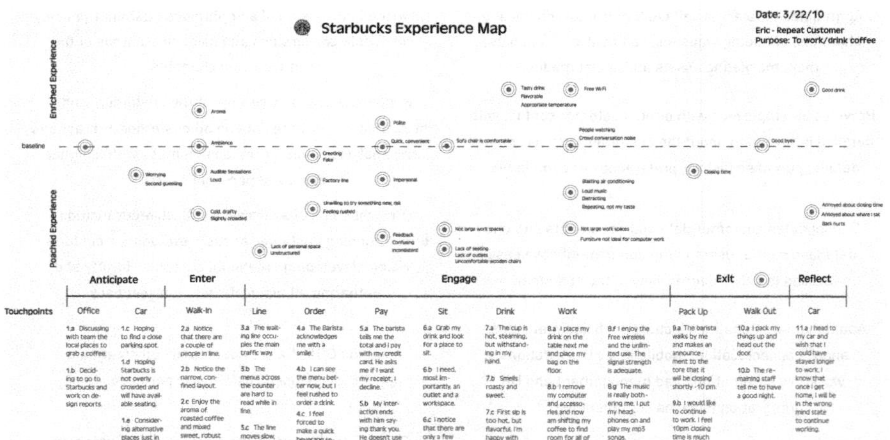

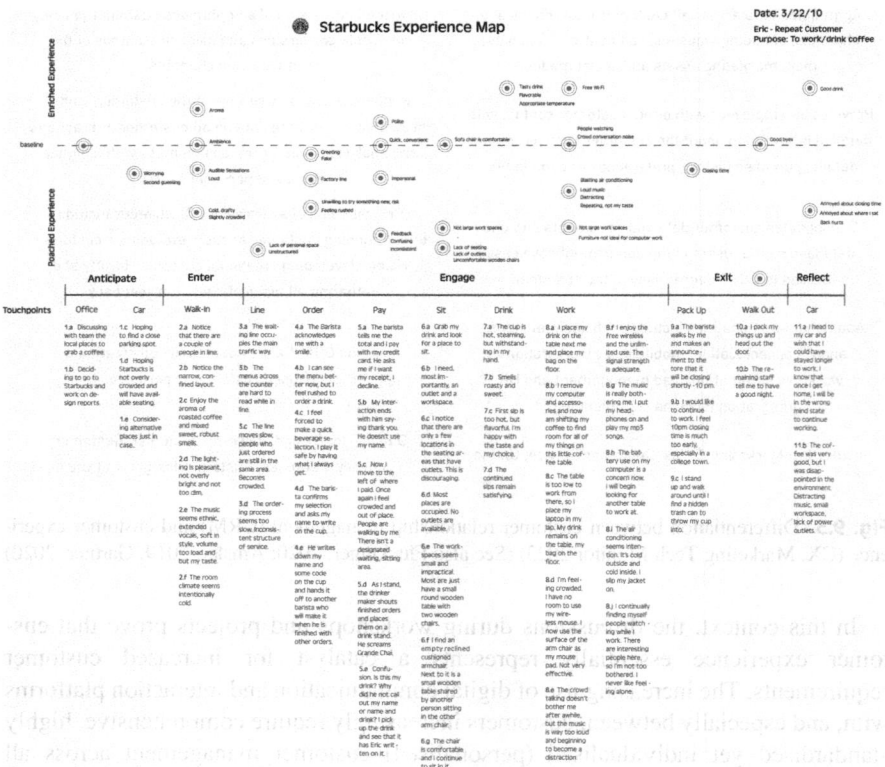

Fig. 9.6 Customer experience map for *Starbucks* (drafted for Marketing Tech Monitor 2022)

The mapping of satisfaction (circles) with the expected effects on business relevant KPIs such as recommendation, Customer Lifetime Value (CLV) or churn rates shows acute need for action (Fig. 9.7). Satisfaction should always be contrasted with metrics to measure business success. For example, customers at *Starbucks* may criticise a long queue, but this has no impact on loyalty because the taste rating of the high-priced coffee overcompensates for the wait (in perception). In other words, aroma and coolness factor are more important than queues and over-boarding prices. For measuring these trade-off relationships (in the sense of a conjoint analysis), the connection to CRM data and BI models is essential. At the core of this is the question of what influences the respective business goals at the single attribute (e.g. satisfaction and recommendation) and experience level.

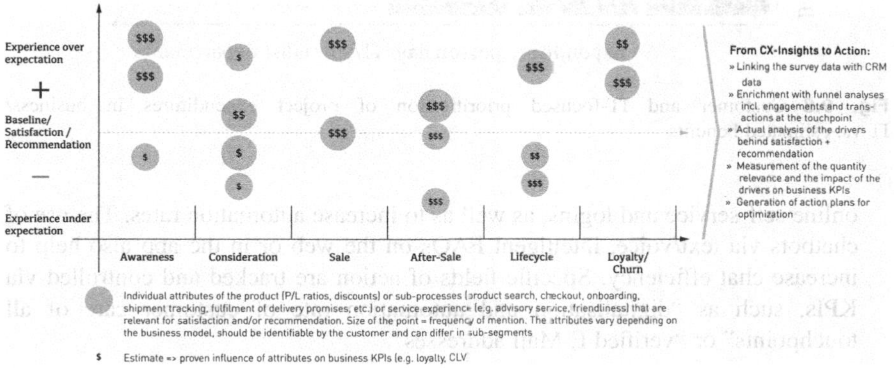

Fig. 9.7 Identification of main drivers of satisfaction and business impact in the life-cycle phases and at the touchpoints (project example in telco)

- *Customer Excellence Board*: All customer-focused IT requirements are prioritised according to IT effort (in estimated man-days of development in IT) and their foreseeable impact on business success, as well as their benefit of providing an expected uplift of business or customer KPI metrics (Fig. 9.8). Issues with a focus on customer satisfaction, service, and digitalisation tend to get more "stage time" and brownie points compared to the frequent focus on short-term sales issues. Control and tracking can be done via Kanban boards, for example in *Jira*.
- *Customer-focused development*: Product owners are divided into different life-cycle phases, and frontends ensure implementation, supported by their own product owner boards (e.g. for backlog monitoring), which can be viewed transparently.
- *Digitalisation of customer journeys in cross-functional teams*: Analyses are made of key journeys of new/existing customers and contact drivers, for instance from a customer care perspective (e.g. to increase the self-service rate). The result are joint quarterly targets, digital (service) processes, traffic measures to increase

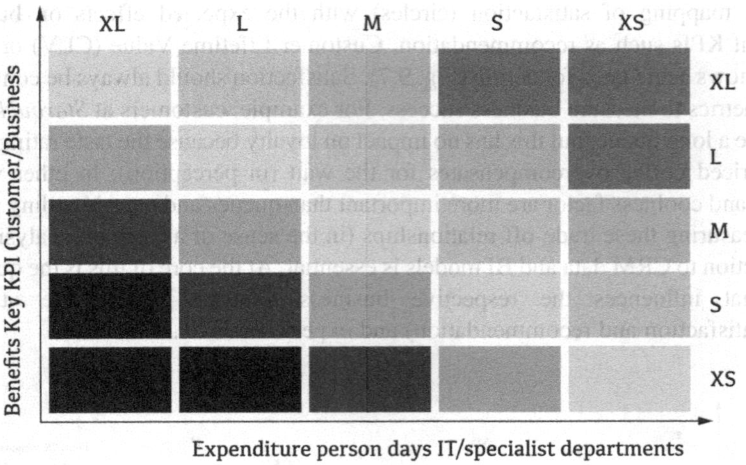

Fig. 9.8 Customer and IT-focused prioritisation of project expenditures in business/IT vs. estimated benefits

online self-service and logins, as well as to increase automation rates. The use of chatbots via text/voice, intelligent FAQs on the web or in the app also help to increase chat efficiency. Specific fields of action are tracked and controlled via KPIs, such as "digitalisation and automation rate of customer care of all touchpoints" or "verified E-Mail addresses".

The goal is to capture as many touchpoints as possible via APIs and to process the insights generated from customer E-Mails and calls via text and voice recognition in such a way that fields of action can already be abstracted from a simple analysis via funnel analyses or sentiments (Fig. 9.9). More sophisticated journey analysis tools

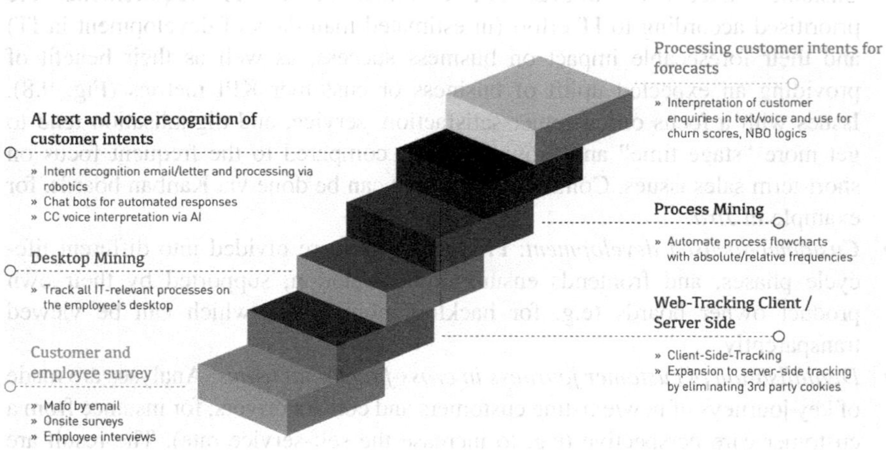

Fig. 9.9 Methods and evolutionary stages in determining user journeys (project example, telco)

such as *CXOmni* allow a direct database connection of the steps along the customer journey and the integration of satisfaction and online surveys, process mining via API connection, trigger actions and task management to support and monitor operational implementation. AI will also reach a higher level of maturity here in the next few years.

The golden rules in the "*House of Cards* of the customer experience" are:

- Customer experience management must be driven out of corporate strategy, with subsequent implementation in processes and organisation. The use of modern IT applications in marketing, sales and service areas is not an end, but (merely) has an optional character ("enabler") that leads to an expansion of organisational design options . . . and not vice versa.
- In strategy and implementation projects, the multitude of dimensions (also from a MarTech perspective) (must) converge, which is why the complexity must be limited in simple steps, for example with the help of a *Customer Experience Audit.*

9.2 Marketing Automation: Unbreak My (Customer) Heart

Burning Man: At its core, marketing automation follows the CRM/CX applications in terms of utilisation: Comparatively high penetration goes hand in hand with only moderate utilisation of all possible application scenarios: 60% of companies already have a MAP solution, while only 5% say they are already able to fully utilise all existing application scenarios. A lack of adoption within the company results in high licence and maintenance costs . . . coupled with a rather low added value for the ongoing business.

While marketing automation tools (MAP) initially focused primarily on E-Mail marketing functionalities, they now cover many functional areas such as the creation and management of landing pages and web forms, campaign management, content marketing, lead scoring with the help of AI, CRM integration, social marketing, and analytics. The focus is on reducing manual activities for massively scalable activities in real time (Lawless Research, 2022). The spectrum of different application scenarios for marketing automation extends accordingly (Fig. 9.10):

- CRM: Automated sales processes and management/access to customer, order, and product data, incl. target group segmentation and targeting.
- E-Mail marketing: Web-based forms and automated responses, incl. analytics.
- Social media management: Publishing, planning, monitoring, and analysis of content and interactions.
- Workflows: Efficient and transparent control of internal processes.
- Lead management: Automated generation, evaluation, and forwarding of qualified customer enquiries (leads).
- Analytics: Patterns in market and customer data, automated upselling/cross-selling activities.

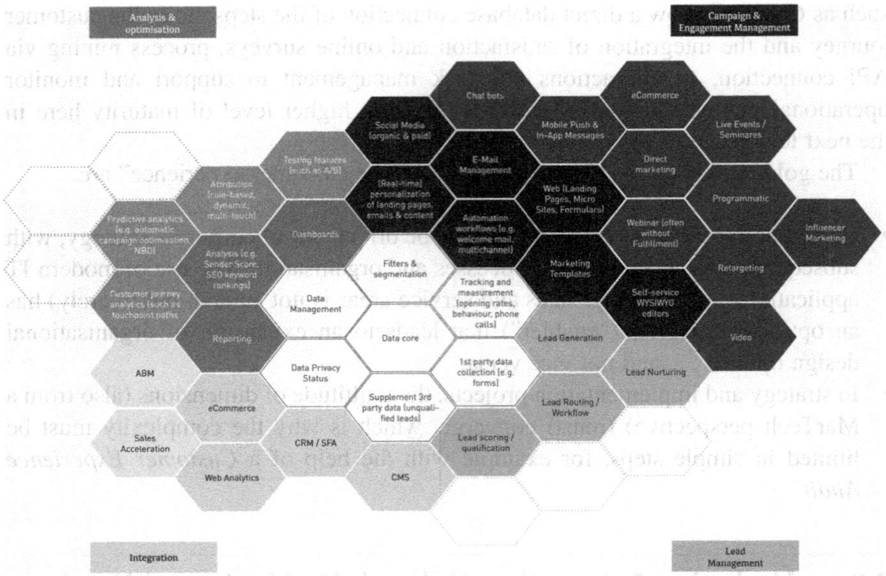

Fig. 9.10 Functional categories of marketing automation (Marketing Tech Monitor 2024)

- Pricing: For instance, via A/B testing or demand estimation.
- Digital advertising and promotion: Optimised and automated for much of the ad creation process and offer strategies across digital channels.
- Loyalty: Customer life-cycle marketing, linking to separate loyalty management engines.

The transition between marketing automation and providers in CRM, MRM, or campaign management is thus fluid—consequently, marketing automation providers have often been taken over by CRM platforms (e.g. *Eloqua* by *Oracle*, *Marketo* by *Adobe*, and the acquisition of *ExactTarget* as an E-Mail engine and *Pardot* by *Salesforce*). The marketing automation market will grow 17.7% annually to $11.5 billion by 2027, although the focus will change over time: (Gartner, 2021)

- Personalised content, AI, chat, and video have been steadily topping the hit parade of the most sought-after features in recent years.
- The alignment between sales and marketing alignment, CDP and behaviour intelligence has seen the biggest growth.
- Trends such as mobile first, predictive lead scoring, and influencers tend to fall behind in comparison.
- User retention and attribution are emerging as the new stars in the marketing automation sky.

One of the most important application scenarios remains *lead management* in both B2B and B2C contexts. A uniform process across different entities (e.g. global/local, marketing/sales) connects sub-processes—from campaign and activity planning, to lead generation, to lead qualification and lead transfer—for example, as an opportunity to the sales pipeline (Fig. 9.11).

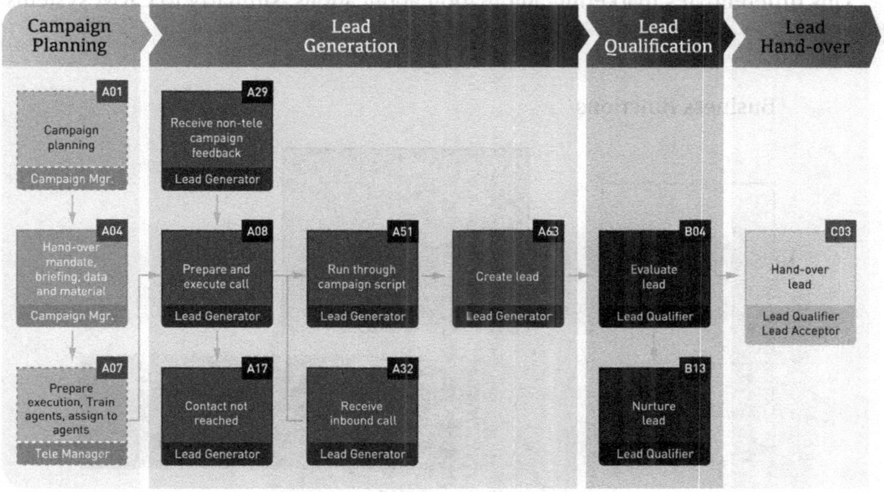

Fig. 9.11 Lead management process (project example, B2B)

> *Lead and campaign management in the B2B context without tool support does not work … we have to get on with this*—Andreas Keiger (Executive Vice President Sales EMEA/India, WIKA)

In terms of functionality, marketing automation platforms have become true "feature monsters" over the last few years and are unlikely to leave much to be desired in terms of efficient support for corporate processes. Lead management and marketing automation projects show that the obstacle to a successful introduction is to be attributed less to the systems (functions) used and more to the following:

- Unclear roles (e.g. campaign manager, lead qualifier, and lead acceptor/account executive) along the process.
- Different interpretations of definitions (MQL, SQL) and lead qualification ("hot"–"cold"–"warm").
- The purchase of (low-quality) leads via E-Mail lists instead of own, organic generation.

- Lead generation content not aligned with each stage of the customer journey—lack of personalisation and smart calls-to-action (CTAs).
- Insufficient use of content formats such as podcasts and studies.
- Lack of website analytics and automated landing pages/forms or similar.
- Lack of automated A/B testing.

This differentiates marketing automation applications, similarly to CRM systems (Fig. 9.12):

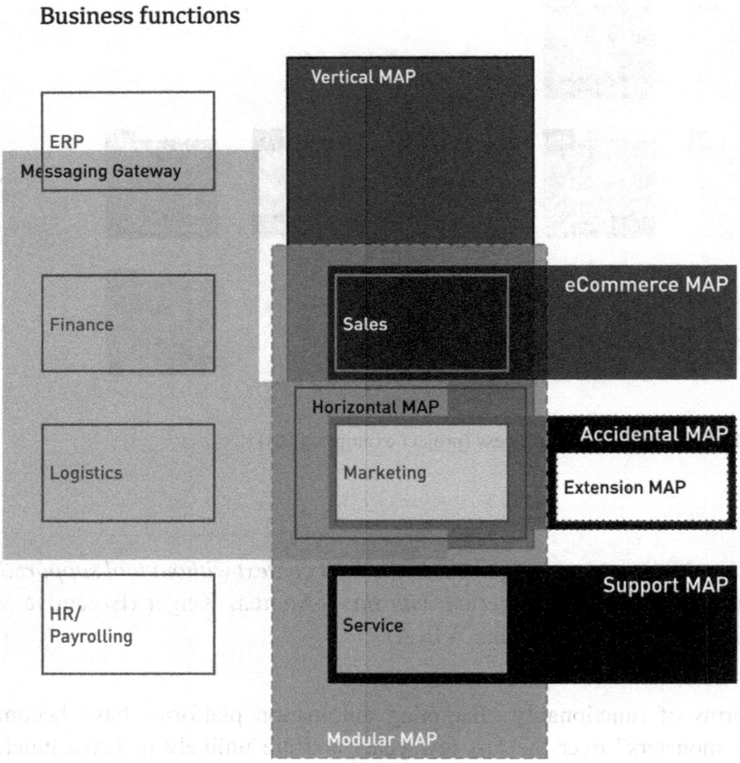

Fig. 9.12 Fields of application and characteristics of marketing automation (MAP; MarTechTribe.com, April 2023; Marketing Tech Monitor 2023)

- *Accidental MAP*: Applications originally designed for a different application area, such as E-Mail/newsletter marketing (e.g. *MailChimp*).
- *Extension MAP*: On a host system (e.g. *Gemelius*).
- *Vertical MAP*: Industry-specific, for example due to legal requirements (e.g. *Herefish.com*).
- *Horizontal MAP*: Stand-alone MAP applications (e.g. *Pipedrive*, *Close*).
- *E-Commerce MAP*: Real-time support for e-commerce automation processes (e.g. *Klaviyo*, *DotDigital*, *Autopilot*, *OmniSend*).

- *Service MAP*: Focus on customer service, contact centre communication (e.g. *Intercom*, *Zendesk*, *Mixpanel*, *Freshdesk*).
- *Messaging gateway MAP*: Support delivery of large E-Mail batches, such as for financial, transactional, and service messaging (e.g. *SendGrid*, *Twilio*, *Vonage*, *MailGun*).
- *Modular MAP*: As one of several software modules (e.g. *HubSpot*, *Salesforce*).

Basic functions such as "E-Mail & Lead Nurturing" or "Campaign Personalisation" are among the Top 10 most used functions … but are also the most missed (Fig. 9.13). The more functions companies have in use, the more critically they rate them.

"Most liked"	"Most used"	"Most missed"
E-Mail & Lead Nurturing	E-Mail & Lead Nurturing	Omnichannel Personalisation
Campaign Personalisation	Deliverability Reporting	Campaign Workflow Automation
Custom Reports	Reporting Including On-site	Campaign Personalisation
Campaign Creation & Design	Custom Reports	Custom Reports
Deliverability Reporting	Campaign Analysis & Optimisation	Predictive Content
Reporting Including On-site	List Management & Segmentation	Revenue Analytics
Campaign Analysis & Optimisation	Campaign Personalisation	Campaign Analysis & Optimisation
Website Visit / Session Tracking	Website Visit / Session Tracking	Reporting Including On-site
Role-based Permissions	Campaign Creation & Design	Campaign Collaboration & Alignment

Fig. 9.13 Analysis and evaluation of the most important marketing automation application scenarios (Top 10) (MarTechTribe, 2023b; G2, 2023)

9.3 Loyalty Management: A Star Is (Re) Born

While loyalty programs gained importance around 2010, thanks to the GDPR and the third-party data discussion, salvation is being sought in loyalty programs, which are experiencing a revival. The catch: the share of users who have signed up for a loyalty program or customer club has stagnated at around 74.5% on average in recent years. Retail Media will further accelerate the move towards loyalty programs, with a broader range of loyalty programs on the supplier side.

The reason for the revival of *loyalty management programs* is the realisation that dissatisfied customers are usually irretrievably lost and can also have considerable negative signal effects in the respective sales market. The retention of satisfied customers, however, requires significantly lower expenditure than the acquisition of new customers and opens additional sales potential (Fig. 9.14). For example, a 7%

Unsatisfied customers	Satisfied customers
Only 4 % of unsatisfied customers actually complain	Customer retention costs are 1/6 of acquisition costs
75-90 % of unsatisfied customers will never return in the future	Satisfied customers are willing to pay more for products and services
Each unsatisfied customer tells another 9 customers	Each satisfied customer tells another 5 potential customers

Fig. 9.14 Comparison of the impact of satisfied and unsatisfied customers (Marketing Tech Monitor 2023) (Tiwana, 2001)

increase in customer loyalty increases the lifetime profit per customer by up to 85% (Brand Keys Customer Loyalty Engagement Index, 2023).

Thanks to the GDPR and the third-party data discussion, salvation is being sought in loyalty programs, which are experiencing a revival. The global loyalty management market will grow by an average of 22.7% to a total of US$13.8 billion by 2026 (Mordor Market Intelligence, 2023). The catch: the share of users who have signed up for a loyalty program or customer club has stagnated at around 74.5% on average in recent years (Wolancke, 2022; Knistr, 2022; Forrester, 2022b; Hoffmann, 2013). Growth has only been recorded in the 18–39 age group (+4.9%). In the age group between 30 and 39, 84% are members of at least one loyalty program. Those who have opted for a loyalty program generally use two to three programs—in total, this is more than 40% of consumers. Only 9.3% of users use four or more programs.

The intensity of use on the customer side has continued to increase in recent years, together with a broader range of loyalty programs on the supplier side, e.g. *Lidl* and *Kaufland, DM, H&M Loyalty Program*, or *Express Insider, Victoria's Secret Credit Card, American Eagle Outfitters*, or *Kohl's Rewards* in the USA. Loyalty program users have demonstrably changed their consumer behaviour significantly. More frequent purchases and longer journeys result in:

- Sales increases of 15–25% annually for active programs participants by increasing frequency or shopping basket (or both)
- Up to 3.5 times more transactions per participant and
- An increase of sales by 25% to 95%, by increasing customer loyalty by just 5% through loyalty programs

A total of 58% of companies report that at least 20% of their total sales are initiated from their loyalty program. The most common uses are instant product discounts (e.g. cash back), points collection mechanisms (e.g. points catalogues), personalised offers, and discount coupons. Three quarters of the programs focus on the more classic approach of collecting points—the "loyalty program cheerleaders"

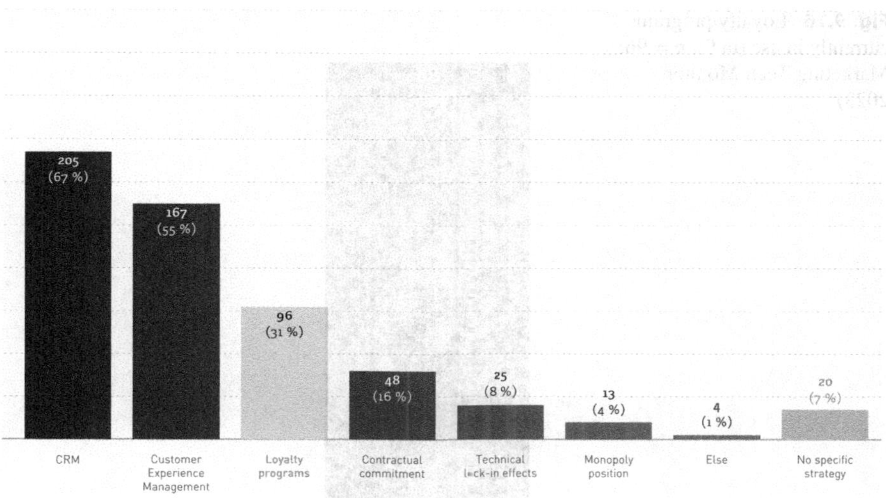

Fig. 9.15 Tools used to gain and maintain customer loyalty/retention (in %, multiple responses, $n = 356$; Marketing Tech Monitor 2023)

are only outstripped by CRM and customer experience management, which ideally (should) go hand in hand (Fig. 9.15) (Forrester, 2022b; Knistr, 2022).

It is estimated that by the end of 2022 already, the volume of unredeemed loyalty points has already exceeded $100 billion worldwide and more than one out of five members in rewards programs will never have redeemed points (The Wise Marketer Research, 2022). "Non redeemers" of points are twice as likely to leave the program as members who have redeemed points in the last 12 months. The two key *challenges* with this (Wadarajan, 2022; Knistr, 2022):

- *Conceptual weaknesses in the loyalty program*: The focus is on the transaction, not the customer. The program structure and reward strategy are often not extremely attractive to program participants. There is no differentiation and personalisation along the customer journey, and consequently no activation on the customer side.
- "*Commodity*": As a further consequence, US-based analyses show that the average consumer is a member of up to 15 programs while they only actually use and utilise 6.5 of them (The Wise Marketer Research, 2022).

Loyalty programs thus present themselves as the catalyst of a first-party data strategy for generating (super-) vital consumer insights. The goal is to convert every customer contact into a (personalised) data point and to activate it. Ideally, hand in hand with retail media. Multi-partner programs (e.g. *Payback*) are rated rather cautiously. The advantages in the simplified design of the program and the breadth of data gained for profiling on the provider side are offset by fewer opportunities for individualisation, whereby the number of partnerships is finite due to exclusivity

Fig. 9.16 Loyalty programs currently in use (in %, $n = 96$; Marketing Tech Monitor 2023)

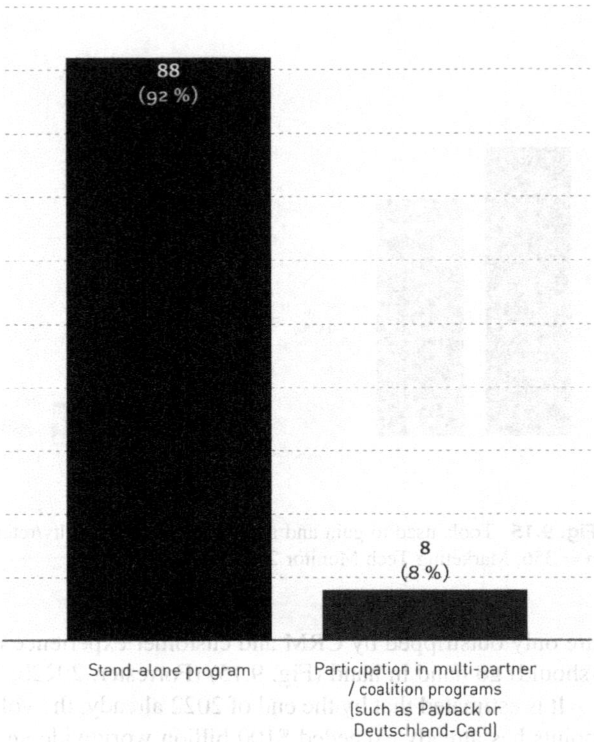

clauses in a coalition program. The consequence: the trend is towards stand-alone programs in connection with own apps (Fig. 9.16).

Advantage-based programs lead the field, followed by transaction-based and referral programs (Fig. 9.17), which mostly occur in mixed forms:

- *Benefit-based*: Exclusive discounts and surprises for loyal customers (e.g. *Nike*, *IKEA*) (special prices).
- *Transaction-based*: Incentivising the transaction, often with a substitute currency (e.g. *Breuninger*, *Starbucks Rewards*).
- *Referral programs*: Building a community of brand ambassadors through benefits and competitions (e.g. *Tesla*, *Lululemon*).
- *Tier-based* (tier levels): Awarding status levels based on cumulative transaction values (e.g. *Sephora*, *Miles & More*, *bahn.Bonus*).
- *Multi-partner programs*: Several partners join to form a program (e.g. *Payback*, *Deutschland Card*).
- *Value-based*: Focus on shared values (e.g. *oekobonus*).
- *Subscription models*: Access to free or special services through an annual fixed fee (e.g. *Amazon Prime*, *Walmart+*, *Costco Wholesale*).

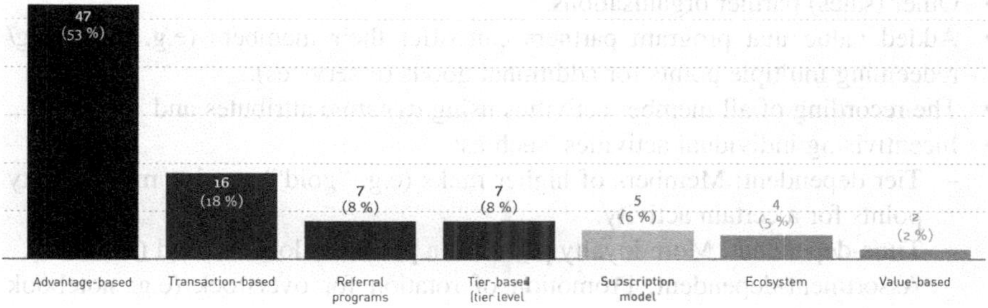

Fig. 9.17 Differentiation of stand-alone loyalty programs (in %, $n = 88$; Marketing Tech Monitor 2023)

- *Ecosystem*: Lock-in effects such as through the product, technology, or service, but also partnerships (e.g. *Apple*, *Amazon*, *Walmart+*).

The core functions of loyalty management applications have remained largely stable over the last 15 years or so and cover program design and set-up (incl. program management and reward rules management) as well as program implementation with processing engines and membership management (Fig. 9.18).

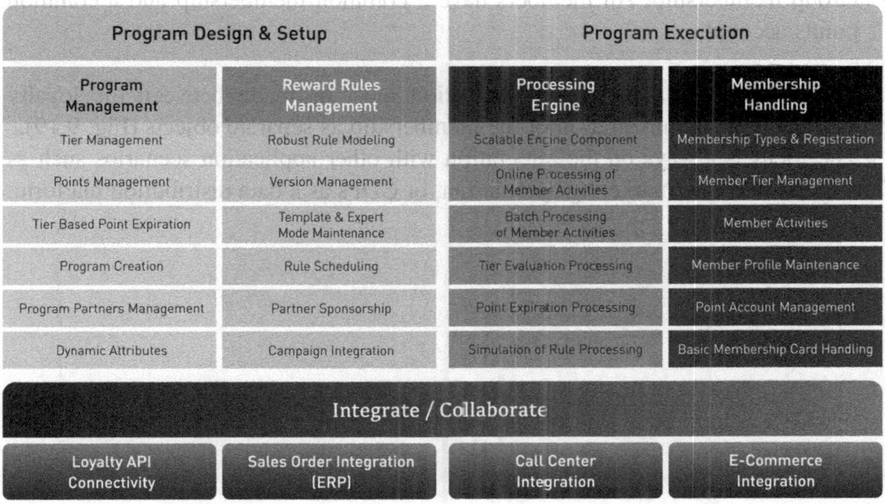

Program Design & Setup
Program Execution
Program Management
Reward Rules Management
Processing Engine
Membership Handling
Tier Management
Robust Rule Modeling
Scalable Engine Component
Membership Types & Registration
Points Management
Version Management
Online Processing of Member Activities
Member Tier Management
Tier Based Point Expiration
Template & Expert Mode Maintenance
Batch Processing of Member Activities
Member Activities
Program Creation
Rule Scheduling
Tier Evaluation Processing
Member Profile Maintenance
Program Partners Management
Partner Sponsorship
Point Expiration Processing
Point Account Management
Dynamic Attributes
Campaign Integration
Simulation of Rule Processing
Basic Membership Card Handling
Integrate / Collaborate
Loyalty API Connectivity
Sales Order Integration (ERP)
Call Center Integration
E-Commerce Integration

Fig. 9.18 Core functions of a loyalty management solution

In *program management*, different membership levels and forms are defined (e.g. "gold status"), as well as the bonus of different user activities (e.g. increased awarding of points for actions) or the expiry of points can be controlled (point expiration, temporal or dependent on user activities). Program management includes:

- Other (sales) partner organisations.
- Added value that program partners can offer their members (e.g. collecting/ redeeming multiple points for additional goods or services).
- The recording of all member activities using dynamic attributes and
- Incentivising individual activities, such as:
  - Tier-dependent: Members of higher ranks (e.g. "gold") receive more loyalty points for a certain activity.
  - Time-dependent: More loyalty points in a period of low demand (seasonal).
  - Assortment-dependent: Promotion of rotation for overstock (e.g. notebook special offer).

Reward rules management determines the rules for the transition from one tier level to another (e.g. "gold status from 200,000 miles earned"), the awarding of base points or the bonus for higher-value activities. Three variants are typically available in *membership management*:

- Personal membership: One member has one points account.
- Shared account membership: Points of different members are managed in one account. "Value points" can be collected and redeemed by any member; "Qualification points" (tier level, such as "gold" status) are still linked to an individual membership.
- Group membership: All members have a common membership and a common points account.

This means that a functional distinction must be made between the loyalty program and the administration of the membership as separate objects (Fig. 9.19).

The focus is always on the integration with other application scenarios such as CRM, e-commerce, marketing automation, or CDPs as a data distribution platform.

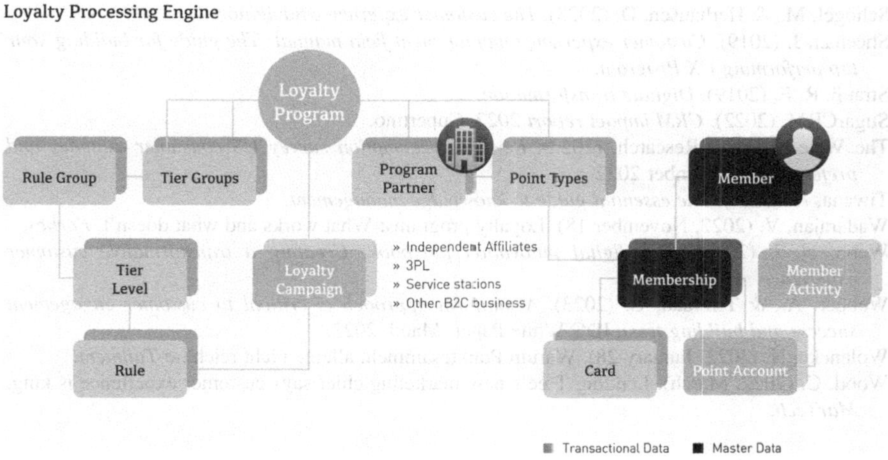

Fig. 9.19 Loyalty management solution between program level and membership administration

References

Alfonso, D. (2021, February). 4 disruptive, uncomfortable, yet inevitable MarTech trends. *MarTech Today*.

Amsler, S. (2019, January). The differences between CRM vs. CX strategy. *TechTarget*.

Brand Keys Customer Loyalty Engagement Index 2023.

Carlzon, J. (1989). *Moments of truth*.

Daniels, J. (2020). *The customer experience playbook: A practical guide for customer experience leaders, independently 2020*.

Fluckinger, D. (2020, July). What is customer experience management (CEM or CXM)? *TechTarget*.

Forrester. (2022a). *Reignite growth with hybrid customer experiences*.

Forrester. (2022b). *Loyalty-marketing & Bonusprogramme—globaler Marktbericht* 2022.

G2 (2023). *Tool evaluation*, March 2023.

Gartner. (2020). *CRM strategy and customer experience*.

Gartner. (2021). Magic Quadrant for B2B Marketing Automation Platforms, September 2021.

Harvard Business Review. (2023). *Die Customer Experience durch interne und externe Maßnahmen transformieren*, March 2023.

Hoffmann, N. (2013). *Loyalty schemes in retailing: A comparison of stand-alone and multi-partner programs*.

Jaffe, J. (2010). *Flip the funnel. How to use existing customers to gain new ones*.

Knistr. (2022). *Retail Loyalty Studie 2022: Was sich Konsument*innen von Loyalty-Programmen wünschen*.

Lawless Research. (2022). Marketing teams that use more tools regularly spend more of their work week on manual tasks, March 2022.

MarTechTribe. (2023a, March). *Global MarTech Requirements Database*.

MarTechTribe. (2023b, April). *Global MarTech Requirements Database*.

Mordor Market Intelligence. Globaler Markt für Kundenbindungsmanagement—Wachstum, Trends, Auswirkungen von Covid-19 und Prognosen (2023–2028).

Priestley, A. (2019). *Customer Experience: 22 international CX professionals share their current strategies for achieving impact and visibility using best practice CX, Writing Matters*.

Schögel, M., & Herhausen, D. (2023). *The customer experience navigator.*
Sheehan, J. (2019). *Customer experience management field manual: The guide for building your top performing CX Program.*
Strauß, R. E. (2019). *Digitale transformation.*
SugarCRM. (2022). *CRM impact report 2022*, Cupertino.
The Wise Marketer Research. (2022). *Rewards redemption survey US consumer attitudes and preferences*, November 2022.
Tiwana, A. (2001). *The essential guide to knowledge management.*
Wadarajan, V. (2022, November 18). Loyalty programs: What works and what doesn't. *Forbes.*
Webb, N. J. (2011). *The digital innovation playbook: Creating a transformative customer experience.*
Webber, A., & Trinidad, G. (2023). *A platform approach is critical to customer engagement success and building trust*, IDC White Paper, March 2023.
Wolancke, N. (2022, January 28). Warum Punktesammeln alleine nicht reicht. *e-Tailment.*
Wood, C. (2022, March). Lending Tree's new marketing chief says customer experience is king. *MarTech.*

10 The New Media Imperative

10.1 The Programmatic Revolution Eats Its Children

Due to the increasing "programmatisation" of all media channels, the paradigm shifts of "customer protection" within the framework of GDPR leads to the fact that large platforms can and will tend to further expand their market power. Due to the elimination of third-party data in 2025 latest, media providers themselves are also coming under pressure, so that on their side—analogous to manufacturing companies—massive efforts to generate first-party customer data can already be observed. Addressable TV (ATV) will be the next evolutionary step.

For most companies, the programmatic trend will (inevitably) reach all channels in the short term … even the "analogue giant TV". The share of advertising that is already programmatically controlled today is approximately 82% of total display advertising. However, studies and the interviews show that instead of intelligent context and interest-based target groups, only simple demographic segments are still booked. This can only be explained by the fact that these generate high volumes (and thus revenues) and cause (comparatively) little work on the side of the media agencies. However, it seems unclear whether there is a lack of sufficient information about consumers to be able to build meaningful targeting segments from them or agencies and advertisers tend to stay away from customised targeting models for other reasons (e.g. ignorance or lack of willingness to experiment). From a technical point of view, much more is possible than what has been used so far.

Overall, the programmatic approach is mainly used for performance (sales) and product communication and less for brand communication. Due to the lack of optimisation models, it is difficult for companies to assess the contribution of programmatic applications. Approximately 89% of marketing organisations are planning to remove programmatic applications from the agency models over the next few years and insource those tasks. The upcoming change is already palpable: most marketing managers and boards expect further growth of programmatic applications. In short, everything that can be programmatically controlled will also be programmatically controlled in the future. If agencies are currently still mainly

R. Strauss, *Data-Driven Customer Engagement*,
https://doi.org/10.1007/978-3-031-64295-1_10

used for this, the trend in the future will clearly be towards "*partial insourcing*". If programmatic purchasing has so far mainly been done via agencies in an outsourcing model, in the future at least partial programmatic purchasing will be done in-house. Only very few companies are planning to go completely in-house. Above all, the:

- Use of corporate data that needs to be protected and used as effectively as possible, as well as
- Cost transparency
- The exploitation of optimisation potential and
- The building-up of one's own competence

crystallise as the main reasons for increasing (partial) insourcing. Overall, the majority 81% of marketing decision-makers expect greater losses due to the ever-increasing data restrictions. The market is split in two: marketing decision-makers one the one side (contrary to agencies) expect the greatest losses the . . .

- . . . larger their annual marketing budget.
- . . . more B2C as a customer segment and omnichannel concepts are in focus.
- . . . more competencies in MarTech have already been built up within their own company.
- . . . more internal company projects have already been launched for the further digitalisation of all marketing processes.

Due to the increasing "programmatisation" of all media channels, the paradigm shifts of "customer protection" within the framework of the GDPR leads to the fact that large platforms can and will tend to further expand their market power. With the tightening of consent regulations (explicit opt-in vs. opt-out), customers are subsequently giving fewer permissions, which means less tracking data is available and previously used attribution models are losing importance. Accordingly, a renaissance of dialogue marketing concepts can be expected for the future.

Addressable TV is attributed the role of a centrifugal accelerator in this case. Smart TV continues to gain acceptance and, with the Internet-capable device equipment, also the possibility for a targeted approach towards the target groups thanks to addressable TV. This means that increased TV broadcasters can use addressable TV for households with smart television sets to realise the advantages of online marketing on the big screen. In the future, they will offer ad-server-based delivery of advertising formats on linear TV, based on the technical device standard *HbbTV*. The consequences of the additional use of addressable TV are, according to studies:

- An increase in awareness of targeted advertising contact by 7%.
- Increased advertising recall, with respondents reached by ATV being able to remember the advertising 10% more often than without additional use.
- A 10% increase in interest in using the products and

- An increase of almost 20% in the recognition of the linear commercial among respondents who were additionally reached by ATV.

Although linear TV still accounts for around 54% of TV consumption, paid services such as *Netflix* and *Prime Video* now account for almost one-third (29%) of TV consumption, and smart TV applications such as media libraries come in at 9%. At the same time, younger target groups are successively more difficult to reach via TV: among 18- to 24-year-olds, only 34% of TV consumption is accounted for by linear TV. Two-thirds of those surveyed, however, use one or more paid TV services. This means that in the short term, *Amazon* and *Netflix* will create two more TV-based walled gardens—with the same restrictions as the walled gardens already online. To make matters worse, no system has yet been established to precisely measure advertising impact across all channels according to uniform standards (i.e. not just as a statistical proxy). The call for standards for reach may be justified but will hardly be realised due to conceptual challenges (e.g. common reference values) and the different economic or political agendas. A step in this direction is the launch of an automated platform (e.g. *VMP Connect*) by *RTL AdConnect* in April 2020, which will make it possible to optimise programmatic pan-European advertising campaigns on the broadcasters' Video-On-Demand (BVOD) offerings. Advertisers will thus have access to the trusted inventory of premium publishers in fraud-free and brand-safe environments across Europe via a single platform. At the same time, it aims to lower the technical barrier to buying BVOD and other forms of CTV/OTT (Connected TV/Over-the-Top).

As a matter of priority, companies need econometric models for which one must methodically master the amount of data and further automation. In addition to short-term sales effects, the brand as an important driver for achieving corporate goals must be integrated into a comprehensive modelling with medium- and long-term effects, especially digitally. The discussions that have taken place in the meantime between brand building (*upper funnel*), on the one hand, and programmatic advertising (*lower funnel*) on the other, focus in essence on the question of whether automated media buying in its current form is rather detrimental to the brand or whether automated systems are simply overtaxed with brand goals. By transferring search metrics to display advertising, advertisers initially used programmatic technologies mainly for performance-driven advertising. Brand building was mainly done via classic I/O bookings (e.g. classic environment planning, direct booking). Years ago, advertisers began to use programmatic applications for the management of their branding campaigns, also under the argument of better measurability. Critical of this is that programmatic branding as an automated system can only be optimised for measurable goals, although branding campaigns often have benchmarks that are difficult to quantify. Accordingly, it seems to be a misconception that a branding campaign can be optimised well if a measurement pixel is available. For example, optimisation along the view through rate (VTR) for videos leads to the exclusion of certain target groups such as users who delete cookies or rarely watch videos in their entirety. Preference is given to people who have already had contact with the brand and therefore already know it. Although the (indirect) assumption is correct that a consumer who has watched a video in its entirety has had more contact with the brand and message than someone who stops after a few seconds, this does not lead to any growth in brand awareness in the upper funnel. In reporting, a campaign may have been successful, but in fact it did not achieve its reach and awareness goals (Marketing Tech Summit, 2024).

The focus here is always on developing own KPIs to measure branding success and optimise campaigns accordingly.

For *Vodafone*, for example, KPIs across all activities come first, especially the cost per qualitative visit (formed, among other things, from dwell time on the page, activities on the page, scrolling, and the use of offers) as the evaluation of the entire interaction of a visitor on the *Vodafone* page (Timm, 2020). For Vodafone, insourcing programmatic advertising has resulted in an average 47% increase in digital advertising ROI after 12 months, excluding agency fees; 80% of this result is due to improved operational campaign management, not media buying savings. Together with insourcing, there is a clear trend towards buying via private marketplaces (PMPs). Even though the prices are higher compared to open auctions, the cost per qualitative visit is more favourable. Open market measures are only selectively supplemented for reach (Priebe, 2020).

It turns out that optimising campaigns in programmatic advertising—even if they pursue branding goals—is always based on clearly measurable metrics. Campaign metrics provided by programmatic systems must be translated into usable branding KPIs. Again, brand awareness or recognition can only be measured retrospectively through market research. However, this does not exclude the fact that programmatic branding can effectively contribute to brand building. Summing up, After all, branding-effective rich media advertising media can increasingly be directed to premium placements via programmatic technologies, analogous to classic I/O campaigns. The same applies to radio, TV, and out-of-home (instore) advertising as well as print mailings, all of which can increasingly be booked programmatically and used for brand building.

In many historically grown companies, programmatic and TV buying are still organised in different areas (performance marketing vs. brand marketing). Consequently, campaigns are not planned and played out "full funnel". However, the brand needs performance and performance need the "new reach" of the brand, so it makes sense to synchronise the media buying of programmatic TV/OoH (out-of-Home) with performance marketing, to plan it together and to optimise it along the entire funnel. The order of the day: team play instead of defending hegemonic claims of ownership.

10.2 Retail Media: The Monetisation of Visitor Traffic and Data

The growth of retail media will continue unabated in 2024+: IAB Europe forecasts an increase in retail media advertising spend to €14.3 bn in 2024 . . . an increase of 35.9% compared to the €10.5 bn in 2022. Euphoric forecasts already expect retail media spend to surpass traditional TV in the coming years. At least 4–5 lines of development are emerging: (1) Non-retailers will build media networks: Due to an increased demand for first-party data, other companies will also enter retail media. Other travel and hospitality companies and quick service restaurants are likely to follow suit. (2) Lack of scale: Not every retail media network (RMN) will be able to stand out from the crowd and scale. Most advertisers state that they do not (want to) work with more than four (larger/relevant) retail data partners. (3) Self-service offerings for advertisers will emerge ("Retail Media as a Service"), and (4) focus on offsite retail media.

The growth of retail media will continue unabated in 2023 and beyond. *Zenith Media* estimates that global ad spend in retail media will increase from $39.2 billion in 2022 to $64.2 billion in 2025—an average growth of 17.8%—making it one of the fastest growing advertising categories alongside video advertising and social media (Zenith Media, 2022). Platforms such as *Amazon*, *eBay*, *Zalando*, and others have laid the concrete foundation for the retail media house for this in two dimensions: (1) the trade promotion principle (as advertising grant/subsidy) has been transferred to the Internet and (2) platforms/marketplaces and large online retailers are not only earning via purely product sales but increasingly also via advertising. On average, the margin generated via advertising revenue is significantly higher than the current retailer margin via purely product sales—for example, at *Amazon* beyond 70%. Retail media has its origins in traditional trade promotions, which manufacturers pay to retailers as a listing fee to get their own products preferentially placed (Fig. 10.1). A special feature is that manufacturers and retailers plan and implement measures together and that the financing is also usually done jointly. While the reach of a retailer was initially defined by footfall (visitor frequency) and POS measures, as

	Trade Promotions (Subsidy)	Retail Media
Content	Subsidies for product listing, unit-linked subsidy for sales or supplementary trade promotions (unit-based)	Paid advertising for communication performance (reach and visibility)
Objective	Sales	Branding and/or product sales
Binding (mandatory?)	Rather obligatory for listing	Voluntary
Budgets of Brands	Classical sales budgets	Sales and marketing budgets
Client	Sales/distribution of manufacturers (brands) selling in the web shop or via the app	Marketing/distribution of manufacturers (brands)/retailers or media agencies on behalf of manufacturers (brands)/retailers

Fig. 10.1 Difference between trade promotions (Trade Promotions/advertising subsidies) and retail media

well as individual media such as flyers or print ads, it is increasingly being extended by traffic on the retailer's own online sites such as shops, content platforms, company websites, E-Mail newsletters, or social media. From the retailer's point of view, the focus is on the extended monetisation of their own reach and customer contacts.

Data-driven marketing can significantly and measurably increase the effectiveness of retail media budgets (Fig. 10.2). The basis is a cycle of data that determines the affinity of potential customers to a product (be it purchase, brand awareness, etc.) up to the collection of data regarding target achievement within selected target groups. Success data in sales flow back into the customer profiles to be able to target the customer approach even more precisely in the next iteration.

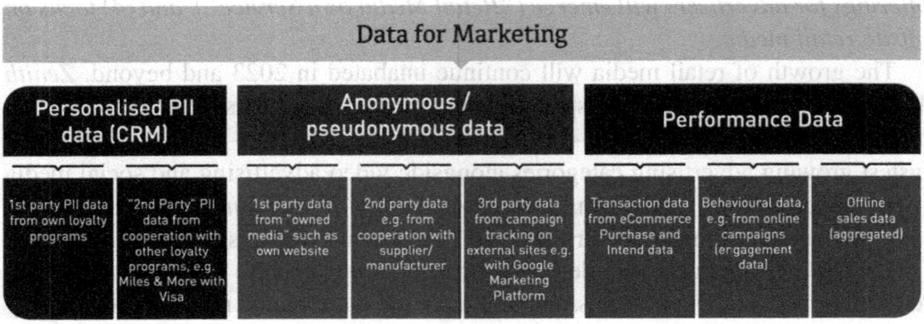

Fig. 10.2 Classification and hierarchy of data for retail media

While *endemic partners* who buy retail media list their products directly on the platform of the retail media provider (e.g. a shop), *non-endemic partners* buy retail media services for their products that have no direct relationship to the product offers of the shop operator and whose advertising therefore also links to offers outside the web shop or app if applicable. It is therefore a completely "normal" form of product advertising, as on publisher pages. The combination of different classes of data and media results in structured fields of action along a retail media strategy matrix. On the one hand, the differentiation of data from pseudonymous to (anonymous) performance data to personalised (PII) data (Fig. 10.3), and on the other hand, the differentiation of reach by "ownership" from owned media on the retailer's pages (properties) to purchased reach of any other website or app, as well as the subsequent evaluation of the possible cases/products according to various criteria such as the monetisation potential or the degree of disclosure and (external) release of the (aggregated) "data crown jewels" on the part of the retailer. It is therefore a very "normal" form of product advertising, as on publisher sites. The combination of different classes of data and media results in structured fields of action along a *Retail Media Strategy Matrix*:

- On the one hand, the differentiation of data from pseudonymous to (anonymous) performance data to personalised (PII) data.

Legend
1 low | 5 high

	Without Media – Data Pure Deal	Owned Media	Purchased Inventories	Owned Media mixed with purchased Inventories transparent)	Owned Media mixed with purchased Inventories (blind)
Data-Free – Media Pure Deal	X	Already in progress: Yes Monetization potential: 2 Additional tech: Already available Feasibility: 5 End user: Direct	Already being done: Yes Monetization potential: 3 Additional tech: Yes Feasibility: 4 End user: Direct	Already being done: No Monetization potential: 3 Additional tech: Yes Feasibility: 4 End user: Direct & Intermediary	Already being done: No Monetization potential: 4 Additional tech: Yes Feasibility: 4 End user: Direct & Intermediary
Pseudonymous User Data	Already being done: No Monetization potential: 4 Additional tech: Yes Feasibility: 4 End user: Intermediary Remarks: Clear Go - Strategic approach and recommendation. Strong leverage on trading own data at low costs.	Already being done: Partially Monetization potential: 2 Additional tech: Not necessarily Feasibility: 5 End user: Direct	Already being done: No Monetization potential: 4 Additional tech: Not necessarily Feasibility: 4 End user: Direct	Already being done: No Monetization potential: 4 Additional tech: Not mandatory Feasibility: 4 End user: Direct	Already being done: No Monetization potential: 5 Additional tech: Not mandatory Feasibility: 4 End user: Direct
PII data from loyalty programs	Already being done: No Monetization potential: Unclear Additional tech: Likely yes Feasibility: 3 End user: Direct and Intermediary Remarks: **Not recommended** as these data are core assets and monetization through "data only" trading is likely to be too low.	Already being done: Partially Monetization potential: 3 Additional tech: Not mandatory Feasibility: 4 End user: Direct Remarks: **No recommendation for Retail Media,** as this is a classic CRM business and already located there.	Already being done: No Monetization potential: 3 Additional tech: Likely yes Feasibility: 3 End user: Direct Remarks: **No recommendation for Retail Media,** as only CRM data offer less potential than combined PII and pseudonymous data.	Already being done: No Monetization potential: 3 Additional tech: Likely yes Feasibility: 3 End user: Direct Remarks: **No recommendation for Retail Media,** as only CRM data offer less potential than combined PII and pseudonymous data.	Already being done: No Monetization potential: 3 Additional tech: Likely yes Feasibility: 3 End user: Direct Remarks: **No recommendation for Retail Media,** as only CRM data offer less potential than combined PII and pseudonymous data.
PII data from loyalty programs combined with pseudonymous user data	Already being done: No Monetization potential: Unclear Additional tech: Yes Feasibility: 3 End user: Direct and Intermediary Remarks: **Not recommended,** as these data without leverage from media in monetization may not be profitable enough.	Already being done: No Monetization potential: 1 Additional tech: Yes Feasibility: 3 End user: Direct and Intermediary Remarks: **Not recommended,** as these data without leverage from media in monetization may not be profitable enough.	Already being done: No Monetization potential: 2 Additional tech: Yes Feasibility: 3 End user: Direct Remarks: **Not recommended,** as these data without leverage from media in monetization may not be profitable enough.	Already being done: No Monetization potential: 2 Additional tech: Yes Feasibility: 3 End user: Direct Remarks: **Not recommended,** as these data without leverage from media in monetization may not be profitable enough.	Already being done: No Monetization potential: 3 Additional tech: Yes Feasibility: 3 End user: Direct Remarks: **Not recommended,** as these data without leverage from media in monetization may not be profitable enough.
[illegible]	Already being done: Yes [illegible]	Already being done: Yes [illegible]	Already being done: Yes [illegible]	Already being done: Yes [illegible]	Already being done: Yes [illegible]

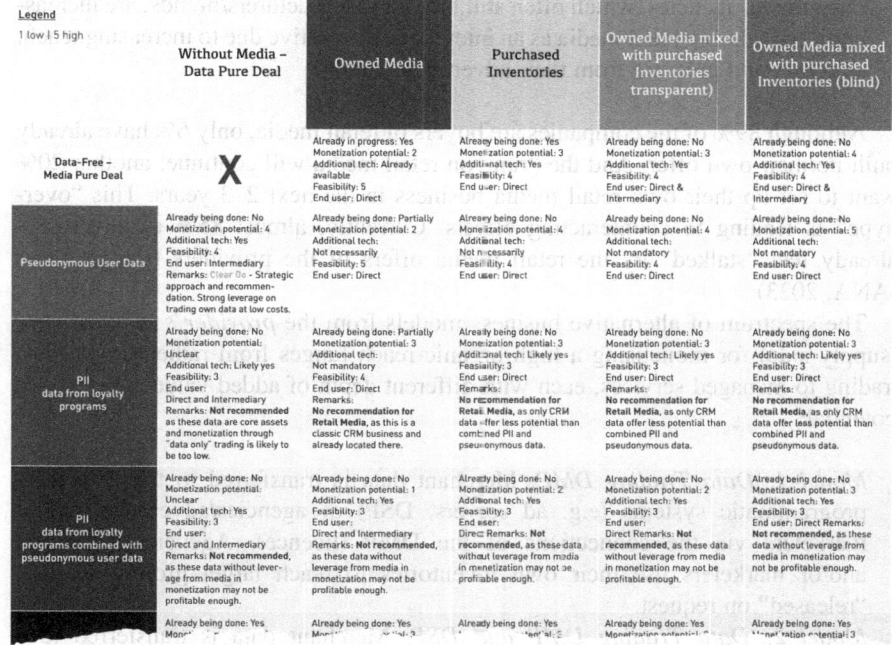

Fig. 10.3 Example of a retail media strategy matrix: evaluation matrix of marketable assets of a trader and possible product offerings from a supplier/trader perspective (project example, retail)

- On the other hand, the differentiation of the reach according to "ownership" of owned media on the pages (properties) of a retailer, for example, up to the purchased reach of every other website or app, as well as the subsequent evaluation of the possible cases/products according to various criteria such as the monetisation potential or the degree of disclosure and (external) release of the (aggregated) "data crown jewels" on the part of the provider.

The *advantages* from the point of view of advertisers (buyers, e.g. consumer goods manufacturers):

- Alternative to constantly rising oligopoly bidding prices and competition on *Google* and *Facebook*, plus an increase in reach along the sales funnel.
- Possibility to influence the purchase decision in a performance-oriented way close to the customer's transaction.
- Obtain targeting data based on real preferences and buying behaviour, which are often much sharper than in traditional digital media buying.
- Return on ad spend is between three and six times greater for brand owners compared to traditional media.
- Increasing maturity of retail media (e.g. via steadily improving self-service booking options and increasingly better reporting/analysis options for paid advertising or performance data).

- Even media agencies, which often still buy for manufacturers/brands, are increasingly considering retail media as an interesting alternative due to increasing reach, maturity, and pressure from their advertising clients.

Although 89% of the companies are buyers of retail media, only 6% have already built up their own offer. And the "run" on retail media will continue: another 20% want to set up their own retail media business in the next 2–3 years. This "over-hype" is leading to counteracting effects. Currently, almost 85% of advertisers already feel "stalked" by the retail media offers of the providers (the retailers) (ANA, 2023).

The spectrum of alternative business models from the *provider's point of view* (supply side) for monetising a high organic reach ranges from rather simple data trading to managed services, each with different depth of added value and revenue potential:

- *Model 1: Data Trading DMP*: Merchant data is transferred to the respective programmatic systems (e.g. ad servers, DSP) of agencies/advertisers and/or marketers via the connections of the DMP (licence). Agencies/advertisers and/or marketers use their own inventories to reach target groups. Data is "released" on request.
- *Model 2: Data Trading DMP and DSP*: Merchant data is transferred to a dedicated DSP (licence/seat) via the connection of the DMP (licence). Agencies/advertisers can access the segments of the provider/retailer via assigned access rights for the campaign display of their own inventories (Fig. 10.4).

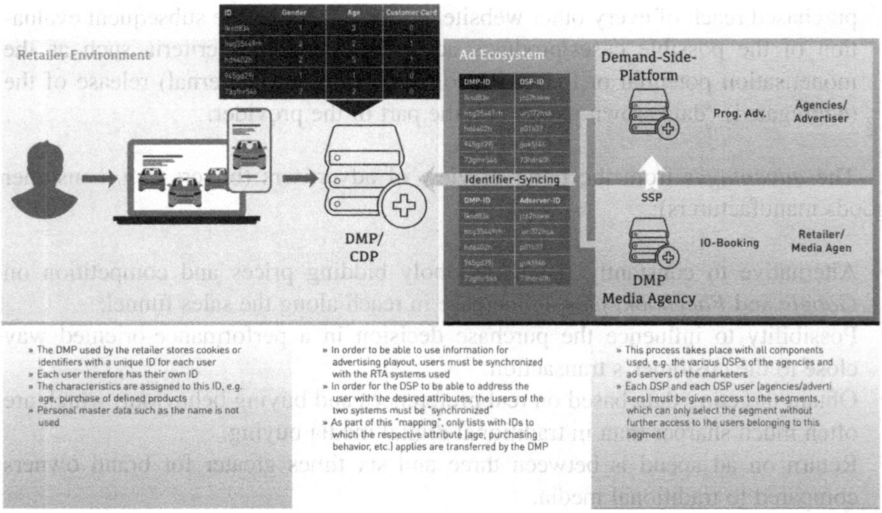

Fig. 10.4 Model 2: Data Trading DMP and DSP: Data exchange/reconciliation between retailer and agencies/advertisers (project example)

- *Model 3: Targeted/Curated Media*: Retailer data is transferred to a dedicated DSP (license/seat) via the connection of the DMP (license). Agencies/advertisers can access the supplier segments via assigned access rights for the campaign display of their own inventories. Advertisers/agencies manage their campaigns themselves in their respective DSP seat.
- *Model 4: Managed Service*: Provider data is transferred to a DSP (licence/seat) via the connection of the merchant DMP (licence), for example. The provider brings together their own and external inventories with their own profiles and offers these as "target group media packages". The complete campaign handling and placement takes place in the form of a campaign management service.

The providers are proceeding very differently in the various business models—these are highly dependent on the degree of maturity, the category, and the respective retail media strategy. The trend is towards managed services, self-services in processing (depending on the respective products), in combination with a maximum of transparency (KPI tracking) (Merkle, 2021). First-party data in certain market segments (especially intent and interest data) will continue to gain in value. The path of open data marketing outside of one's own ecosystem is taken rather rarely. Mostly, data is marketed in combination with space and then offered either as a self-service (e.g. *Amazon Advertising Services*, *OTTO* with product listing ads, or *Zalando* influencer marketing) or as a managed service ("all-in carefree package") for advertisers. Multichannel providers also include offline transactions in this case, for example via customer cards for multi-touchpoint sales attribution.

Besides a (supposedly) simple redistribution of trade promotions, two opposite effects arise here:

- Firstly, the retailer runs the risk of receiving a lowered CPC from manufacturers in the future, as they (can) receive digital, data-driven offers from other retailers or platforms in return for their CPC investment. The focus is on who can offer the advertiser the best "conversion" or return on advertising spend (ROAS). As a rule, these are the providers who hit the "right" audience through good data and segmentation. This means that the advertising budgets do not simply "disappear" but are placed by the manufacturer with a competitor . . . if necessary. The retailer thus loses two things: access to the trade promotions feed trough and, in the medium term, possibly market share due to the better capitalisation of competing market participants.
- Secondly, in addition to the trade promotion budgets controlled (mostly) by the sales departments, there are marketing budgets that are usually controlled by media agencies. These usually do not have access to the inventories (booking sites) of the retailers. However, the promise of retail media is, due to the proximity of customer contacts to the actual buying process, better customer insights and thus more effective customer contacts, which retail media offers better than media agencies ever could with the inventories they manage—further away from the (digital) point of sale.

The guidelines for retail media always include compliance with GDPR, avoidance of using third-party data (cookie loss), as well as the keeping of the "data crown jewels" without data leakages. The technical data exchange between retail and advertising customers therefore might use four different *options for a technical data exchange* within retail media:

1. *Cooperation with a demand-side platform (DSP)*: Retailer/provider segments are transferred to DSP and could be made available to the respective agency and advertisers. While this solution is easy to be set up, the downside comes with a lower sales potential (bound to DSP), using predominantly third-party data, and the potential reach of the identifier cannot be determined in advance, plus the potential of "piggy backing" with data leakages between advertisers.
2. *Identifier/via data management platform (DMP)*: DMP-centred approach that can support and process the various identifier solutions. Extended to include users of one or more ID solution(s) and the provisioning of segments to DSPs and possibly also SSPs. Billing via selected DMP. Advantages are in sales for demand and sell-side solutions, hand in hand with high revenue shares for DMP and DSP, and ID solutions, but facing low matching rates and therefore also low reach. The further development and market penetration remains uncertain.
3. *Data clean room (DCR)*: Market reach depending on the number and type (login volume) of advertising partners involved. Opens joint sales opportunities with publishers and other advertisers/suppliers. The downside is when transferring the data to DSPs/SSPs, data becomes third-party data again, suffering from cookie loss. Again, potential "piggy backing" with data leakages between advertisers.
4. *First-party tag integration with publisher*: Ad and tracking tags implemented on the website by the retailer themself to be able to address retailer first-party data on publisher sites. From the perspective of the retailer, this solution allows the own management and implementation of tracking tags, without the integration of external advertising networks or analysis platforms required (Fig. 10.5).

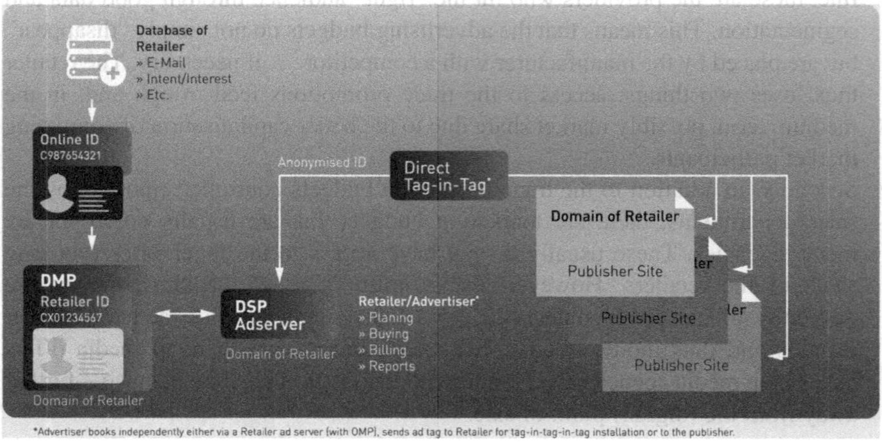

Fig. 10.5 Option 4: First-party tag-in-tag integration (project example)

In case of option 4, the advertiser books independently via the ad server of the retailer (with order management platform, OMP), and then sends the ad tag to the retailer for tag-in-tag-in-tag installation or to the publisher. Advantages range from solving the third-party cookie problems to gaining a higher degree of privacy and data security, combined with a higher sales potential. The downside is that a "new" method requires high initial efforts to convince publishers for cooperation. The final decision will largely depend on the role the retailer wants to play in the market itself, alongside the different process steps (Fig. 10.6).

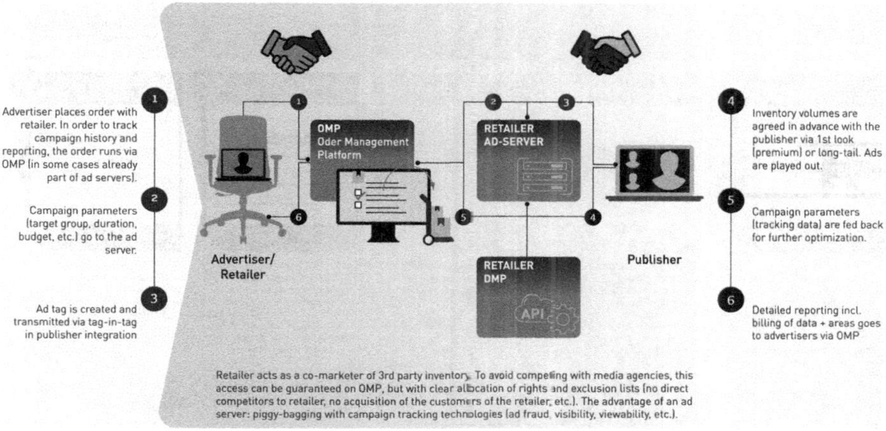

Fig. 10.6 Roles of a retailer in retail media—data and inventory (project example)

The marketing budgets of the manufacturers/brands can therefore have a complementary effect and are not a mere substitute for classic trade promotions. From the retailer's point of view, this opens another treasure chest in the form of the marketing budgets on the part of the manufacturers, which have so far presented themselves more as a "military restricted area à la Area 51". Against this background, retail media appears attractive for companies with a high organic reach. The implementation follows ten steps (Fig. 10.7):

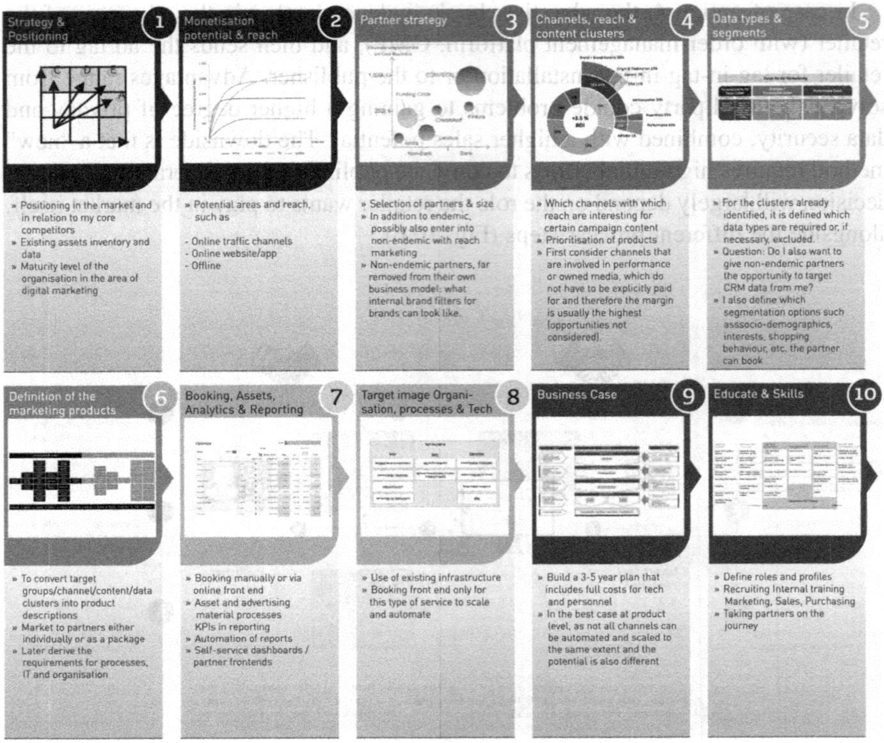

Fig. 10.7 Procedure model for setting up retail media (project example)

The focus is still on purely data exchange (74%), followed by exclusive (endemic) landing pages at the retailer and the creation of cross-selling/upselling campaigns (Fig. 10.8). The fewest companies are "clueless in retail media Seattle" (7%).

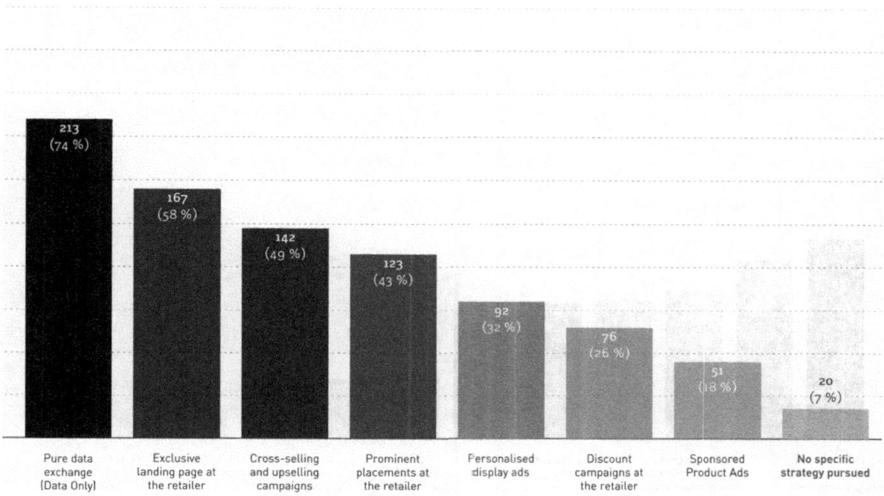

Fig. 10.8 Retail media collaborations used between brands and retailers (in %, multiple responses, $n = 356$; Marketing Tech Monitor 2023)

With each channel added to the retail media mix, providers have created new platforms to help retailers manage and monetise these media. The increasing number of providers in a fragmented technology landscape generates more problems such as IT integration and the exchange of data in compliance with the GDPR, and it increases the lack of qualified personnel. In other words, while the use of all other media channels is already legion, retail media is currently still in a pain therapy clinic due to:

- Unresolved legal issues
- The multitude of possible business models
- Mostly insufficient reach in the case of singular offers by individual retailers and
- The proof that it can also be used meaningfully in the upper funnel (awareness, Fig. 10.9).

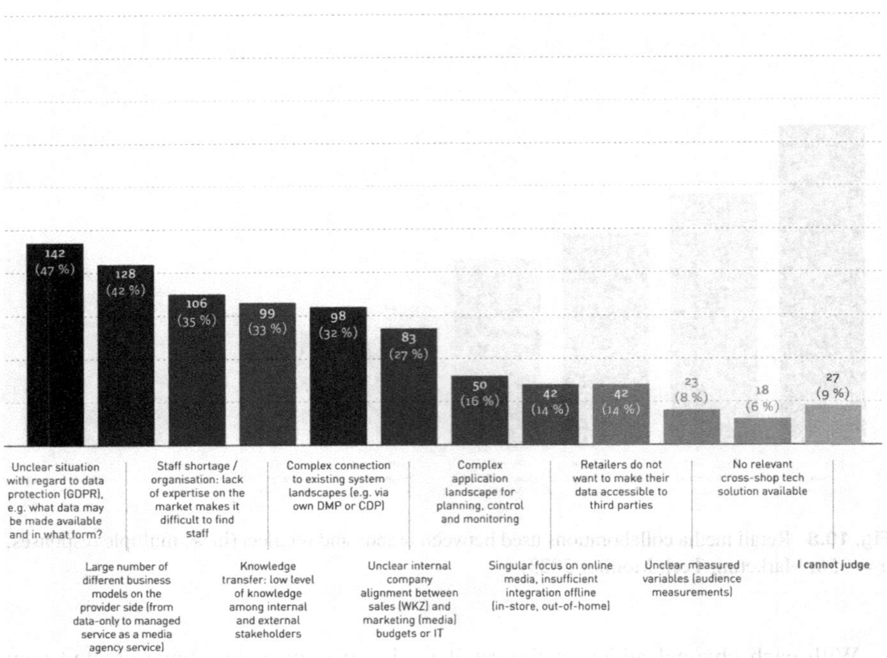

Fig. 10.9 Biggest challenges in retail media (top 3, in %, multiple responses, $n = 356$; WKZ = trade promotions, Marketing Tech Monitor 2023)

This requires the establishment of a technological infrastructure. The depth of the implementation of the corresponding MarketingTech components depends on the individual starting point of the retailer. This can range from a simple connection of an ad server to a full-stack implementation (e.g. SSP, DSP, DCO, analytics, attribution, CRM connection; Fig. 10.10). The challenge is the conversion of the mostly manual trade promotion booking mechanism to data-driven retail media, which counteracts established processes, responsibilities, system worlds, and data management (ownership) on the part of both the retailers and the manufacturers involved.

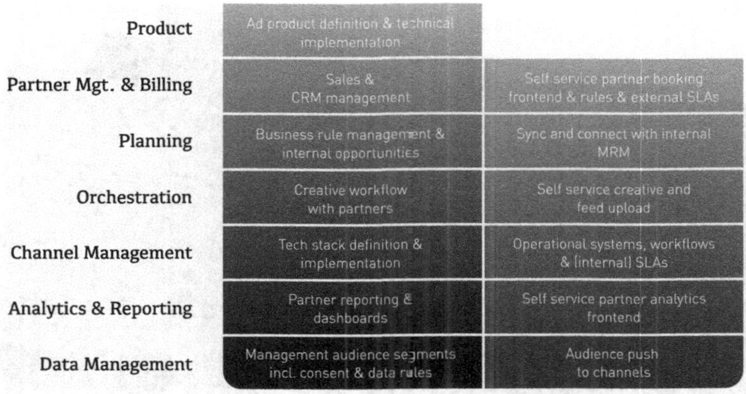

Product
Ad product definition & technical implementation
Partner Mgt. & Billing
Sales & CRM management
Self service partner booking frontend & rules & external SLAs
Planning
Business rule management & internal opportunities
Sync and connect with internal MRM
Orchestration
Creative workflow with partners
Self service creative and feed upload
Channel Management
Tech stack definition & implementation
Operational systems, workflows & (internal) SLAs
Analytics & Reporting
Partner reporting & dashboards
Self service partner analytics frontend
Data Management
Management audience segments incl. consent & data rules
Audience push to channels

Fig. 10.10 Components of retail media development (project example)

The shift towards programmatic TV/radio/DOOH will increasingly take up and link first-party data from data providers (e.g. retailers such as *OTTO* in cooperation with *Ströer* and *Adition* or *Virtual Minds* around Digital Out-of-Home (DOOH)). Innovative formats will develop both off-site and on-site in social and video channels, including the intelligent linking of sales measures financed by the advertiser (e.g. vouchers and reviews). Initially, fundamental questions need to be clarified along various building blocks (Fig. 10.11), such as:

- The quality and quantity of the 360-degree customer database in a Data Lake or CDP.
- Data-driven products and services and the resulting targeting opportunities.
- Transparent KPIs and dashboards (vs. non-transparency in trade promotions).
- Convincing approaches of an AdTech programmatic partner with experience in ID management and first-party synchronisation/management, which at the same time are already planning for new programmatic opportunities in TV, audio, or DooH (Digital Out-of-Home) (road map)—usually a DSP/ad server as well as a docked DMP or via a data clean room is necessary.
- Clear control of the agencies involved—especially before the discontinuation of other remuneration models (e.g. kickbacks).
- Heterogeneous KPIs and reporting standards—in terms of the tools used (currently still *PDF*, *Excel*, CSV files, up to dashboards) as well as in terms of a uniform nomenclature of KPIs, such as ROAS (e.g. on revenue same article, same brand, all brands) and
- Processing—for self-service bookings, larger market participants tend to use in-house solutions/frontends for brands/agencies or rely on outsourced platforms (e.g. *Criteo*).

Fig. 10.11 Retail media in a box—toolbox for providers (data providers) and retailers alike

The challenge is the conversion of the mostly manual trade promotion booking and accounting mechanism to data-driven retail media, which counteracts established processes, responsibilities, system worlds, and data management (ownership) both on the part of the data providers (e.g. retailers) and the advertisers involved (fast-moving consumer goods manufacturers).

10.3 A Brave New World: Audience Verification, Brand Safety, and Visibility . . . The New Reach Measurements and Currencies

While MarTech is growing, AdFraud as well. Studies estimate the damage caused by fake traffic at a total of up to $700 billion annually. Converted into budgets and spendings, this results globally of almost $697 billion wasted globally each year due to data distortions, $42 billion in lost revenue per year due to invalid data traffic, and $115 billion in labour costs for invalid sales leads. DoubleVerify even reports a 70% increase in fraud between 2021 and 2022.

Next to viewability and brand safety, the danger of ad fraud is a defining issue. Cases of ad fraud are already legion in the market but are still often ignored (Fig. 10.12).

More than 20 different techniques for defrauding advertising money ensure that in some cases, only just under 20% of the budgets used end up with the target group in an advertising-effective way. Accordingly, *CHEQ* estimates the damage caused by fake traffic at a total of up to $700 billion annually (CHEQ, 2023):

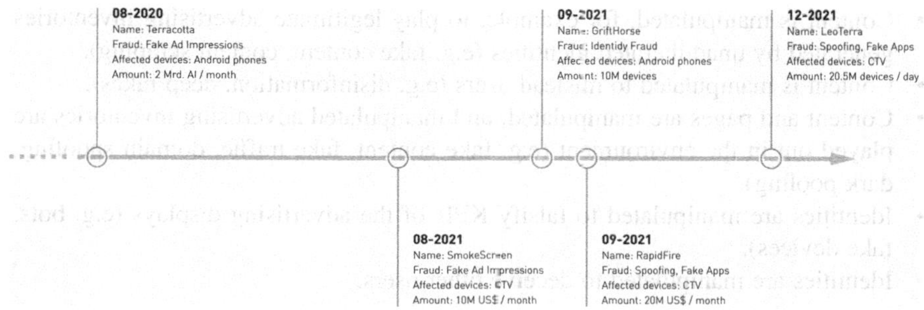

Fig. 10.12 Prominent cases of ad fraud since 2020 (Marketing Tech Monitor 2022)

- 27% of organic traffic is fake
- 32% of organic/direct traffic from mobile phones or in the retail sector is invalid

Converted into budgets and spendings, this results globally, in *CHEQ's* view, of:

- $697 billion wasted globally each year due to data distortions
- $42 billion in lost revenue per year due to invalid data traffic and
- $115 billion in labour costs for invalid sales leads

DoubleVerify even reports a 70% increase in fraud between 2021 and 2022 (DoubleVerifiy, 2023).

Ad fraud thus accounts for approximately half of global programmatic display advertising investment. The game variations of ad fraud are manifold (Fig. 10.13):

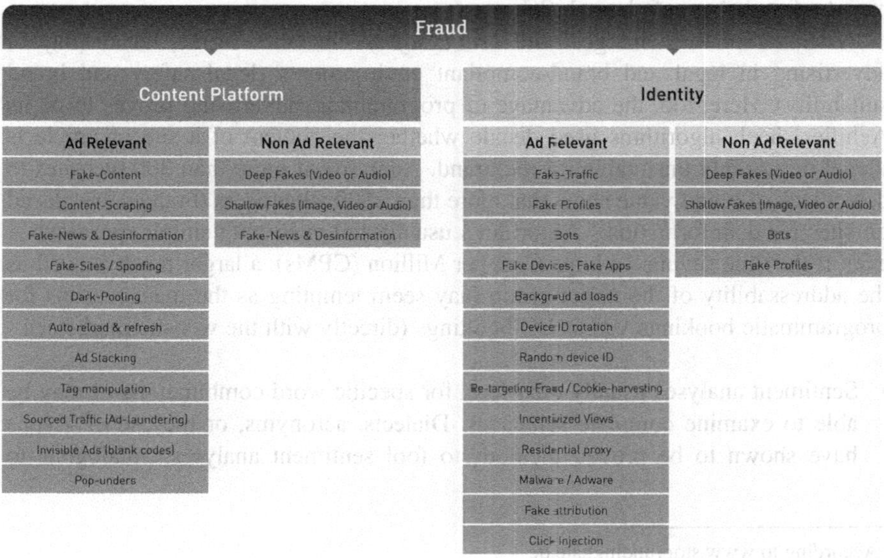

Fig. 10.13 Forms of ad fraud (Marketing Tech Monitor 2021)

- Content is manipulated, for example, to play legitimate advertising inventories generated by unadulterated identities (e.g. fake content, content scraping).
- Content is manipulated to mislead users (e.g. disinformation, deep fakes).
- Content and pages are manipulated, and manipulated advertising inventories are played out in the environment (e.g. fake content, fake traffic, domain spoofing, dark pooling).
- Identities are manipulated to falsify KPIs of the advertising displays (e.g. bots, fake devices).
- Identities are manipulated to deceive other users.

To make things worse, it seems important to differentiate whether manipulation takes place on the content or platform side or whether the manipulation takes place on the "user" or "advertising medium" level. In addition, advertising-effectiveness losses occur due to ad blockers, inaccurate attribution, and missing viewability.

A vivid example is *fake device ID fraud*, in at least two variants: in the case of *random device ID fraud*, frequency caps based on device IDs are booted out. A new device is played to the fraud detection technology so that advertising is delivered by default. Frequency caps are bypassed because the filters used assume "different" and thus "new" devices. In the case of *replayed device ID*, valid device IDs are "harvested" from real devices and sent to fake devices or apps to replicate the IDs and thus also circumvent fraud filters. *Viper Bot*, for example, focuses primarily on the connected TV and mobile video channels. With this, fraudsters remove the code that verifies the ads and then redirect this code through real devices to hide the fraudulent activity and remain undetected. According to analytics platform *DoubleVerify*, this is used to spoof more than 5 million devices and up to 85 million ad requests per day. Analysts assume that the share of site, device, and app fraud is already over 57%, while the known and certified fraud detection providers only report a fraud share of about 1–2%.

A similar picture emerges with *brand safety*—in other words, the display of advertising in legal and brand-compliant environments (legal safety and brand suitability). Here, too, the advantage of programmatic advertising proves to be its Achilles' heel: algorithms used decide whether the content of a site or article is illegal or possibly unsuitable for the brand. Analyses of more than 300 websites to detect lack of brand value show that more than 2500 advertisers (brands) are placed on sites for disinformation.[1] Algorithms usually fail even with simple questions—even if the time savings, a huge Cost per Million (CPMs), a larger reach as well as the addressability of the target group may seem tempting as the main reasons for programmatic bookings versus I/O bookings (directly with the website marketer):

- Sentiment analyses usually only look for specific word combinations or may be able to examine complete sentences. Dialects, acronyms, or the use of glyphs have shown to be proven methods to fool sentiment analyses. Analogous to

[1] According to www.stopfundinghate.de

contextual targeting, the next evolutionary leap is expected to be based on artificial intelligence, machine learning, and natural language processing.

- A provider can artificially increase the ratio between mainstream content and disinformation (e.g. via stock indices, sports results, horoscopes) to be able to claim that most of its content is legitimate.
- Audio manipulation (i.e. a real existing voice is cloned) can hardly be identified as such, which makes brand safety in programmatic audio seem practically impossible.

AI in the AdTech industry is the culmination of a decade of black box algorithms happily spending advertisers' digital budgets without a clue about how to market. AI algorithms maximise the profits of Adtech companies rather than the business outcomes of the marketers they are supposed to serve—Dr Augustine Fou (Fou Analytics)

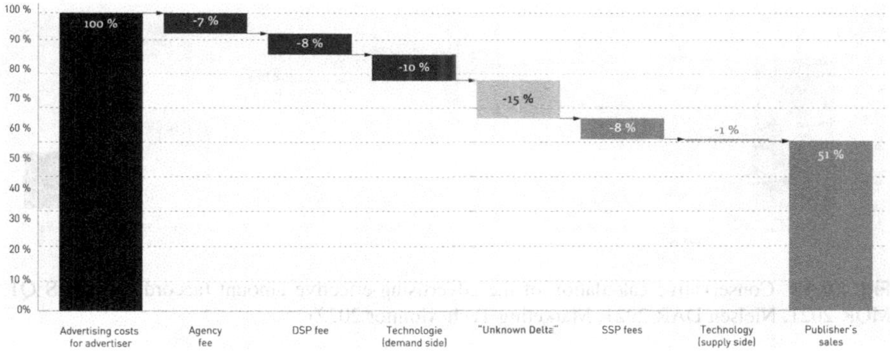

Fig. 10.14 Advertising costs vs. booking volume on the part of publishers (ISBA Programmatic Supply Chain Transparency Study 2020; Marketing Tech Monitor 2022)

The consequence is that the effective CPM for advertisers is significantly higher. If one subtracts the costs incurred for the ad stack and the fees of all intermediaries, the difference between advertising volume and booking volume at the publisher becomes apparent (Fig. 10.14):

- Almost 50% of the advertising investments had no visible effect or cannot have an advertising effect (advertising-effective Euro).
- Service and technology fees on the agency side accounted for 25% of the costs on average (e.g. ad server, DMP, trading desk, verification, other administrative costs).

- On average, 15% of the invoiced costs could not be allocated. It is assumed that these are caused by cost discrepancies between the winning bid in the DSP and the asking price in the SSP.
- Only 12% of the ad impressions were clearly identifiable.

Assuming (conservatively calculated) that 1% of this 51% is deducted due to domain spoofing, 1% due to ad blocking, 2% due to invalid traffic (IVT, e.g. bots) measured by ad fraud detection providers, and 1% due to banners that are not displayed correctly or not at all, only 48% of the advertising money invested remains. *IAS*, as a brand safety and ad fraud detection provider, also calculates with a non-visible or off-target share of just under 40% (Fig. 10.15). Under these circumstances, the effective advertising amount is only 19%.

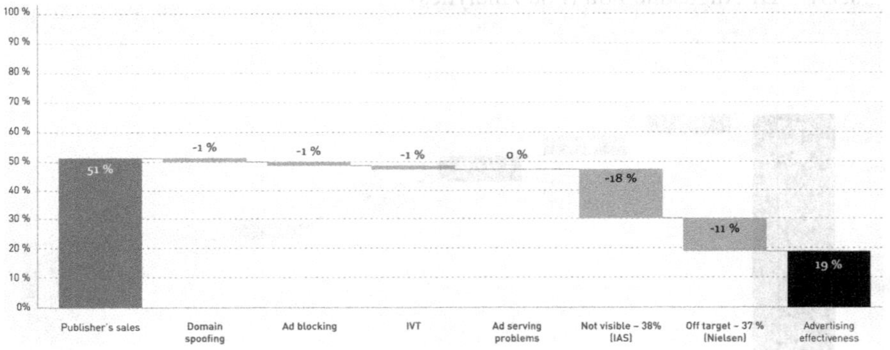

Fig. 10.15 Conservative calculation of the advertising-effective amount (according to IAS Q1 MQR 2021, Nielsen DAR 2021; Marketing Tech Monitor 2022)

Even with comparatively smaller programmatic campaigns (open market, 5 million to approx. 10 million AI per month), it is not uncommon for advertising to be displayed on more than 20,000 domains. Media audits show that on average, up to 6000 domains are targeted to (supposedly) generate the necessary reach. The technically induced cookie loss due to the spread of *Firefox* and *Safari* alone is around 37%, and the share of *iOS* devices is around 38%. In other words, only about 60% of the target group could technically be addressed by targeting at all.

The established ad verification tools on the market can only capture a part of these fraud mechanisms:

- One weakness is to analyse the traffic in the pre-bid before the actual auction is completed. Domain spoofing is used, for example, to pretend to be a news site, although the site is just an accumulation of nonsense content with countless advertising placements ("made-for-advertisement pages").

- User agent spoofing can cause the information collected about web browser usage to become inaccurate. Fraudsters' bots can easily spoof the HTTP_USER_AGENT and change it to any value to disguise themselves. Ad fraud verification providers that use HTTP_USER_AGENT to detect bots thus miss 100% of these bots because the user agent is reported as "valid" or "normal".
- Fraudsters block analytics tags and/or fraud detection tags or modify measurement data to avoid identification.

Since mid-2022 at the latest, ad fraud has also reached the audio environment through streaming, on account of the *BeatSting* scam (Priebe, 2023). *BeatSting* uses server-side ad insertion (SSAI). Via SSAI, advertising spots are delivered personalised (i.e. with the right targeting) in video and audio streams. In contrast to client-side ad insertion—where the stream stops, a spot is delivered, and the streaming is then resumed—the ad is inserted into the stream before it is sent to the viewer's or listener's device. The spot is thus integrated into the audio or video content by the SSAI server, which is interposed in the communication with the other advertising platforms, and then seamlessly delivered together with the stream. The advantage of this is greater efficiency, especially in the case of programmatic auctions.

In the context of *BeatSting*, fraudsters set up such an SSAI server themselves and linked it to inconspicuous apps to generate inventory there, the origin of which is deliberately concealed (spoofing). In this way, they make it appear that the inventory is from large audio platforms. In the next step, access to the content of the apps is generated, the origin of which is also disguised so that different IPs and devices appear as senders. With their self-constructed SSAI servers, manipulated apps, and simulated accesses, the fraudsters ultimately generated bid requests that were sent to supply-side platforms, ad exchanges, and networks. Advertisers bid there with their respective buying technology and were made to believe that they were buying high-quality inventory. The fraud is only noticed when apps do not receive an update for a longer period, do not stream relevant content and, at the same time, generate a conspicuous amount of traffic. However, even the applications already established in the market in audience or ad verification are—with all their inaccuracy—punished with ignorance in most companies—only 34% of companies use ad verification and only 14% audience verification.

A solution can hardly get around independent measurements and audits. By analysing the traffic, the first indications of fraud can be identified:

- High visitor frequency/traffic at night.
- Most visits do not come from the intended target region, despite geo-targeting.
- Traffic peaks always occur at the same time.
- Device distribution that does not correspond to that of the overall population or the target group.

The analyses and prevention of fraud require at least five steps:

1. Quality checks of the websites that media planners have selected for the campaigns can be carried out with the service of *DeepSee.io*, among others. Here, for example, the number of pop-ups, unsolicited redirects, excessive referrals, or ads.txt entries (authorised digital sellers) is checked. ads.txt, as a text file, defines those companies that are authorised to sell their advertising space.
2. Detailed analysis of ads.txt entries is performed. Dubious site operators or marketplaces make incomplete or false entries in the ads.txt or, in the case of marketers, in associated sellers.json files. sellers.json allows standard advertisers to identify and verify those companies that are either direct sellers or intermediaries of the selected digital advertising opportunity to be purchased. This involves verifying the identity of the publishers, including the name, domain name, and seller ID. The time required for this is usually a maximum of 1 week.
3. A brand value check follows, in terms of ownership, funding sources, networking, and verifiability of content, including the presentation of opinions as facts or discriminatory content (e.g. database-supported via providers such as *NewsGuard*).
4. Next comes analytics, for instance with regard to the near time ad fraud rate or viewability (e.g. via *Fouanalytics*). Own analytics tags uniquely identify each instance in terms of time and allow these to be checked for manipulation. Even if it were copied, changed, and repeatedly attacked, only a single page view or impression would be affected—and thus easy to detect and remove.
5. Permanent monitoring and optimisation are performed to detect deviations, for example via dark pools and domain spoofs, from the include list, as well as preferred SSPs and marketplaces are defined.

Whether those pages or apps are served that the customer really booked is determined, among other things, by an *ancestorOrigins* analysis or the measurement of delivery after each winning bid. The read-only property of *ancestorOrigins* is a static DOMStringList that contains, in reverse order, the origins of all predecessors' browsing contexts of the document associated with the specified location object. One uses this string to determine, for example, where a document (banner) is delivered in a frame of a site and on which site it is delivered. In this case, the banner should explicitly not(!) be delivered on gaming, lottery, or game apps (Fig. 10.16).

Fig. 10.16 In-ad measurement, app names, and share of impressions (in %; FouAnalytics; Marketing Tech Monitor 2023)

mobile_app_name 99.8%
5,039 out of 5,047 (11% of 46,608)

Percent	Count	Mobile App Name
16.4 %	826	com.productmadness.cashmancasino
13.7 %	691	com.peoplefun.wordcross
8.5 %	428	net.supertreat.solitaire
8 %	403	com.productmadness.hovmobile
7.6 %	383	com.playstudios.myvegas
6.8 %	342	com.gamebility.onet
4.4 %	223	com.productmadness.tightninglink
4 %	201	com.jellybtn.boardkings
3.6 %	183	com.fluffyfairygames.idleminertycoon
3.5 %	175	com.loop.match3d
3.1 %	155	com.playstudios.mykonami
2.8 %	143	com.mars.avgchapters
1.7 %	84	pch.apps.pchsweeps
1.3 %	67	com.kongregate.mobile.throwdown.google
1.3 %	67	com.pch.lottoblast
1.3 %	66	com.etermax.preguntados.lite
1.2 %	62	com.pixel.art.coloring.color.number
1.1 %	56	com.wooga.pearlsperil
1 %	50	com.jellybtn.cashkingmobile
0.8 %	38	scratch.lucky.money.free.real.big.win
0.6 %	30	com.appcraft.number.puzzle
0.5 %	26	com.peoplefun.wordflowers
0.4 %	18	com.imvu.mobilecordova
0.3 %	17	com.inspiredsquare.blocks

The permanent implementation in the regular process usually requires an independent controlling unit:

- To provide complete site reports from the DSP, including at the domain and ancestor-origin level, planned and ex post.
- To audit digital campaigns not only for brand safety, but also for ad fraud and other KPIs.
- To delete domains, vendors, and publishers who do not meet the requirements from both a brand and performance perspective and
- To create an include-list of sites and partners who are regularly reviewed and fit the brand.

Due to the unique features of campaign structures and media placements, company-specific measurements are usually necessary.

A newer approach is the use of *shared campaign identifiers* (*SCID*), especially to uncover data foibles. These arise, for example, when using audience or context targeting, brand safety or verification tools. Some demand-side platforms (DSPs) also charge for certain features such as optimising the auction mechanism. For example, fees for data usage or brand-safety technology can be charged twice on both the buying and selling sides. Technically, the SCID uses a standard campaign identifier field in the OpenRTB protocol. This is defined by the DSP at the creative level and passed down the chain to the publisher. The ID can therefore be broken down to such an extent that the creative ID is appended to the campaign identifier. In this way, all the fees that were charged along the entire chain become visible. If in doubt, all auction data should be analysed in more detail: SCIDs appear at the end in the log-level data and can be transferred from there to reporting. There are fewer hurdles from a technical point of view than in the bilateral coordination between advertisers and publishers, who must agree with each other on how much initial budget has been allocated for a campaign and how much has finally arrived—which greatly increases the complexity with an increasing number of partners.

References

ANA. (2023). *Retail media networks: A forced marriage or perfect partnership?*, January 2023.

CHEQ. (2023). *The state of fake traffic 2023*, March 2023.

DoubleVerifiy. (2023). *DV brand safety and suitability solution allows major fashion brand to safeguard its brand reputation without limiting scale*, March 2023.

Marketing Tech Summit 2024, September 2023.

Merkle. (2021). *The evolution of retail media networks*, October 2021.

Priebe, A. (2020, May 11). Programmatic Advertising Inhouse bei Vodafone: Das Ergebnis ist noch besser als erwartet; *ADZINE*.

Priebe, A. (2023, February 3). Ad Fraud erreicht Audio. *ADZINE*.

Timm, F. (2020). Optimierung auf falsche Ziele—Branding zu schwierig für die Maschine? *ADZINE*, February 25

Zenith Media. (2022). *Zenith forecasts 4.5% growth for 2023 after 7.3% uplift in 2022, marking continued healthy growth*, December 2022.

On the Way to Composability: The Changing Role of IT

11

11.1 It's About the Integration, Stupid! . . . The (New) Necessity of Integration Architectures

The more individual strategies for building and expanding a technology stack are followed, the more singular, individual applications (best-of-breed), which (should) cover the respective, specific requirements based on the processes in the best-possible way; and composability has been defined as the focus of the IT strategy, the more integration as service-oriented architectures come into play.

With increasing experience and exposure to MarketingTech strategy and implementation, and the associated internal knowledge building, user companies (users) are increasingly focusing on:

- Individual strategies for building and expanding a technology stack.
- Singular, individual applications (best-of-breed), which (should) cover the respective, specific requirements based on the processes in the best-possible way and
- From more comprehensive suite offerings (as a service), selecting and using only those application scenarios that they need to cover their specific requirements.

The consequence of this is that the focus is increasingly on the process and IT integration of the "patchwork" and higher-level IT strategy principles such as cloud first, the automation of business processes, and the establishment of (service-oriented) integration architectures (Fig. 11.1). Accordingly, the ability to integrate with existing applications ranks at the top of the criteria for the purchase of IT applications, after the trustworthiness of the provider and a professional appearance of the seller in the sales process (Gartner, 2023).

The interviews impressively prove—as does project experience—that it is still due to a lack of integration approaches, under the term *Enterprise Application Integration*, that digitalisation and business applications used for this purpose turn to the dark side of MarTech power as a "spaghetti landscape" (Linthicum, 2004).

R. Strauss, *Data-Driven Customer Engagement*,
https://doi.org/10.1007/978-3-031-64295-1_11

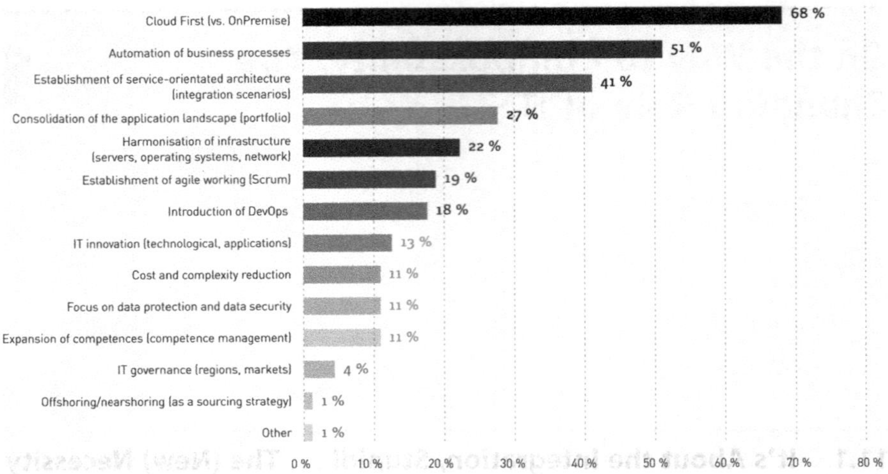

Fig. 11.1 Prioritisation of IT strategy principles as the basis for data and a MarTech strategy (in %, $n = 295$; Marketing Tech Monitor 2022)

The goal is to connect IT processes and support IT applications using defined formats and protocols. Studies by *Gartner* show that 34% of CIOs in the USA are increasingly allocating more budgets to integration technologies, APIs, and API architectures (DiLemmo, 2022). No wonder: even smaller companies with 500 or fewer employees have 172 apps in use, according to analyses by *Zylo* in 2023, and medium-sized companies with 501 to 2500 employees have an average of 255 apps and large companies have an average of 664 SaaS applications in use (Zylo, 2023). On average, more than 6.2 SaaS applications are added to the application landscape every month … despite all efforts to consolidate. Enterprise application integration can take place at the level of data, applications, and processes (Fig. 11.2). A higher-level integration on the third process level builds on other methods for a comprehensive overall integration.

> *The best thing marketers can do to move this forward is to insist upon better integrations in the evaluation of MarTech tools before you purchase (or renew) them*—Scott Brinker (Editor, Chiefmartec) (Brinker, 2021)

A (comparatively simpler) *data integration* makes sense if different applications access the same data and there is or should be only one "truth". For the integration of different applications on the data level, there are options such as (Hohpe & Woolf, 2012):

- *File-based integration*: Data transfer via CSV files between applications, for example via SFTP.

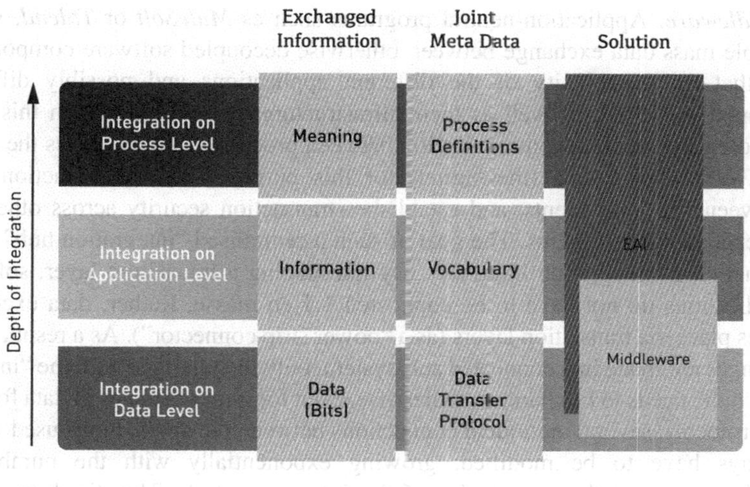

Fig. 11.2 Structure of integration platforms (schematic)

- *Common data storage* (CDS): Data integration via common access to a data warehouse for all data.

An *application integration* is suitable if a common use of a central data storage is not an option and/or an application needs special information from another application to fulfil tasks. For an integration of two applications, there are possibilities such as:

- *Native integration (application-based integration)*: As a standard interface for 1:1 integration between two applications.
- *API (application programming interface)*: Programming interface to exchange information between an application and individual program parts in a standardised way. The transfer of data and commands is structured according to a previously defined syntax. Individual program parts connected via an API fulfil specific functions and are clearly separated from the rest of the application. The communication of individual program modules is only possible via the precisely specified interface. An API can be technically implemented via XML web services or representational state transfer (REST) interfaces.
- *Web service*: Software application that is uniquely identifiable and whose interface can be defined, described, and found as an XML artefact. A web service supports direct interaction between software applications using XML-based messages through exchange via Internet-based protocols.

In addition to the classic peer-to-peer integration methods, several applications can also be connected to each other, for example via:

- *Middleware*: Application-neutral programs such as *MuleSoft* or *Talend*, which enable mass data exchange between otherwise decoupled software components, so that the complexity of the different applications and possibly different technologies used, as well as their infrastructure, remain hidden. In this way, middleware supports communication between processes and organises the transport of complex data (messaging) for this purpose, mediates function calls between the components, and establishes transaction security across otherwise independent sub-systems. The goal of such a centralised "integration hub" is the reduction of integration interfaces. By introducing a translation layer, software applications do not have to be connected 1:1 en masse. Rather, data exchange takes place via translation layers (as a "power strip connector"). As a result, when changes are made in a connected sub-system, only the interface with the "integration hub" needs to be changed. Otherwise, even for minor changes in data formats or protocols, several individual connections between the applications used would always have to be modified, growing exponentially with the number of applications and the complexity of the integration task. The disadvantage of middleware in practical projects is usually the size and cumbersomeness of the middleware—the complexity of the *n:m* individual connections between software components is usually reflected (even if only disproportionately) in the complexity and size of the required middleware and corresponding matching patterns.
- *Business bus or integration platform*: The functionality of a so called business bus is characterised by the possibilities of data exchange—analogous to the middleware—and additionally the mapping and control of processes along the value chain (Enterprise Architecture Integration (*EAI*) *backbone*).

A *process integration* focuses on the integration of all business processes across several functional domains and applications. Middleware does not enable process integration but can be extended by a dedicated process management tool.

Over the last few years, *Integration Platform as a Service* (iPaaS) has gained prominence with a variety of automated tools across public and private clouds. Typically, an iPaaS platform offers pre-built connectors, business rules, maps, and data transformation tools (The Art of Service, 2021; Churchville & Bigelow, 2021). Some iPaaS providers offer custom development kits for connecting legacy applications, mobile services, social media platforms, or master data management, such as *Integrate.io*, *Appypie (connect)*, *Uipath*, or *Zapier*. In most cases, an iPaaS provider hosts application servers and infrastructure data and provides integration tools and middleware that help developers create, test, deploy, and manage software in the cloud. Data exchanges can be configured to be multi-tenant via pre-built connectors and business rules. Most iPaaS platforms and tools support the same methods for integrating a wide variety of applications, platforms, and systems, even if they do not all share the same integration patterns (Fig. 11.3). Common iPaaS features tend to include:

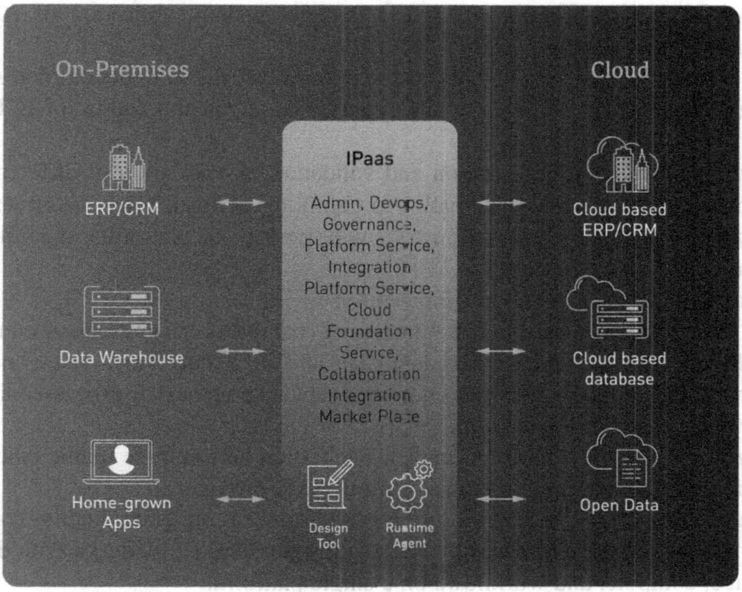

Fig. 11.3 Basic principle of integration Platform as a Service (iPaaS, schematic; Marketing Tech Monitor 2023)

- Ease of use in platform deployment, data integration and processes for managing multiple applications.
- Scope of integration tools and pre-built data connectors.
- Scope of support for SaaS and locally hosted applications.
- Support for different protocols such as HTTP, FTP, Open Data Protocol, and Advanced Messaging Queuing Protocol.
- Flexibility to create custom connectors and change access mechanisms.
- Ability to process, cleanse, and transform data in formats such as XML and JSON.
- Support for processing even large-scale data operations.
- Support for real-time processing and batch data integration.
- Monitoring of failures, latency, resource utilisation, and workflow performance and
- Security mechanisms for access control, data encryption (providing integrated monitoring, threat detection, and observation tools), and single sign-on.

iPaaS frameworks allow the seamless integration of applications across multiple clouds and between cloud and legacy applications. The spectrum of application scenarios is correspondingly diverse:

- *Application-to-application integration*: Pre-configured interfaces across different applications.

- *Microservices integration*: Automatic generation and publication of APIs to support microservices.
- *B2B integration*: Integration with different third parties, without common API or custom integration, while enforcing security standards and audits for B2B data flows.
- *Data integration*: Administration and validation of translation of different data formats in real time as an alternative to traditional scripted batch data transfers.
- *Platform integration*: Integration of a wide variety of platforms, regardless of location and cloud concept.
- Internet of Things (*IoT*) *device integration*
- *Big data integration*: Implementation of complex integrations around BI, machine learning, or AI, such as data lakes and cloud data warehouses, analysis, and visualisation tools, as well as time-critical data that must be processed in large quantities and with low latency.
- *Multiple cloud integrations*: Complex integration between the public cloud and services with other clouds, such as various SaaS providers.
- *Integration event streams*: A central platform to integrate highly complex interactions in an event-based design of microservices (serverless), with diverse storage, compute, and workflows on a single platform.

iPaaS providers can be broadly divided into four groups for this purpose:

1. Older integration vendors that have adapted their applications for cloud services, such as *Microsoft*, *Tibco*, *OpenText*, *Informatica*, *SnapLogic*, or *IBM*. Other providers such as *Oracle* or *SAP* have developed their own iPaaS to handle end-to-end integrations for large (ERP) platforms.
2. A second group of iPaaS providers has emerged as cheerleaders of the cloud era, such as *Jitterbit*, *SnapLogic*, *Boomi*, *Talend*, or *MuleSoft*. The focus is on the use of innovative technologies such as artificial intelligence or real-time data analytics. More recently, these providers are increasingly supporting low-code programming.
3. A third group of providers uses innovative integration methods: *Integrately*, *Zapier*, *SyncApps*, or *Notion*, for example, offer "one-click" and low-code workflow integration, regardless of whether it is a 1:1 integration or more complex application landscapes. Vendors such as *Martini* and *Tray.io* take an API-centric approach to automating workflow integrations, manual processes or even the implementation of specific business rules. Many of these newer providers are available as free open-source versions.
4. The fourth group of large cloud platform providers offers a wide variety of native integration tools for applications, data, and services (also from third parties), such as *Amazon AppFlow*, *EventBridge* and *AWS Glue*, *Azure Logic Apps* and *Data Factory*, as well as *Data Fusion* and *Data Flow* in the *Google Cloud*.

The focus is always on deciding whether local or cloud integration is primarily required, or whether there is a need to support more decoupled workloads, such as via service-oriented architectures and microservices (Fig. 11.4). Pretty often,

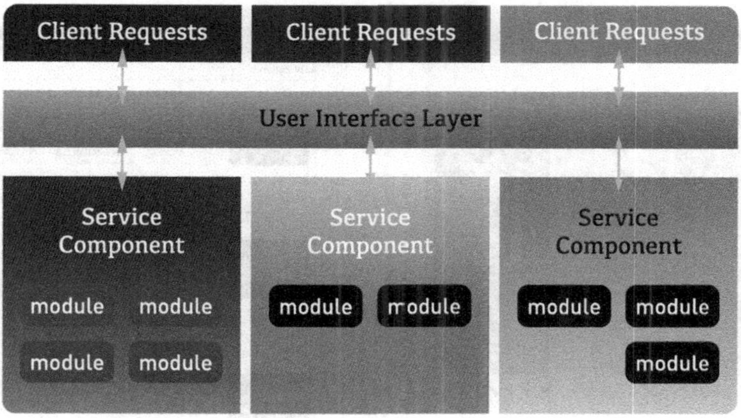

Fig. 11.4 Scheme of a microservices architecture (See also Richard, 2015)

integration via iPaaS is cheaper than via Enterprise Service Bus (ESB), offers more scalability and allows integration outside the company's own boundaries.

The focus is on the establishment of a *service-oriented software architecture* as the ideal model for the integration of fragmented MarTech landscapes. Here, existing IT components such as databases, servers, and websites are encapsulated as services and coordinated (orchestrated) in such a way that their services can be combined into higher-level services and made available to other organisational departments or external customers. They are encapsulated as services, and all are provided with APIs for internal or external access. Service-oriented architectures are thus a deliberately chosen structure for integrating applications, in that the complexity of the individual applications remains in the background behind the standardised interfaces (APIs). By composing individual services of lower abstraction levels, IT services of higher abstraction levels can be created quite quickly, flexibly and with the greatest-possible reusability. SOA compositions should avoid "single points of failure", otherwise the entire "lasagne" composition collapses. What is required for implementation—especially in heterogeneous, long-standing, and complex IT application landscapes between marketing, sales, the call centre (service ticketing), and e-commerce—is decoupling, service connection, and optimisation in several steps. For this purpose, a *microservice* is defined as a software architecture that can be implemented with web services, while *web services* are only one technology (of many) for providing services via the web or HTTP (Fig. 11.5).

Service-oriented architectures are therefore a deliberately chosen structure for integrating applications, in that the complexity of the individual applications remains in the background behind the standardised interfaces (APIs). By combining individual services of lower abstraction levels, IT services of higher abstraction levels can be created quite quickly, flexibly and with the greatest-possible reusability. Taking this concept further: in a composable architecture, especially for omnichannel business models, services (headless) are abstracted from their underlying applications and used in the cloud via web-based interfaces (REST) (Gartner,

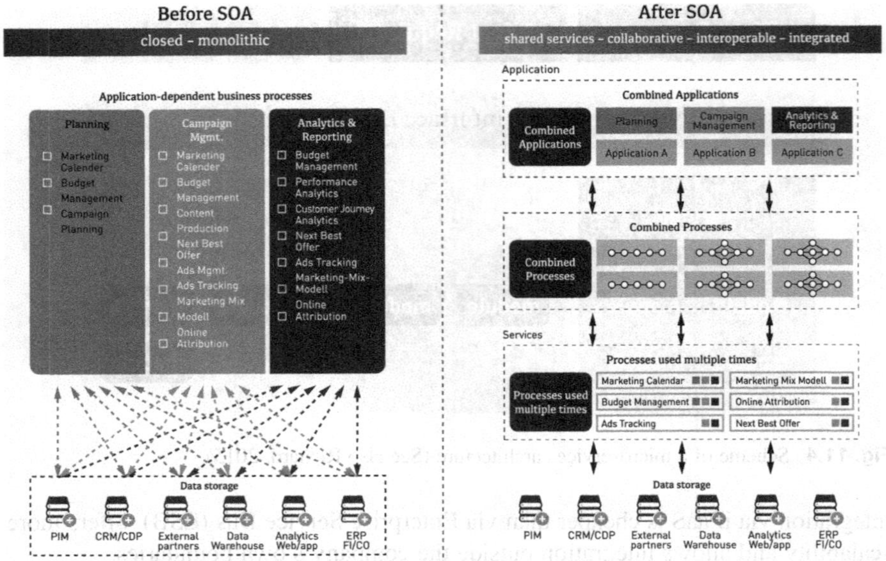

Fig. 11.5 From a monolithic, complex "spaghetti architecture" to clean "lasagne layers" as an integrated service-oriented architecture (SOA)

2020). The *composable architecture* thus also allows the possibility of person-to-system integration, in which all services are integrated in a common user interface, as well as B2B integration across company boundaries with partners. Based on the microservices, API-first, cloud-native, headless (MACH) principles, the saviours promise nothing less than more speed, higher flexibility, and long-term cost efficiency.

A complete composable concept consists of a collection of loosely coupled services that communicate with each other via standardised interfaces and simple protocols. In a monolithic approach, however, front-end and back-end components are tightly coupled. "Composable" is thus a more comprehensive approach than "headless", where, for example, in the case of "headless commerce", the front-end of a web shop is decoupled from the backend. Headless architectures enable companies to innovate faster in the front-end, while composable architectures represent a fully customisable system platform. The advantage of the composable architecture is that the necessary changes, due to changing customer preferences, can be implemented by changing a specific microservice instead of having to redesign an entire application. Small, independent components (microservices) can be operated in a composable architecture in the cloud in an elastically scalable manner (DevOps). According to *Gartner*, companies that follow a composable approach can implement new functions 80% faster and usually have a usage-based pricing model.

The *disadvantage* of implementing a service-oriented architecture is that more initial effort is required than with the development of monolithic program structures due to the decoupling of services. Both the initial and the permanent orchestration are time-consuming because processes and interfaces must be recorded exactly, and all dependencies must be considered. This applies to a composable approach:

- *Complexity*: Composable architectures (may) consist of many independent components that need to communicate and interact with each other, which can also make troubleshooting difficult.
- *Maturity*: Is unsuitable for digitally immature organisations.
- *Portfolio management*: Requires managing diverse providers and maintaining a critical "connective tissue" between them.
- *Security*: Communication between the different components can be a gateway for external attacks.
- *Performance*: Communication between the different components takes time and resources and thus comes at the price of performance. Insufficient planning or implementation of the communication between the components can lead to latency problems and bottlenecks.
- *Availability*: If one of the components is not available, this can affect all applications and lead to downtime (monitoring and redundancy strategy).
- *Know-how*: Usually requires an experienced IT development team.
- *Architecture*: Requires a modern technology architecture as a basis and does not mix well with proprietary legacy systems.
- *Component dependency*: Can lead to strong component dependency; if one component is changed or updated, this can affect other components.
- *Sprawling architectures*: This often tempts users and companies to build elaborated things (like interfaces) ... simply because they can.

SOA compositions should avoid "single points of failure", otherwise the entire "lasagne" composition collapses. For this to be implemented—especially in heterogeneous, long-established, and complex IT application landscapes between marketing, sales, the call centre (service ticketing), and e-commerce—it is necessary to decouple, service connect, and optimise in several steps. The definition of a business blueprint includes organisational units, master data, and business scenarios, down to the level of individual process steps.

Especially in complex integration projects, joint process and IT modelling is performed using a domain model (Moser & Riha, 2019; Vernon, 2013). With a *domain model* (e.g. at *Volkswagen*), the IT applications, the basic concepts, and elements of a domain as well as their relationships are modelled (Fig. 11.6).

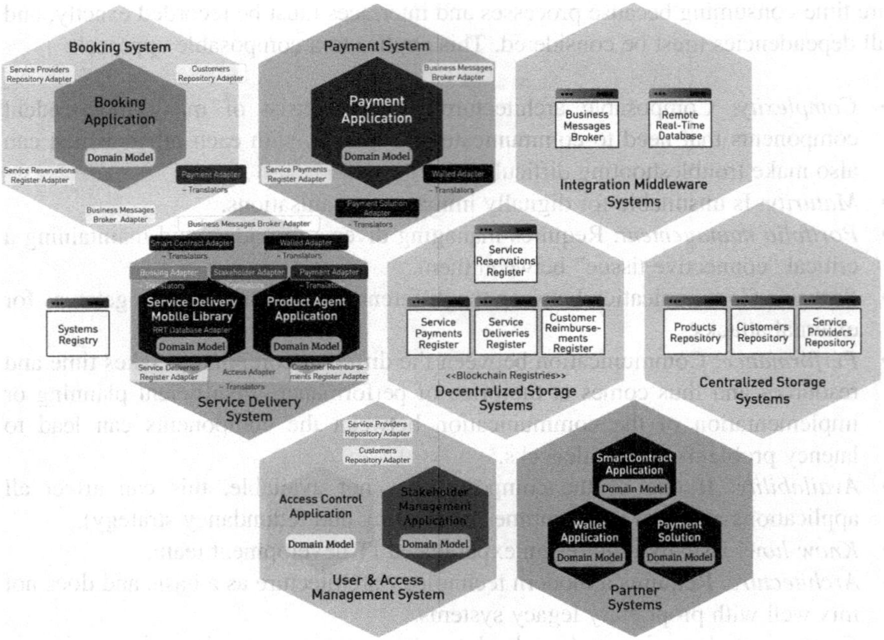

Fig. 11.6 Domain-driven design in the IoT application example (Marketing Tech Monitor 2022)

Domain modelling and the *architecture* based on it are characterised by (Fig. 11.7):

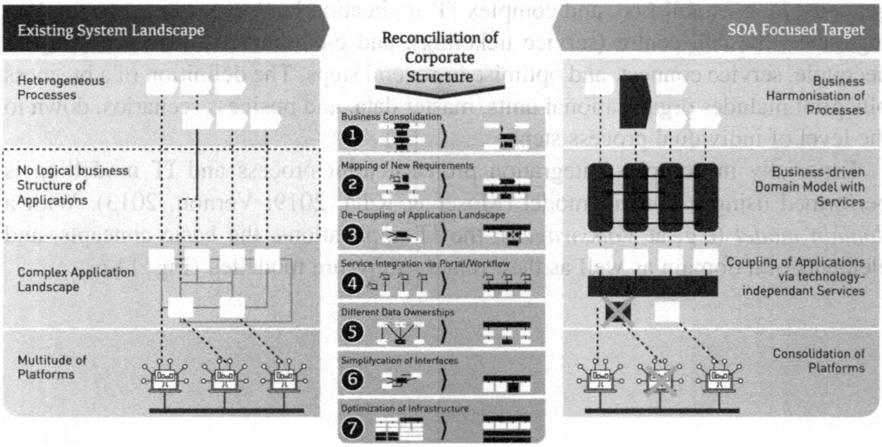

Fig. 11.7 Procedure for developing and implementing an integrated, service-oriented IT target architecture

- *Professional consolidation*: Includes the vision of the professional necessity and process steps as well as the associated goals. This context overview provides a comprehensive overview of all models, their respective boundaries, and interfaces, as well as functional overlaps. In this way, the context boundaries of a domain become apparent, for example in relation to the team assignment, the purpose of use, or the underlying database schemata. For example, a sub-domain "Customer Relationship Management", the capability "Business Partner Maintenance", and the function "Create Business Partner" are uniquely assigned to the domain "CRM". Other parts of a domain model serve to support this core functionality or to enrich it functionally. This provides the basis for
- *Mapping of new requirements*: New requirements are raised by the department and recomposed as "services", for example, and must always be assigned to a domain and function. Only in this way is it possible to prevent functional-procedural redundancies—and thus subsequent redundancies in the IT applications used.
- *Decoupling the application landscape*: Dependencies and redundancies in the application landscape are eliminated to be able to further optimise the IT applications and their assignment to functional domains and process steps.
- *Service connection via portal/workflow*: The integration of different processes and applications can take place via uniform user interfaces (e.g. portal) or via workflow, whereby the primary focus should be on avoiding double entries and media discontinuities along the business process. All changes to a domain model and the applications involved must be continuously coordinated or integrated with each other and tested (automatically) against the existing technicality.
- *Separation of data sovereignty*: Data responsibilities are precisely assigned and the existing—mostly database-driven—workflows are replaced.
- *Simplification of interfaces*: Interfaces in the application landscape are standardised and the overall complexity is reduced for, finally, ...
- *Optimisation of the infrastructure*: Harmonising the underlying infrastructure, including the hardware platforms, and operating systems involved.

Agile working methods and DevOps (i.e. the interlocking of software development and IT operations) are already common practice in many companies. In future, DevOps will only be a component of an overarching XOps landscape for all applications up to and including control and security (SecOps). The usual sprints and iterative progress will be replaced by a continuous optimisation process.

In reality, the implementation of the IT strategy often fails because of the project organisation (lack of experienced project managers), the interface between business and IT (use cases, derivation of precise requirements) and also the conceptual planning and implementation of integration scenarios (Fig. 11.8). The project managers are sometimes described in the interviews as "greenhorns" who roam through the world of MarTech and SalesTech like *Sam Hawkens* once roamed through the Wild West. Only: *Sam Hawkens* was funnier.

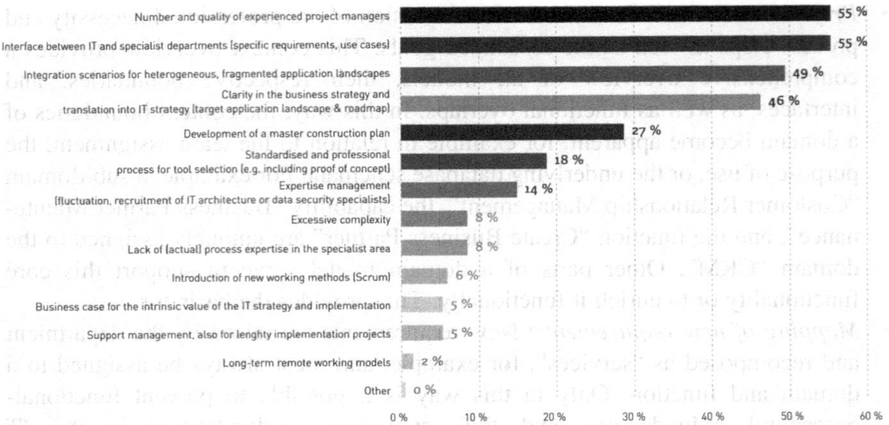

Fig. 11.8 Challenges in implementing the IT strategy in the next 2–3 years (in %, $n = 295$; Marketing Tech Monitor 2022)

The journey of the integration architectures represents—like the drive-through at *McDonald's*—the volatility of modern MarTech developments. The (integration) marriages in the drive-through chapel are of a fast-moving nature thanks to AI, microservices and gradually establishing blockchain application scenarios (Fig. 11.9) (Illa, 2018). The development is thrusting towards "self-defining integration", oscillating in perspective between the shelf life of *Frank Sinatra's* marriages (less than 2 years) and that of *Britney Spears* (13 h).

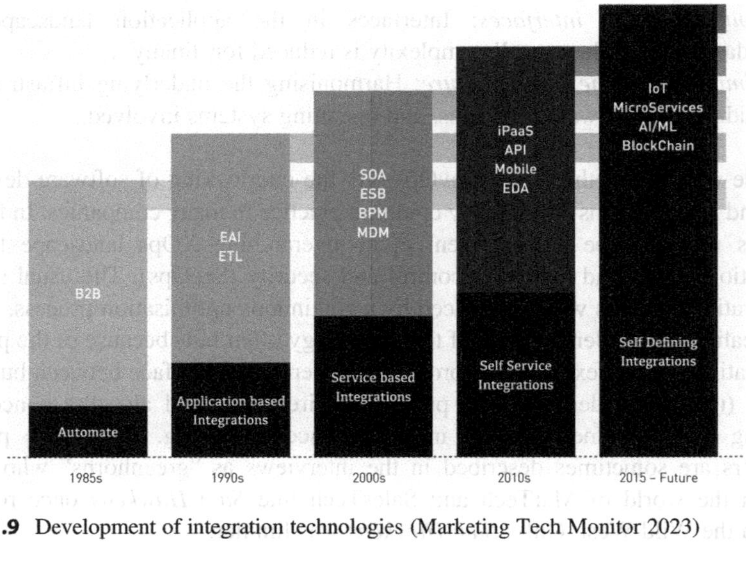

Fig. 11.9 Development of integration technologies (Marketing Tech Monitor 2023)

11.2 Pay as you Use: Shift in Paradigm in Software Licensing

Licensing models for IT applications are a combination of different parameters that determine how software can be used. Licensing models combine different licence attributes into logical groups that determine the form in which a protected application is provided and used. These attributes are generally defined properties (incl. name, data type, and possible scope of use) of a licence. Since the mid-1980s, licensing models have gradually moved from *perpetual licensing* to user-based licensing and, subsequently, through a myriad of different combination forms in the direction of feature or volume-based licensing:

- *Public domain*: Freely available, without limitation.
- *Demo/trial licensing (time-limited licence)*: For in-depth evaluation, for example in the context of a proof of concept (POC).
- *Lesser General Public Licence (LGPL)*: Developers can include open-source libraries in the source code, which in turn can be used under any other licence type. The LGPL-applicable component should be made available under the same LGPL licence.
- *Perpetual licensing*: One-off purchase (acquisition of ownership), possibly extended by an annual maintenance fee. Advantage: stable pricing, no surprises due to price changes (e.g. in the subscription model), mostly on premise. Extensions as flexible subscription models (e.g. *Microsoft Office*).
- *Named user (single-user licence)*: The number of licences purchased is based on the number of users specified by name (via login). Simple to administer, more complicated in multi-user application environments (e.g. with shift work) and changing requirements over time.
- *Concurrent user (multi-user shared licence)*: Multiple licences for all employees using one licence code (analogous to metered licences for the number of log-ins). Disadvantage: software providers carry out periodic surveys, whereby the licences used are compared with those acquired in accordance with the software licence agreement, and demand relicensing if necessary.
- *Network licensing*: Based on a client/server architecture, whereby licences can be activated in a sub-network. Licence requests and the request for a licence code from the clients are answered by the server.
- *Feature-based licensing*: Licensing based on the features purchased for use with the respective licence code. Licences can be personalised according to the needs of the individual employee or user.
- *Floating-feature licensing*: Several licences are purchased, and the simultaneous use of certain features by users is restricted. Advantage: certain features can be flexibly selected and used according to need.
- *Volume-based licensing*: Licensing is dependent on the number of business partners (entries in the database), possibly extended by application scenarios used such as pipelines (in feature-based licensing, e.g. with *HubSpot*). *Oracle CX Unity* calculates features per user (master IDs are the named user);

additionally for the CDP, *Intelligence IQ* is required, which is calculated per number of sessions (i.e. "traffic-based") (Fig. 11.10).

Application Scenario	Provider (examples)	Licence Model	Pricing Scheme
Marketing automation	*HubSpot* (Marketing Hub)	• Baseline of licence costs for required features in 4 packages (Free, Starter, Professional, Enterprise) – incl. unlimited number of users. • In addition, there are staggered, volume-dependent additional costs per package, depending on the number of "marketing contacts" – e.g. Professional includes 2,000 such contacts at no extra charge.	• "Starter Marketing Hub" from €41/month (€497/year) • "Enterprise Marketing Hub" from €2,944/month (€35,328/year) • "Starter Marketing Hub" from €41/month (€497/year)
CDP	*Salesforce*	• 3 licence editions (Corporate, Enterprise, Enterprise Plus) • Depending on volume/needs (e.g. number of profiles, messages, segment publication)	• "Enterprise" with 500,000 profiles and 150 million messages for $50,000/month (approx. €550,000/year)
Data warehouse / Data lake	*Google BigQuery*	• Analyses, incl. SQL queries or scripts • Data storage (loading and exporting is free of charge) • 2 price models: On-demand according to the number of bytes or monthly/yearly flat rate	• Short-term storage for $0.02 per GB/month • Flat rate from $ 1,700/month for a dedicated reservation of 100 slots (~€19,000/year)
	Microsoft Azure	• In *Azure Data Lake*, volume-dependent costs for data storage, storage capacity reservation and transactions (write and read) • Versions: Premium, Hot, Cold, Archive	• Data storage "Hot" for $0.0184/GB • Storage capacity reservation "Cold" (1 year) for $840/month for 100 TB • Read operations (every 4 MB, per 10,000) "Hot" for $0.0052 and "Archive" for $6.50

Fig. 11.10 Examples of licensing in marketing automation, CDP, and data warehouse/data lake (status as of May 2022, Marketing Tech Monitor 2022)

Traditional licensing models limit flexibility on the company side and tend to lead to over-licensing (frequency of use vs. costs) or, in the case of concurrent users, to painful re-licensing in the event of measurements. CRM suites or CDPs are often over-licensed by up to 25–30%, partly motivated by

- The over-ambitious initial business case at the start of the project
- A clever packaging of the side of the vendor as "Marketing Cloud"
- or partly simply due to the dollar signs in the eyes of the vendor's sales force staff

From the providers' point of view, overly rigid licensing models inhibit the adoption rate in the market. The availability of usage data by means of log file analysis via self-developed scripts or dedicated software licence management tools (SLM) allows detailed tracking of functions used and the incurred expenses (e.g. for internal service charging).

There will always be a need for on premise(s) technology instances or some permutation of that and thus one-time licence sales (tied to annual or longer-term maintenance contracts so there is recurring revenue even in on premise [s] licence sales). But the cloud and subscription-based models are defining how technology systems (and much more) are being licensed and are the most prevalent model now and will be going forward. In fact, it, too, is advancing from what was Software as a Service (SaaS) to the early stages of XaaS (Everything as a Service) (again too broad a subject to go into here). Going forward, this will only get to be a bigger and bigger and, ultimately, totally dominant model for how software licences are sold. Software has, for the most part, been redefined as a service, and this will only solidify over the years— Paul Greenberg (Author of *CRM at the Speed of Light*)

On this basis, newer metered/consumption-based licensing models have emerged, such as: (See also Jiang et al., 2007)

- *Classification model*: Extension of the named user model. Here, users are divided into usage categories with different rights and access to functions (features) or also the number of sessions within a period. Actual use is recorded via monitoring and true ups are tracked.
- *Time-based pay-per-use*: Licensing based on the actual usage based on the usage log file analysis (following usage time or CPU cycles).
- *Transaction/traffic-based pay-per-use*: Focus on use (either as an e-commerce transaction as with *Shopify* or as data volume traffic as with *Tealium*), without considering the duration.

Changing business requirements are mapped in *remix licence models*. The licensing of a technology allows access to multilayered application scenarios, with simultaneous flexibility in the number of licences (remix):

- *Static remixing*: Periodic analysis of usage patterns and adjustment of licensing.
- *Continuous real-time remixing (token-based licensing)*: Instead of purchasing individual features in different usage scenarios, a generic token feature is purchased. A value of tokens is attributed to each feature, which is then billed based on usage via log file analysis.

Other models such as *technology partnerships* ("all you can eat") provide for a longer-term cooperation with unlimited access or a (multi-year) development partnership with the provider based on (fixed) licence fees. Sometimes there are also mixed models with a fixed (annual) baseline and usage-based billing.

I think the biggest question that I constantly get, ... when is the software industry going to change its pricing model? ... I mean, subscription models are hard. And, constantly I get asked the question, when will this industry move to a pay-as-you-consume model? And it's a valid question at the end of the day. Why should in this day and age, when you look at how things are built, if I use the hyperscaler, I get billed for what I consume, and it's pretty darn accurate down to the second, usually? But if I use an SFA app, I'm getting charged a subscription. And depending on which company it is, it could be anywhere from $150 to $800 a month. And the question really is a valid one. When will the industry change? Why can't I just pay for what I use at the end of the day? ... Subscriptions are killing because customers can't afford to keep paying the subscriptions, especially when their business is faltering. Why does the industry make me pay from the time I sign the contract? Why is it not that I'm paying from the time I go live? These are valid questions that I think the software industry really has to do some soul searching on (Howlett, 2020)—Bob Stutz, (former President CRM Siebel/Oracle, Microsoft, Salesforce and SAP)

The next evolutionary leap in software licensing will be *pay-as-you-use* (usage-based). In SaaS, providers must go this way. Per-usage services increase the complexity of management on the client side, which must be tracked via scripts or dedicated SLM tools such as *Slascone*, *Revenera*, *Zylo*, or *10Duke*. It is worth noting that indirect time recording and tracking must be checked, at least in Germany according to the Works Constitution Act (subject to approval by the works council, Section 87, Paragraph 1, No. 6 of the BetrVG), as well as the difference between pricing according to the price list and discounts as a "street price" in the range of 30–45%.

References

Brinker, S. (2021, April). Wait, more MarTech tools create more manual tasks?! *Chiefmartec*.

Churchville, F., & Bigelow, S. J. (2021, June). What is iPaaS? Guide to integration platform as a service. *TechCrunch*.

DiLemmo, L. (2022, March). Why the business automation market is poised to explode. *MarTech*.

Gartner. (2020, June). *Composable commerce must be adopted for the future of applications*.

Gartner. Digital Markets 2023 SMB Software Buying Trends Survey.

Hohpe, G., & Woolf, B. (2012). *Enterprise integration patterns. Designing, building, and deploying messaging solutions*.

Howlett, B. (2020, October). SAP's Bob Stutz rips off the enterprise software pricing Band-Aid as DSAG reports significant redlines in member revenue. *diginomica*.

Illa, P. K. (2018, July). What's next for the next-generation iPaaS? *DZone*.

Jiang, B., Chen, P.-Y., & Mukhopadhyay, T. (2007, November 1). *Software licensing: Pay-per-use versus perpetual.* SSRN: https://ssrn.com/abstract=1088570

Linthicum, D. S. (2004). *Next generation application integration. From simple information to web service.*

Moser, C.; Riha, K. (2019). Digitalisation of information-intensive logistics processes to reduce production lead times at ENGEL Austria GmbH: extending value stream mapping with subject-oriented business process management. In N. Urbach & M. Röglinger (Eds.), *Digitalisation cases. How organisations rethink their business for the digital age* (pp. 293–312).

Richard, M. (2015). *Software architecture patterns.*

The Art of Service. (2021). *IPaaS a complete guide.*

Vernon, V. (2013). *Implementing domain-driven design.*

Zylo. (2023, April). *Drive business impact with insights from the 2023 SaaS Management Index.*

12 The Organisation Remains the Digital Construction Site

12.1 Navigating Over the Competency Gap

Adequate organisational structures and high-performance teams are needed to ensure cooperation and coordination along the web-based value creation processes, as well as the willingness to innovate. Some of the interviewees repeat that "getting/enhancing talented people to do our job!" is their top priority. Increasingly, a leadership style is required that is characterised by inspiration, reputation, and a high degree of cooperation, up to the maximum level of a "leaderless organisation" (holacracy). By being open to the use of newer tools, leaders demonstrate that they themselves want to use these tools, be more agile, network within the company and let employees participate more in processes.

The disillusionment after an initial "digital drunkenness" as well as the migration of employees of traditional companies to "start-up cultures" causes organisational performance to attract increasing attention as a "digital permanent construction site". While classic structures are each geared to a status quo and optimised, new organisational forms try to make change and adaptability the structural core and to develop maximum innovative power. To prevent its own marginalisation, an "adapt or die" approach applies to the marketing function more than ever before. But there is no "one master solution".

Against this backdrop, a trend towards *insourcing* has been observed for about 2 years now, whereby specialised competences are built up in separate departments. The reason: many of the topics such as data analytics or MarTech/SalesTech are gradually becoming a mandatory *core competence* that must be built up in-house immediately. At the same time, *Gartner* predicts that more than half of the companies will tend to further centralise over the next 2–3 years against the background of the required (scarce) competences—60% of the marketing organisations have already centralised some or all functions in the pursuit of operational efficiency (centralisation).

In other words, the future of the marketing organisation is likely to be centralised, with a high degree of internal vertical integration and centralised provision of

R. Strauss, *Data-Driven Customer Engagement*,
https://doi.org/10.1007/978-3-031-64295-1_12

processes and IT platforms—with all the implications for both the internal organisation and external partners (agencies). The focus is on end-to-end processes for efficient customer interaction and collaboration with IT (Fig. 12.1).

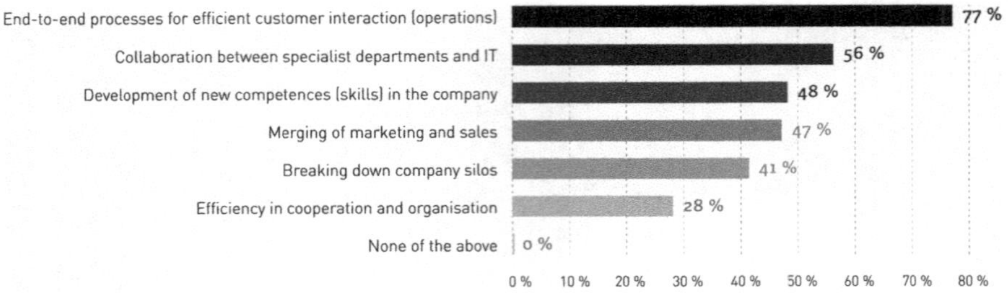

Fig. 12.1 Challenges in the marketing organisation for the implementation of MarTech/SalesTech and data-driven marketing (in %, $n = 295$; Marketing Tech Monitor 2022)

Adequate organisational structures and high-performance teams are needed to ensure cooperation and coordination along the web-based value creation processes, as well as the willingness to innovate. Some of the interviewees repeat that "getting/enhancing talented people to do our job!" is their top priority. Increasingly, a leadership style is required that is characterised by inspiration, reputation, and a high degree of cooperation, up to the maximum level of a "leaderless organisation" (holacracy). By being open to the use of newer tools, leaders demonstrate that they themselves want to use these tools, be more agile, network within the company and let employees participate more in processes. "User-centricity" thus refers not only to (external) customers, but also to the (internal) company organisation. This implies a higher proportion of self-organisation and a "fail faster mindset", instead of ancient Roman autocracy and a strict alignment with rigid hierarchical bureaucratic structures.

At the same time, the role profiles and competences sought are becoming more differentiated. The starting point is the definition of the strategic focus (Fig. 12.2). Here, a clear distinction must be made between a more market-oriented commitment with a customer focus (*external orientation*) and the goal of improving the company's internal processes and stakeholders (*internal orientation*). In parallel, it must be determined whether the focus is more on improving the efficiency of existing internal and external business relationships in the sense of *process orientation* (e.g. workflows, customer journeys) or whether the focus is more on technologies (*technology orientation*). The orientation along the four fields is not exclusive, but rather overlapping and possibly also become complementary over time. For example, the start in MarketingTech can be characterised by an external orientation and process focus, while experience and the building up of know-how in a second wave can lead to a more internal orientation regarding technologies.

Fig. 12.2 Characteristics of marketing technology roles according to *Brinker* (Marketing Tech Monitor 2022) (See also Brinker, 2020)

Examples of different skillsets and associated archetypes can be found, for example, in:

- *Brand/Demand Builder*: "Marketers" or "marketing mavens" who regularly use MarTech to complete their tasks within campaigns and programs. Typical role title: marketing manager. Technical skills: Spreadsheet, HTML/CSS, SQL.
- *Operations Orchestrator*: "Maestros" or "infrastructure architects" design and control workflows and reports, define the requirements on the business side and the MarketingTech development plan. Key decision-makers in the buying centre for MarketingTech. Typical role title: marketing operations, CRM power user or admin, marketing planning and steering. Technical skills: Spreadsheet, HTML/CSS.
- *Analytics Architect*: "Modeller" or "data divas" who dive more comprehensively into data and application structures, for example also in the environment of business and customer intelligence (data quality). Typical role title: marketing analyst, data scientist, data engineer. Technical skills: SQL, JavaScript, Python.
- *Marketing Maker*: "Makers" develop applications (increasingly as no-code). Typical role description: web/app developer, marketing engineer. Technical skills: HTML/CSS, JavaScript, SQL, PHP.

In some cases, these archetypes are supplemented and expanded by specific forms, for example as: (Brinker, 2014)

- *Content Curator*: Focus on content creation and curation, social media marketing and PR.
- *Experience Engineer*: Focus on in-store experience, mobile app development, e-commerce technologies, and product/service design.

- *Media and Marketing Analyst*: Identification of target groups and markets, media/marketing mix modelling.

Newly established *customer experience managers* are positioned between maestro and marketer because they act both in the direction of "product development/maestro" and "brand builder campaigning". The competency gap is usually defined as the lack of staff with experience in the areas of . . .

- . . . *maestro* (i.e. MarTech/building planning and requirements engineering)
- . . . *modeller* (i.e. analytics and data sciences) . . .

. . . and lamented accordingly. In general, employees cite staff shortages significantly more than the respective marketing managers and Board members, especially in the service sector. Feedback from headhunters shows how conflicting the balancing act is between personnel needs and executive search consultants the actual approach to recruitment. On the one hand, there is a desperate need for employees with specific skills, but at the same time there is no willingness to pay them accordingly or to pay bonuses due to unfavourable geographical location ("bush allowance"). In the operational design, "MarTech experts" are still increasingly required in addition to data scientists. *Action heroes* are being sought to fix things. The challenge is to prevent new hires from being "streamlined" by corporate culture and leadership behaviour . . . and to forcibly reproduce adapted "corporate soldiers" or "clone warriors". Top-of-mind is building new competencies (skills) in the company (71%), followed by end-to-end processes for efficient customer interaction in marketing operations (57%)—which are also said to have the highest risk (64%).

While the industrial age was characterised by "authoritarian leadership through hierarchical power", the demands on leadership are changing dramatically today. In the mechanistic and deterministic image of leadership and organisation, employees were in demand who showed up on time, completed their (largely) predetermined tasks in a disciplined manner and exchanged as little as possible with colleagues in carefully delimited cubicles. The goal of organisational design measures in leadership and corporate culture is to ensure organisational flexibility. The focus is on increasing the speed of decision-making for operational and strategic tasks that arise. In summary, the following can be identified as guidelines and parameters of leadership:

- The *delegation* of responsibility to the lowest-possible levels (self-organisation).
- The flexible and autonomous assumption of roles and tasks by all employees (especially *self-coordination*).
- The rapid formation of teams and *cross-functional interaction* across hierarchical levels and functional areas (e.g. marketing, sales, service).
- A culture that *allows for mistakes*.
- Incentive systems for *internal entrepreneurship*, for example in the form of bonus payments or stock option programs, which are directly linked to the success of marketing activities or the success of the company.

The focus of organisational design is thus on setting conditions for the realisation of self-organisation, such as planning and information systems, wage systems or the management structure. Hierarchical superior roles usually suffer a lasting change in the implementation of self-coordination compared to previous possibilities of influence and design. The leadership of self-organising units changes to the role of a "facilitator" along the value creation and learning processes and is limited to setting the formal conditions à la

Leading others to lead themselves (Manz & Sims, 1989).

This implies a higher proportion of self-organisation and a "fail faster" mindset instead of ancient Roman autocracy and strict alignment with rigid hierarchical bureaucratic structures. In contrast to the hierarchical coordination mechanisms often found, self-organisation opens a variety of options for the realisation of digital organisations and a "digital culture":

- The relief of the otherwise necessary hierarchical coordination and thus the reduction of formal, vertical communication processes.
- Increasing motivation on the part of employees, stimulating additional joint learning processes ("organisational learning").
- Increases the flexibility of the organisation.

The practical implementation of self-organisation takes different forms (Fig. 12.3):

- *Self-leadership*: Employees' responsibility extends not only to the correct execution of (hierarchically) assigned activities, but also to the permanent monitoring and control of task execution along the overarching processes. Associated with this is the self-coordination between different members of a work group on the distribution of tasks within the group.
- *Self-structuring*: Organisational members also have the possibility to independently define and design the organisational structure as well as the interfaces to other groupings (e.g. IT or category management).
- *Unit that sets its own goals*: Realistically, this is reserved for participative goal setting, usually at the management level.

Since the 1960s, concepts and analyses of leadership and organisational development, such as organisational learning or cross-functional teamwork, have increasingly found expression in everyday business life. Agility is currently the greatest hope when it comes to countering the dynamics of disruptive change. In the latest *State-of-Agile Marketing Report*, 51% of companies state that they have implemented elements of agile working (Fryrear, 2021). But the well-known agile methods and processes such as Scrum, Kanban, and Design Thinking only address the team level—the underlying organisational models remain in hierarchical agony.

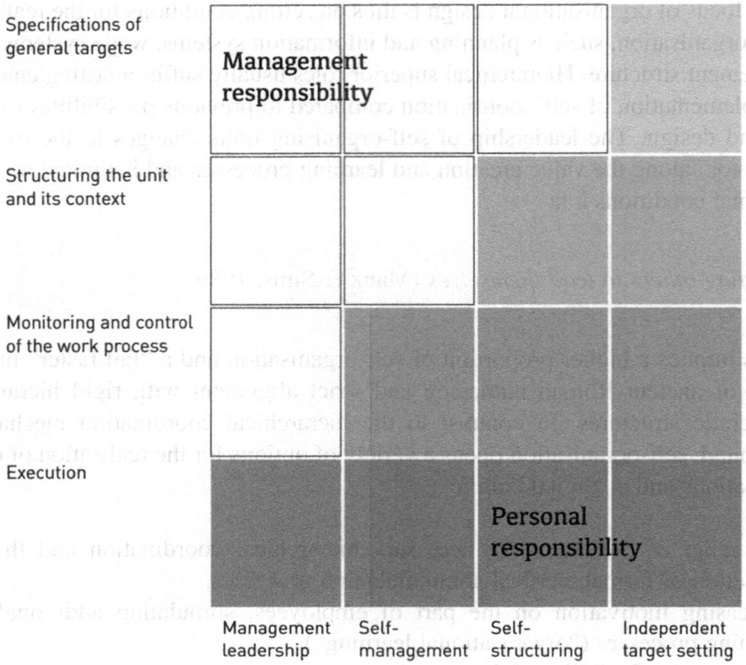

Fig. 12.3 Forms of self-organisation according to Hackman (1986) (Marketing Tech Monitor 2022)

A mixture that leads to problems. No matter how well teams can work in an explorative manner and complete their tasks in a self-organised way, there is bound to be friction with structures and management routines that still follow an old pattern, including silo thinking and coordination deficits. This puts the marketing organisation and the motivation of the employees to the test. Agile organisational models are therefore in demand. But their essential feature is to dissolve rigid hierarchies. In many companies, however, these are too deeply anchored to be easily abolished without overburdening those involved and the organisation. In addition, there are areas in many companies that still need hierarchies to function. Quick and radical approaches are therefore hardly an option ... even though "wannabe new work apostles" like to call for them again and again.

The mantra of agile working is currently the greatest bearer of hope when it comes to countering the dynamics of disruptive change. *Agile Marketing* is based on principles such as self-organisation, learning through mistakes, simplicity, and transparency (Agile Marketing Manifesto, 2021; Ackermann, 2021; Strauß, 1996). But agile methods and processes such as Scrum, Kanban, and Design Thinking only address the team level, the underlying organisational models remain in hierarchical agony. It often turns out that:

- After a phase of being an "agile saviour", agility is not or cannot be a panacea for everything.
- Often, "agility" is intuitively equated with "chaos", although agile collaboration methods also require a high degree of "ownership".
- It becomes clear that agility has a lot to do with "mindset", and "mindset" is often confused with "method" (e.g. Scrum).
- Self-organisation and fast processes tend to be counteracted by existing management and incentivisation processes and systems.
- Agile tends to be understood as "chic" and "hip," without being based on systematic success criteria à la OKR.
- The focus in the implementation of agile principles is mainly on daily stand-ups, user stories, and retrospectives (Fryrear, 2021).
- Agile principles can hardly be taught in a one-day seminar, and the learning success can hardly be measured only by the volume of sticky notes.

For the implementation of principles of self-organisation in the form of an "agile organisation", the Scrum method already outlined has been used for some years in the context of IT project management. The goal is the fast, cost-effective, and high-quality completion of a project or the completion of a product that is to follow a vision formulated at the beginning. *Scrum* thus represents the operationalisation of a self-organising, agile organisation as a counter-design to the command-and-control organisation in which employees are to be given the most precise work instructions possible. Instead, Scrum relies on highly qualified, interdisciplinary project teams that are given clear objectives but are solely responsible for their implementation. The motto is to establish "tents instead of palaces" or rather "small speedboats in the form of SWAT teams".

Agile marketing planning, for example, cascades through goals (wildly important goals [WIGs], derived from OKR), road maps, and initiatives to the "last responsible moment" as a decision and calibration of planning and activities in the context of daily stand-ups (Fig. 12.4). More traditional instruments in planning set the framework, which is flexibly controlled in detail using agile methods.

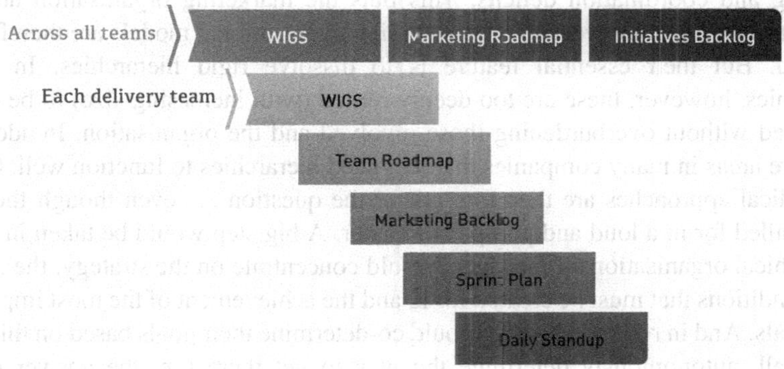

Fig. 12.4 Agile marketing planning for the "last responsible moment" (Marketing Tech Monitor 2022) (Ackerman, 2022; Gartner, 2022)

They are looking for action heroes with new, digital competences—who are supposed to fix it, but without any influence or budgets, and who thus run the risk of getting caught between the worlds. The challenge: to prevent new hires from "streamlining" in line with the corporate culture and lived leadership behaviour—and forcibly reproducing adapted "corporate soldiers" or "clone warriors", for which a change in leadership culture seems necessary. It is even more astonishing that managers themselves—as well as companies—make comparatively little effort to build up the necessary competences, for example through *training*. Again, the topic is rarely addressed systematically and in a structured way in training courses. In some cases ("fig leaf"), trainings take place, but then more on "fancy lifestyle" topics à la "digital life". The almost schizophrenic chicken-and-egg problem: the exchange of experiences needs experienced and competent discussion partners, who, however, can hardly exist without the appropriate system and the teaching of specific competences. In the estimation of the decision-makers, further postponement of the unanimously proclaimed need for training goes hand in hand with the danger of recklessly squandering existing competitive advantages.

The agilisation of the organisation is seen very differently. While management assesses the degree of agilisation much higher than the employees (rating of 4.2 by management compared to 5 by employees, with 10 being the best value), companies that have already successfully implemented data-driven marketing and sales are also presented here as those that want to actively take up the basic organisational requirements (rating of 5.8 compared to 3.6 in other clusters). Groups have already taken up this trend to a much greater extent, mostly due to a greater involvement with modern organisational concepts and a more extensive portfolio of service providers in this topic environment. The pure B2C sector is clearly lagging (rating of only 4.8). Agility is currently the greatest hope when it comes to countering the dynamics of disruptive change. But the well-known agile methods and processes such as Scrum, Kanban, and Design Thinking only address the team level—the underlying organisational models remain in hierarchical agony. A mixture that leads to problems. No matter how well teams can work in an explorative manner and complete their tasks in a self-organised way, there is bound to be friction with structures and management routines that still follow an old pattern, including silo thinking and coordination deficits. This puts the marketing organisation and the motivation of the employees to the test. Agile organisational models are therefore in demand. But their essential feature is to dissolve rigid hierarchies. In many companies, however, these are too deeply rooted (with increasing size) to be easily abolished without overburdening those involved and the organisation. In addition, there are areas in many companies that still need hierarchies to function well. Quick and radical approaches are therefore out of the question … even though they are often called for in a loud and pompous manner. A big step would be taken in many hierarchical organisations if managers would concentrate on the strategy, the necessary conditions that must be created for it, and the achievement of the most important KPI goals. And in return, the teams could co-determine their goals based on this and, above all, autonomously determine the way to get there (i.e. the answer to the question "*Which measures will get me to the goal*"?). The interference of managers in the "how" at the operational level often makes agile work drift towards chaos.

	Total	Successful companies (leaders)	Stuck in the middle	Non-successful companies (followers)
"Rather Yes" (top 3 boxes)	10 %	25 %	2 %	1 %
"Rather No" (bottom 3 boxes)	42 %	15 %	57 %	56 %

Fig. 12.5 Active personal involvement in restructuring marketing processes in the sense of agilisation (in %, $n = 195$; Marketing Tech Monitor 2022)

Successful companies are also characterised here (Fig. 12.5) by the fact that they . . .

- . . . actively shape further agilisation and make considerable efforts to overcome organisational silos (25%).
- . . . manage to create a mindset of a future-oriented "we" in their own organisation, beyond the individual "me" function optimisation and the protection of existing, long-established power bases.

The question about the organisational attachment of all MarketingTech and optimisation topics is mostly answered with a staff position at the marketing management or the top management level (management, Board). From the respondents' point of view, this is the only way to ensure that:

- Access to the necessary resources (e.g. budget, personnel, especially availability of internal knowledge carriers) is ensured.
- The strategy for digitalisation with the help of MarTech is bindingly specified (i.e. successful MarTech implementations are based on a clear, binding, formal, and hierarchical decision) and
- Overarching guidelines and standards (e.g. master construction plans, blueprints for the uniform integration of different application scenarios, the joint use of platforms/synergies) are followed.

The market research company *Gartner* predicts that more than half of the marketing organisations will tend to decentralise their execution over the next 2–3 years. Decentralised structures are most likely to make change and adaptability the structural core and to develop the maximum innovative power. In other words, the future of the marketing organisation is likely to be decentralised in operations, with a high degree of internal vertical integration (insourcing) and the centralised provision of processes and IT or MarTech platforms, or as decentralised self-service MarTech.

> *The technology must be a basic structure used across the whole organisation. This is central, not individual solutions* (Head of Activation Marketing, Strategy & Infrastructure, Food Retail)

In addition to its own performance, the efficient management of the interfaces to other areas comes into the limelight as a field of activity. If the challenge of the interface to IT (focus topics: development planning, integration scenarios, availability) is already legion, this is extended by the context-related management of the interface in the direction of controlling (focus topics: savings, cost efficiency).

> *Success control is central. First, the methodology must be in place, then you can measure in a structured way. Only a common, harmonised database and consistent dashboards can bring added value to what is just floating around. A lot of things just don't seem measurable at first ... but working on this will also be a new role for the CFO*—Andreas-Christoph Hofmann (Vice President Marketing & Product/CMO, Hyundai Motor Europe)

Diffuse interests and undifferentiated tasks make interaction difficult in many cases. It depends on outstanding individuals, whether they are young talents, experienced employees, the CEO themself, or the CMO. Again, what is needed are "*action heroes*" who can fix things. In the operational design, "MarketingTechnology experts" are increasingly required in addition to data scientists. Again, the challenge is to prevent new hires from being "streamlined" and (having to) adapt in the medium term due to the lived leadership behaviour and corporate culture. The analysis of current job advertisements shows that the sought-after role profiles mostly abstract to five different roles (Fig. 12.6):

Role	Most important fields of activity
MarketingTech Specialist	• Deployment and management of existing MarTech • Design of the MarTech stack – development planning and road map for MarTech transformation • Development/consolidation of use cases / requirements • Carrying out fit gap analyses based on defined requirements from the business units and selection/recommendation of new MarTech products
Roll-out Manager	• Roll-out planning, implementation, quality assurance and success assurance of new MarTech in the organisation (local, global) • Project management, resource planning, monitoring of project progress and milestone achievements. • Communication and change support in the organisation, incl. training, support, and implementation support, User Acceptance Testing)
Data Manager (Data Engineering)	• Organisation and management of all data from different sources, thereby standardisation of data (e.g. definition, syntax, semantics) • Procurement and merging (matching/stitching) of data, setting up of data pipelines and storage in central data repositories (data warehouse, data lakes) as well as preparation for extraction. • Oversees the development and use of data and systems, considering data quality and data security
Data Analyst (also Business Analyst)	• Preparation of basic statistics, descriptive evaluations based on structured data (DWH) • Evaluates existing data (history) for the businsess department on a routine or ad hoc basis. • Applications of Tableau, Excel, PowerBI, SQL, Google Analytics, etc.
Data Scientist	• Application of statistics, ML algorithms, analysis, and mathematics based on unstructured data (e.g. DWH, data lake) • Supports the department in gaining explorative knowledge and solving problems and in interpreting data and its significance (including future-oriented forecasts) • Use of Python, R, hadoop, AWS, Google Cloud, Azure, etc.

Fig. 12.6 Role profiles of currently most sought-after roles in MarketingTech

12.2 Pretty Best Friends (The Untouchables) ... Marketing Meets Information Technology

To paraphrase Woody Allen, collaboration between business and the IT department is often like a marriage: "trying to solve the problems together that you can't solve alone". The marriage between marketing and sales as business departments and IT therefore remains a challenge in any case. Couple therapy clearly starts here with a gloomy assessment of the state of domestic co-operation at the first session on the therapist's couch. Almost half of the companies rate the collaboration as "rather bad" and lament the tribal feuds and petty squabbles that have usually been lovingly cultivated over the years.

One reason for the often-tense relationship between IT and business departments lies in a "disconnect" on several levels—only in abstraction do we recognise the energetic elemental forces that are act in opposition here:

- *Time horizon*: Marketing and IT usually work according to different time schedules. IT usually works on a six-month project time frame (e.g. containers in development). The success/non-success only becomes apparent after project completion. In contrast, marketing and sales work in a quarterly cycle and measure results continuously.
- *Objective*: From the IT perspective, multilateral security is the focus ... both in the implementation of the projects and in terms of security architecture and guidelines. From the marketing and sales perspective, the focus is on generating business results along the customer journey.
- *Process alignment*: No integrated process between business and IT; the larger the organisation, the more both functions are driven into a competitive mode—chasing budget supremacy, reputation, and decision-making power as the dominant driver, with unclear roles and responsibilities in terms of "*what*" should be done and "*how*" something should be implemented.
- *Syntax meets semantics*: Different and non-comparable metrics deepen the divide and separation. If "SQL" in marketing stands for "Sales Qualified Lead", the same acronym in IT represents a structured database query ("Structured Query Language").
- *"Problem bear meets actionist"*: Striving for successful implementation of projects and compliance with security standards usually comes across as a trip to the dentist and the IT manager as a "problem bear" for the business department, focused on timely implementation. The interaction sometimes bears the traits of a real-life satire.

Loosely based on *Woody Allen*, the cooperation between the functional areas often presents itself like a marriage: "*Marriage is trying to solve the problems as a couple that you don't have alone*". The marriage between marketing and sales as business departments and IT thus remains—analogous to the couple *Jennifer Lopez* and *Ben Affleck*—a challenge in any case. After all, the narcissist loves himself above all. Couple therapy clearly starts here with a gloomy assessment of the state of

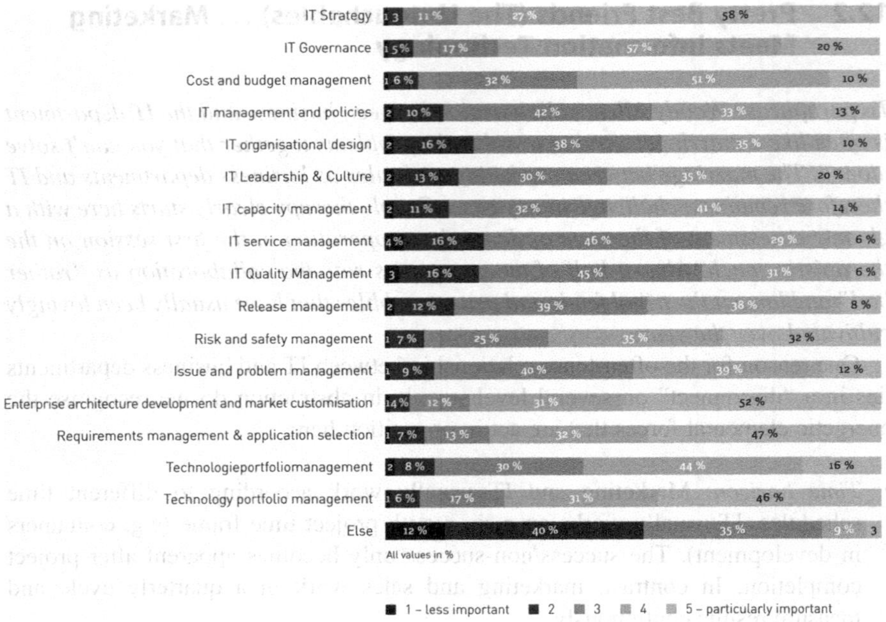

Fig. 12.7 Most important issues in collaboration with IT that require clear, shared goals, transparency, and common processes and strategies (in %, $n = 356$; Marketing Tech Monitor 2023)

domestic cooperation at the first session on the therapist's couch: almost half of the companies rate the collaboration as "rather poor" and lament the tribal feuds and petty squabbles that have usually been lovingly cultivated over the years. Consequently, the focus of cooperation lies in clear, common goals along the IT strategy, in enterprise architecture development and the fit of selected tools as well as the successful implementation of applications (Fig. 12.7). Especially for the cluster of "managers", implementation is the biggest challenge, while the "newcomers" do not have the topic on their radar at all. Cynically formulated (following the French philosopher *Nicolas Chamfort*), this cluster is apparently characterised by: "*Stupidity is the most peculiar of all diseases. The sick person never suffers from it*".

The focus is on end-to-end processes for efficient customer interaction and collaboration with IT. For the cooperation between marketing/sales and IT, the establishment of a "project management couple" has proven to be efficient across various projects. The business department and IT manage the project with joint, cross-functional responsibility. The advantage is the shared responsibility for both the "what" and the "how".

> *Why should I waste my time with IT when they don't have any suggestions for solutions and tend to present themselves as problem bears ... similar to the data protection officer?*—CMO of a Fast Moving Consumer Goods company

Here, too, risks of insufficient cooperation crystallise in areas such as IT strategy, architecture, and application implementation (Fig. 12.8). The internal perception is always shaped by IT leadership and culture.

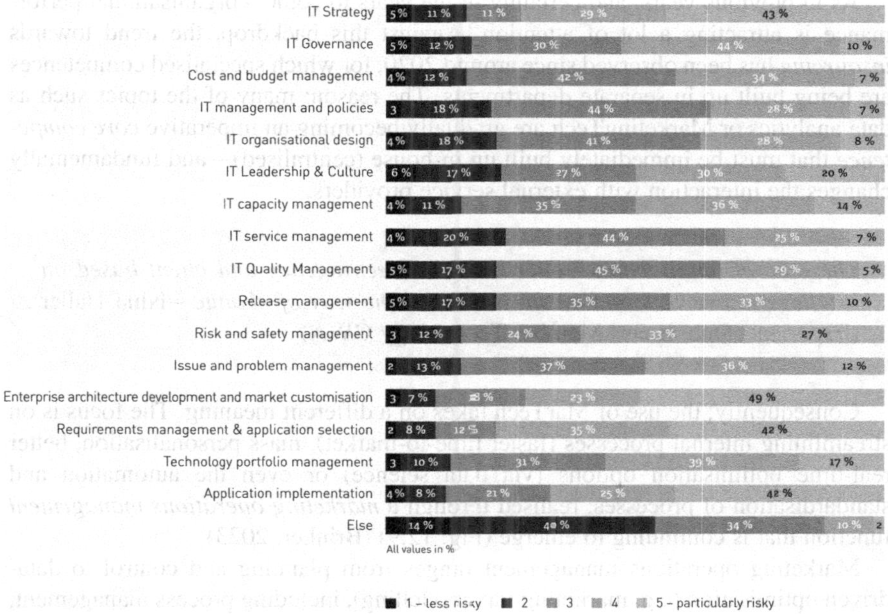

Fig. 12.8 Biggest risks for the further development of the marketing organisation considering the cooperation between marketing/sales and IT (in %, $n = 356$; Marketing Tech Monitor 2023)

A lack of common "ability to discuss" does not lead to greater efforts being made to build up the necessary competences, for example through *training*. The almost schizophrenic chicken-and-egg problem also persists: the exchange of experience requires experienced and competent interlocutors, who, however, can hardly exist without a corresponding system and the teaching of specific competences. This applies to the basic cooperation between the business areas and IT, successful cross-functional projects as well as the effective use of applications once they have been introduced. A tried-and-tested method in the context of "marriage counselling" is the *Enterprise Architecture Management* (EAM) approach. The focus is on the utilisation of IT in various facets along all value creation processes, which requires consistency between corporate and IT strategy.

12.3 Marketing Operations Management: Expedition into New Organizational and Role Model Worlds

Many of the topics such as data analytics or MarTech are gradually becoming an imperative core competence that must be immediately built up in-house (centralised)—and fundamentally changes the interaction with external service providers. Consequently, the use of MarTech takes on a different meaning. The focus is on streamlining internal processes (faster time-to-market), mass personalisation, better real-time optimisation options (via data science) or even the automation and standardisation of processes, realised through a marketing operations management function.

As in previous years, and certainly in the years to come—organisational performance is attracting a lot of attention. Against this backdrop, the trend towards *insourcing* has been observed since around 2020, for which specialised competences are being built up in separate departments. The reason: many of the topics such as data analytics or MarketingTech are gradually becoming an imperative *core competence* that must be immediately built up in-house (centralised)—and fundamentally changes the interaction with external service providers.

> *The time of unidirectional interaction between agency and client based on briefings is over ... and mostly stands in the way of change*—Nina Haller (ExperienceOne, Board Member Technology GWA)

Consequently, the use of MarTech takes on a different meaning. The focus is on streamlining internal processes (faster time-to-market), mass personalisation, better real-time optimisation options (via data science) or even the automation and standardisation of processes, realised through a *marketing operations management* function that is continuing to emerge (Fig. 12.9) (Brinker, 2023).

Marketing operations management ranges from planning and control to data-driven optimisation (e.g. marketing mix modelling), including process management, control of new product launches, customer journey management (incl. customer activation), and the development of the application landscape such as the implementation of a CDP or a CRM system based on use cases.

Tasks such as data-driven optimisation, smooth cooperation with IT (e.g. via

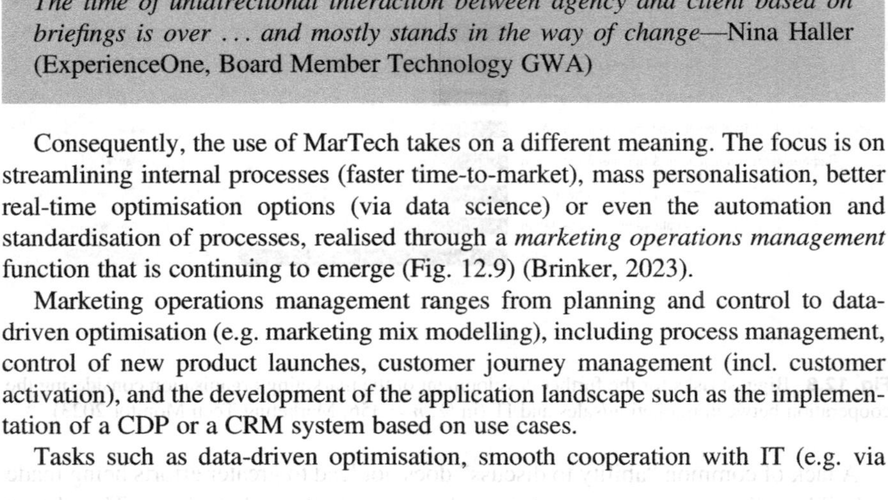

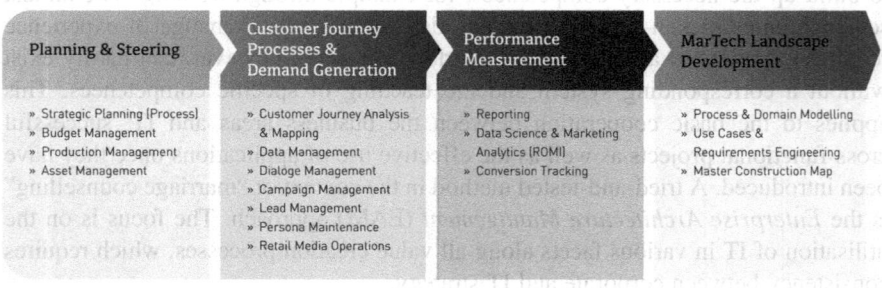

Fig. 12.9 Range of tasks in marketing operations management

requirements engineering), increasing the number of customer interactions or implementing systematic data management represent the latent background variables for the implementation of MarTech, bundled in a dedicated marketing operations area (Fig. 12.10). Organisations with a dedicated marketing ops team show an up to 41% higher revenue per employee.

Rotated Component Matrix[a]	Data Scientist	Risk and security management	Leadership, Culture and Value Management	Customer interaction (it security)	Business Value Management	the right method and collaboration models in requirements management	Change Agent	Data management, -maintenance analysis	Quality Management
Retail Media: Major Challenges: I cannot assess	-0,786	-0,353	-0,004	0,118	-0,054	-0,021	-0,086	-0,082	-0,023
Features important in marketing optimization programs: Availability of sales (promotions/prices) vs. media insights (touchpoint allocation)	0,582	-0,215	0,044	-0,015	0,215	0,102	0,296	0,218	-0,051
Key features in marketing optimization programs: Ability to perform frequent model updates (e.g., monthly)	0,449	0,043	0,143	0,196	0,373	-0,097	0,047	-0,145	-0,037
Retail Media: Major Challenges: Knowledge Transfer: Low knowledge among internal as well as external stakeholders	0,396	-0,156	-0,175	0,367	0,032	0,216	0,011	0,289	0,297
Retail Media: Utilization of marketing collaborations between brands and online retailers: Pure data exchange (Data Only)	0,387	0,299	0,178	0,218	-0,120	-0,073	0,373	0,232	0,182
Greatest risks in the collaboration between marketing and IT: Requirements management & application selection	0,387	0,379	0,349	0,366	0,047	0,100	0,096	0,166	-0,078
Retail Media: Major Challenges: Unclear situation regarding data protection (GDPR)	0,009	0,710	-0,092	-0,129	0,151	0,132	-0,011	0,072	0,072
Challenges in cross-functional collaboration with other departments: Integration of marketing and customer service	-0,192	-0,567	-0,026	-0,101	-0,146	0,272	-0,034	0,045	-0,020
Greatest risks in the collaboration between marketing and IT: IT strategy	0,446	0,500	0,344	0,346	0,145	0,029	-0,083	0,054	-0,077
Greatest risks in collaboration between Marketing and IT: Issue and problem management	-0,044	0,406	0,175	0,235	0,124	0,369	0,267	0,107	0,024
Greatest risks in collaboration between Marketing and IT: Risk and security management	0,051	0,377	0,357	0,127	0,115	0,016	0,284	-0,004	0,114
Focus for marketing organization in 2023: Change management	0,081	-0,105	0,696	0,129	0,037	0,051	0,189	0,055	-0,027
Focus for marketing organization in 2023: Project management	0,030	0,180	0,600	0,217	0,109	-0,003	0,020	0,114	0,175
Focus for marketing organization in 2023: Leadership, culture, and value management	0,067	-0,089	0,502	-0,200	-0,002	0,462	0,138	-0,141	0,100
Greatest risks in the collaboration between Marketing and IT: Enterprise architecture development and MarTech adaptation	0,273	0,301	0,428	0,309	0,214	0,245	0,136	0,178	-0,072
Goals of the technology and data strategy: Create higher frequency in customer interactions	0,098	-0,058	0,094	0,655	0,156	0,081	0,103	-0,052	-0,006
Retail Media: Major Challenges: Retailers are unwilling to share their data with third parties	0,228	-0,161	-0,18[illegible]	-0,634	-0,035	0,103	-0,278	-0,190	-0,154
Important features in marketing optimization programs: Dashboard solution	-0,008	0,200	-0,065	0,155	0,750	-0,020	0,077	-0,141	0,081
Important features in marketing optimization programs: Integrated simulation and optimization tool	0,149	0,020	0,054	0,029	0,725	-0,011	0,062	0,164	-0,088
Focus for marketing organization in 2023: Business value management	0,001	0,072	0,206	-0,163	0,415	0,282	0,207	0,344	0,102
Focus for marketing organization in 2023: Performance management	0,310	0,343	0,266	0,293	0,392	-0,148	0,207	0,078	0,146
Correct methods and collaboration models found in requirements management	0,095	0,029	0,21[illegible]	0,082	0,118	-0,764	0,017	0,136	-0,138
Greatest risks in the collaboration between Marketing and IT: IT leadership and culture	0,173	0,047	0,238	0,243	0,062	0,655	-0,101	0,169	-0,061
Focus for marketing organization in 2023: Campaign management, operations management	0,021	0,152	0,11[illegible]	0,068	0,195	-0,056	0,679	-0,019	0,111
Focus for marketing organization in 2023: Other	-0,038	0,139	0,12[illegible]	-0,022	0,091	0,134	-0,541	-0,280	0,466
Greatest obstacles in change management: The necessity and successes of a change are less tangible (compared to IT expenditures, for instance).	0,175	-0,076	0,09[illegible]	0,144	0,067	0,143	0,363	-0,040	0,024
Forecast increase in marketing budget next year: Data management, maintenance, analysis	-0,024	0,000	0,015	-0,002	0,022	0,068	0,054	-0,846	0,028
Utilization of AI/Machine Learning: ROI optimization / media optimization / cost optimization	-0,023	0,030	0,055	-0,094	0,101	0,022	-0,160	0,022	-0,766
Focus for marketing organization in 2023: Quality management	-0,100	0,045	0,257	-0,316	0,211	0,169	-0,265	0,156	0,474

Fig. 12.10 Rotated factor loading matrix (according to principal components/Kaiser method, variance explained 57.3%; Marketing Tech Monitor 2023)

Feedback from HR consultants shows how conflicting the balancing act is between staffing needs and the actual approach to recruitment.

12.4 Change Management: Colorful Sticky Notes, Quick Failures?

Inadequate or missing change management is one of the main reasons for the failure of projects to implement data-driven customer interaction. It is not about sticking post—it's on in an agile process, but rather about anchoring new structures, processes, and systems in an organisation in the long term—and learning from mistakes. Resistance to the implementation of data-driven marketing & sales usually has many different reasons, from macroscopic (organisational) to microscopic motivations.

Project experiences and studies show that insufficient or missing change management is one of the main causes for the failure of projects in the field of data-driven marketing and sales using MarTech (Cameron & Green, 2012). The change process towards data-driven marketing in most organisations is subject to considerable fluctuations and phases. After a phase of initial information about upcoming changes and the subsequent shock, after the phase of denial come insight and realisation, which slowly increase until finally new structures and processes are accepted (Fig. 12.11).

Stay curious! … and: don't give up … but also don't underestimate the change process!—Thorsten Schapmann (Global Media Director, Beiersdorf)

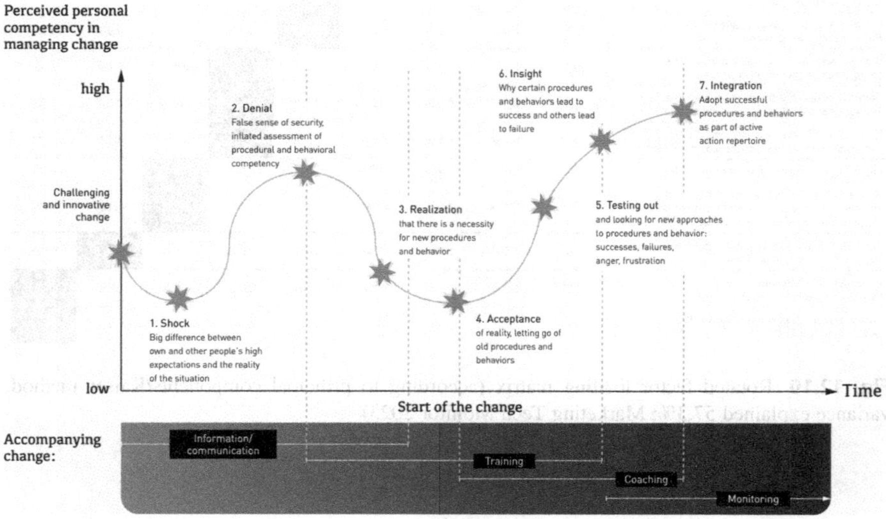

Fig. 12.11 Change management cycle for implementing change (Marketing Tech Monitor 2022)

Depending on the phase, the changes should be accompanied by different instruments in a comprehensive change management system. This is not about the atmospheric sticking of sticky notes in an agile process, but about sustainably anchoring new structures, processes, and systems in an organisation … and also learning from mistakes (Hofert & Thonet, 2019). The more companies have dealt with the challenges on the way to data-driven marketing in terms of content and concept—and have already had to accept setbacks in partial projects—the more they emphasise the need for active and permanent change management and learning from mistakes. They take a page out of *Voltaire's* book: "*Love truth, but pardon error*".

This is not about the atmospheric sticking of sticky notes in an agile process, but rather about sustainably anchoring new structures, processes, and systems in an organisation—and learning from mistakes (Hofert & Thonet, 2019).

Because it is the (systemic) relationship of the parts to each other, their interaction, that drives a certain dynamic and a development that produces undesirable results or errors. If you want to change this, you first must understand this interaction. (Göpel, 2022a)

The most important obstacle to successful change management and the implementation of data-driven marketing is the focus on individual topics combined with a lack of understanding of the systemic interaction (77%), followed by a lack of know-how and understanding of the underlying content (46%), which is then difficult to communicate in a tangible way (25%, Fig. 12.12).

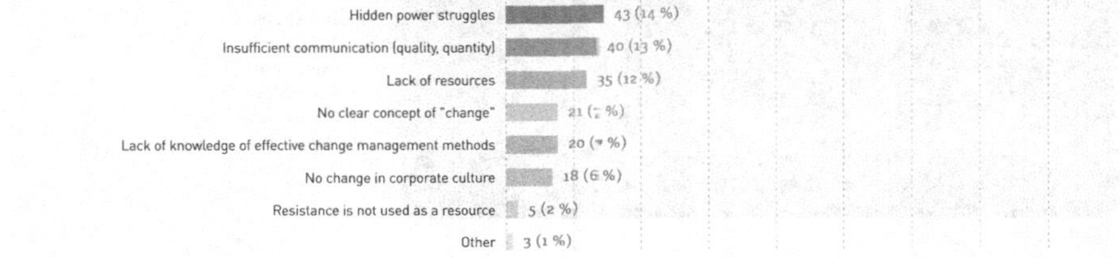

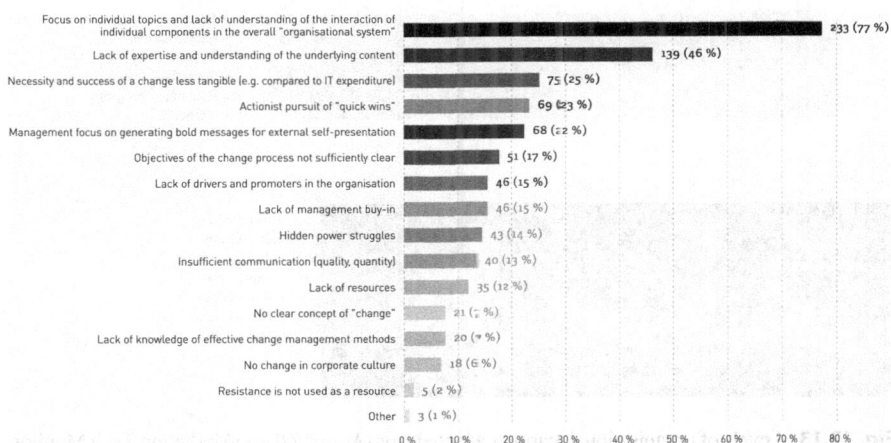

Fig. 12.12 Biggest obstacles in change management (in %, multiple responses, $n = 356$; Marketing Tech Monitor 2023)

The first step is not only to react at an early stage, but also to really understand the problem (in terms of its content). (Göpel, 2022b)

Failure by design: the required learning process thus already fails in understanding the problem or the necessity in the content (conceptually).

The understanding of a company as a system rejects singular, linear models of thinking in which attempts are made to analytically break down the necessary change into individual parts and then "conjure up" the implementation with a few (actionist) measures . . . while "*Once Upon a Time in the West*" by *Ennio Morricone* plays softly in the background.[1] The entropy of the system prevents simple solutions . . . by definition.

> *We break it down into its building blocks and believe that if we have understood all the individual parts well or make them 'whole', the big whole will behave like the sum of the parts . . .* (Göpel, 2022a)

As tempting as "quick wins" may sound . . . they usually only serve as Viagra for the construction of Potemkin villages. Or to put it in the words of former *Lufthansa CEO Wolfgang Mayrhuber*, "*Too much incense blocks the saint's view of what is essential*".[2]

The *resistance to change* that arises in the context of the introduction of MarTech and organisational change usually has complex reasons. At the (microscopic) level of *individual employees*, phenomena can be found such as (Fig. 12.13):

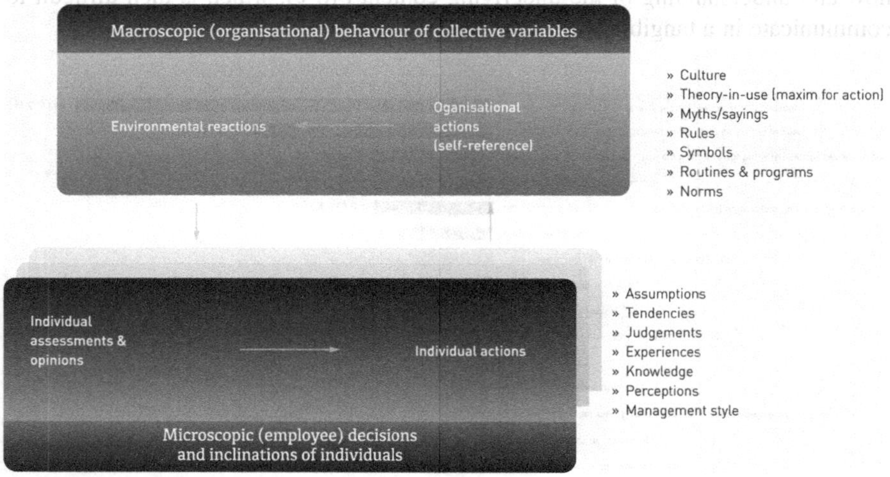

Fig. 12.13 Levels of organisational learning adapted from *March/Olsen* (Marketing Tech Monitor 2023) (March & Olsen, 1976; Neck & Manz, 1994; Strauß, 1996)

[1] Nonaka & Takeuchi (2007); Daft & Huber (1987).

[2] Deutscher Marketing Tag (2008).

- (comfortable) ingrained habits.
- A selective perception of information that does not fit into the usual frame of reference.
- A high dependence on the values, attitudes, and beliefs of the most important reference persons (opinion leaders).
- A social-psychological fear of a still unspecified "new", in the sense of "Nobody likes change—except wet babies"; according to the philosopher *Peter Sloterdijk*, "*Past and present . . . form the incubation period of a monster that appears on the horizon under a deceptively harmless name: the New*".
- Insecurity and regression, such as fear of losing one's job, the danger of de-skilling, or the loss of influence (budgets, headcounts, access to decision-makers) . . . even if curiosity about "the new" correlates with exasperation about the present, for the feudalists of the existing system it feels like "survival" and
- Digitalisation, which comes on top of day-to-day business, pre-programming conflicts of objectives in implementation.

> *Agility is all well and good . . . but I didn't slave away for years doing corporate politics to get leadership—I certainly won't give that up now . . . .*—Senior Manager of an Airline

Resistance in groups, however, occurs more frequently when the group members have a high sense of belonging and superiority. At the (macroscopic) level of the *organisation*, resistance occurs due to, for example:

- Non-conformity with existing organisational norms and traditions, the common maxim of action ("theory in use") and established "mental models".
- Interdependencies with sub-systems that are hardly manageable or containable and
- Privileges, taboos, or resistance to external ideas ("not invented here").

> *The implementation of MarketingTech means a competition for scarce internal resources and the endurance of sometimes fierce reactances*—CMO of an Airline

For this reason, as the size of the organisation increases, the transformation of the existing organisation is often accompanied by *specialist/business promoters* who, independent of their position and task, and parallel to any reorganisation measures that may have already been started, take care of the dissemination of digital know-how and the implementation of the requirements. These expert promoters (or "*change agents*") do not usually have the right to issue instructions to the functional areas, but actively try to give impulses for the realisation of a holistic "digital organisation" by bundling know-how and transferring experiences from other company areas. By using expert promoters, it is easier to overcome differences between different functional areas, such as IT and marketing, and to establish a common, overarching understanding of the potential and the necessary implementation steps. The support of *political/power promoters* is essential, even if they usually do not play an operational role in the implementation process.

The *Myers–Briggs type indicator* (MBTI), a classic of personality diagnostics, helps in analysis and implementation by distinguishing between eight dimensions of a personality. The starting point is the conviction that one of the following categories usually predominates in people:

- *Intraversion and Extraversion* (I/E): The extrovert is more outgoing and ready to act, whereas the introvert is more concentrated and intense.
- *Intuition and Sensing* (N/S): The intuitive type relies more on gut feeling and speculation, whereas the sensing type is more detail-focused and realistic.
- *Feeling and Thinking* (F/T): Here a distinction is made between how decisions are made. The Feeling type (F) makes judgements subjectively and takes ideals and emotions into account, the Thinking (T) makes them rationally and by means of logic.
- *Judging and Perceiving* (J/P): This describes the certainty of the decisions made. The Judging (J) decides quickly, sometimes before they have all the information, and sticks to the decision unswervingly, while the Flexible (P) acts more spontaneously and is prepared to adapt based on new information.

Studies by *Ashridge University*, among others, from 2012 with 22,000 European managers show that the most common type tends to be the ESTJ manager (approx. one-fourth of all managers), followed by ENTJ (15%), ISTJ (14.2%), and ENTP (11.2%).[3] The types that are less common in management are INFP, INFJ, ESFP, and ISFP. Of the four most common types of managers, all interact harshly and of the four rarest types, all interact more cooperatively. This shows that interacting harshly is rather a typical characteristic of leaders: egocentric, profit-oriented thinking, making tough decisions, not avoiding conflict, and representing one's own opinion also to others. Empathic behaviour, however, tends to be weaker in many leaders. The virtues of leadership are decisiveness, thinking rather than feeling, always oriented towards facts and figures, and less towards intuitive judgement. This tends to dominate as personality types that follow the ISTJ pattern in the sense of "Controller, reduce costs, proceed correctly!" or with ESTJ the "Driver, increase sales, speed!". "STJ" means that everything must be processed quickly, cost-effectively, according to plan, process-oriented, methodically, analytically, logically, "ISO-9000-compliant". ISTJ tend to focus on bureaucracy and obsessive under stress, ESTJ overtime stress and actionism.[4] The real power in a head office is usually held by introverts in staff functions or in finance accounting. Other personality traits such as "feeling" (F), "spontaneous" (P), and "intuitive" (N) are usually less understood in view of the clearly structured power relations and tend to be excluded as "strange". Conversely, this leads to new challenges such as MarTech causing problems:

---

[3] Dück (2016).

[4] Emre (2018).

- Innovation needs intuition.
- Change, especially the digitalisation of customer interaction, requires intuition and flexibility.
- Problem that in chaotic change, past figures cannot be used to infer the future ("bankruptcy of linear planning").
- Familiarity and closeness to the customer along with a feeling for the customer (F) are required or also a culture of trust among employees (F).

These problems can be better addressed by managers who have a stronger expression in the N, F, and P areas. Intuition, feeling, and spontaneity, however, tend to be rejected by STJ-influenced management. Here, attempts are made to solve problems with plans, methods, numerical quotas, and processes because, seen collectively, management thinks and acts in this way and can (and will) hardly allow other thought patterns collectively due to the inherent personality structures. The consequence: the attempt to press intuition, feeling, and spontaneity into methodical and planned idea management as well as innovation/change processes, "big data customer intelligence", and brainstorming. In other words, to counter non-linearity with even more linear process models. In some cases, attempts are being made to methodise creativity again under the heading of "agility" or using "design thinking" methods, to pour it into rigid processes—while intuitive work towards a great result is being stifled in new "STJ rules".

The challenge lies within the *content* of the exponentially developing world, which is created in the realm of feeling, intuition, and spontaneity. Innovations and new things also for MarTech require intuition, imagination, and trial and error in addition to methods and processes. STJs, in contrast, are focused on *form*. They can produce what is known in the best possible form quickly and well. But they cannot deal with the unknown and cannot understand well that which cannot be directly represented by facts and figures in their system of experience and values. The high value of STJ only comes into play when one knows what one wants. Once you know what you want, STJs consider how much you want and how fast, etc. An STJ-influenced management culture is thus in danger of systematically leading one's own business model to change in the wrong direction in a very methodical and planned way and with attention to all processes, with untold overtime and constant analysis to the best of one's knowledge and conscience.

The phenomenon of "self-reinforcement" thus plays a vital role in the development and maintenance of existing competences. A (previously) successful ability that has been widely congratulated in the organisation becomes a self-perpetuator. Because a behaviour and field of competence are viewed positively, it is used more and more widely. The decisions of other members of the organisation are trusted or only a certain standard is (insidiously) supported via the leadership structures. The good reputation of an employee further reinforces this effect. However, such a competence path can also lead to the fact that all organisational members can no longer help but act as they did yesterday and the day before. The organisation thus finds itself in a "*lock-in*" of its own success (*innovators' dilemma*). If the organisation were to abandon its own path to success, this would appear nonsensical in the short term and would be difficult to communicate to the organisation (Christensen et al., 2011). The greater the existing spread of knowledge and rituals on the macroscopic level, the greater the subjectively perceived benefit from the application of the existing knowledge base, existing processes and tools (avoidance of cognitive dissonance) (Bandura, 1979). In essence, a frequency dependency effect with lock-in or "competency traps" (analogous to the innovators' dilemma) emerges:

Everybody is watching (the group) while being watched (Allen, 1988)

This means that the implementation of a new action maxim or theory in use, for example for the application and use of a CRM application, follows the company's internal diffusion (Fig. 12.14). The greater the degree of diffusion of a certain knowledge about application scenarios and "mental models" in data-driven marketing, the greater the perceived (subjective) benefit that is perceived from the application or change of the existing knowledge base (Bandura, 1979). In other words: away from the prevailing paradigm of "*Why do we need a CRM application and why should I maintain my personal contacts and activities here*?" to "*The others are already using it and raving about it … I would like to be part of this*" across the entire organisation (*Fear of Missing Out, FOMO*). In other words, creating

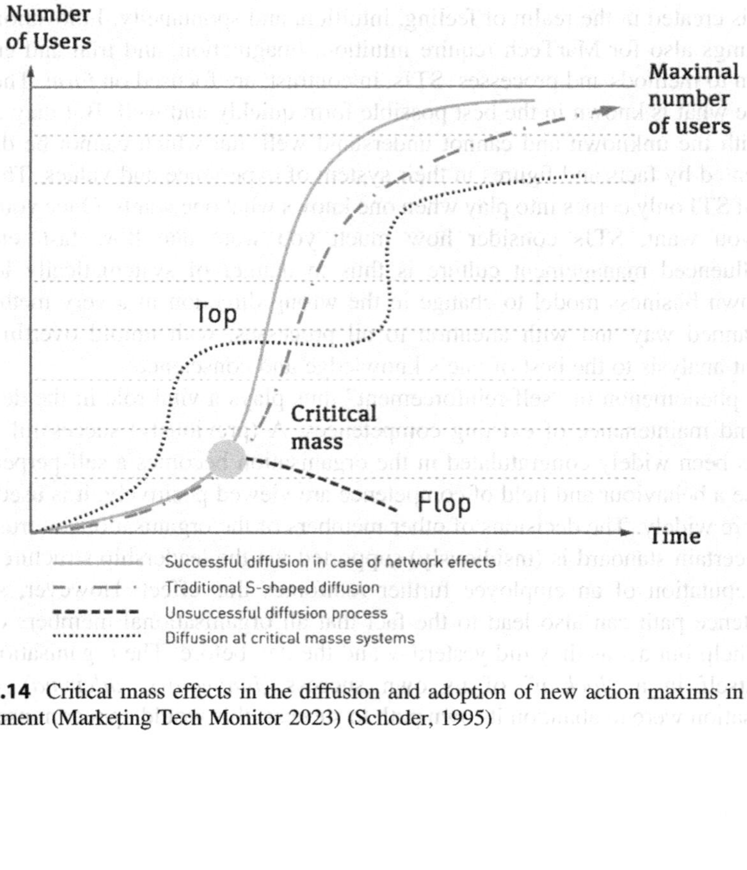

Fig. 12.14 Critical mass effects in the diffusion and adoption of new action maxims in change management (Marketing Tech Monitor 2023) (Schoder, 1995)

desirability by means of beacons instead of (supposedly) training the ratio in a *PowerPoint*-driven way.

The change in the behaviour of the members of an organisation thus depends on the marginal change in the relative frequency of behaviour within the organisation from the macroscopic variables of (observable) relative frequency. Simplified, this means that the choice of a certain behaviour by the individuals depends on how often this behaviour is already represented and observable in this organisation (*frequency dependency effect*) and exceeds a threshold value in the perception (*critical mass*) to become "top" or "flop" (Probst & Büchel, 1994). The benefit and the perceived relative attractiveness of a maxim of action or the use of an application scenario increases with the number of participants who make its application evident through their observable behaviour.

Like a wave that passes through people's bodies and culminates when everybody synchronises himself with the wave. (Nonaka, 1994)

The area around the critical mass point (the physical bifurcation point) is critical in that minor fluctuations and the influx of other organisational members (e.g. the use of MarketingTech by in-house innovators and opinion-leaders) can have a lasting impact on propagation.

Diffusion, plus the expansion of capacity to take effective action, defines collective learning. (Tompkins, 1995)

Change management thus essentially requires "unlearning" and the adoption (leap) to a new organisational, process-related, or application-related maxim of action (Hedberg, 1981).

Willingness to adopt new processes, routines, digital technologies, and business models is fostered by:

- *Relative advantage*: The relative advantage compared to existing practice.
- *Compatibility*: The compatibility with existing values, routines, and maxims of action.
- *Complexity*: The perceived complexity.
- *Trialability*: The ability to be tested in a definable environment.
- *Observability*: The observability for others.

Depending on the phase, the changes should be accompanied by different instruments in a comprehensive change management system.

> *Without change management, projects fail ... and these are ongoing, be it through new channels, technologies or even mergers and acquisitions!*—Nina Haller (ExperienceOne, Board Member Technology GWA)

Change management methods are as diverse as they are varied, ranging from *Lego Serious Play*, employee mobilisation, coaching, incentives, train the trainer, and competence management to combining change methods with psychological assessments such as MBTI (Cameron & Green, 2012; Emre, 2018). Employee narratives and metaphors have proven effective in change management to provide information about the company culture and to uncover costly process weaknesses. Compared to abstract information based on facts, stories have the advantage of being more comprehensible, more memorable, and able to create meaning and identity. To counteract this, the communication of an abstract "Why" embedded in a narrative frame story has emerged as an effective instrument for transformation according to *Sinek*:

> *The narrative's content and structure inspire people, dispel unbelief and compel transformation ... When used properly, a story can help people see the future and can transform them from adversaries into advocates working hard to create that future.* (Sinek, 2014; Furr et al., 2018)

Companies that have already successfully implemented data-driven marketing and sales are also worthy of their leadership role here, as this group is more likely to have a meaningful "strategic narrative" and to implement it systematically as part of the transformation. Thus they ...

- ... are much more likely to ensure internal alignment in the form of constructive cooperation with neighbouring departments (e.g. IT, legal).
- ... to convince management of the need for the upcoming changes.
- ... to support them in the further development of their assessment competence, if necessary, also by using 1:1 coaching.

Accordingly, the consequence is that these companies put forward less resistance from their own colleagues—they present themselves as more open-minded (36%). Stories are strategically used to convey traditions, values, and corporate culture, to awaken resources, but also to make internal and external conflicts pictorially and emotionally tangible in a metaphor and to point out possible solutions (Smith, 2012). It is not what has been achieved which counts but what has been told that is enough. It is about telling poignant stories that inspire thought and action.

> *It is usually the case that if you think that everything has been understood, it does not mean that something has been understood . . . it starts with terminology, where there are different understandings*—Adriana Nuneva (CDO, Head of Marketing & Sales, CWS International)

Compared to abstract information, stories have the advantage of being more comprehensible, more memorable, and able to create meaning and identity. Corporate stories feature traditional elements and structures of narratives such as actors, events, places, temporal and logical progressions, and action patterns that support the organisation's identity, attention, and interpretation management.

> *In any form of change and transformation, expectation management is one of the biggest challenges . . . which is best carried into the organisation in the form of small successes or stories and metaphors*—Andreas Ehspanner (Head of CRM/OneCRM, Mercedes-Benz Sales)

Storytelling describes a method with which the knowledge of employees about incisive events in the company (e.g. a pilot project) is recorded, evaluated, and processed in the form of a shared experience story from the most diverse perspectives of those involved. In essence, according to *Sinek*, it is about communicating an abstract "why" embedded in a narrative framework.

> *The narrative's content and structure inspire people, dispel unbelief, and compel transformation . . . When used properly, a story can help people see the future and can transform them from adversaries into advocates working hard to create that future.* (Furr et al., 2018)
>
> *Humans are meaning-seeking and cooperating beings. Their societies are founded on stories with which they design and explain the world and make and justify their decisions . . . What is important in these times is to set clear priorities that give us orientation for what is desirable and possible, give meaning and are contagious.* (Göpel, 2022c; Smith, 2012)

In addition to storytelling, *Lego Serious Play* (LSP) has proven to be an effective tool in projects for the development and expansion of data-driven marketing or MarTech as one of the few strategic management methods that both open up the problem space, show alternative solutions, focus on possible solutions (solution space), and guarantee the participants work in a psychologically protected space (psychological safety). LSP is essentially a facilitated and time-box structured method for conducting strategic workshops at the management or team level (Fearne, 2020). A certified facilitator clarifies the workshop objectives with the sponsor and plans the different levels of reflection. They guide the participants through the method in the workshop and lead them through the problem definition with methodically structured questions. Strategic decisions and problem solutions are gained through the construction and metaphorical interpretation of models. In the business environment, LSP uses *Lego* models to promote innovative ideas, improve communication, and accelerate problem-solving. LSP is based on psychological principles:

- *Flow*: People work most effectively when they are in a feeling of complete immersion (concentration) and complete absorption in an activity, the "flow", which is experienced as pleasurable, for example when playing a game or visiting a website (Carlson et al., 2013).
- *Serious play*: In purposeful thinking with the hands, clarity can be created for contexts that are difficult to master linguistically; complexity can be mapped in a new, simple form; and collaborative, creative, new ideas and innovative solutions to problems can be found, along with central anchor points for joint action. Through models and metaphors, the object of the game takes on a specific meaning and abstract concepts become more understandable. In this way, informal relationships—which would otherwise be difficult to capture in language—can be made concrete. It is important that the participants do not draw up a kind of "construction sketch" in advance in their heads before building their own model and then simply try to implement this. The special effect of LSP is since the metaphor and its interpretation only emerge during construction.
- *Constructionism*: People learn especially when they construct something, be it designing a product, building a model ship, or writing a computer program. During the construction of real things, theories and knowledge are simultaneously designed in thought. This new knowledge enables the construction of far more complex real things, which in turn leads to a further gain in knowledge.
- *Hand-brain connection*: This is particularly strong in sensory and motor terms. Thinking processes combined with physical movement and sensation—and especially with the hands—lead to a deeper and longer-lasting understanding of the environment and its possibilities. In addition, manual work with *Lego* bricks creates an emotional connection between the builder and the model. It is "their" model, "they have created" it. Decisions thus acquire a greater binding force.

Through the constant handling of the *Lego* bricks and the building of metaphorical models, the topics dealt with are not only visualised, but literally become "tangible". The models therefore primarily serve as visual anchors for discussions and conversations. At the same time, the abstraction to a model prevents thinking in functional areas and the participants build a common model from the parts of the individual models, adding further aspects (bricks) if necessary, including all the necessary connections.

References

Ackerman, S. (2022, March). MarTech's agile marketing for leaders.
Ackermann, S. (2021, November 26). Living the 10 principles of agile marketing. *MarTech*.
Agile Marketing Manifesto; October 29, 2021.
Allen, D. (1988). New telecommunication services – Network externalities and critical mass. *Telecommunications Policy*, 257–271.
Bandura, A. (1979). *Sozial-kognitive Lerntheorie* (pp. 100–161).
Brinker, S. (2014, September 30). Discoveries from our marketing technologist survey. *Chiefmartec*, 8.
Brinker, S. (2020, January). The many splendid varieties of marketing technologists in 2020: MarTech roles and archetypes. *Chiefmartec*.
Brinker, S. (2023, April). Marketing ops careers are good today – and likely to get much better; here's the latest data on these roles. *Chiefmartec*.
Cameron, E., & Green, M. (2012). *Making sense of change management* (3rd ed.).
Carlson, J., Ahrholdt, D., Sridharan, R., & Simatupang, T. (2013). New insights into consumer loyalty of website-services: The quadratic effect of flow. In H. El-Gohary & R. Eid (Eds.), *E-Marketing in developed and developing countries: Emerging practices*.
Christensen, C. M., Matzler, K., von den Eichen, S. F. (2011). *The Innovator's Dilemma: Warum etablierte Unternehmen den Wettbewerb um bahnbrechende Innovationen verlieren*.
Daft, R., & Huber, G. (1987). How organisations learn: a communication framework. In N. Ditomaso & S. Bacharach (Eds.), *Research in the sociology of organisations* (pp. 1–36).
Deutscher Marketing Tag 2008, Munich.
Dück, G. (2016). DD263: STJ-Menschen dominieren methodisch analytisch nach Plan. *Omnisophie*, 13.
Emre, M. (2018). *The personality brokers: The strange history of Myers-Briggs and the birth of personality testing*.
Fearne, M. (2020). *The LSP method: How to engage people and spark insights using the LEGO serious play method*.
Fryrear, A. (2021, April). Agile acceleration: 4th annual state of agile marketing report. *Agile Sherpas*.
Furr, N., Nel, K., & Ramsoy, T. Z. (2018). *Leading transformation. How to take charge of your company's future*.
Gartner. (2022, April). *Build an agile marketing strategy*.
Göpel, M. (2022a). *Wir können auch anders* (p. 27).
Göpel, M. (2022b). *Wir können auch anders* (p. 228).
Göpel, M. (2022c). *Wir können auch anders* (pp. 101–102).
Hackman, J. R. (1986). The psychology of self-management in organisations. In M. S. Pallak & R. O. Perloff (Eds.), *Psychology and work: Productivity, change, employment*. Washington (pp. 89–139).
Hedberg, B. L. T. (1981). How organisations learn and unlearn. In P. Nystrom & W. Starbuck (Eds.), *Handbook of organisational design*, No 1 (pp. 3–27).
Hofert, S., & Thonet, C. (2019). *Der agile Kulturwandel: 33 Lösungen für Veränderungen in Organisationen*.
Manz, C. C., & Sims, H. P. Jr. (1989). *Super leadership. Leading others to lead themselves*.
March, J. G., & Olsen, J. P. (1976). *Ambiguity and choice in organisations*.
Neck, C. P., & Manz, C. C. (1994). From Groupthink to Teamthink: Toward the creation of constructive thought patterns in self-managing work teams. *Human Relations, 47*(8), 929–952.
Nonaka, I. (1994). Dynamic theory of organisational knowledge creation. *Organisation Science, 5*(1), 24.
Nonaka, I, & Takeuchi, H. (2007). The knowledge-creating company. *Harvard Business Review, 85*(7/8), 162.
Probst, G. J. B., & Büchel, B. S. T. (1994). *Organisationales Lernen*.

Schoder, D. (1995). *Erfolg und Misserfolg telematischer Innovationen—Erklärung der kritischen Masse und weiterer Diffusionsphänomene*.

Sinek, S. (2014). *Frag immer erst: Warum: Wie Top-Firmen und Führungskräfte zum Erfolg inspirieren*.

Smith, P. (2012). *Lead with a story. A guide to crafting business narratives that captivate, convince, and inspire*.

Strauß, R. E. (1996). *Determinanten und Dynamik des Organisational Learning*.

Tompkins, T. C. (1995). Role of diffusion in collective learning. *International Journal of Organisational Analysis, 3*(1), 70.

13 Case Studies: Lessons Learned from Other Companies

13.1 "Lifting The Data Treasure" . . . for Customers, Partners, and Business Through a Strong Omnichannel Loyalty Program at *COOP* (CH)

The year 2020 was the year in which everyone, inevitably and due to Covid, spent significantly more time at home and in their own kitchen. In Switzerland, *COOP* is a basic supplier who serves their customers with their wide range of food retail products, both offline and online. Those who used to have only pasta Bolognese and scrambled eggs on their menu may have become more experimental in the Covid years. Food retail was also a winner during the Covid crisis in Switzerland. *COOP* achieved a turnover of CHF 30.2 billion in 2020. The *COOP* supermarkets benefited, with sales growth of 14.3%, gaining market share (Statista, 2021). In terms of turnover, *COOP* is the number one in Switzerland in overall food retailing. In online grocery retailing, *COOP* was able to record not only a renewed growth in market share to 44.2%, but also a significant leap in turnover to a total of CHF 232 million in 2020 (Fig. 13.1). For 2023, 34.7 billion Euro revenue have been reported (offline and online).

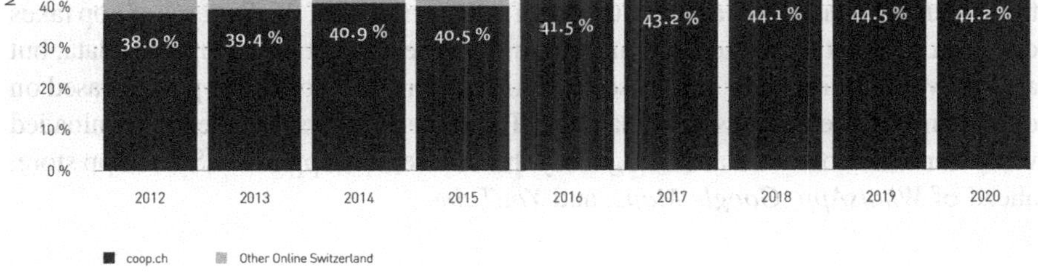

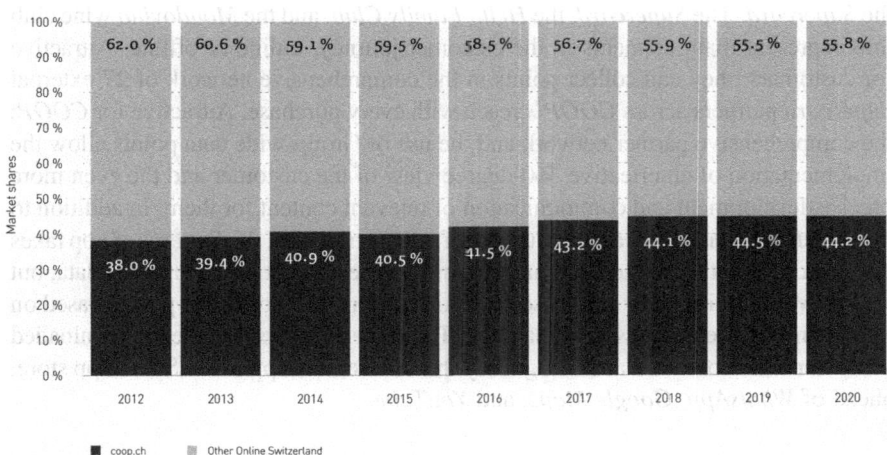

Fig. 13.1 Market shares of online food trade in Switzerland 2012–2020 (Statista, COOP, Marketing Tech Monitor 2021)

R. Strauss, *Data-Driven Customer Engagement*,
https://doi.org/10.1007/978-3-031-64295-1_13

Fig. 13.2 The *Supercard* customer card and special interest clubs as well as partners of the customer programs (Marketing Tech Monitor 2021)

While *Lidl* focuses on app and digital reach, this is already everyday life at *COOP*. *COOP* manages to reach about 85% of Swiss households with its *Supercard*. Building on the *Supercard* and its customer base, *COOP* has developed two more special interest clubs, the *"Hello Family Club"* and the *"Mondovino"* wine club. Both clubs have their own market development and content strategy. The focus here is on building relationships between the customers and the brands. Accordingly, there are many members of up to three *Coop* clubs. An extensive partner network increases the attractiveness of the *Supercard* for customers and the benefits for the *Coop Group* (Fig. 13.2).

The key figures are impressive, because in addition to the high penetration of Swiss households, over 70% of the total turnover can be allocated and evaluated via the *Supercard*. The *Supercard*, the *Hello Family Club*, and the *Mondovino* wine club thus represent main elements in the customer journey, online or offline. Attractive for customers: they can collect points in the comprehensive network of 27 external *Supercard* partners across *COOP's* reach with every purchase. Attractive for *COOP*: the comprehensive partner network and the use of Group-wide data points allow the implementation of an effective 360-degree view of the customer and the even more precise development and communication of relevant content for them. In addition to the systematic generation and evaluation of transaction data, the *Supercard* app takes on a special function in the dialogue with users. The app not only generates data, but also provides individually prioritised coupons, offers, and collective passes based on online and offline purchasing behaviour. The *Supercard* app has been downloaded well over 2 million times and is regularly the number one app in the Swiss app store, ahead of *WhatsApp*, *Google Maps*, and *YouTube*.

The high reach owned media channels such as the *COOP* newspaper (>60% weekly household reach) and the various newsletters represent a forceful communication mix with which the *Supercard* program is supported in terms of communication. In other words, the *Supercard* is positioned as "glue" and "fuel" for omnichannel purchases, with over 3 billion scans per year. But the omnichannel portal Coop.ch and the Coop.ch app do not only play a decisive role for online transactions and all basic services from the *Supercard* program, but also support the preparation of purchases as well as simplify shopping and the post-processing of purchases, in which the sales slips or the guaranteed certificates are stored digitally and centrally. The shopping experience is rounded off by the *Fooby* content platform. This inspires customers with a variety of cooking recipes and the opportunity to eat more creatively, and it conveniently offers the option of integrating the ingredients directly into the shopping list on Coop.ch or in the *COOP*.ch app, or to buy online.

Another key to success is the close and trusting cooperation with the fast moving consumer goods (FMCG) industry. *COOP* allows its partners, manufacturers, and brands to benefit from the comprehensive information and insights they gain from their data and works closely with them on the further development of new services and benefits for customers. An example: in 2020, *COOP* launched a new retailer portal that offers brand manufacturers the opportunity to create detailed evaluations based on the respective sales data, repurchase rates, buyer segments, etc. This enables real-time time comparisons to be made. This means that time comparisons, category comparisons, sales share of promotions, but also statistics on the descriptive buyer segments (aggregated) are available in real time. Based on this data, brand owners can significantly optimise product development, action planning, and communication campaigns.

The next development step: outside the "*Supercard* data universe" there are still numerous data points whose potential should be tapped for segment-specific customer processing. Examples of this are on-site movement data and sometimes also transaction data, which are not yet considered for the calculation of segments, characteristics, and attributes. In addition, some of these data sets are fragmented and distributed over several data pools, so that a 360-degree view of the customer is not possible without major manual effort on the part of the analytics teams. These data sources must now be systematically integrated—in compliance with the new and significantly more restrictive Swiss data protection legislation—and the calculation logics for algorithms for the calculation of individualised content must be adapted or refined accordingly. This is the basis for controlling further triggered campaigns and content in the shop and in the app in real time in the future. *COOP's* aim is to use the constantly growing data on customers to better understand their interests, affinities, and buying behaviour, which can also change over time (Fig. 13.3), in order to increasingly provide their customers with a better user experience through individual prioritised offers and content on their preferred channels.

The engine—the heart—is being overhauled and modernised: *COOP* has so far relied on a best-of-suite approach in its MarketingTech strategy. In addition to *SAP*

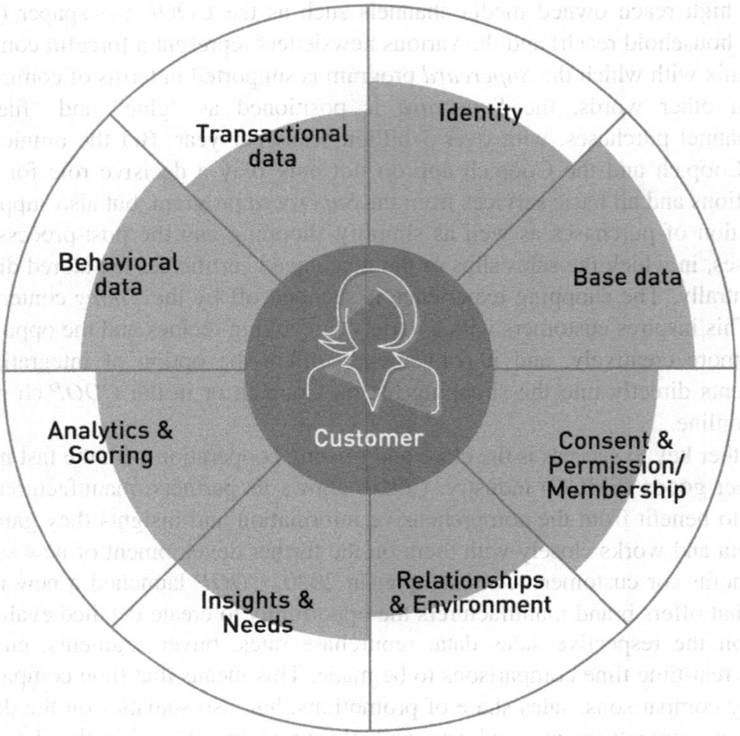

Fig. 13.3 Segment cluster: the profile should be continuously expanded and refined over the duration of the customer relationship (Marketing Tech Monitor 2021)

are *Salesforce*, *Adobe*, *SAS* (segmentation), and the *Google Marketing Platform* in use (Fig. 13.4). The current development plan has analytical CRM with *SAS* at its core for the selection of target groups. The *Google Marketing Cloud* is used to link offline and online identification data, which is also used for individualised 1:1 communication on third-party sites after data enrichment with various IDs to identify the users. On third-party sites, a differentiation is made between customers and non-customers in the advertising material. All data flows back into the analytical CRM from *SAS* and is used for feature refinement and profile expansion. The *Google Marketing Cloud* serves as a central ID hub—a link between the online and offline worlds—to ensure the consistency of the target groups of the *COOP* advertising partners and to maximise the reach.

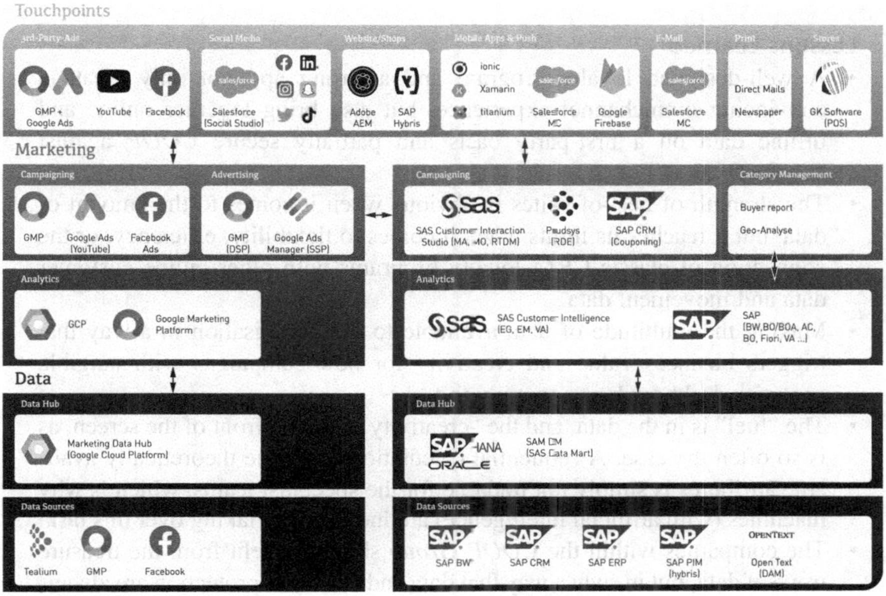

Fig. 13.4 MarTech map for *COOP* (Marketing Tech Monitor 2021)

The data of the performance marketing disciplines is stored in the *Google Marketing Data Hub* of the *Google Cloud Platform*, on which online analytics is also based and from which data for different digital marketing channels is activated. A separate DSP complements the tech stack. All other back-office data is stored in *SAP* (e.g. transactions, customer card data, incl. a data mart) in the PIM or also in the DAM system. On the owned media side, marketing automation is performed via *SAS* with a direct channel connection to E-Mail, mobile push, and print. *Tealium* is used as a tag management solution in the shop and *Adobe Experience Manager* as a CMS solution.

Above all, the criterion of scalability has dominated the decision-making so far. Nevertheless, over time it became apparent that the current structure also had disadvantages in terms of flexibility, efficiency and customer data that was still distributed in data silos. The next development step with the goal of building a Group-wide centralised customer database giving a 360-degree customer view has already been tackled. The best-of-breed approach is being consistently pursued. This is also accompanied by a paradigm shift, in which the analytical CRM environment is no longer based exclusively on the *Supercard* data, but which unites all data of the *COOP Group* centrally and thus enables an overall view of all customers (with/without card programs). All channels are to have access to a central customer view. The already existing analytical CRM front-end will be rebuilt and play a significant role in combination with a CDP.

Lessons Learned

- A well-designed loyalty program and a strong app not only create a convincing omnichannel experience, but also bring together online and offline data on a first-party basis and partially secure *COOP* against "cookiegeddon".
- The strength of best-of-suites is obvious when it comes to the amount of data, but it reaches its limits when it comes to flexibility, efficiency, or the connection of classic CRM loyalty programs with other online customer data and movement data.
- Making the multitude of data available to the organisation in a way that triggers business value and creativity for new campaigns with tangible analytics dashboards is a mammoth task.
- The "fuel" is in the data, and the "creativity" sits it in front of the screen, as is so often the case. A sequential calculation of all the theoretically available attributes is simply not tradable for the specialist teams, which is why machines (with artificial intelligence) are increasingly taking over this task.
- The companies within the *COOP Group* should benefit from the treasure trove of data, but in such a way that data and customer protection are always ensured.

13.2 The Democratisation of the MarTech Landscape at *Philips*

Royal Philips is a leading provider in the field of health care technology. Headquartered in the Netherlands, the company's mission is to improve people's health and well-being by providing products and solutions that support them in all phases of the health continuum: from healthy living to illness prevention, diagnosis, and therapy, to home care. The development of these integrated solutions is based on advanced technologies and a deep understanding of the needs of healthcare professionals as well as of consumers. The company is a leader in diagnostic imaging, image-guided therapy, patient monitoring, and health IT, as well as consumer health products and home care.

Hand in hand with a stronger customer-centric focus came challenges to establish efficient, data-driven customer interactions:

- Insights from the respective audiences could not be efficiently implemented.
- Knowledge and responsibilities in the areas of D2C, D2B, and digital platforms were fragmented throughout the organisation.
- No integrated, only product-centred planning (inside-out) vs. customer-centred (outside-in).
- Insufficient know-how in the areas of experience design or data-driven marketing.

- Multiple work in activities, channels, and creation as well as insufficient focus and management of media spend.
- Lack of a mutual understanding of the way of working or responsibilities.

The implementation in the direction of data-driven marketing takes place using MarTech as a technical enabler and the basis for the implementation of capabilities. The goal is to establish a democratised MarTech landscape in the company by 2023 (Fig. 13.5) that:

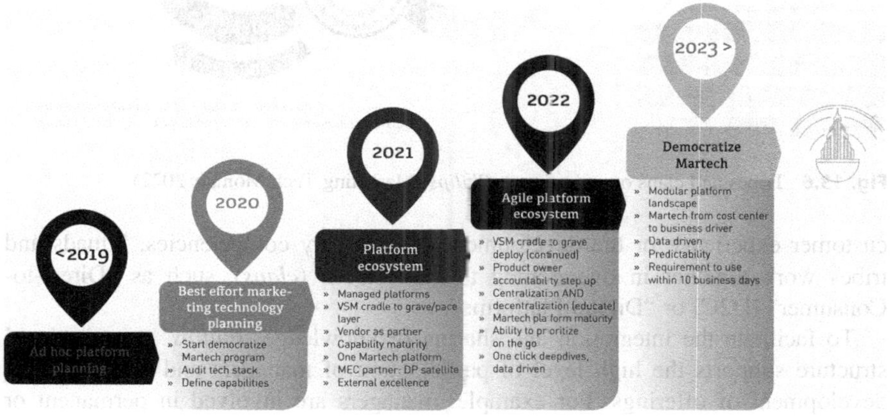

Fig. 13.5 High-level road map (Marketing Tech Monitor 2022)

- Follows a modular and transparent architecture
- Enables fully data-driven decisions with maximum predictable outcomes
- Achieves a time-to-usage of 10 days and thus
- Moves from being a cost centre to a business driver

The successful development and use of MarTech is inextricably linked to the capabilities of the employees in the company and the organisational structure. *Philips* is set up as a project-centric organisation with clans, tribes, squads, and chapters (Fig. 13.6). Employees are grouped into *squads*, which are then subdivided into tribes (e.g. "Customer Care and Engagement" or "Experience and Conversion"). This approach is designed to maximise the benefits of pooling shared knowledge and skills. Each tribe has a *tribe lead* and a product owner assigned to different tasks (e.g. "Digital Activation Policy" or "Mobile Platforms"). Another organisational structural element is the implementation of permanent or temporary groupings of employees from different areas and functions with the aim of continuously improving operational procedures, processes, and structures. For example, in the marketing structure of the company, there are defined groups (*chapters*), each of which is made up of employees from different squads or tribes and have certain things in common, such as programming languages or activities that relate to the improvement of the

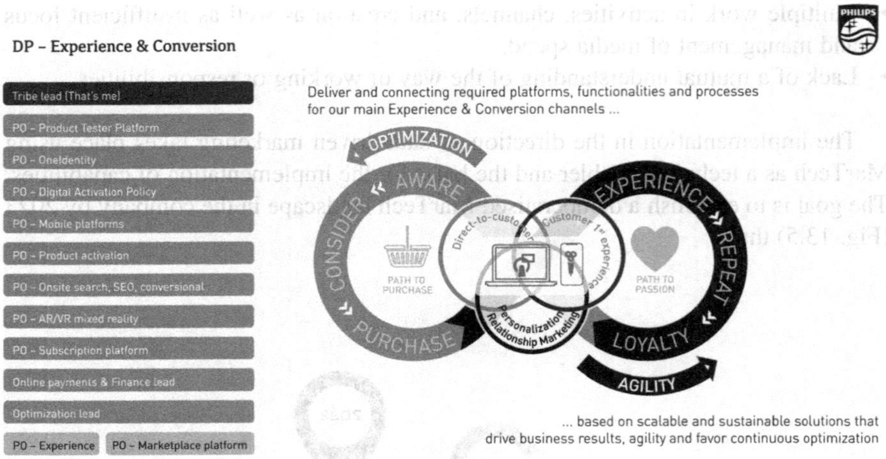

Fig. 13.6 Tribes and clans organisation at *Philips* (Marketing Tech Monitor 2022)

customer experience or the development of necessary competencies. Squads and tribes work together in overarching thematic areas (*clans*), such as "Direct-to-Consumer" (D2C) or "Digital Platforms".

To facilitate the integration and sharing of knowledge, *Philips'* organisational structure supports the high level of participation of managers and leaders in the development of offerings. For example, managers are involved in permanent or temporary project-based working groups (e.g. for mobile app development), which emphasises the value of each individual employee and the perspective of equality. Based on these structural features and characteristics, *Philips*' organisational structure has a strong heterarchy, with considerable variability and flexibility. For example, an employee could be a group member in a mobile application development project and at the same time advise another work group.

The *Digital Platforms* clan is responsible for building the extensive MarTech landscape, focusing on an integrated architecture as a "best-of-service" due to functional coverage and integration benefits (Fig. 13.7). In other words: best-of-breed applications are used if they cover specific requirements, and suites if they can combine multiple requirements. The focus is on the best-possible efficient use of applications that are otherwise only 58% utilised. From *Philips'* point of view, an utilisation rate of 70% already offers the option of generating a 20% higher ROMI and thus bottom-line results. Particularly noteworthy for the success is the remarkably close dovetailing with the business and market functions and the corporate IT, which, on the one hand, enables maximum utilisation of the technology and maximum value creation, and, on the other hand, enables a consistent "cradle-to-grave" approach and prevents unused legacy systems.

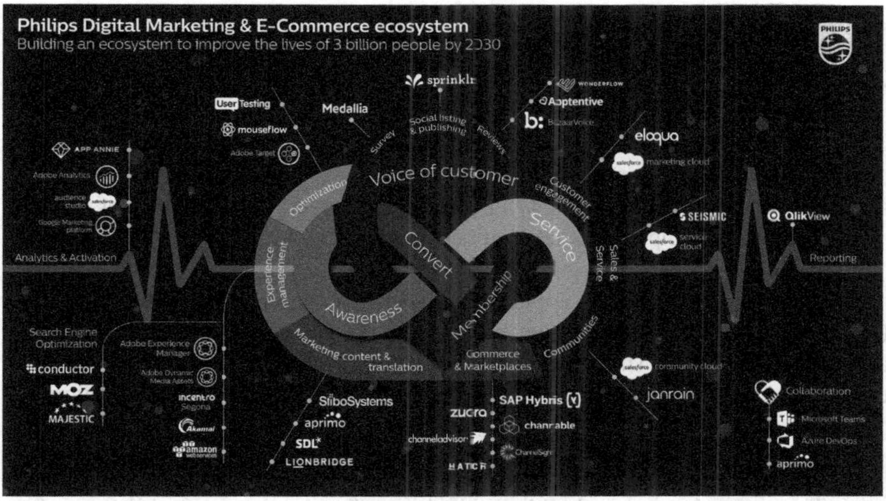

Fig. 13.7 The iServer MarTech construction plan at *Philips* (Marketing Tech Monitor 2022)

For the selection of the different MarketingTech applications, questions such as the full costs of an application, its expected life cycle and the measurability of the results are important. The economic success of the MarketingTech platform is measured according to four central criteria (Fig. 13.8):

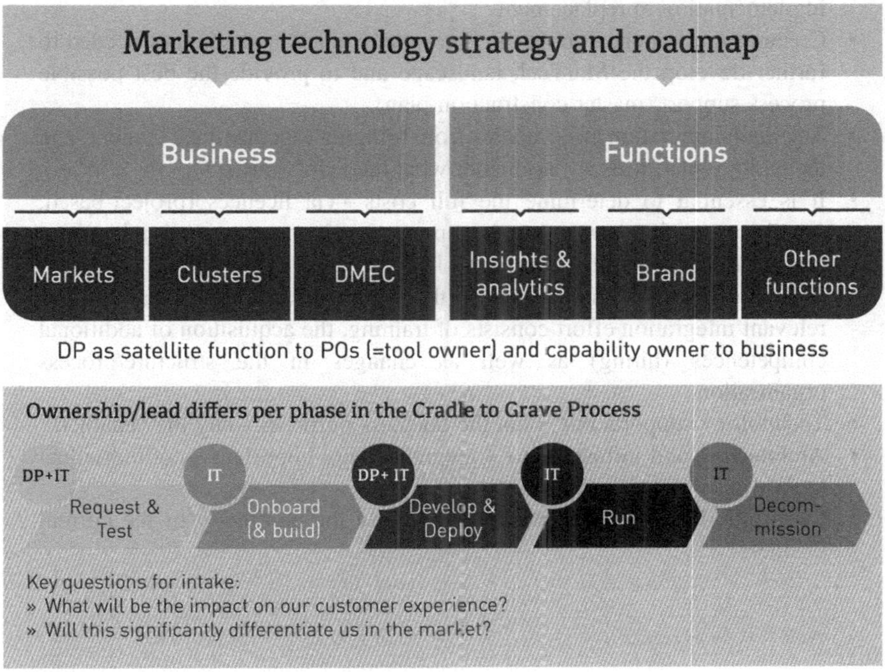

Fig. 13.8 ONE Philips MEC for MarTech (Marketing Tech Monitor 2022)

1. *Product activation (process)*: Number of days from product activation to availability for purchase online (add-to-cart).
2. *Platform utilisation (ROI)*: Percentage of features used by end users and integrated into IT landscape/processes.
3. *Platform satisfaction (end user)*: Satisfaction measurement of key platforms (by primary/tier 1 users).
4. *Capability maturity (strategic fit)*: Percentage of coverage or maturity of required competencies compared to external best practices.

The selection of MarTech applications follows a classic step-by-step procedure (selection process)—from a target picture, requirements engineering, and fit gap analysis based on this. The focus is on questions such as the scope of integration, the existence of native connectors, or the extensibility of the respective applications.

Lessons Learned

- The most important building block in the development and use of MarketingTech is the teams and their capabilities, both in selection and implementation as well as in use.
- It requires a central department that works closely with IT—both for the development of the requirements (in the business blueprint) as well as the selection of the tools and the integration or implementation.
- The purchase of a licence is only the first step ... much more important is the focus on the entire life cycle of an application—from purchase to implementation to replacement.
- Creating transparency about the investments made and changes needed to further develop the MarTech landscape and to provide the best possible process support (master construction plan).
- The main integration effort comes from bringing together data, content, and technology platforms ... no matter what the theory says.
- It is essential to determine the full costs—via licences (project-based, ongoing operation, service, and support), development costs, implementation, roll-out or even training (e.g. UAT).
- The purchase of an application is the comparatively easiest part ... the relevant integration effort consists of training, the acquisition of additional competences (hiring) as well as changes in the structure/process organisation.
- Technology supports but is not the business purpose—only the "enabler".
- Architecture and infrastructure (integration) are important—not individual tools.
- Do not under any circumstances jeopardise the continuity of the current business.

13.3 The Evolution of the MarTech Development at *Volkswagen*: The Marketecture

Traditionally, car manufacturers such as *Volkswagen* have established a three-tier distribution model:

- Manufacturer (OEM), with 120 production plants in 29 countries in *Volkswagen's* case.
- Wholesalers/importers in one country, often distributing several brands and in some cases being legally independent.
- Dealers, around 95% of whom operate as legally independent concessionaires, albeit under the manufacturer's name or, as in the USA, as entirely manufacturer-independent multi-brand dealer organisations.

In most countries, the customer data is owned by the dealers, so that the ultimate buyer or user is not known at the manufacturer or wholesale level. This is even worse for company cars (fleet). The company's internal "user chooser" is completely unknown to the local dealer, as well as to the OEM due to existing fleet contracts. Accordingly, a 360-degree view of the customer remains nothing more than lofty wishful thinking.

However, direct sales are also gaining momentum in the automotive industry and are becoming increasingly visible in its various facets in the sales landscape, and they are also becoming a true reality in the individual customer business. More and more manufacturers are announcing that they want to introduce D2C in whole or in part as a form of distribution. With the introduction of the *ID series*, *Volkswagen* is also moving in the direction of D2C/omnichannel. In the new sales model, car dealerships act as intermediaries for sales to private and small commercial customers. They take care of acquisition, advice, test drives, transaction processing and delivery in coordination with *Volkswagen*. The dealer named by the customer at the beginning of the sales process receives the commission and bonus analogous to the stationary business, even if the vehicle is purchased on the Internet directly from the manufacturer. *Volkswagen* also sets the price for the vehicle. This eliminates complicated price negotiations. The danger of a discount battle is also defused. The brand also takes over the financing of the cars and bears the risk for returns and residual value. The goal for all OEMs is to create a consistent and uniform customer experience across all online and offline touchpoints, from the information phase to the purchase phase to service.

In most cases, the multi-level sales model is compounded by media discontinuities along the entire customer journey. Local dealers operate their own websites and campaigns in their region, which may not be synchronised with the national activities of the manufacturer or the distributors. In most cases, there is no end-to-end tracking of the customer journey and lead management—via the brand website, auto-configuration, and targeting of a specific dealer. If a user configures a product on the brand's website, the best that can be done is to suggest retailers in the user's geographical vicinity, due to a lack of knowledge about a possible preference and customer history with a particular retailer.

Even simple use cases such as the purchase of a new car in combination with the trade-in of a used car usually present themselves at the retail level as a process flow with several process and data interrupts ("media breaks"), for example:

- The creation of the customer
- The enquiry about the valuation of used cars (e.g. via the *Schwacke* list in Germany)
- The checking of the creditworthiness of the buyer in the case of financing (via *Schufa* information, for example, for customers)
- The query of the expected delivery (in the case of "build-to-order") in the order management and distribution (OMD) system or
- The query of available cars in the dealer's own dealer management system ("build-to-stock", DMS as an ERP derivative)

Process analyses show up to seven media breaks, where the dealer must create the respective customer data anew each time. Two different data objects are always carried along the process: customer data and vehicle data (vehicle identification number [VIN]).

An almost inevitable result of this fragmented process landscape in marketing was, in *Volkswagen's* case, more than 50 applications in use, for example in CRM, SEA/SEO, CMS, DMPs, hosting or analytics, a multitude of objectives and the associated KPIs—with the challenge of being able to control and evaluate all marketing activities in a targeted manner only with difficulty. Experiences from previous projects have led *Volkswagen* to consciously refrain from a best-of-breed strategy due to the complexity of the constellation "brands—markets—dealers". A best-of-suite approach (based on *Adobe* and *Salesforce*) is intended to ensure that lengthy discussions about requirements (e.g. level of detail, weighting) or development plans and blueprints (e.g. the discussion of which is the leading system in retail, CRM, or DMS) are reduced to a minimum. The focus is on the use of standard functionalities and the acceptance of an "80% version". Lengthy customising is only permitted in exceptional cases. The focus on the best-of-suite approach serves as a flexible framework that is to be questioned or adapted repeatedly along newly arising use cases and the associated requirements. The goal of the resulting *Volkswagen Marketecture* (marketing business architecture, Fig. 13.9) is to generate more traffic, leads, and sales, to make all marketing activities traceable across the entire customer journey, to increase the volume and value of all transactions, and, finally, to increase the lifetime value of each customer. The focus is on a high degree of integration as well as continuous measurability and scalability across all markets and customers.

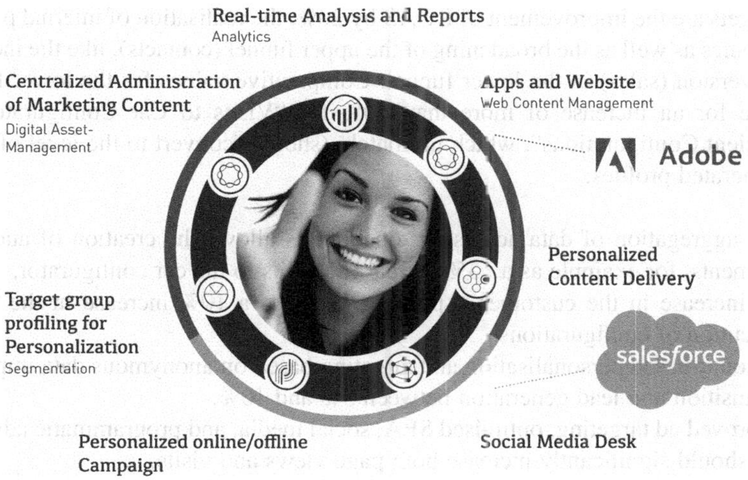

Fig. 13.9 Cornerstones of Marketecture at *Volkswagen* (Marketing Tech Monitor 2022)

Whereas traditionally, due to the multi-level sales model, the focus has been on personalised information (e.g. from campaign and journey management, dealer tools), the area of anonymised data is now also being addressed, via personalised websites, web tracking and analytics, tag management or CMS, and programmatic advertising (incl. DMP). With the brand-related development plan from the headquarters' point of view, the subsequent roll-out to the markets was immediately planned, with roll-out teams in the "Center of Excellence" in Wolfsburg (Fig. 13.10). Whereas earlier digitalisation projects were carried out as large-scale projects with detailed business cases, milestone planning, and steering committees, the brand structure serves more as a target picture that is gradually developed in smaller individual projects and POCs.

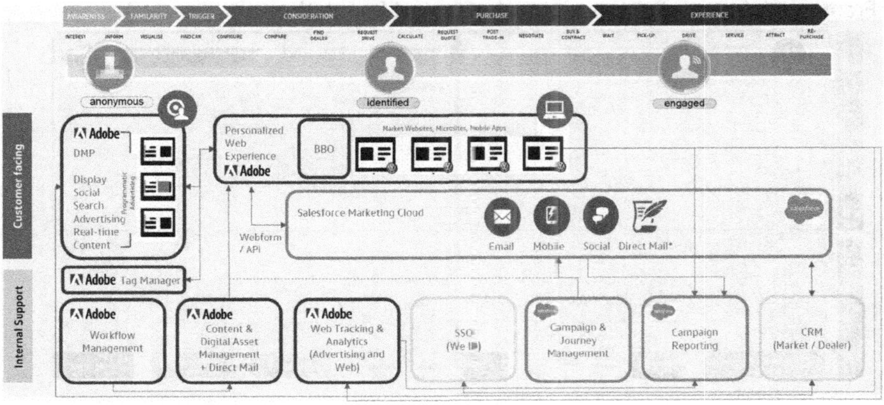

Fig. 13.10 Target picture Marketecture at *Volkswagen* (Marketing Tech Monitor 2022)

Targets are the improvement of ROAS by 20%, the realisation of internal process efficiencies as well as the broadening of the upper funnel (contacts), like the increase in conversion (sales) in the lower funnel. Comparative values for the lower funnel provide for an increase of more than 40% for "Visits to Car Configurator" or "Sufficient Configurations", which ultimately (should) convert to the level of leads via generated profiles:

- The aggregation of data across all touchpoints allows the creation of audience segments, for example as a 15% increase in visits to the car configurator.
- An increase in the customer experience leads to a 10% increase in the actual execution of configurations.
- Account-based personalisation and targeting based on anonymous data improves acquisition and lead generation between 5% and 10%.
- Improved ad targeting, optimised SEA, social media, and programmatic advertising should significantly increase both page views and visits.

The "PowerHouse" concept, where employees from different silos come together and work in a concentrated manner on the completion of a topic, project, or campaign, considering the results of A/B testing, for example, has proven itself here. "Roll-out suitcases" for the markets include concrete plans for testing, parameterisation/customising in the respective country, task lists, or integration scenarios. The devil is in the detail: the greatest challenges arise primarily in the gradual replacement of individual applications, some of which are also operated in the (external) agency model. Financing is done centrally to avoid discussions with local markets about scope, requirements, and cost allocation keys within the Group.

Following the successful launch in 2019, *Marketecture 2.0* (Fig. 13.11) was adopted at the beginning of 2020 as a closed-loop model of customer management to be expanded by 2023, with the aim to:

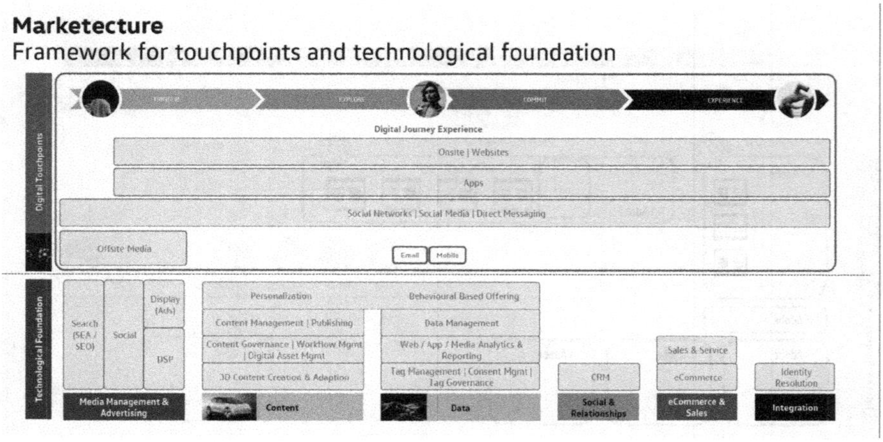

Fig. 13.11 Target Picture *Marketecture 2.0* at *Volkswagen* in 2023 (Marketing Tech Monitor 2022)

- More clearly take the step towards comprehensive data analytics along the entire customer journey
- Establish a high degree of marketing automation
- More strongly separate technologies and services and
- Individualise content along all touchpoints

The separation into domains such as "Data", "Content", "eCommerce & Sales", and "Media Management & Advertising" allows a stringent allocation of the functional coverage. Based on data collected, AI-based recommendations are subsequently to be made to customers. This goes hand in hand with a tendency towards stronger business process insourcing.

The next step is to include other brands of the *Volkswagen Group* (e.g. *Audi*, *Škoda*, or *Porsche*). For this purpose, business capabilities in marketing (business capability level 2) and "advertising and promotion" (business capability level 3) are further subdivided up to business capability level 4 (e.g. as "display and programmatic advertising)" and compared with the other Group brands in terms of application scenarios such as ad server, ad verification, DCO, or DSP about comprehensive use.

Lessons Learned

- Large projects with multiple interdependencies are more likely to be replaced by target pictures and the development of a flexible framework.
- A "best-of-suite" strategy is followed—unless the effort to introduce other applications seems reasonable due to the functional coverage.
- The decision about what makes sense must always be made at the content level; the IT application is only the "enabler" ... nothing more and nothing less.
- Before a roll-out in the countries (markets), the own area should first follow the established strategy.
- A lack of expertise (e.g. in retail processes) cannot be compensated by "fancy" applications.
- Governance is necessary for the implementation of a master construction plan/target picture with gradual roll-out into the markets.
- The main shortcoming is usually experienced project managers who can also say "no" and (can) steer the projects qua expertise and seniority.
- Business owners "at arm's length", as technical drivers, with authority and decision-making power, who can prioritise qua seniority/authority in the event of requirements getting out of hand.
- Think big, start small—take small steps to reach the goal and make the benefits clear on a permanent basis. Projects are not an end in themselves.

13.4 A New AI-Optimised World of Communication at *Tchibo* Every Week

A strong online shop with thousands of articles, plus thousands of shelves in supermarkets, and a network of hundreds of its own branches in numerous European countries—the traditional company *Tchibo* has grown mightily since it was founded in 1949. The business with coffee and a changing, carefully curated non-food range generates a good 3 billion euros in turnover every year. To ensure success, consumer insights are gained with the help of data, thus increasing customer satisfaction and the efficiency of the marketing measures used. To develop consumer insights, primary and secondary data are systematically linked, and growth potential is determined based on this (Fig. 13.12). AI methods have found their way into *Tchibo's* market research already since years.

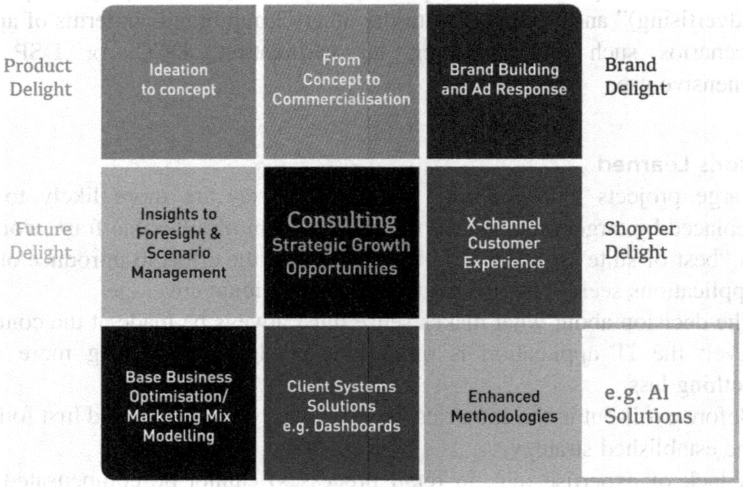

Fig. 13.12 Linking primary and secondary data at *Tchibo* (Marketing Tech Monitor 2023)

In principle, AI solutions offer countless possibilities to derive insights from millions of data points from different touchpoints with the customer. The decisive question here is at which point in the value chain AI approaches deliver the greatest added value. "Off-the-shelf solutions" will hardly bring the desired success. Market research at *Tchibo* has also gone its own way with:

- Flop identification
- Semantic engine and
- Ad pre-testing

The objective of *flop identification* for non-food products is to catch those products as early as possible in the development process of the *Tchibo's* weekly "new worlds" that are highly unlikely to bring the desired success, and to do this in a differentiated way according to the three retail channels of web shop, supermarket, and branch. Here, several thousand explicit survey results on content (e.g. spontaneous associations, likes/dislikes) for products as well as historical sales data are linked to form a forecast model. The basis is a large language model tailored to *Tchibo*. Flop identification is now an integral part of the non-food process at *Tchibo* and is used approximately 40 weeks before the market launch of a weekly world. The prediction quality is high at 75% to 80% depending on the channel. So, if the tool predicts a flop, it is highly likely to happen. Early placement in the launch process enables product management to react accordingly (Fig. 13.13).

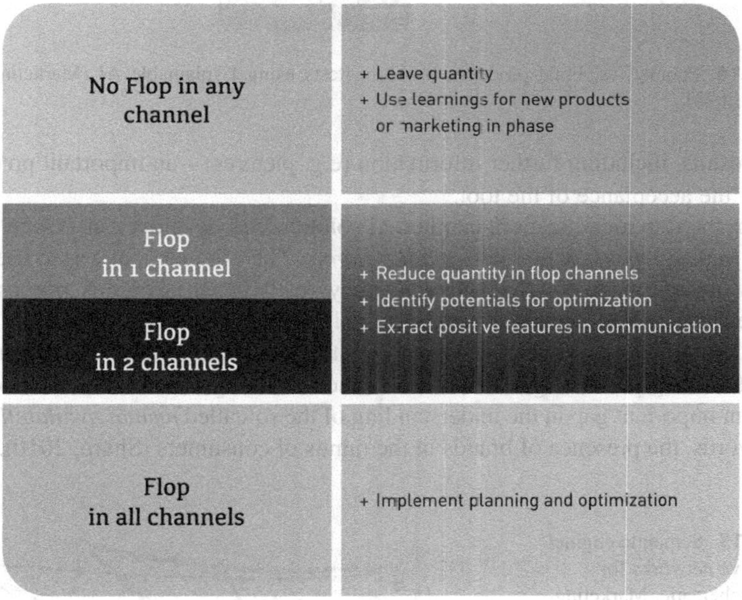

Fig. 13.13 AI-based recommendations for assortment planning (Marketing Tech Monitor 2023)

Today, the tool has reached a high level of maturity. However, this was a long road for the market research team, along which the model had to be constantly tested, trained, and improved. But one thing was clear early on: the human assessment of the future success of a non-food product could never come close to the precision of an AI solution. Too many aspects define success or failure, and human assessments are too subject to cognitive biases. Here, data must "speak", and it does so by means of two important advancements: explainable AI and a special front-end. *Explainable AI* serves to break down the success or failure factors of a product into understandable components (e.g. likes/dislikes on colour, cut, shape, functionality, implicit and explicit price perception, the fit to the motto of a weekly world), which product management can directly address (Fig. 13.14). The front-end enables intuitive access

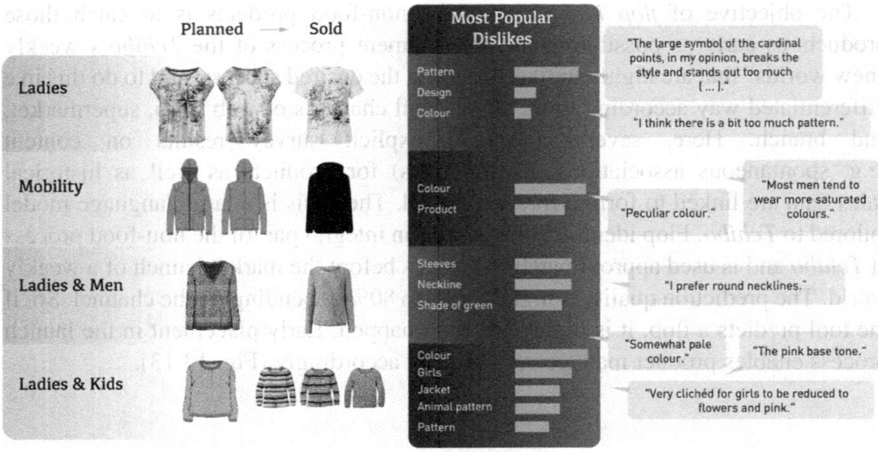

Fig. 13.14 Planned vs. Final products, based on tests using Explainable AI (Marketing Tech Monitor 2023)

to the results, including further information (e.g. pictures)—an important precondition for the acceptance of the tool.

From the flop identification, another AI solution was developed at *Tchibo* which is used in many ways today: the *semantic engine*. The original goal was to use AI to identify what consumers say and what they really mean. For this purpose, the so-called associative networks were used (Fig. 13.15), which were initially based on the tens of thousands of open mentions that consumers made about non-food products during pre-testing. Transferred to the marketing context, this method now closes an important gap in the understanding of the so-called *mental availability*—in other words, the presence of brands in the minds of consumers (Sharp, 2010). What

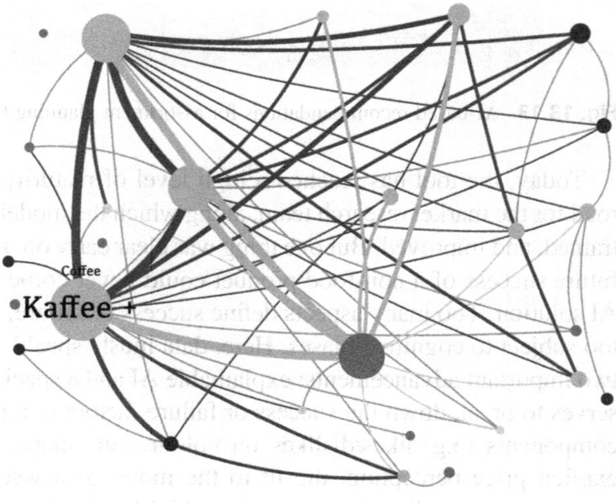

Fig. 13.15 Semantic engine/associative networks for coffee (schematic, Marketing Tech Monitor 2023)

images of brands exist in the minds of consumers that can be called up at the POS when needed? Which "distinctive assets" have made it into the mind? How are these connoted? Once again, it is a question of breaking down and structuring associations based on a language model and strong visualisation. And once again, this only succeeds with a front-end from which the user can quickly draw insights from the networks.

Such AI solutions help to understand all forms of content and open feedback, and to use them in their respective emphases and meanings or context (sentiment analysis), as well as for forecasting models (Binet & Feld, 2013). Ultimately, these solutions will eventually translate the results of surveys into reliable assessments of the success and failure of products in real time. They will shorten the expensive, cumbersome, and error-prone path from consumer statements to consumer insights.

Tchibo is currently also working on the AI-based optimisation of communication. Ultimately, it is strong campaigns that bring good products "to the people". Once again, AI will play an important and probably decisive role here in future. The quality of the creative artwork largely on the effectiveness and efficiency of the advertising budget used. Without strong copy, even the best assortment cannot be successfully brought to the target group. Classic pre-testing (surveys) today delivers good predictions on the effects of advertising on sales and brand, but it is expensive and therefore hardly scalable. This is where prediction models come into play, which have been trained based on the results of hundreds of classic pre-tests of advertising media and can now quickly and cost-effectively evaluate copy in terms of complexity, memorability, and sales impact. The focus is on whether copy and images can quickly convey the intended message—and if possible, in a real environment (e.g. city light posters in road traffic). AI-based, automated, and cost-effective test processes will not only deliver more results quickly in the future, but they will also help to improve the underlying models via these economies of scale.

And AI makes another important contribution to increasing the efficiency of advertising media: by linking it to marketing mix modelling. *Tchibo* has several years of practice with such models. The entire marketing mix, all divisions (e.g. coffee, non-food, mobile), all media, and all retail channels have been modelled for years. Basic sales and media-driven sales have long been precisely decomposed. However, one important component could not be meaningfully grasped until now: the effect of the creative performance—in other words, the monetary value of the creative performance that is contained in every advertising medium (Fig. 13.16).

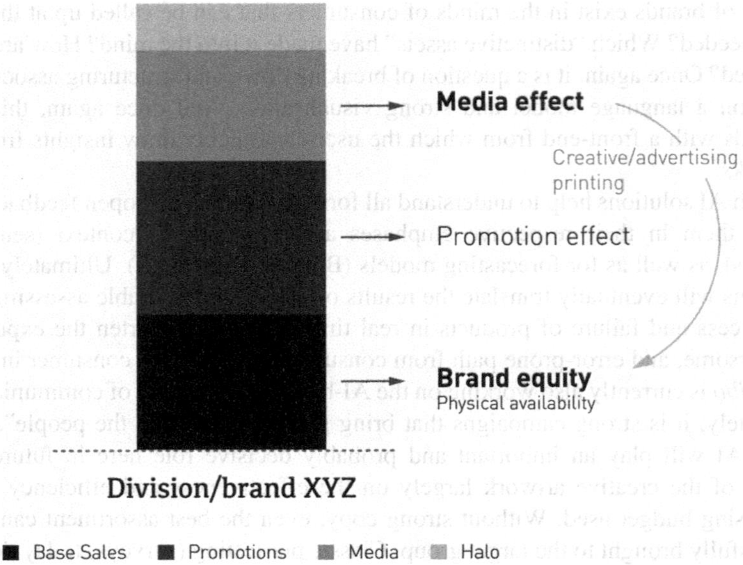

Fig. 13.16 Influencing factors on marketing mix models (schematic, Marketing Tech Monitor 2023)

With the economies of scale of AI-based solutions described above, it will be possible to pre-test many more advertising media, collect many more data points, and close one of the last big gaps in marketing mix models. Giving the value of creative performance "a price ticket"—a big step towards increasing advertising efficiency (Fig. 13.17). *Tchibo's* market research has long since embarked on this path and is currently testing diverse options.

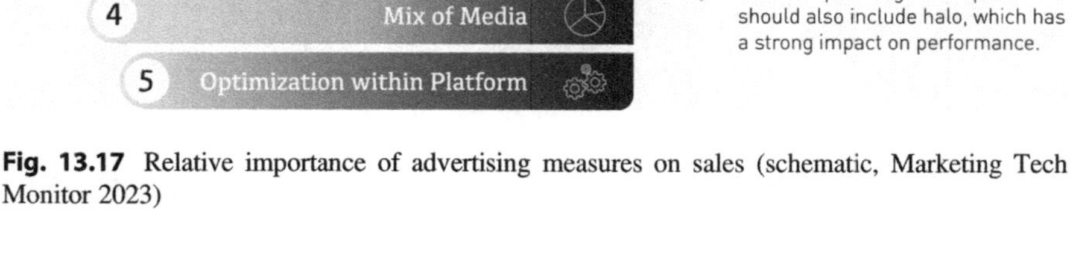

Fig. 13.17 Relative importance of advertising measures on sales (schematic, Marketing Tech Monitor 2023)

Lessons Learned

- Artificial intelligence has long since found its way into the field of consumer insights. Previous methodological approaches will hardly be able to survive in the future.
- However, not everything that glitters "AI" is gold. Solutions must be developed for one's own area of application. Patience, time, and budget are needed in this respect.
- Results must be checked and validated repeatedly. Test, learn, train.
- If an AI solution is not stable, the classical approach is good enough.
- Correlations are not causalities. But in causalities lie scalability.
- An understanding of the underlying methods, such as multivariate statistics, is indispensable today—otherwise, models are often "black boxes" that defy their own assessment of their quality.

13.5 Setting Up a Content Engine at *Deutsche Bank*

Deutsche Bank has fundamentally changed its business model since 2019. The bank is now entering a phase of sustainable growth, in which it will benefit from a leaner and more focused set-up. The focus is on the goal of further expanding *Deutsche Bank's* position as a "global house bank". As the leading bank in Germany with strong European roots, a global network, and a broadly diversified product offering, *Deutsche Bank* wants to become the first point of contact for even more clients in all financial matters. *Deutsche Bank* wants to navigate its clients through geopolitical and macroeconomic changes and accelerate the transformation to a sustainable and digitalised economy.

From *Deutsche Bank's* perspective, the establishment of a unified content engine is of crucial importance. "Content" is defined as an ecosystem of technology, processes, and people that ensures the interaction of thematically charged brand experiences across all channels (e.g. digital, analogue, existing, and emerging). The MarTech components used should ensure that the right content (e.g. relevant and "convenient") is published globally at the right time, to the right user (e.g. target group, existing customers, and/or non-customers) and in the right way (e.g. emotional, rational, formal, dramaturgical-temporal, or dramaturgical-spatial). In this way, the content engine should be a future-proof, media-neutral technology backbone to ensure the business with relevant content about and around products and the brand. The premises for the "target operating model":

- Flexible responses to changing user behaviour and proactive enrichment of the lives of customers and prospects.
- A maximum of consistency and automation of the integrated, cross-media and staggered campaigns.

- A brand-adequate and "best-in-class" user experience with significant business impact through the real-time consideration of the customer/user context.
- Support for day-to-day marketing and processes, strategically and operationally as well as efficiently and ergonomically.

The enormous number of applications used in combination with heterogeneous processes meant that before the content engine was established, the creation of an E-Mail newsletter took up to 4 weeks. The challenge in this case was that while BI analyses could already show in detail where the customer was in the respective life cycle and how this could best be addressed, content and channel management could hardly pick up on these insights and implement them (Fig. 13.18).

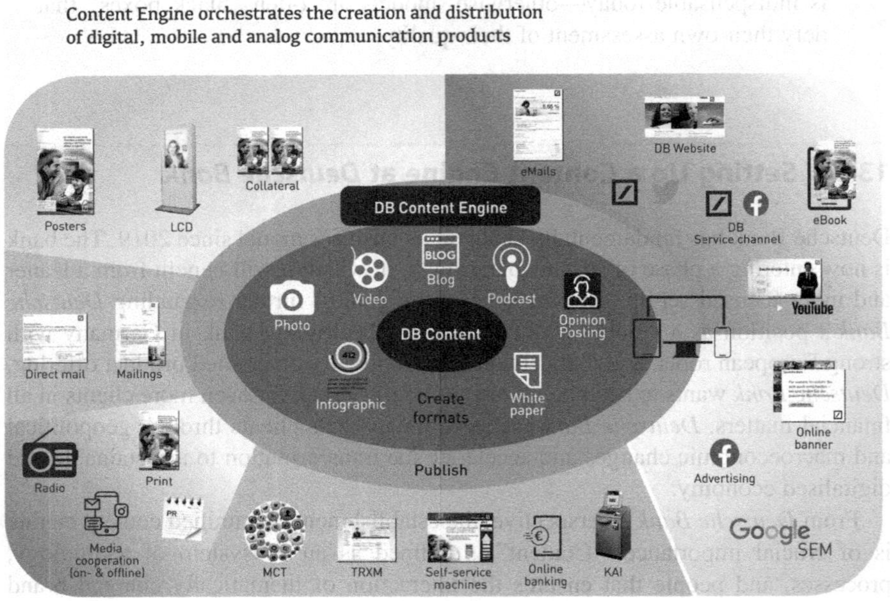

Fig. 13.18 *Deutsche Bank* content engine functions (Marketing Tech Monitor 2023)

In the selection process, eight central use cases were initially defined, which were agreed with the most important countries (focus markets) and handed over to selected providers. The criteria were, on the one hand, the fulfilment of the functional requirements, such as the support of the use cases, the user experience (from the employees' and agency's point of view), and the chance of a "faster time to market". From an IT perspective, the focus was on compliance with existing standards, the understanding of all required components, a high degree of reusability of already existing components, compliance with all IT security and control standards, cost transparency, and a complete (agile) proposal for integration/migration. This was supplemented with a commercial view regarding the positioning of the provider, costs (terms and conditions), competences on the part of the provider as well as the availability of reference customers. The cross-functional project team was deliberately kept small, with seven participants, to ensure that all the necessary competences could be incorporated into the process, but at the same time the complexity remained manageable and there was a high level of personal commitment. Since suite providers could hardly meet the detailed requirements, different providers were selected for different subject areas (as "best-of-function") (Fig. 13.19).

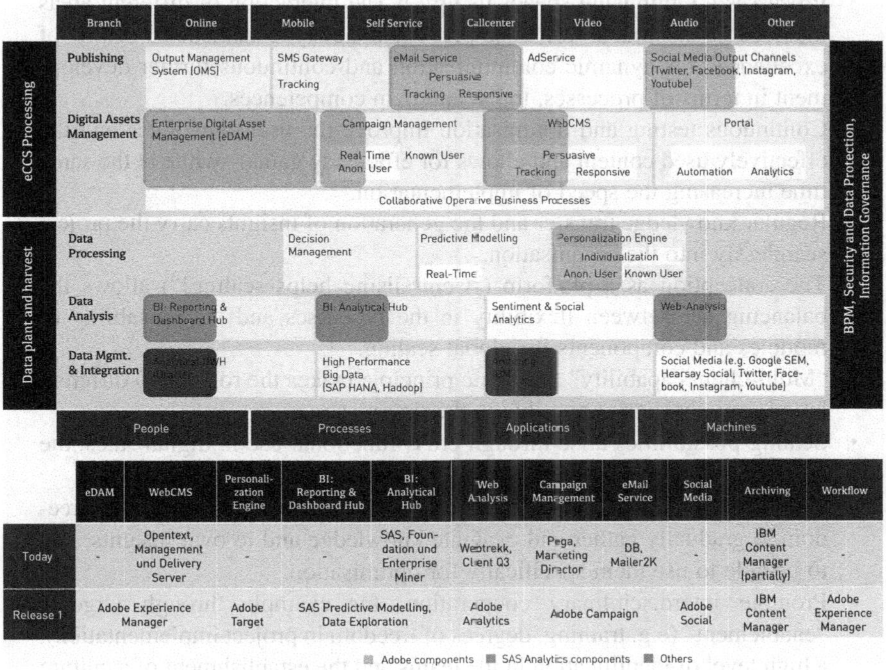

Fig. 13.19 Changes in the architectural landscape using the content engine (Marketing Tech Monitor 2023)

The core of the introduction—analogous to the introduction of on-site analytics—was viewer and editor training, accompanied by a regular, cross-departmental exchange across segment marketing, website management, product management, media, and web analytics as well as digital sales. As a result, the process was standardised and automated as far as possible:

- Newsletter dispatch: From manual control to dark processing (automated dispatch after content approval).
- More detailed reporting: Control based on data (open/click rates for E-Mails).

- Personalised content playout: E-Mailings on the customer group level, websites on dynamic (cookie-based) communication (no multiple copies of pages).
- Structure of DAM: All the necessary assets for communication on the channels are stored in a "single source of truth".
- Effectiveness of "user flows" can now be checked and optimised much more quickly using analytics tools.
- Report call-up reduced from originally 20 min to 2 min.

Lessons Learned

- Processes ("Optimising speeds us up!"): The interaction of different areas must be orchestrated, for example via a newly established "centre of excellence" for dynamic communication and continuous further development in terms of processes, tools, and own competences.
- Continuous testing and optimisation improve the user experience and the effectively used content and allows for efficiency gains—while at the same time increasing the speed of implementation.
- Regular knowledge transfer and the generation of insights carry the project seamlessly into the organisation.
- The conception as a platform ("Centralising helps scaling!") allows the balancing act between flexibility in the processes and the reusability of modules and components for global scaling.
- "Multi-client capability" as a basic principle makes the roll-out to different brands or subsidiaries possible in the first place.
- Scaling possibilities arise through cross-functional use in digital sales, the acquisition of new customers and for retention measures.
- People ("Creativity beats rules!"): Allow and promote creativity and freedom to gradually gather and evaluate knowledge and to own insights, and to be able to use them specifically for optimisation.
- Promote interdisciplinary cooperation, for example through targeted "enablement" (e.g. training, degrees of freedom in project implementation), a high level of identification in the teams and the establishment of a culture of error.
- Creating internal "desirability" is more important than rational arguments.
- The basic funding of a template by a market or the head office lowers the entry hurdle for adoption on the ground.
- Incentives are necessary to generate and reward the right mindset of "rethinking".
- A small cross-functional project team with selected experts and a high level of commitment proves to be the most important ingredient for project success.
- Promises made by many providers have usually turned out to be at least rather "questionable".

13.6 Marketing Steering Framework (MSF) and Econometric Modelling at *Lufthansa*

The *Lufthansa Group* is one of the largest airlines worldwide and the leader among the European airline groups. The *Lufthansa Group's* goal in this role is to continue actively shaping the global airline market. In doing so, it makes targeted use of innovation and digitalisation potential to develop customer-oriented offers and increase efficiency. Against the backdrop of changing supply and demand structures, the further strengthening of the customer focus is thus a central core element of the Group strategy. The focus is on customers and their individual wishes and needs. Through an increasing individualisation of selectable product components, an improved travel experience, an interactive and personal dialogue, a solution-centric and available customer service as well as fast digital solutions, customers are to be individually valued along the entire travel chain and receive tailor-made solutions. In this context, the focus is placed on all topics that are highly relevant for customers, which influence repeat purchases and that, subsequently, secure long-term value generation for the *Lufthansa Group*.

As part of the digital transformation and the changeover to a (process-oriented) matrix organisation, the separate function "Marketing Steering, Intelligence and Processes" was established to answer the question of "What contribution does marketing make to the company's success?". The objective was to understand and systematically establish strategies, processes, technologies, and investment modelling as growth drivers. The focus here is on tasks such as:

- Harmonisation of MarketingTechnology across several airlines of the *Lufthansa Group* (LHG)
- Optimisation and Digitalisation of work processes
- Marketing measurement and controlling
- Establishing transparency about cause-and-effect relationships with the help of econometric modelling and attribution
- Recommendations for optimal budget use
- Introduction of system platforms such as MRM (finance and planning) and DAM (digital asset management) and
- Overarching harmonisation of technologies, methods, and processes to exploit efficiency potentials

Against the background of an extremely heterogeneous and historically grown technology and data landscape, the need arose not only to harmonise infrastructure and processes within a new process organisation and to make the interdependencies between marketing measures and corporate goals transparent, which would subsequently allow (budget) optimisation potentials to be realised (Fig. 13.20). Within the framework of the attribution analysis and modelling, it became clear that a systematic approach to digital marketing transformation is necessary, under challenges such as:

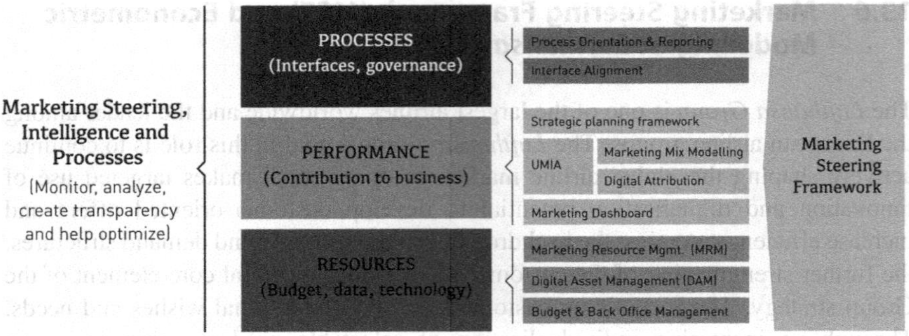

Fig. 13.20 Transformation levels and individual projects (Marketing Tech Monitor 2021)

- Only limited transparency due to a multitude of different technologies and applications for multiple overlapping tasks
- Limited steering capacity and independence from other areas due to limited access to data and
- Only limited (de facto) independence, as relevant task areas are predominantly managed by agencies

To analyse the as-is situation and to create a target picture, the marketing steering framework (MSF) project was initiated, which was carried out across all departments of the individual airlines of the *Lufthansa* Group. For this purpose, a cross-functional project team was established right at the beginning together with representatives from the areas of IT, data management, e-commerce, and media purchasing of all participating airlines. The transformation then took place in three steps (Fig. 13.21): (1) As-is analysis (technology landscape), (2) Development of a target picture based on solution issues (solution design, development plan), and, finally (3) Launch and realisation of individual implementation projects.

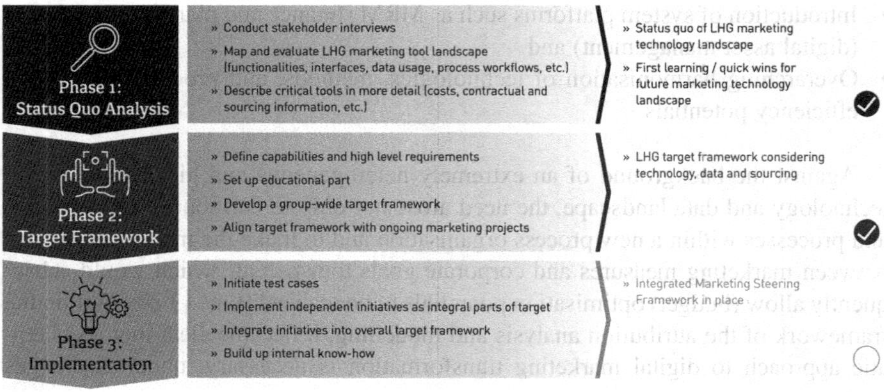

Fig. 13.21 Project phases of the marketing steering framework (MSF; Marketing Tech Monitor 2021)

Within the as-is analysis, a complete technology map was created as part of the inventory, including the functions of the respective tools and applications, their functional affiliation (e.g. marketing, sales, content, BI, IT), their affiliation to certain functional areas ("ownership") and support models (e.g. in-house, agency) as well as the data used in each case (Fig. 13.22).

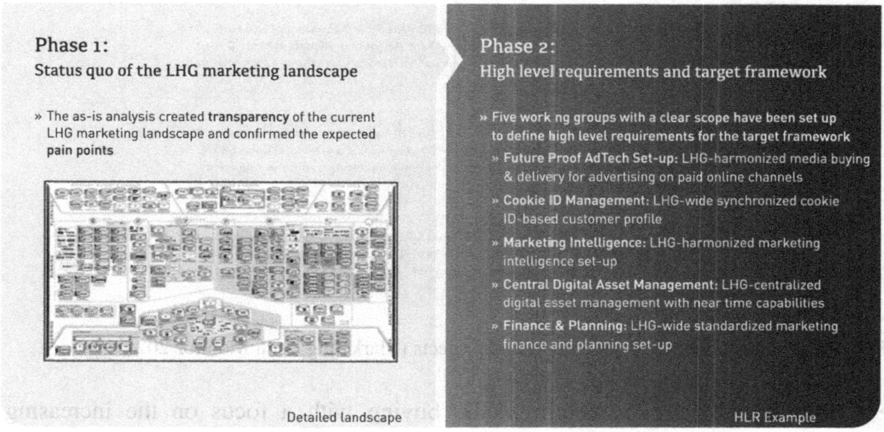
Phase 1:
Status quo of the LHG marketing landscape
» The as-is analysis created transparency of the current LHG marketing landscape and confirmed the expected pain points
Detailed landscape
Phase 2:
High level requirements and target framework
» Five working groups with a clear scope have been set up to define high level requirements for the target framework
» Future Proof AdTech Set-up: LHG-harmonized media buying & delivery for advertising on paid online channels
» Cookie ID Management: LHG-wide synchronized cookie ID-based customer profile
» Marketing Intelligence: LHG-harmonized marketing intelligence set-up
» Central Digital Asset Management: LHG-centralized digital asset management with near time capabilities
» Finance & Planning: LHG-wide standardized marketing finance and planning set-up
HLR Example

Fig. 13.22 Functional areas and technology map (Marketing Tech Monitor 2021)

Five strategic fields of action were defined based on the MarTech map, and the corresponding high-level requirements were developed for each field of action. For each field of action, a cross-functional work group was started, which worked out requirements and solution issues in detail and identified the redundancies as well as the functional gaps, based on which a technological solution design (development plan) integrated into the existing system landscape was created for the next 3–5 years across all airlines of the *Lufthansa Group*. Within the design for the overarching target picture, functional sub-target pictures were worked out for individual areas and process domains and the connections between the functions were described on a functional and process-related level. The subsequent implementation projects covered five central elements along the processes (Fig. 13.23):

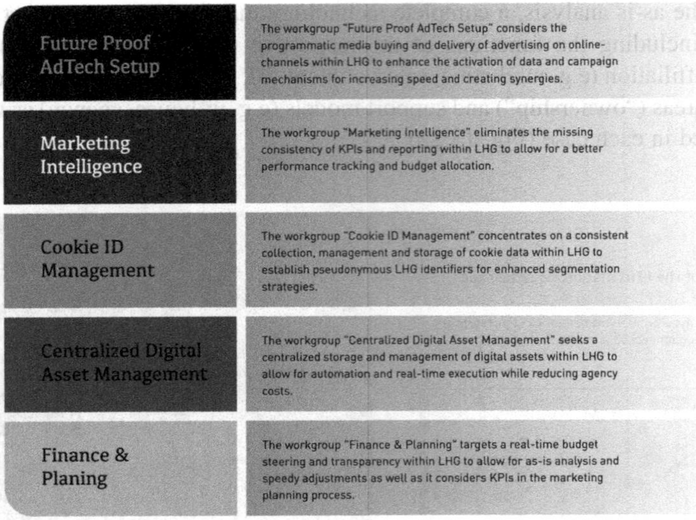

Fig. 13.23 Functional areas and individual projects (Marketing Tech Monitor 2021)

- Future-proof AdTech Set-up: Media buying with a focus on the increasing "programmatisation" of advertising. The aim is to create transparency within the systems, ensure conformity with in-house strategies, and support the connection to data platforms with the aim of automated optimisation.
- Marketing Intelligence: Data management, incl. development of an own marketing data platform (Hadoop, plus development of data pipelines of own business data, agency and third-party data) within the Group platform. Based on this, econometric models and attribution modelling were started to gradually optimise media investments based on data. This is seconded by the introduction of a uniform and KPI-based strategic planning process with a focus on the effect of individual measures on the company's success. The developed marketing mix model fully maps the business process and integrates sales effects (lower funnel) as well as medium- and long-term brand effects (upper funnel) and is methodically and systemically linked to digital attribution. Cross-marketing dashboards have been integrated to increase transparency.
- Cookie ID Management: The collection and management of user data and IDs, and the exchange and modelling of data using segmentation and predictive analytics.
- Centralised Digital Asset Management: Central production control and asset management (e.g. administration, real-time release), incl. the automated processing of personalised advertising with interfaces to media buying, dynamic content, and rights management.
- Finance and Planning: Harmonisation of work processes and budget control through tool-based marketing planning and KPI management with the help of marketing resource management, incl. connection to ERP FI/CO (cost centre).

Implementation takes place within individual projects based on further detailed individual initiatives (Fig. 13.24).

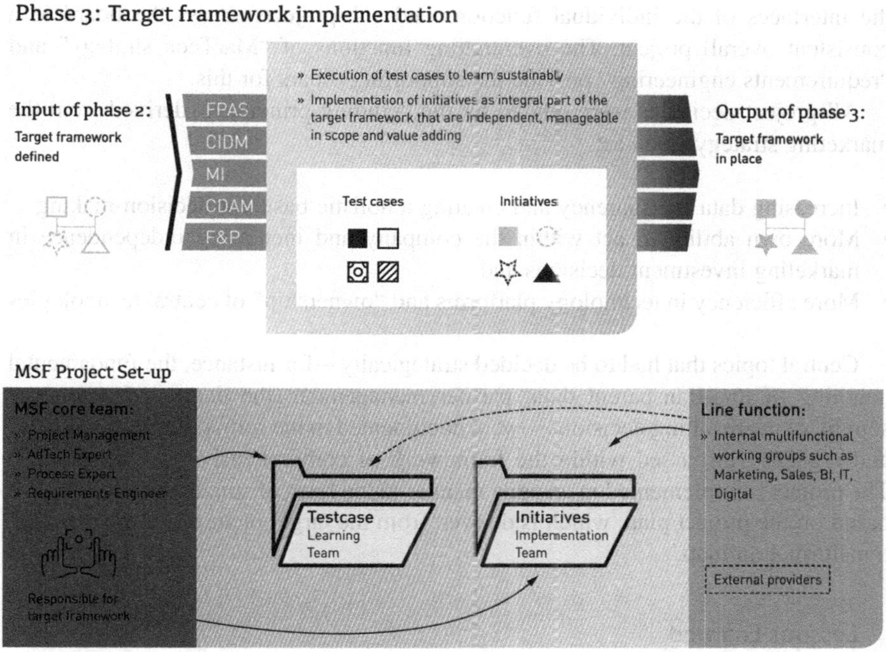

Fig. 13.24 From the target picture to individual implementation initiatives (Marketing Tech Monitor 2021)

Central to the success of the project was the definition of a strategic framework (common understanding of goals) and a "digital culture" that guides all individual decisions to be made. This includes, above all, the goal of creating harmonised data and consistent results chains as well as end-to-end transparency across the customer journey (Fig. 13.25). The core project team, which was set up to ensure consistency among the individual projects, had the main task as program management of leading

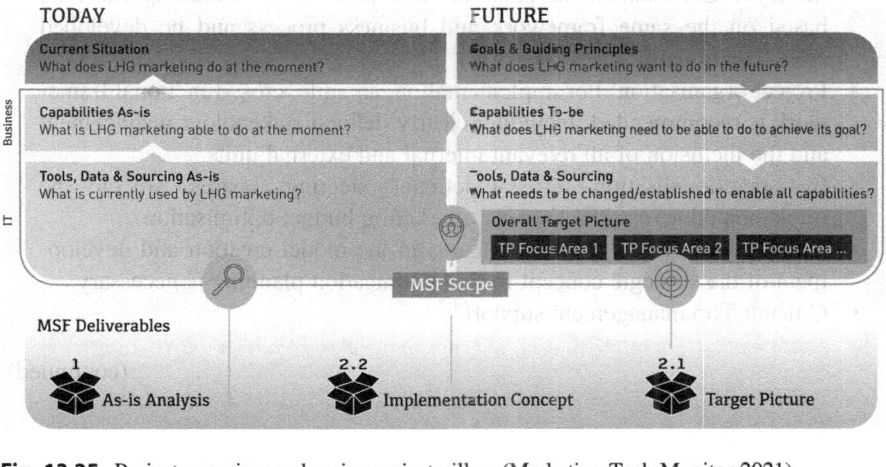

Fig. 13.25 Project overview and major project pillars (Marketing Tech Monitor 2021)

the interfaces of the individual functions and sub-projects across the board to a consistent overall project. The overarching functions of "MarTech strategy" and "requirements engineering" provide the supporting pillars for this.

All project decisions were guided by the "guiding principles" derived from the marketing strategy, such as:

- Increasing data transparency and creating a holistic basis for decision-making
- More own ability to act within the company and increasing independence in marketing investment decisions and
- More efficiency in technology platforms and "ownership" of central technologies

Central topics that had to be decided strategically—for instance, the fundamental handling of non-transparent data, partner management, the degree of autonomy sought, or the resulting decisions—were documented in the form of "solution issues" and regularly discussed within the framework of comprehensive steering boards. The project is implemented in an agile manner in the form of small individual sprints based on the project plan, which is derived from the target picture and the resulting transformation map.

Lessons Learned

- The creation of "solution issues" is a central success factor: Which strategic decisions do we have to make that are action-guiding for the description of the respective function?
- Requirements must be created on a cross-functional basis. The overall target picture plus detailed requirements serve as the basis for the subsequent control of all individual projects.
- The introduction of consistent data concepts in terms of semantics and syntax/data structure is central, as is the alignment of naming conventions.
- The introduction of GDPR and new framework conditions in digital data management requires the adaptation of methods used.
- Strategy: Communication planning and investment modelling must be based on the same framework and business process and be developed cross-functionally.
- Project organisation: For implementation, an agile, cross-functional framework is recommended, including clearly defined stakeholder management and the inclusion of all relevant internal and external units.
- In operationalisation, cross-functional steering boards are to be implemented across all channels (marketing budget optimisation).
- Close integration of the media teams in the model creation and development of the strategic concept for communication planning is necessary.
- Crucial: Top management support.

(continued)

- Overarching requirements: Integration of data and technology requirements into agency contracts is necessary to ensure systematic and frequent exchange processes as well as structured data delivery.
- Change process: Measures to support the change process must be implemented.

13.7 Scalable Data Architecture at *Lufthansa*

Before establishing a new data architecture, *Deutsche Lufthansa* was faced with the challenge of having to combine a wide variety of data, such as commercial data (e.g. customers, bookings) or ops data (e.g. airline operations such as flight plans, baggage tracking, punctuality). Each airline and domain within the *Lufthansa Group* had historically grown data landscapes and its own data warehouses (e.g. the airlines *Swiss*, *Lufthansa*, *Austrian*). The consequence: unless a key identifier is available (e.g. via *Miles & More Ident*), customer data and the associated preferences could hardly be merged. The 360-degree customer perspective (e.g. CLV calculations, a golden record) then fails directly at the data boundary of the respective domain. Due to the lack of integration, it could also be the case that passengers who had just lost their baggage (operations) were sent an offer for baggage protection by marketing (commercial). The respective data warehouses were usually maintained by (several, different) external providers, so that there was no complete know-how on the part of the *Lufthansa* Group—from data engineering to the level of simple administrative tasks.

This created a situation in which:

- Different technologies and standards—such as SOAP, REST, JMS, data formats, open frameworks, and proprietary interfaces—collided.
- Different programming languages and platforms such as Java, .NET, or R are used.
- Across different application architectures such as service-oriented architectures or microservices and
- Different communication paradigms such as batch processing, (near) real-time, request-response, or fire-and-forget existed.

The *One Data Platform* was used to implement a cloud-native infrastructure in *Microsoft Azure* (cloud-based insourcing) where new use cases were first built on an access layer. On the *One Data Platform*, all application scenarios were developed completely from scratch; there was no porting from legacy systems. In a second wave, all existing legacy data warehouses are now to be integrated into a cloud-native lakehouse. On the one hand, the lakehouse enables the cost-effective storage of data, and on the other hand, it supports ACID transactions (atomicity, consistency, isolation, and durability, i.e. parallel reading and writing of data, among other things) and thus offers the core functionality of a classic data warehouse. At the same time, higher-value analytics scenarios are being established, for example for machine learning. The transition from distributed database systems took place gradually, with a focus on the use cases throughout the process (Fig. 13.26).

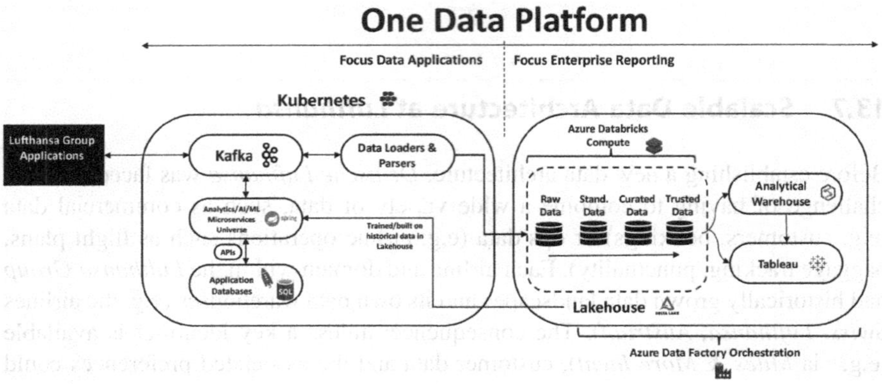

Fig. 13.26 Data architecture of the *Deutsche Lufthansa Group's One Data Platform* (Marketing Tech Monitor 2022)

For the integration of the lakehouse with the operative applications of the *Lufthansa Group*, the Group relies on *Kafka*, a streaming platform for integration. *Kafka* uses events as its core principle. One sees these events in the constant (data) flow and in the processing of the data while they are in motion. The features of a streaming platform include:

- Event-based data flow as the basis for real-time processing.
- A scalable central nervous system for events between any number of sources and sinks across the entire *Lufthansa Group* as a scalable, distributed infrastructure.
- Out-of-the-box connectors for all common database products or programming languages such as *Java* or *Python*, which enable the uncomplicated connection of existing legacy applications, but also newly developed microservices and
- The modelling of stateless services and of stateful business processes. Business processes typically operate as stateful processes, and design patterns such as event sourcing help to implement this in an event-driven streaming architecture.

The advantages of a streaming platform like *Kafka* are (elastic) scalability in terms of nodes, volume, and throughput as well as a flexible architecture for building small services, large services, or monoliths. Asynchronously connected microservices model complex business processes and move data to where it is needed (event-driven microservices). At the same time, there is openness for technologies and data formats, as well as independent and decoupled business services and multi-client capability.

For the *Lufthansa Group*, the application scenarios of a streaming platform range from:

- Event-driven processing of large data sets (e.g. logs, social feeds, web clickstream) and
- Business-critical real-time applications (e.g. bookings, customer experience) to
- A microservices architecture, for example for machine learning

Lessons Learned

- Close cooperation with *Microsoft* as a technology partner, which also has a fully integrated platform with *Azure*.
- The onboarding of the colleagues concerned could have been expanded—in addition to the *Azure* self-learning offer could have been training for the translation into the *Lufthansa* context.
- It was necessary to subdivide the data lake due to data protection.
- Tools must mesh seamlessly, otherwise the advantage of individual applications is directly lost again.
- The change in data architecture also entails a change in the tools and applications used, for example from *SQL* queries to *Python*.

13.8 Automated Activation of Customers at *Lufthansa*

The demand for quality with "premium" as a central building block of *Lufthansa's* business model should be reflected in automated, high-quality and high-frequency customer interaction and communication across the various channels. After setting up an entire planning and steering framework and a scalable data platform, the *One Data Platform*, the next step was to focus on the use of all acquired data points and insights across all communication channels, including the segmentation and activation of differentiated segments and audiences.

For this purpose, all available first-party data is aggregated across all touchpoints and applications (e.g. CRM) and the respective consent is checked (Fig. 13.27). Alongside third-party data, this forms the basis for enterprise data model and marketing analytics use cases based on it. The integrated data is transferred to the customer data platform for the event stream, predictions, and the creation of customer profiles (segmentation). Anonymous customers (unknown customers) are identified via tag management and cleaned via clickstream ingestion for transfer to other applications and subsequent activation. The CDP used ensures that all available data points are aggregated, including data from flight ops (e.g. flight movements, flight delays), while other data first enters individual segments/audiences and thus cannot generate unfiltered activities in the various channels.

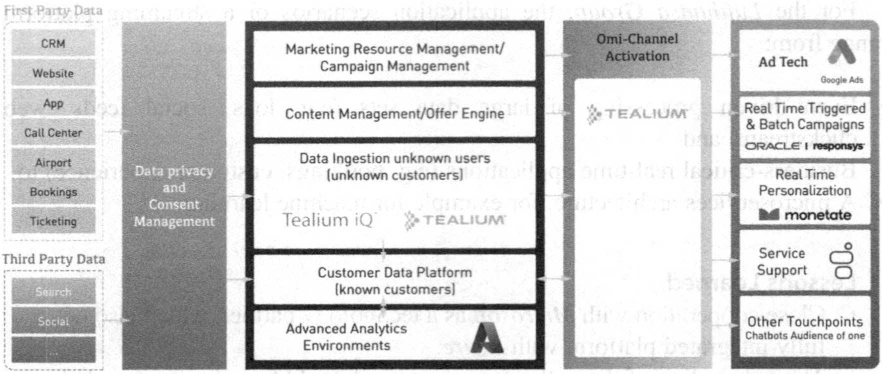

Fig. 13.27 MarTech application landscape for omnichannel activation at *Deutsche Lufthansa* (Marketing Tech Monitor 2023)

In the context of omnichannel activation, audiences (i.e. target groups) are then formed from, for example, anonymised web sessions and first-party data, and business rules for communication are defined. In this way, the *Lufthansa Group* achieves a significantly more relevant and personal approach to customers in terms of content, design, timing of communication, and communication channel.

The orchestration across the communication channels is (prospectively) controlled in real time by means of AI. Target audiences are addressed programmatically within the framework of channel control, for example via connected DSPs, or also via personalised E-Mails, the *Passenger Lufthansa App*, or text message. At the same time, the information will be available in the future as attributes for individualised call centre interactions.

Decisive for the success of customer activation through segmentation is the creation of specific content, the creation of the respective communication channel, as well as the selection of the right time of publication depending on the audience by the marketing and communications department of the *Lufthansa Group*. These departments also play a special role in generating and developing strategic lifetime customer journeys. Professional know-how and data-driven decision-making are complementary.

To ensure that the resources deployed are used effectively, all potential use cases are carefully examined to determine whether they offer a clear and comprehensible return on investment (ROI). This means that expected increases in turnover, cost savings, and efficiency gains from the planned measures are analysed and evaluated in detail.

Furthermore, the strategy of the *Lufthansa Group* is also considered. Paid media measures must be in line with the overarching corporate goals, such as the focus on "premium". Care is taken to ensure that the selected use cases are integrated into the *Lufthansa Group's* digital marketing mix and that synergetic effects are achieved with other marketing channels.

The strict application of ROI criteria in the selection of paid media use cases ensures a data-driven and results-oriented approach to digital advertising measures. This enables an optimal allocation of resources and a continuous improvement of the *Lufthansa Group's* digital marketing activities.

Lessons Learned

- An end-to-end view of the entire value chain in a cross-functional delivery team is essential.
- The focus should always be on the lifetime customer journey.
- Automated campaigns can be used to determine, at least in near real time, whether or what additional bookings a campaign has generated and in which booking classes.
- Manual activities are gradually reduced, such as the creation of ad hoc audiences or the sending of push notifications.
- AI-driven orchestration requires a step-by-step approach and learning along the way, for example using machine learning for scoring across all customer data based on clickstream analysis or also the right timing for an approach or the selection of the preferred channel from the customer's point of view.
- The size of the audiences is crucial for scaling the marketing campaigns.
- The use of first-party data is financially "relevant".

13.9 Setting Up Our Own Data Science Landscape (DSML) at *HUK24*

HUK24 is the leading German online insurance company, with over 2.4 million customers, and the digital and price spearhead in the *HUK-Coburg Group*. As a pure online provider, the orchestration of customer and analytics data via its own data platform (DSML) is a particular focus of *HUK24*. The objective: to provide real-time product and content recommendations based on multiple data sources. Depending on the application, an analytics engine decides whether customer or transaction data is more relevant and uses these data points to provide specific content to users. The marketing and tech strategy thus focuses on the broad, mass advertising of products for highly specialised (individualised) target groups, in particular the targeted addressing of young and affine target groups for the additional module "Telematik Plus" in car insurance. Analytics data is used to divide website users into interest segments, which receive a website tailored to them via the audience layer so that *HUK24* can display all insurance products for the relevant target groups.

The discussion about a MarketingTech build-up at *HUK24* was triggered, on the one hand, by the need to defend market leadership. After 18 years, as the leading online insurance company, they were challenged to adapt technologies to defend their ancestral market leadership. The vision is clearly defined: to be the online "insurance engine" generating the most online insurance deals in 2025. Pain points were the insufficient possibilities to analyse how users behave on the website or to perform A/B testing between different website variants. The objective for the considerations was therefore the desire to gain a precise understanding of user behaviour in a purely online business model with only few interaction points (mainly characterised by annually cancellable car insurance policies), which makes a precise addressing of potential customers in the real-time website momentum imperative. Necessary for this is:

- The creation of a data platform and corresponding data quality
- The possibility to check changes quantitatively and
- The inclusion of best practices from other digital companies (e.g. e-commerce)

The goal is to achieve the highest possible level of automation, with a large part of user communication and interaction being automated, with detailed user analyses at the push of a button (and not through log file analyses) and with optimisations that are automated as far as possible but still traceable.

Analogous to other companies, the MarTech development was started with an analytics solution. For this, preliminary work had already been done and experience gained with Adobe Analytics. Subsequently, a testing and personalisation tool was introduced to be able to implement website changes on a larger scale. From a proof of concept (PoC) with two different providers, the better integration with the existing analytics and CMS solution ultimately tipped the scales. Parallel to this, a DMP was set up to be able to leverage user data in real time and for displaying ads (Fig. 13.28). The PoCs launched for this did not produce a clear winner, which is why, against the background of the experience with the testing solution, the decision was once again

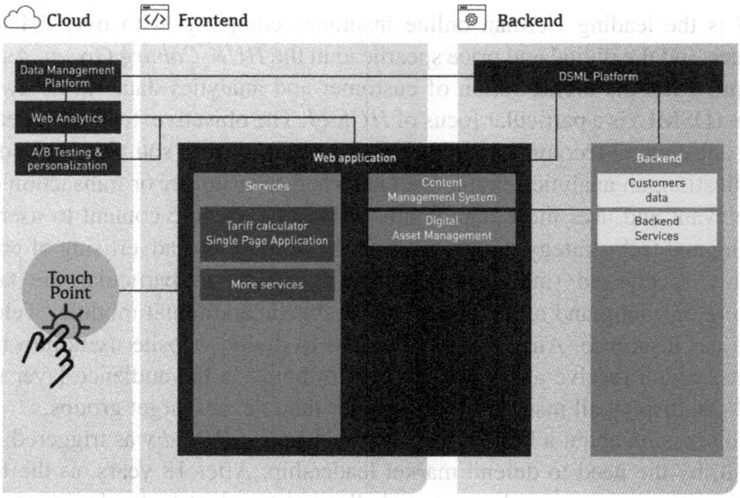

Fig. 13.28 MarketingTech development at *HUK24* (Marketing Tech Monitor 2021)

made in favour of the solution that harmonises best with the existing analytics solution. The next step is to introduce an orchestration engine to be able to distinguish between customer and transaction data in real time and to address the customer in the best feasible way based on a Situational Relevance Index (SRI).

Currently, an analytics solution is used for near real-time dashboards and continuous monitoring, with ad hoc analyses for current developments, segment identification for A/B testing and personalisation, and a DMP for off-site activities with first-party data and initial real-time personalisation. As before, there are challenges in data quality: business figures according to controlling and web analytics solutions sometimes differ greatly, which ties up resources for maintenance and research that could and should be used for optimisation. As a result, the credibility of both systems decreases. In practice, data collection based on DSML is rather complex due to the required consent management—extensive data collection is only possible with user consent. Despite standardised interfaces and the selection of a preferred vendor as technology provider, the integration of the systems sometimes takes several months. Even if manufacturers suggest that they have integrated their own solutions natively, the reality paints a clearly different picture. The reason for this is that the platforms of individual providers have emerged from—yet still not—integrated acquisitions. While the presentation layer (i.e. UI) has mostly been harmonised, underlying data models, processes, and structures have remained the same. In some places, integration is further complicated by internal IT security requirements. The ROI for the use of a DMP presented here appears questionable. The development towards third-party cookie blocking and the implementation of the ePrivacy Directive could make this MarTech segment completely superfluous. The experience gained in the development of the MarTech landscape brings the decision of own purchase versus agency model back into focus.

So far, *HUK24* has been able to achieve an increase of 70% in new business in the sales focus product "home contents" in 3 years, which can be attributed to several factors such as a contemporary CX through single-page application, the data-driven optimisation of online marketing measures for new customer acquisition, and the targeted approach to existing customers to increase upsell rates. In parallel, the process for several A/B tests per month was established, with alerting/monitoring of all relevant KPIs in mobile/desktop and per channel, so that outliers can be quickly identified and further offers made. The time span for the implementation of optimisations, from the identification of a weak point to the live setting via A/B testing, is now only 2 weeks. In the future, the aim is to integrate customer data more strongly for website personalisation and trigger communication, as well as to use web data to trigger communication.

Lessons Learned

- PoC with individual providers shows more opportunities/risks than the most detailed analysis of feature sheets and questionnaires.

(continued)

- Setting up the other tools with the analytics solution at the core seems to make sense.
- Think about the further development process right from the start . . . or also: the use cases first emerge during the application.
- Early integration of programming, IT security, and data protection significantly accelerates the selection and implementation process.
- There are no global MarketingTech requirements. These must be developed specifically for each company.
- The focus for all solutions was strongly on integration capability.
- Integration with analytics is essential for personalisation.
- When selecting a DMP, focus more on the campaign benefits.
- Quality needs time: In retrospect, the introduction of analytics, personalisation, and DMP within 12 months was perhaps too fast. This meant that no extensive testing of different implementations could be carried out (e.g. client-side vs. server-side).

13.10 Marketing Automation at *QIAGEN*

QIAGEN is the world's leading provider of sample preparation and testing technologies for molecular diagnostics. This involves the extraction, preparation, and analysis of biological samples of all kinds. Its customers, among them numerous Nobel Prize winners, come from research, the pharmaceutical industry, and applied diagnostics in medical institutions and laboratories from around the world. For some years now, *QIAGEN* has been pursuing a multimodal sales strategy in which digital marketing and sales channels increasingly play an integral role. The company's own aspiration is to offer B2B customers a customer experience that is comparable to or even better than the one they are used to in their private B2C environment. The digital transformation of marketing and sales at *QIAGEN* is also based on the fundamental idea that in marketing automation, the goal is to efficiently set up and execute B2B campaigns across all channels and to be able to precisely evaluate them afterwards. Automation functions that facilitate tasks or take them over completely help to concentrate on the essentials: the conception of appealing campaigns and content.

The challenge from the marketing point of view at the time of the launch was only low efficiency in all marketing processes, comparatively excessive costs, and a lack of transparency about performance across all teams involved. The goal was therefore to increase efficiency, generate more leads at lower costs/resources, and increase the customer experience and customer loyalty through personalisation—in other words, to design relevant content across all touchpoints as a "seamless experience". From a customer experience perspective, a customer has on average about seven offline/online touchpoints along the customer journey before making a purchase. Customer loyalty should be increased through the launch of the customer engagement portal *My QIAGEN*, including the tracking of relevant key figures on the user experience, and the resulting continuous improvement measures, along the entire customer journey across all touchpoints and data sources (Fig. 13.29).

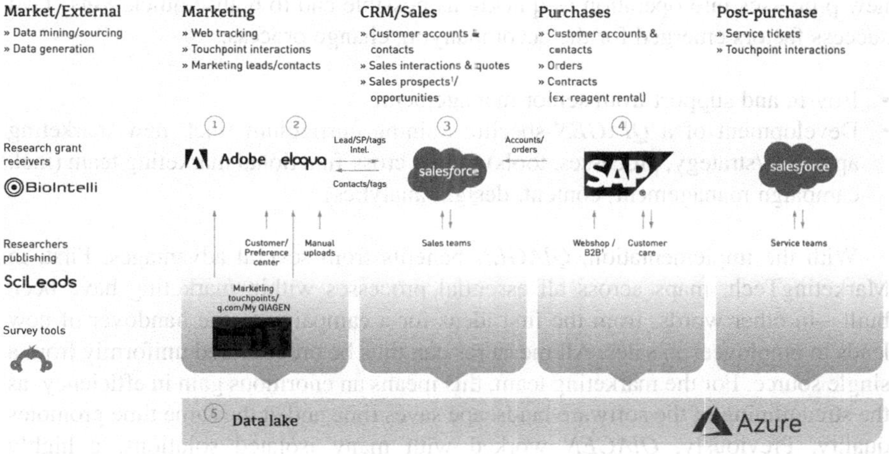

Fig. 13.29 Customer data source systems along the customer journey at *QIAGEN* (Marketing Tech Monitor 2022)

At the beginning, there were no firmly established, globally standardised processes, which had lasting implications for the process model:

- Centralisation of marketing execution in a centre of excellence (*QIAGEN Marketing Agency*) with highly specialised teams of experts (e.g. campaign management, channel experts, content, design, marketing analytics, and automation teams)
- Definition of globally standardised marketing processes by experts as well as the complementary development of the marketing IT infrastructure (e.g. automation of campaigns, performance reporting)

QIAGEN has chosen a suite approach to realise the benefits of further automation in marketing—the drivers for this decision:

- Centralised control and optimisation
- Avoidance of targeting conflicts
- Optimal pre-qualification of leads for sales through central scoring
- Efficiency gain through maintenance/administration/IT workflows in a single suite instead of various individual tools.

The project started with the development of standardised processes by the marketing expert teams and the determination of requirements for the subsequent IT development. Smaller, cross-functional project teams were responsible for implementing the requirements (e.g. final solution design, implementation, testing).

A dedicated marketing automation team was formed cross-functionally from performance marketing experts (point-of-contact to marketing teams) and platform experts (governance and maintenance). The roll-out took place in phases to be able to put new processes into operation as quickly as possible and to realise quick wins. Two success factors emerged for the accompanying change process:

- Buy-in and support from senior management
- Development of a *QIAGEN*-specific training curriculum (incl. new marketing approach/strategy, processes, tools) for the cross-functional marketing team (incl. campaign management, content, design, analytics)

With the implementation, *QIAGEN* benefits from several advantages. First, in MarketingTech, maps across all essential processes within marketing have been built—in other words, from the first ideas for a campaign to the handover of new leads to employees in sales. All measures can thus be orchestrated uniformly from a single source. For the marketing team, this means an enormous gain in efficiency, as the streamlining of the software landscape saves time and at the same time promotes quality. Previously, *QIAGEN* worked with many isolated solutions, a highly fragmented tool landscape and all the challenges this entailed. In retrospect, several factors stood out in the approach:

- Technical centralisation of processes together with the establishment of an internal marketing agency that benefits from the established applications, which has indirectly strengthened cross-functional cooperation ("everyone pulls together").
- Digital-first approach: Prioritising more efficient digital marketing channels over traditional marketing tools (e.g. creating content primarily for digital purposes).
- Common goals were set as a basis for good cooperation between the expert teams during the roll-out phase.

From a data perspective, the focus is thus on gaining a 360-degree view of the customer across all touchpoints (Fig. 13.30).

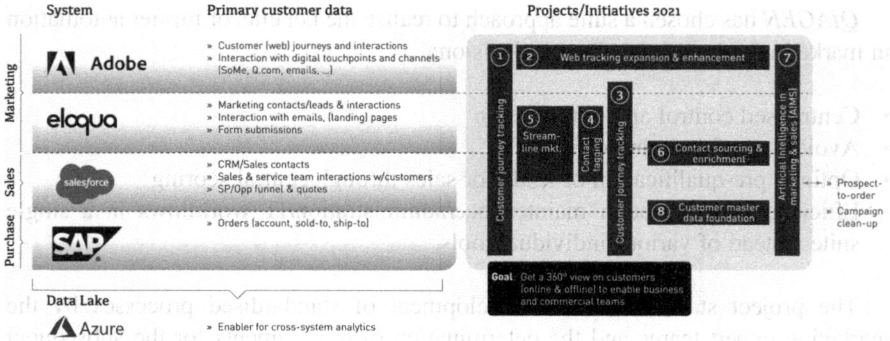

Fig. 13.30 Initiatives to obtain and improve customer data at *QIAGEN* (Marketing Tech Monitor 2022)

All this progress can be measured quantitatively and objectively. For example, instead of 60–80, 400–500 marketing campaigns per year are now possible—mainly thanks to the use of integrated automation. All functions sum up to a heterogeneous MarTech stack (Fig. 13.31).

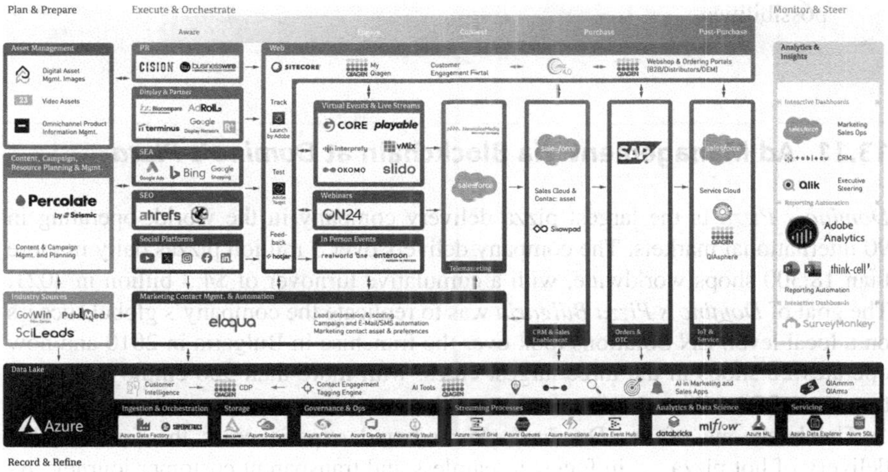

Fig. 13.31 *QIAGEN's* MarTech stack (Marketing Tech Monitor 2022)

Thanks to marketing automation, *QIAGEN* can tailor its campaigns much more specifically to individual target groups. The qualitative result:

- Increase in opening and click-through rates by 50%, with decreasing opt-out numbers.
- Increase in leads passed to sales and resulting opportunities by 200%.
- Higher engagement (more likes, views, comments, forwards) at the digital touchpoints through better addressing of the target group and targeted communication of the marketing campaigns.

Lessons Learned

- Organisational structure with centralised, global experts is an essential building block.
- Process organisation "high level" defined by the project team, but detailed elaboration by the later responsible marketing process experts (definition of own future work processes was also an important element of the successful change process).
- A cross-functional marketing automation team is an essential component (i.e. marketing experts, suite/system experts as well as IT technical experts).

(continued)

- Only recognised in the second step: Need for dedicated experts per (digital) marketing channel with a clear mandate: (1) to advise internal marketing stakeholders, (2) to ensure best practices, and (3) to continuously develop the channel and channel performance, also regarding automation possibilities.

13.11 Ad Management Via Blockchain at *Domino's Pizza*

Domino's Pizza is the largest pizza delivery company in the world, operating in 90 international markets. The company delivers over 3 million pizzas daily in more than 18,300 shops worldwide, with a cumulative turnover of $4.3 billion in 2021. The goal of *Domino's Pizza Bulgaria* was to replicate the company's global success on a local level. LN Solutions took over the franchise in Bulgaria in 2010 and now operates 22 shops in the three largest cities, with more than 900 employees and a turnover of 28 million euros.

The backbone of the *Domino's Pizza* brand experience is the fast, reliable delivery of hot pizza ... in focus: a seamless and transparent customer journey. As part of a consumer-centric digital strategy, *Domino's* has relied heavily on MarTech and innovation over the years. At the same time, the pandemic has led to strong growth in sales and revenue ... and thus increased pressure on existing end-to-end processes. *Domino's*—in contrast to other suppliers—relies on vertical integration with its own drivers, its own kitchens, and its own dough. The goal being the overarching process chain control to deliver hot, fresh pizza on time. However, with a small side effect: reducing dependence on food aggregator platforms, which often see the Pizza Mogul as a competitor and are happy to respond to this with increased advertising pressure on their part.

To be able to recruit the number of employees required for growth, not only the brand but also the "way of working", including all the processes that make up the brand, were to be made accessible to a wider public. For this purpose, a docu-reality web series with well-known actors was initiated, in which real employees of the company were portrayed, including their experiences with the high-quality production processes at *Domino's*. The series was distributed via OOH/platforms. The series was promoted via OOH/posters, flyers as well as social media ads. An early indicator of success is that the pizza associated with the series (and named after the main character) now accounts for almost 10% of *Domino's* sales, making it the second best-selling pizza. Alongside the expansion of the menu, a rebranding exercise was also initiated in terms of the perception of *Domino's Pizza*—moving away from fast food to fresh food, free from artificial preservatives, flavours, and colours, including vegetarian and gluten-free options.

The ability to measure performance, assess current customer engagement in real time, and quantify success is proving critical to data-driven decisions at *Domino's*.

For example, heat maps are used for A/B testing to analyse how people interact with different displayed ads and to determine which product generates higher sales with which creative. As part of automated replenishment, these data points flow directly into the buying strategy and forecasting of all orders and ingredients. The focus is on "digital empowerment". It is not just about digitalising the buying process, but also going beyond that to use technology to increase the efficiency of all business processes.

Domino's Pizza addresses increased data protection requirements through two mechanisms: on the one hand, the existing customer base was incentivised to register and participate in loyalty programs, thus generating first-party PII data. By using *Domino's* own channels, advertising expenses are reduced, and organic traffic is generated at the same time. On the other hand, attention was paid to maximum efficiency (ROAS) in marketing with a broad customer profile, for which a blockchain-based display ad management system was initiated, with *AdHash* as a provider of contextual advertising technology.

The focus is on addressing customers at the right moment, using deep learning technologies and real data. Contextual targeting does this by using natural language processing to scan text and images, capture the meaning and sentiment of items, and determine the level of relevance. It is also important for assessing brand safety. Using blockchain, the majority of AdTech middlemen were eliminated, allowing *Domino's* to significantly reduce online advertising costs while benefiting from greater transparency. An A/B test with a leading DSP showed that *Domino's* was able to reduce their cost per click by 44%. At the same time, 25 times more budget was invested in premium publisher (rather than long-tail) sites. Higher-quality traffic led to a 92% higher engagement. Subsequent campaigns further improved engagement by integrating contextual and real-world data targeting (Fig. 13.32). In contextual targeting, an algorithm considers factors such as the relative weight of negative words, the length of the article, word combinations and more to eliminate erroneous

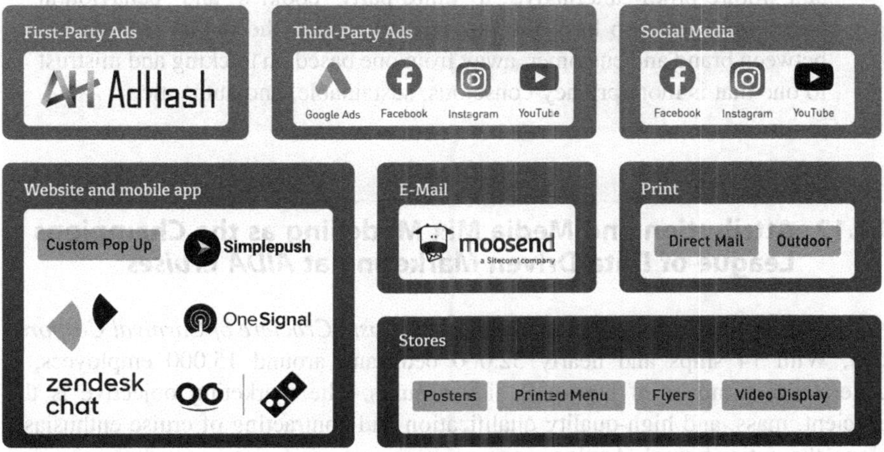

Fig. 13.32 MarTech landscape at *Domino's Pizza* (Marketing Tech Monitor 2022)

ad delivery. Again, it becomes apparent that rudimentary blacklisting based on simple keywords and "if–then" statements is hardly effective and significantly limits reach. Unsafe page impressions are blocked before a bid is made, not after *Domino's* has won the bid and the ad has been programmatically displayed. Most AdTech platforms block irrelevant pages only after the bid has been made. Using "real-world" data targeting, live triggers were permanently integrated into the ad displayed, such as weather data (e.g. rain), financial data, sports data (incl. sporting events and teams playing at the time), the latest film releases, or even breaking news. The combination of contextual and real-time data allows for a comprehensive picture of where customers are in their customer journey.

Since March 2020, *Domino's* has been experimenting with contextual AI with a focus on recipe pages and recipes that take more than an hour to prepare. With the message "Hungry now? Order pizza!", engagement increased by nearly 75%. Weather targeting that automatically triggered a home delivery campaign in the event of rain led to such high demand that restaurants in each region struggled to fulfil orders.

Lessons Learned

- Vertical integration (with own drivers, own kitchen, own dough, etc.) offers the highest level of control, especially when the customer experience is central.
- It is crucial to stay relevant through innovation—whether that innovation comes from within the company or from external partners. By working with innovative, tech-savvy, and agile partners who understand the changing AdTech landscape, *Domino's* can focus on what they do best: pizza.
- Blockchain-based ad management offers higher ROAS as well as privacy compliance.
- Contextual and real-world data targeting provides an ethical, cost-effective, and future-proof alternative to third-party cookies and behavioural targeting. They also have the potential to change the online relationship between brand and customer, away from one based on tracking and mistrust to one that is more privacy-conscious, sustainable, and authentic.

13.12 Attribution and Media Mix Modelling as the Champions League of Data-Driven Marketing at *AIDA Cruises*

AIDA Cruises offers cruises as a subsidiary of *Costa Crociere of Carnival Corporation*. With 14 ships and nearly 32,000 beds and around 15,000 employees, it generates a turnover of almost 2 billion euros. The marketing objective is the efficient, mass, and high-quality qualification and contracting of cruise enthusiasts along the entire funnel. Analogous to pregnancies, cruises (as a product requiring intensive consultation) are characterised by a comparatively long customer journey of up to 9 months from the first contact to the booking to the start of the journey. For *AIDA*, the focus is on data-supported decision-making around media planning, hand in hand with media success control (i.e. calculation of media efficiency as ROAS). Data-driven decision-making also focuses on agency management and thus on decisions about media investments. A comprehensive optimisation across online and offline measures requires the standardisation of the calculation bases (comparability) to be able to stringently evaluate and decide on budget allocations to different media channels (intermedia comparison) and individual placements (intramedia comparison) within the channels. Technically speaking, this means the linking of digital attribution and marketing mix modelling, including events, sponsorships, re-branding of travel agencies, CRM measures, price and utilisation plans, or product placements. The prerequisite is the creation of a database on which scenarios and forecasts for media planning can be created (Fig. 13.33).

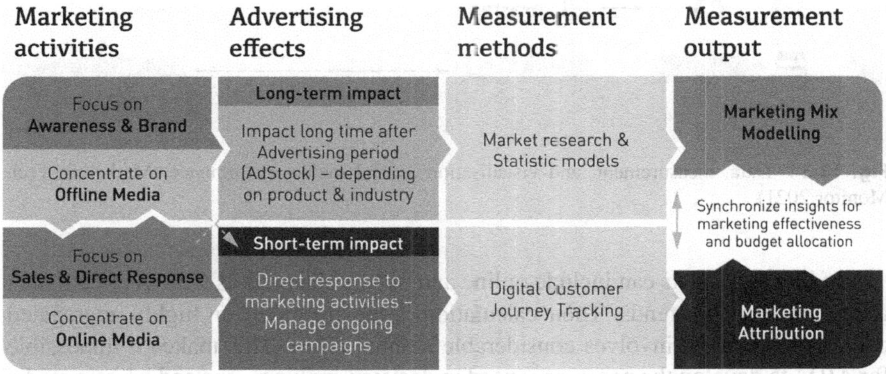

Fig. 13.33 Interaction of marketing attribution and marketing mix modelling at *AIDA* (Marketing Tech Monitor 2021)

The challenges were manifold: the planning was based on an incomplete and not very valid database, which was compounded by the lack of integrated processes between media planning and (strategic) performance measurement. An overarching KPI framework for online and offline marketing had to be developed first as a condition, as channels were controlled individually. Consequently, it was difficult to determine and calculate valid scenarios. All forecasts and efficiency considerations were based purely on volumes and market shares of historical data. The long customer journey to (in terms of purchase) "birth", the product requiring intensive consultation with a wide variety of design variables (e.g. *AIDA Premium*, *AIDA Vario*, and diverse cabin types) as well as a broad media mix increase the need for comprehensive marketing mix modelling and a visualisation of the results for navigation (Fig. 13.34).

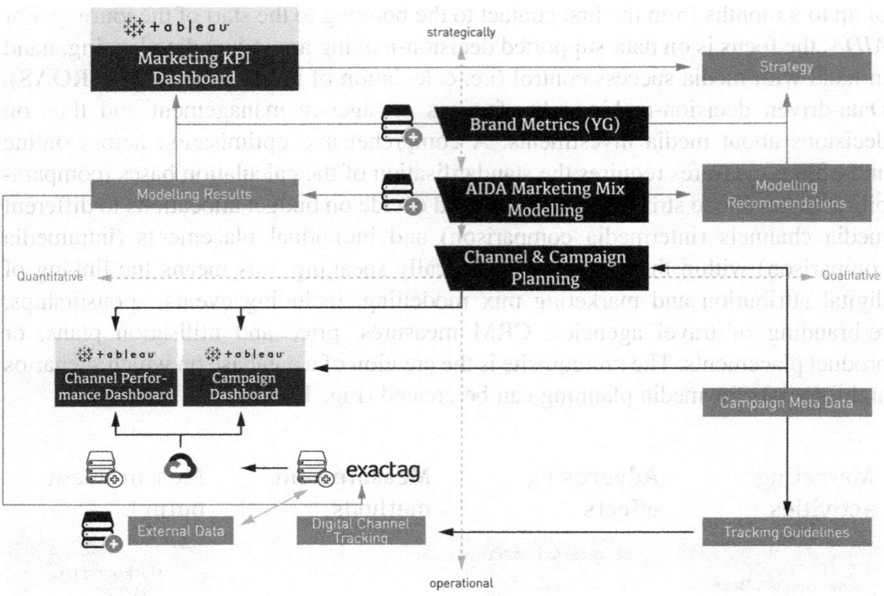

Fig. 13.34 Data, measurement, and visualisation around media performance (Marketing Tech Monitor 2021)

Media mix models can include online and offline channels as well as effects such as seasonality and trends. Their calculation is mostly based on highly aggregated data, which usually involves considerable manual effort. This makes it impossible for *AIDA* to develop the necessary speed in decision-making—instead, classic media mix models are at best recalibrated on a quarterly basis and the necessary workflows for faster model adaptation are often not in place. With the Covid crisis, however, the conditions are changing. Under these circumstances, a classic media mix model can only document the situation with a delay of a few months. At the same time, stand-alone, multi-touch attribution models at the user level lack the ability to consider the long-term effects on sales. A compromise between "speedboat" and "aircraft carrier" is sought.

Against this background, *AIDA* has been building up two complementary fields of action since 2018:

- *Digital attribution (since 2018)*: The experience of all digital customer contact points and the use of TV attribution via data reconciliation lay the foundation for automating data flows in a second step with the help of APIs (e.g. to *Google, Criteo*, Fig. 13.35). The objective was to ensure a high level of granularity, a high degree of topicality, and a low level of deviation in the data at the same time. In a third step, the dovetailing of digital attribution with marketing mix modelling (MMM) was launched, so that MMM results are used for the presentation of a baseline and correction of digital attribution. In a fourth step, digital tracking will

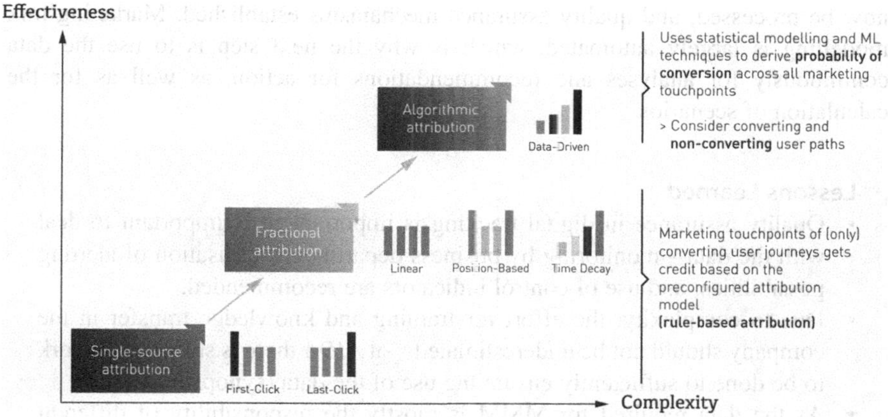

Fig. 13.35 Developmental steps of digital attribution

be converted to future-proof technologies with a focus on first-party and server-side tracking, the use of aggregated (instead of personal) cookies to reduce dependence on cookie consent, and aggregated view tracking with large partners (e.g. *Google Ads Data Hub*).

- *Marketing Mix Modelling (since 2019)*: Started with a statistical (one-off) marketing mix modelling, which examines all influencing variables (e.g. media, prices, brand, competition, call centre, seasonality, capacity) on cruise bookings. In a second step, the static MMM was expanded to dynamic modelling, for which all data streams are automatically stored on a central server (hot folder) monthly, and the modelling and results based on it are automatically updated. Digital tracking data including digital attribution is automatically integrated into the MMM. In a third step, a standardised visualisation of all consolidated monthly modelling results was established by June 2021, directly linked to revolving media planning. Finally, as a navigation aid, in the fourth step, the MMM will be cascaded to a more fine-grained level (incl. campaigns, target areas of the ships) as well as the inclusion of other secondary models (e.g. brand analysis or direct marketing activities) to further increase the variability of the models.

The implementation at *AIDA* has turned out to be a cruise in difficult waters. Data reconciliation in digital tracking is particularly time-consuming and nerve-racking, many different influencing factors, differences in the data (as well as between different tools), and many "bugs" in the data allocation can usually hardly be found and clarified in the required speed. This goes together with shoals due to quite complex quality assurance in digital tracking, but also in the complex field of offline media data, which (acc. to *Nielsen*) have a different temporal availability. Data loss due to lack of user consent limits the meaningfulness of quantitative results.

By the end of 2021 already the first three steps for digital attribution have been almost completely implemented, so that the technological adjustments (step 4) must now be processed, and quality assurance mechanisms established. Marketing mix modelling is largely automated, which is why the next step is to use the data continuously for analyses and recommendations for action, as well as for the calculation of scenarios.

Lessons Learned

- Quality assurance in digital tracking is important: it is important to deal with the data—monitoring by business departments, utilisation of alerting possibilities, and use of control indicators are recommended.
- Due to complexity, the effort for training and knowledge transfer in the company should not be underestimated—at *AIDA* there is still a lot of work to be done to sufficiently ensure the use of the data (synopsis).
- As the data required for MMM is mostly the responsibility of different departments in the company, agencies, third parties, a lot of coordination effort, and good project management skills are sometimes required.
- A lot of knowledge transfer to the partners involved is necessary, as *AIDA* has a very complex product, and the data sources are mostly decentralised in the company. Long purchase decision processes of potential customers complicate the analysis and the generation of insights.

13.13 End2End . . . From Customer Interaction to Route Planning and Optimisation at *Flaschenpost* Home Delivery Services

Since its founding in 2016, *Flaschenpost* is now active in 190 German cities and delivers over 200,000 beverage crates per day with the help of around 16,000 employees. The more than 1,000,000 monthly active customers are served by a fully integrated end-to-end process and a proprietary system landscape.

Consideration: Long-term planning for maximum service quality in delivery
At *Flaschenpost*, the entire planning and production process starts long before a customer is acquired. The reason for this is that in order to guarantee delivery in compliance with reliable delivery times, precise order forecasts based on predictive analytics have to be created, which make it possible to plan both sufficient inventory and sufficient delivery capacities (drivers and vehicles) in good time (Fig. 13.36). Seasonal effects, upcoming events, weather, holidays, and general growth are considered. A short- and long-term forecast extends accordingly to the level of weekly shift planning for existing employees (short-term FC), HR marketing and the high-volume recruitment process, where the application and hiring process for 2000–3000 new employees per month is managed in advance (long-term FC). The available delivery capacities (drivers and vehicles) are fed back into the marketing planning to be able to grow sustainably in line with the delivery capacities—assuming good service quality. For this purpose, budgets for all marketing activities

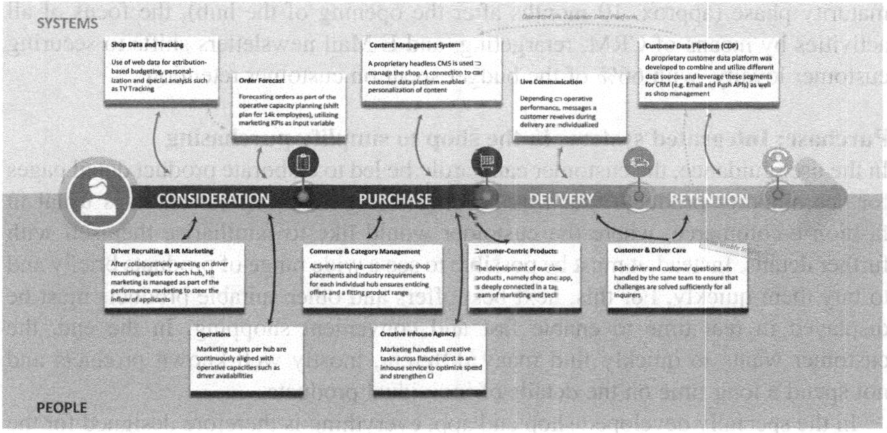

Fig. 13.36 Process/organisational and technical integration with operational business processes at *Flaschenpost* (Marketing Tech Monitor 2022)

are based on the attribution and mix modelling, which accesses web and app tracking data, but also all other information from the data infrastructure and the deep analytics area. The focus is on the inflow of new customers within the framework of delivery capacities according to shift planning.

Supply chain planning and scheduling is integrated with marketing and sales planning so that it is clear a priori which marketing activities (e.g. promotions) generate which uplift in sales and which stocks and warehouse capacities (incl. storage locations and warehouse staff) must be available for this. For this purpose, action planning and category management are linked to supply chain planning and scheduling. This planning is highly automated down to the item level to be able to deliver on special occasions—for example, the algorithm recognises that family-driven holidays (e.g. Easter) generate different requirements than event-driven holidays (e.g. Labour Day). A beer offer before Labour Day is accordingly treated with a stronger sales uplift than beer offers before Easter, as Labour Day is generally associated with more beer consumption than the Easter holidays.

Excursus: Strategic hub ramp-up in three phases

The marketing goals and budgets are adjusted according to the growth phase of the respective location/(hub) life cycle in addition to the capacity available. After opening a location (growth/ramp-up phase), the focus is on generating reach and customer acquisition, for example via flyers, OOH, or promotions. The focus is on actively making the service known, even if the customer is not (yet) actively looking for it. At the beginning, a maximum of 33% of the budget is used for customer retention. In the following phase (semi-mature, between four and 9 months), the focus is on the further acquisition of new customers, while at the same time increasing marketing efficiency. For this purpose, the "word-of-mouth" effect initiated in the first phase is addressed via channels that pick up on the purchase intention. Thus, the focus is increasingly on SEA and retargeting measures. In the maturity phase (approx. 10 months after the opening of the hub), the focus of all activities by means of CRM, retargeting, and E-Mail newsletters shifts to securing customer loyalty, with 66% of the budget spent on customer retention.

Purchase: Integrated systems in the shop to simplify purchasing
In the user guidance, the customer can hardly be led to elaborate product detail pages for "commodity products" such as beverages (e.g. mineral water), as is usual in fashion e-commerce, where the customer would like to familiarise themself with further details. Instead, it must be possible to see a wide range of products briefly and to buy them quickly. For this, next best offers and other suitable products must be displayed in real time to enable fast and convenient shopping. In the end, the customer wants to quickly find many different, mostly well-known products and not spend a long time on the details of individual products.

In the specially developed shop and app, everything is therefore designed for the specifics of food and beverage shopping, with the aim to be able to easily put together shopping baskets with dozens of items, without long and time-consuming click routes. At the same time, a separate content management system makes it possible to dynamically compile the content for each order (like in a construction kit). This content can be dynamised and targeted via the company's own customer data platform. In addition, specially developed recommendation engines (e.g. provision of next best offer) help to configure large shopping baskets quickly (Fig. 13.37). This AI-based real-time approach not only considers which items other customers frequently buy together, but also considers the customer's order history and even the current shopping basket. This involves continuous A/B testing to find the right algorithm for the right area. The different advantages of the various approaches tested mean that the different algorithms work differently well in different parts of the website. For example, complementary recommendations are made on the product page (buy *Coke* and get *Fanta* recommended), whereas recommendations for regularly purchased products are favoured in the order history

Fig. 13.37 Characteristics of A/B testing in the recommendation engine (Marketing Tech Monitor 2022)

and a "virtual quench zone" is set up in the check-out. The AI-based real-time approach set up here shows immediate success: these higher-quality analysis processes have a success rate (measured by the shopping basket) that is up to 30% higher and allow multilayered cross-selling.

Delivery: Transparency during delivery and active communication
In the operations team, route planning including load planning is carried out directly based on the order, supported by the product information management system (e.g. restrictions in terms of payload and available volume). If problems occur during delivery, the delivery management usually directly accesses the live communication APIs to inform the customers via E-Mail or push. In the case of minor delays, there are automated mailings accordingly. In the case of major deviations, the delivery management team accesses the ticketing of the customer and driver support team. This team, which deals with both customer enquiries and support for the delivery drivers, can then contact the customer personally and resolve the issue individually.

Retention: Before the order is after the order
Retention management is not exclusively a matter of marketing. The "success of the delivery" is ultimately measured by customer feedback, but also by hard operational factors (e.g. punctuality). This information is used to prioritise the customer in question for the next order in case of errors in the delivery process, so that there are no repeated "slips". For example, if a customer receives their delivery too late, they will be given extra punctuality and priority for the next order. In addition, the customer care team has the possibility to "flag" customers who were not satisfied with an order, so that they are given priority for future orders. Processes and rules for this are mapped in operational retention management.

In addition, deeply integrated systems are used in marketing to retain customers. The comprehensive customer data platform (CDP), which can also influence the content management system during the ordering process, is also used here (Fig. 13.38).

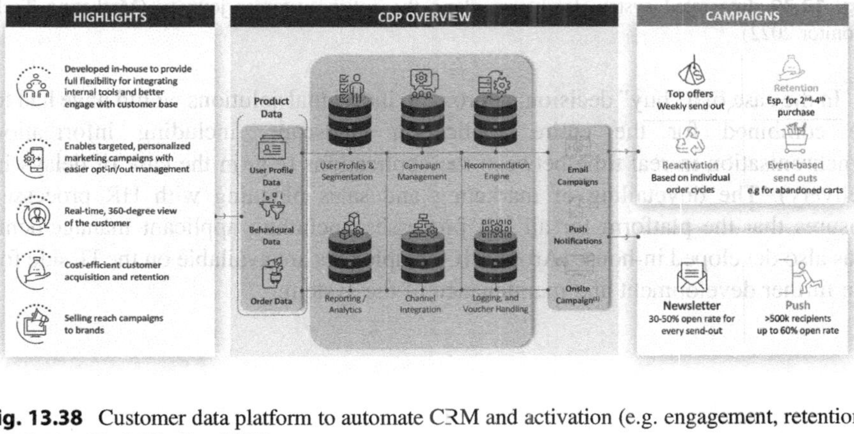

Fig. 13.38 Customer data platform to automate CRM and activation (e.g. engagement, retention; (Marketing Tech Monitor 2022)

The system was also developed in-house to be able to store the multitude of algorithms and logics directly in the data infrastructure (segmentation and formation of audiences or in-depth analytics such as churn probability scores). The integration of external tools would foreseeably have been too slow and too costly. The CDP directly controls the content retrieved from the CMS. In addition, the company's own communication APIs are used to send marketing campaigns, which in turn take over the sending of E-Mails and pushes. The CDP can also use personalised product recommendations (recommendation engine). There is also an interlink to the operative retention management system to make all necessary customer data available.

The entire system as a MarTech stack, including the web shop, but also the picking handhelds in the warehouse and the complete merchandise management system, was developed in-house (Fig. 13.39). Apart from a few individual "best-of-breed" solutions such as *Zendesk* in customer support or application-related solutions such as *MS Dynamics* in finance and accounting, there are hardly any "off-the-shelf" solutions.

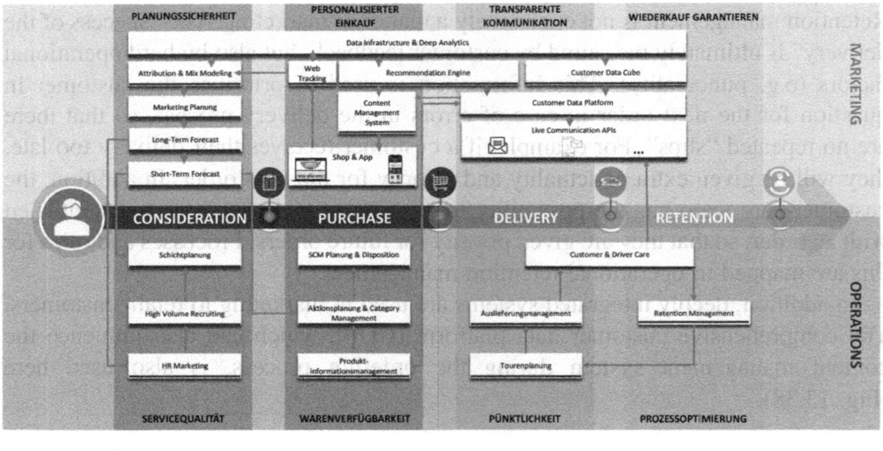

Fig. 13.39 Integrated system landscape along the entire customer journey (Marketing Tech Monitor 2022)

In the case of a "buy" decision, approx. 30 individual solutions would have had to be combined for the entire application landscape, including information synchronisation in real time between the applications (e.g. in the case of delays in delivery). The dovetailing of marketing and sales planning with HR processes ensures that the platform for all HR processes, including applicant management, was also developed in-house. Around 100 employees are available on the IT side for the further development and maintenance of the system.

Lessons Learned

- Depending on the specific requirements, a "make" approach is to be considered even in components with high standardisation (e.g. CMS or PIM). Functional integrity is often surpassed by the integration capability of all components.
- In an agile organisation, it seems hardly possible from a management point of view to follow and control all details—a high degree of ownership and technical understanding of the functional departments is required to develop solutions together with product management.
- It is important to start small and simple and form de-limitable packages that can nevertheless be integrated well in the right places.

13.14 Ad-Optimisation and In-Housing at *Vodafone*

Vodafone is one of the pioneers in bringing programmatic advertising expertise in-house. Since 2019, the telecoms giant has dispensed with agencies and manages its programmatic branding campaigns itself with the help of specially selected technologies. The in-house approach was driven by the desire to:

- Not be dependent on external service providers for core processes as an innovative technology provider
- Bring data sovereignty in-house, also to be 100% GDPR-compliant
- Have maximum transparency across all value chains and
- Further automate and standardise to contain the myriad of manual activities that would otherwise be required

For the development of the in-house AdTech platform, a greenfield start was made, and all major components were re-tendered—from DSP to ad verification to dynamic creative optimisation (DCO). The entire process of transforming the MarTech landscape started back in 2018 (Fig. 13.40). The basis for the business

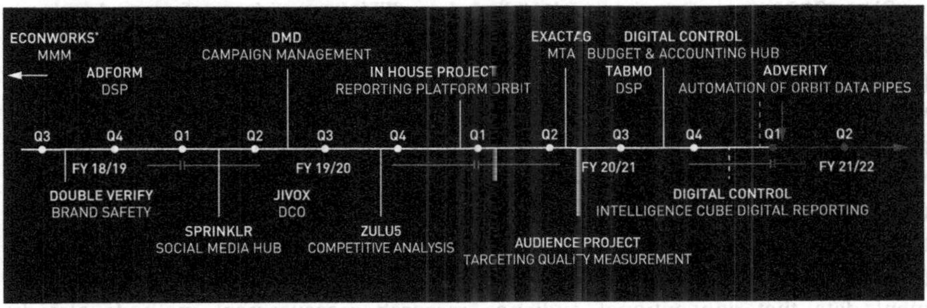

Fig. 13.40 Development of the MarTech landscape at *Vodafone* (Marketing Tech Monitor 2022)

case for in-housing is the replacement of employees who would otherwise be employed in external agencies, as well as the outcome optimisation of the campaigns carried out.

The focus in all new tenders was on the best-possible user experience and integration scenarios, without the need to operate several different systems with (manual) media breaks. The integration for planning and steering was ensured via the Digital Media Hub (in-house developed MRM application), with a focus on campaign management, planning, and budget control. The entire AdTech stack was connected to this MRM component via APIs, including internal booking/accounting in ERP (SAP Ariba in Procurement and FI/CO as cost centre). An integrated process now includes KVAs of all participating service providers, the actual booking, the release of the ads, and the final invoicing. *Adverity* was implemented as a data hub to harmonise all incoming data and then transfer it to *Google Data Studio*. Data management was transferred to *AWS*. The cooperation with IT is coordinated via the "Owner AdTech" committee, where issues of development planning, data security, and integration scenarios are discussed, such as the use and integration of *Tealium* as a customer data hub across all touchpoints (Fig. 13.41).

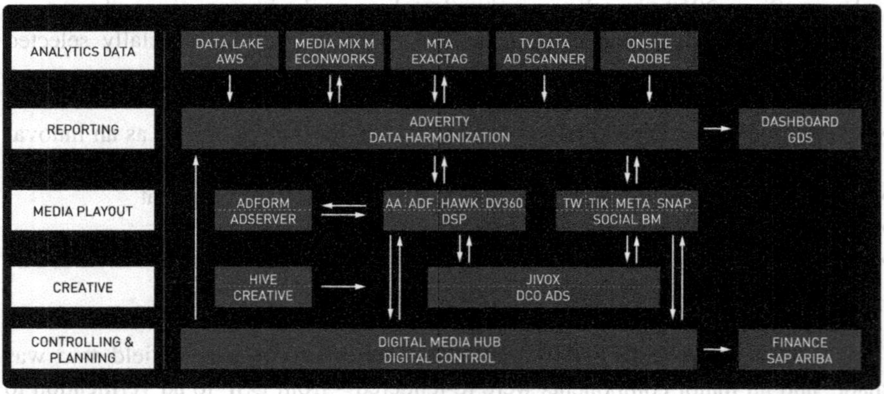

Fig. 13.41 Functional components of the MarTech landscape at *Vodafone* (Marketing Tech Monitor 2022)

Since 2021, a cooperation with *AdScanner* (TV recognition software) has been launched for reach measurement based on pseudonymised data. The goal: more precise key figures to increase the efficiency of campaigns. The self-learning software automatically recognises TV campaigns and TV content and generates parallel performance values and target group analyses based on the interactions of TV viewers with the TV program. Via a central cockpit, proprietary audience measurement KPIs based on representative IPTV households can be used to analyse second-by-second insights into placement, reach, view-through rate, and interest groups (who saw the commercial on TV). These results expand and deepen the measurement data that conventional audience research measurement methods already provide today. In addition, the cockpit can integrate correlations via its own as well as external data streams such as traffic, sales, or weather data.

All initiatives are driven by the desire for independence and self-determination through the generation of first-party data, so that there are also plans to build up their own targeting along the lines of viewing behaviour in the future. While the digital media hub has been developed, all other components are to be modularly interchangeable in their functionality. Four different DSPs are used for this purpose: *AdForm* for display and video advertising, *DV360* for *YouTube*, *Tambo* for mobile, in-app as well as programmatic radio and out-of-home, and finally *Amazon* for *Amazon Advertising*. In analytics and reporting, *Zulu5* is used for competitive analysis in online spend and campaigns, *Audience Project* for quality measurement in targeting and measuring the impact of digital campaigns on brand equity. *Econworks* uses data modelling to determine the ROI of each individual media channel, while *Exactag* is used to determine multi-touch attribution—in other words, the effects of campaign performance across the customer journey touchpoints and attributed online sales.

Within the "MarTech guild", CRM application scenarios and use cases are also discussed in-house between colleagues from CRM and IT, as well as brand, performance, or digital marketing. The focus is on personalisation—how, for example, propensity scores can be developed or churn predictions as input in next best offers. For *Vodafone*, KPIs across all activities are at the top of the list, especially the "cost per qualitative visit" (e.g. formed from the time spent on the page, activities on the page, scrolling, use of offers) as the evaluation of the entire interaction by a visitor. The insourcing of programmatic advertising has resulted in an average 47% increase in digital advertising ROI after 12 months, excluding agency fees. A total of 80% of this result is due to improved operational campaign management—not media buying savings. Hand in hand with insourcing is a clear trend towards buying via private marketplaces (PMPs). Even though the prices are higher compared to open auctions, the "cost per qualitative visit" is more favourable. Open market measures are only selectively supplemented for generating reach (Priebe, 2020). Overall, the output of all marketing activities was increased by 41.6%.

In addition to the quantitative KPIs, there is a higher level of involvement on the part of the employees involved. Only the status of all projects is discussed on a weekly basis, so that every employee always knows where all projects stand and what the necessary next steps are. A time frame of only 4 months was deliberately set for the recruiting/onboarding of new staff (and the expiry of existing agency contracts) to ensure that the process does not "fray" in terms of time. In an elaborate training program, all new hires at the (previous) agencies and technology partners received a 2-day deep-dive program on all relevant platforms. Important and painful learning in the context of recruiting new staff: open postings on platforms and advertisements generated comparatively few relevant applications compared to direct approaches to interesting candidates from the (extended) network. The interviews always focused on the question of which platforms the respective candidates had already worked with and what concrete operational experience existed. In other words, less lofty theory, and more practical implementation experience, for example around social media management.

Lessons Learned

- The combination of recruiting new employees and competences in combination with a clear mission (goal) in the direction of maximum self-determination ensures that even junior managers know the complete tech stack, including all the use cases implemented in it and the phases for implementation.
- The process model is strictly content-centric to involve many new colleagues and related operational areas at the same time and to ensure that everyone has the same understanding of the content.
- A plea for diversity: Heterogeneous team compositions may be more time-consuming in the coordination of procedures and tasks, but they produce above-average results.
- A single headcount for data science will hardly be able to handle the spectrum of topics in personnel union—from data engineering and modelling to the creation of dashboards and the conceptual consulting of colleagues for activities.
- Formal job advertisements hardly yield any results—it seems more important to approach interesting candidates directly through one's own network.
- The reporting infrastructure (MRM application scenario) was started too late—the revision of the MarTech stack should have been built up more from the target to be able to act before the replacement of DSP, etc., in marketing planning and steering.

References

Binet, L., & Feld, P. (2013). *The long and the short of it: Balancing short and long-term marketing strategies.*

Priebe, A. (2020, May 11). Programmatic Advertising Inhouse bei Vodafone: Das Ergebnis ist noch besser als erwartet. *ADZINE.*

Sharp, B. (2010). *How brands grow.*

Statista, 23 February 2021.

14 Steps Towards MarketingTech Strategy and Implementation

14.1 The "Rocky Horror Project Show": Pitfalls on the Way to Data-Driven Marketing

The success or failure to enter and prosper in data-driven customer interaction is determined by the success or failure of the respective project setup. Hence, experience shows the success or failure of projects is defined right from the start as part of the project DNA, reaching from experienced project leads to clarity in methodologies, as well as managing expectations.

"*It's not easy having a good time. Even smiling makes my face ache*". As in the classic *Rocky Horror Picture Show* film with *Dr Frank-N-Furter*, the interviews and implementation projects reveal some down-to-earth craft errors in the strategy and implementation projects. The problems in the implementation of MarTech are rather the projection screen for other challenges such as an insufficient project set-up, problems in the operational processes, or insufficiently detailed requirements engineering in terms of content. Success or failure is usually already anchored in the project DNA "by definition" at the start of the project.

Overall, only 9% of marketing managers state that they have invested sufficient time in all phases and fields of action. This means that the conceptual, content-related foundations are often missing right from the start. The survey of 252 CIOs shows that only just under 46% of the projects are classified as successful and bring the expected ROI (Userlane, 2023). A challenge in the supposedly agile project approach: even if the term "agile" suggests that there are no rigid specifications, an agile process model (e.g. Scrum) is one of the most structured and rigid project methods of all.

The most common mistakes in MarTech projects (Strauß, 2019):

- *Development process*: Lack of a common process model, neglect, or inadequate organisation of the early development phases (e.g. which content and sub-processes can be tested in early releases as part of a user acceptance test [UAT]).

R. Strauss, *Data-Driven Customer Engagement*,
https://doi.org/10.1007/978-3-031-64295-1_14

- *Communication*: Poor communication (and collaboration) between all stakeholders.
- *Knowledge*: Insufficient knowledge and understanding as well as insufficient insight of those involved about the intended overall system, and, very often, missing, or insufficient knowledge in the specialist area about detailed process flows and the resulting requirements.
- *Insufficient clarity in the methodology* (e.g. the required granularity and precision of a use case or requirement).
- *"Head to toe"*: Insufficient support from the departments and IT involved, as the rationale ("reason why") as well as the responsibility and urgency or importance was not clearly communicated at staff level. The individual incentive for support, besides the ongoing daily business, remains rather nebulous.
- *Lack of actual management support*: Beyond the steering committees, which are often dominated by their own internal and power-political interests.
- *"Too much, too soon"*: Too many projects are tackled at once (e.g. in a retail/wholesale company, four POCs are set up in parallel . . . which inevitably leads to "bogging down". Multitasking may have become obsolete as proof of personal commitment, but it usually has fatal effects on the quality of the individual projects and the state of mind of those involved in the project.
- *Documentation*: Faulty, incomplete, or inaccurate documentation of requirements.
- *Project management*: Inadequate management of people and resources, so that, for example, important key people ("go-to persons") are not on board or can only give insufficient time to this project. Prioritisation means, above all, deliberately not doing something (Nieto-Rodriguez, 2016).
- *Politically motivated pro-forma staffing*: Due to political pressure, projects must be staffed—not according to competence and knowledge but according to the criterion of "dispensability" or "availability" of the seconded colleague.
- *"Youth in research"*: Instead of experiential knowledge, harsh PowerPoint romanticism dominates because experienced project leaders are lacking. There is usually a positive correlation on the projects between insufficient experiential knowledge and depth in content versus the number of PowerPoint slides generated.
- *Agile is hip*: Even though the term "agile" suggests that there are no rigid specifications, an agile process model (e.g. Scrum) is one of the most structured and rigid project methods ever.
- *False expectations*: The idea is that everything can be done faster and more cost-effectively with agility and Scrum, that clean project planning becomes obsolete, that requirements can be changed "on demand" at any time, or that the door is opened to total control over all activities of all employees. The "downside" of agile methods: a substantive approach with maximum involvement of all employees as well as the overcoming of outdated maxims and patterns of action requires more time and effort, but at the same time is rewarded with higher-quality results. Otherwise, according to *Botho Strauß* in his essay *"Herkunft"*: "*. . . one has essentially lived according to patterns and consumed oneself according to patterns*".

- *Lack of or unclear objectives*: If you don't know the objective, no path is the right one. Unclear objectives prevent effective orientation from the outset.
- *Inadequately staffed team roles*: In many cases, the roles of the Scrum Master and of the product owner are underestimated. As a result, the roles are often not filled with dedicated people, or they lack the necessary qualifications. Here, too, "availability" beats the criterion of "knowledge" or "experience".

> *... I am unlikely to nominate my best colleagues for a cross-functional, overarching project like CRM, where a, we don't know what the outcome will be and b) such a project traditionally falls victim to the ritual tribal feuds within the company anyway*—CMO of an Automotive OEM

- *Insufficient planning*: Poor agile requirements engineering inevitably leads to poor quality user stories. They are often not clearly described or incomplete (e.g. acceptance criteria are missing, or they do not correspond to the "definition of ready" adopted at the beginning). The same applies to buffers for unscheduled tasks such as coordination meetings, support, or hot fixes, so that these are (or must be) omitted as a result. Too tight, overambitious schedules and missing milestones (several times) tend to lead to frustration on the part of those involved in the project.
- *Lack of discipline*: No timeboxing in planning and team meetings and insufficient moderation by the Scrum Master. Consequently, the backlog of the current development sprint is not stable, new requirements are added several times or are changed "on the fly". To avoid maximum confusion, teams usually fall back into traditional patterns such as completing tasks "on demand".
- *Omitting important process steps*: Basic process steps such as refining, planning, daily stand-up, implementation, review, or retrospective are part of an agile process model according to Scrum. These process steps are essential for Scrum and cannot be left out arbitrarily. A retrospective ensures learning from experience to improve both the process and the resulting product.

In the interviews, as in the analyses of the *Marketing Tech Monitor* editions in previous years, it was repeatedly critically noted that the implementation of MarTech requires internal know-how, for example around possible IT integration scenarios, as well as the development of a *master construction plan*. In addition, there is the precise collection of technical requirements for a differentiated evaluation of different providers/platforms as well as the necessary integration. The challenge being only rarely or rudimentarily available competences and experience to accompany the interface between business and IT applications, for example regarding:

- The definition and granularity of a limited (prioritised) number of use cases, as well as
- Process modelling and from this

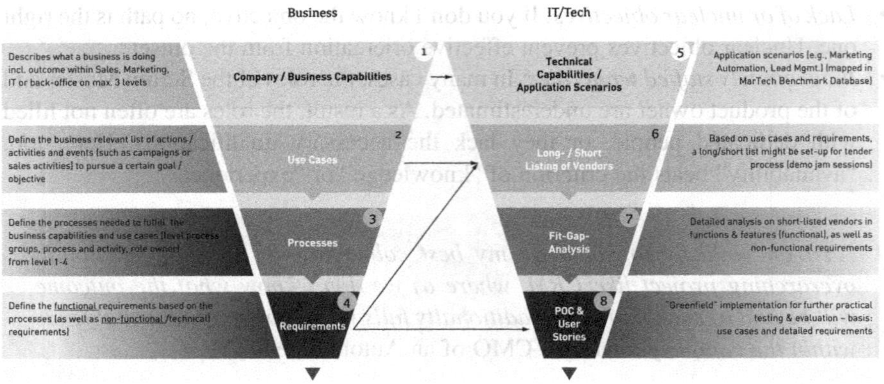

Fig. 14.1 Levels and relationships between capabilities, use cases, process modelling, requirements engineering, and translation into a fit gap analysis and POC (schematic)

- The derivation of requirements (functional/non-functional requirements) or
- Their translation within the framework of a POC (Fig. 14.1)

> *. . . we have to try out a lot of things . . . and try them out again . . . and see how they fit into the IT landscape . . . this will continue to evolve*—Tobias Lorenz (Head of Marketing, E.ON)

The often occurring "minor quibble" in the context of *requirements engineering*: lived processes are hardly formally described, so that it is difficult to see which functions and application scenarios from an extensive catalogue are really "absolutely necessary" or "(super-) vital". The challenge: MarTech competence is still not an integral part of marketing teams, which is why there is not a sufficient overview of the market nor enough methodical knowledge of how to proceed. Instead of elaborate requirement descriptions and subsequent pitches, a pragmatic proof of concept (POC) with a provider is more often found, based on which the requirements are also derived retrogradely on the "living object" so to speak (based on the standard processes mapped in the tool by a provider). Here, too, a lack of content-related or methodological know-how tends to create a vacuum that wanders freely.

Accordingly, for the majority of marketing managers and CMOs, the detailed and professional description of the requirements and the discussion of detailed use cases (42%, Fig. 14.2), coordinated with an overarching target picture in the overall infrastructure (i.e. master construction plan) (40%), repeatedly emerge as the centrepiece for the successful implementation of MarketingTech.

> *MarTech providers have solutions for everything . . . but in detail problems remain unsolved*—Thierry Pool (former Global Head Digital & Data Marketing, Credit Suisse)

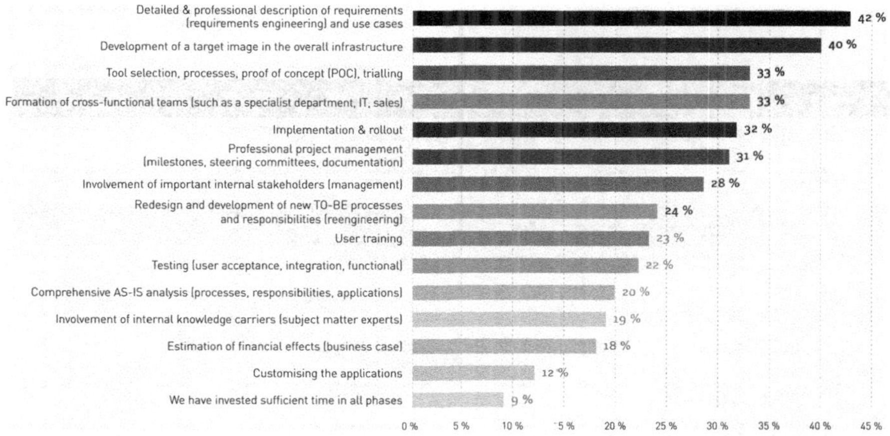

Fig. 14.2 Topics in which, in retrospect, more time should have been invested in the MarTech projects (in %, multiple responses, $n = 257$; Marketing Tech Monitor 2021)

Requirements management essentially includes the definition of requirements from requirements elicitation, requirements documentation, and requirements validation, while requirements management includes all activities for controlling, monitoring, and managing requirements (i.e. risk management, change management, and implementation management). The objective should be to achieve at least a common basic understanding of a system to be developed right at the beginning. In the context of requirements engineering, requirements must not only make statements about desired properties, but must also describe criteria for how these properties can be verified (acceptance criteria).

At the same time, the management of requirements means that processes are defined and implemented by updating the requirements documentation throughout the course of the project and (can) be used at the end as a basis for the creation of test cases. The requirements interchange format (ReqIF) has established itself as a standard for the uniform exchange of requirements. ReqIF is defined by an XML schema and is a format and data model that contains structures for requirements, their attributes, types, access rights, relations (links), and similar. The result can be several hundred requirements, which subsequently must be consolidated and prioritised (Fig. 14.3).

These criteria, known as test cases, are not only used for quality assurance, but also essentially determine the quality of the requirements themselves, as the description of an acceptance criterion forces an immediate review of the content of the requirement, if necessary, supported by *rapid prototyping*. The focus is on the simple, automated and, above all, rapid implementation of a prototype to enable a "test living" in a simple way starting in the early phases.

The detailed requirements serve as the basis for the request for information (RFI/RFP), as well as for the fit gap analysis that builds on this. Here, possible providers and IT platforms are examined to see to what extent they fulfil the detailed requirements directly in the standard or, if applicable, which extensions must be

	Process Level 1	Process Level 2	Process Level 3	Roles	Roles to be Supported		Use Data & Formats	Priorization	Release Planning
	Process Details				System Requirements (high-level)			Importance	
#	Process Group	Process	Activity	Marketing Role (R - Carries out)	How the MRM-System should support the activity	How data is generated	Data Source/ Format	Priority	Release
2.1.1.1.	Marketing Communication Strategy	Analyze Status Quo of Marketing and Sales Activities	Collect and analyze marketing communication performance reports	Communication Planner	- Making market research and consumer insights/feedback available	Upload by user	PPT, XLS	3 - could have	2 - Q1/2019
2.1.2.1.	Marketing Communication Strategy	Analyze Status Quo of Marketing and Sales Activities	Analyze marketing communication channels	Communication Planner	- Making results of marketing communication channel analysis available	Upload by user	PPT, XLS	3 - could have	3 - Q2/2019
2.1.2.2.	Marketing Communication Strategy	Analyze Status Quo of Marketing and Sales Activities	Analyze marketing communication channels	Communication Planner	- Enabling „What-if"-analysis	System-to-system interface	Mktg. Mix Modelling Tool	3 - could have	3 - Q2/2019
2.1.2.3.	Marketing Communication Strategy	Analyze Status Quo of Marketing and Sales Activities	Analyze marketing communication channels	Communication Planner	- Enabling customer-journey analysis	System-to-system interface	Mktg. Mix Modelling Tool	3 - could have	3 - Q2/2019
2.1.3.1.	Marketing Communication Strategy	Analyze Status Quo of Marketing and Sales Activities	Develop marketing communication strategy improvement plans	Communication Planner	- Making marketing communication strategy improvement plans (HQ/area, market) available	Upload by user	PPT	3 - could have	3 - Q2/2019
2.2.1.1.	Marketing Communication Strategy	Set Marketing Communication Targets	Define mktg. communication targets and target groups	Marketing Communication Strategist	- Entering or selecting marketing communication targets and target groups (HQ/per market) in the system	Manual data entry	MRM Tool	1 - must have	1 - Q4/2018
2.2.1.2.	Marketing Communication Strategy	Set Marketing Communication Targets	Define mktg. communication targets and target groups	Marketing Communication Strategist	- Informing stakeholders about defined marketing communication targets and target groups	Automated	Email Notification	1 - must have	1 - Q4/2018
2.2.1.3.	Marketing Communication Strategy	Set Marketing Communication Targets	Define mktg. communication targets and target groups	Marketing Communication Strategist	- Automatically generating targets/target categories drop-downs for budget allocation	Automated	MRM Tool	2 - should have	2 - Q1/2019
2.2.2.1.	Marketing Communication Strategy	Set Marketing Communication [illegible]	Define mktg. communication KPI monitoring & steering [illegible]	Communication Planner	- Entering or selecting marketing communication KPIs/metrics in the system	Manual data entry	MRM Tool	1 - must have	1 - Q4/2018

Fig. 14.3 Requirements elicitation (project example: MRM)

made with what effort (*effort estimation*) in the context of parameterisation or customising. By comparing them with the existing application landscape and architecture, statements can be made about the "fit" with the once defined master construction plan (as a target picture) and the further application development, and integration scenarios including the interfaces required here can be discussed.

In the later phases, it is advisable to follow a *Minimum Viable Product* (MVP) approach. The basic idea in creating an MVP is to create a product as quickly as possible with only the most necessary functions, such as a landing page. This is then published immediately, and feedback is first obtained from (potential) customers. This feedback is then used to expand and improve the MVP. As a rule, any further functions are left out of the MVP. Only those functions that are necessary to enable the actual purpose of the product are integrated.

Otherwise, an insufficient methodological and content-related foundation in the further course of the project ensures corporate stories about the "*rise and fall of the house of MarTech*" (loosely based on *Edgar Allen Poe*) around the (virtual) campfire, such as (Byrne & Gingras, 2017):

- *Political/Hierarchical decision*: The selection is made according to the gusto or "good feeling" of the respective managing director and Board member. There is no substantive justification and validation—rather a (formal) fig leaf for a rationalisation after the fact.
- *"Available anyway application"*: Technologies are used that are already licensed, regardless of concrete needs and requirements, as they are already available due to a previous licensing.
- *"Horse race"*: The selected application is in the top quadrant of an analyst's market study . . . the famous "upper right-hand quadrant".

- *"Puppy love"*: After a mostly superficial (click) demo, a love decision is made without a comparison against the precise requirements.
- *Politically motivated decision*: The multitude of possible application scenarios is used (for self-protection/self-justification) as a bogus argument for the selection of a certain provider—according to the pub slogan: "You can't go wrong there".
- *Over-promise, under-deliver*: The noble and full-bodied (brand) promise of a certain provider is followed, while any necessary detailed functionalities are not actually available. This results in the euphoria at the beginning, due to the rapid project progress, being over-compensated by political "finger-pointing" when functional gaps are uncovered.
- *"Window shopping"*: Detailed requirements for a new software are not defined with sufficient precision—consequently, the selection is rather superficial, following the motto, "Let's see what's available here".
- *The "hope principle"*: Instead of a step-by-step incremental forward strategy, there is hope that the intended application scenario can be achieved after all . . . and must first "mature" further (like a good wine).
- *Project implementation*: The introduction is stuck in the organisation, as training and change management prove to be more complex (even with comparatively simple application scenarios) than initially predicted (Fig. 14.4).

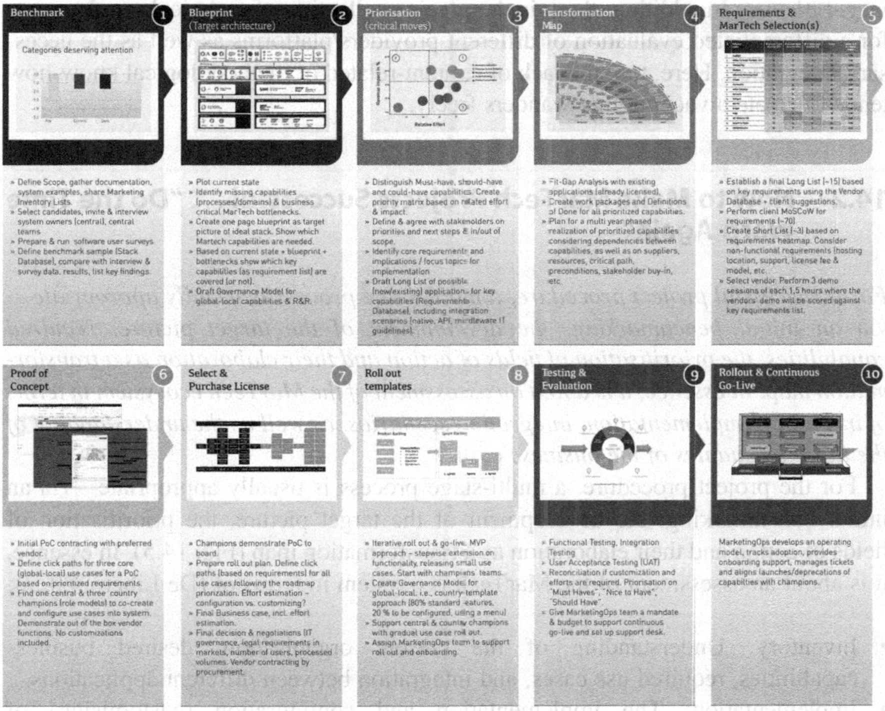

Fig. 14.4 Development planning with benchmarking and software selection (project example retail)

As a rule, most MVPs do not require extensive knowledge of programming or similar. For example, there are construction kits (e.g. *Zapier* for integration scripts or *NinjaForms* for data collection) that can be used to create rudimentary applications for a concept test even without extensive knowledge of web development. Similarly, more and more companies are using a *feature-based design approach*: applications start with a basic set of functions (features), and the range of functions is successively expanded. Further requirements can be discussed/prioritised on a regular basis via a change board and subsequently incorporated.

> *The important thing is to get started—even with the knowledge that this is not yet the perfect tech stack, the perfect tech landscape, because it doesn't have to be perfect from the start. You need a clear vision—and then you get started step by step*—Stephanie Wölfel (Head of Digital Business, Ernsting's Family)

The summary for this is provided by *Albert Camus*: "*The absurd only makes sense insofar as one does not resign oneself to it*". Accordingly, it was critically noted in the accompanying interviews (as in previous years) that the implementation of MarTech requires internal know-how, for example around possible IT integration scenarios, as well as the development of a separate *master construction plan* and *target picture*. In addition, there is the precise collection of technical requirements for a differentiated evaluation of different providers/platforms as well as the necessary integration. Here, too, the lack of content-related or methodological know-how tends to create a vacuum that wanders freely.

14.2 How to Make MarTech Projects Successful ... "Do the Time Warp Again"

For a successful project procedure, a multi-stage process is usually appropriate— via *an initial benchmarking, the development of the target picture, required capabilities, the prioritisation of fields of action and their elaboration as a transformation map. In essence, it is about an assessment of the MarTech ecosystem in terms of inventory, implementation, integration scenarios, as well as the understanding of the basic mechanics of the business case.*

For the project procedure, a multi-stage process is usually appropriate—via an initial benchmarking, the development of the target picture, the prioritisation of fields of action and their elaboration as a transformation map (Fig. 14.5). In essence, it is about an assessment of the MarTech ecosystem in terms of (De Libero, 2022):

- Inventory: Understanding of the current organisation, desired business capabilities, required use cases, and integration between different applications.
- Implementation: The implementation and configuration (customising) of platforms and individual applications.
- Integration scenarios: Via APIs, native connectors, or middleware.
- Utilisation: The actual use of implemented applications.
- Investment and ROI: As the basic mechanics of the business case.

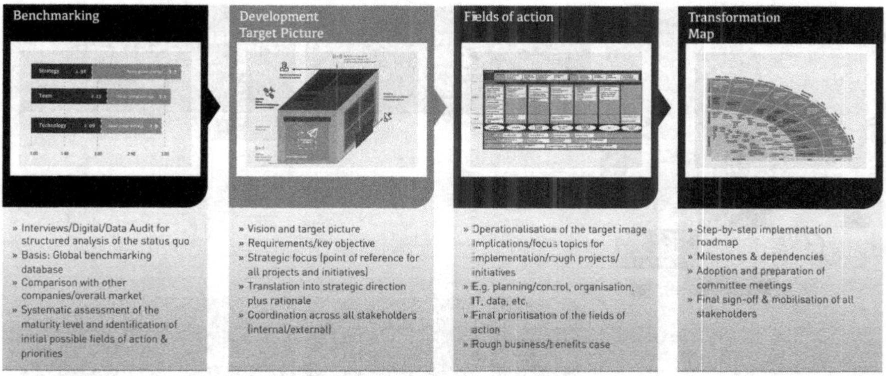

Fig. 14.5 Process model and phases of the development of a MarTech target picture and transformation map (project example: fast moving consumer goods, FMCG)

Competitors and MarketingTechnologies used—and thus also as an impulse for the development of a strategy for further digitalisation—serve as a *MarketingTechnology benchmarking*. This is understood to be an analysis procedure that, based on structured interviews and surveys, examines the existing organisation, processes, tools, and applications used (as well as the integration into the IT application landscape) and their compatibility and usability in the (current/possible future) business model. The *benchmarking database* that can be used for this purpose and is continuously updated consists essentially of three components (Fig. 14.6):

- *Vendor database*: Collection of all 14,000 vendors (in May 2024) in the relevant subject area, incl. basic company information.
- *Stack database*: Collection of meanwhile currently 1400+ MarTech stacks (in May 2024) from a wide range of companies and industries. This can be used to answer the question of what differences there are between one's own tool landscape and a) the overall market or b) the sub-industry segment "retail company" or "consumer goods manufacturer".
- *Requirements database*: Collection of currently just under 4500 detailed requirements in the most diverse application scenarios. This can subsequently be used to answer the following questions, amongst others:
  – Which IT application best covers the requirements (has the best "fit")?
  – Which requirements can only be covered by third-party applications?
  – Which requirements are not included in the respective standard (necessity for customising, if necessary, incl. subsequent *effort estimation*), to reduce the actual effort thus considerably . . . and potentials for errors?
  – For the target picture and the subsequent fields of action, access to almost 400 ROI studies can also be taken from the benchmarking database, for example to answer the question: "*What is the average ROI of a CDP*"?

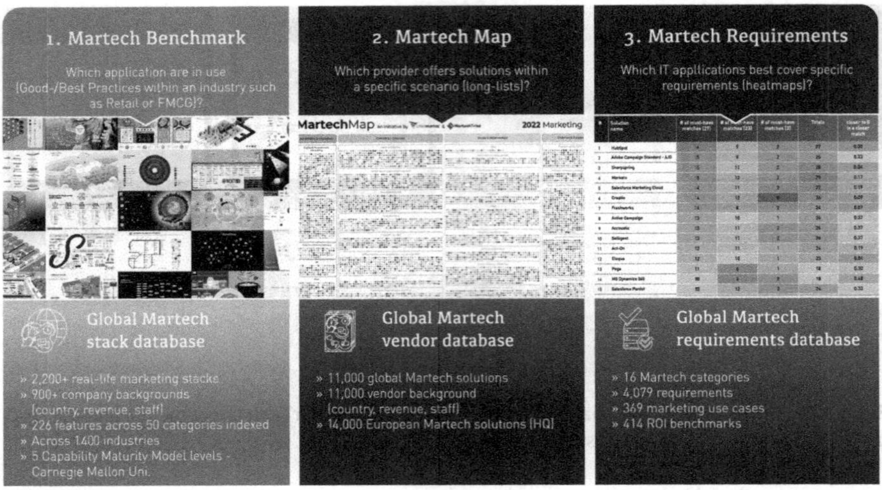

Fig. 14.6 Global MarTech Benchmarking Database (Marketing Tech Monitor 2024)

As a result, benchmarking can produce insights in a structured form for a variety of questions and dimensions, such as

- *Stack completeness and integration*:
  - Overarching analysis of MarTech development versus benchmarks.
  - Number of tools covering the specific topic and application scenarios.
  - Analysis of the level of integration of technologies and data (e.g. native, iPaaS, or API).
  - Alignment of the MarTech application landscape with the business model, application scenarios, and business-critical processes.
- *Strengths and weaknesses analysis*:
  - High or low level of coverage in relation to specific application scenarios.
  - Extraction of specific questions for individual application categories.
- *Maturity*:
  - Maturity in terms of coverage of specific application scenarios (i.e. the real use of licensed applications).
  - Comparison of the overall market, with the respective industry segment such as "financial service provider" and with own company.

As part of the two-stage benchmarking process, about 15 (qualitative) interviews are usually conducted and a survey is sent to all stakeholders directly involved in the MarTech stack (e.g. marketing staff, related areas). In some cases, it is also advisable to (selectively) include external customers. Based on this analysis and the basic understanding of the business model and the current/planned application scenarios, first rough recommendations for applications in different topics can be given (Fig. 14.7). Through the interviews, structured target pictures of individual stakeholders and, if

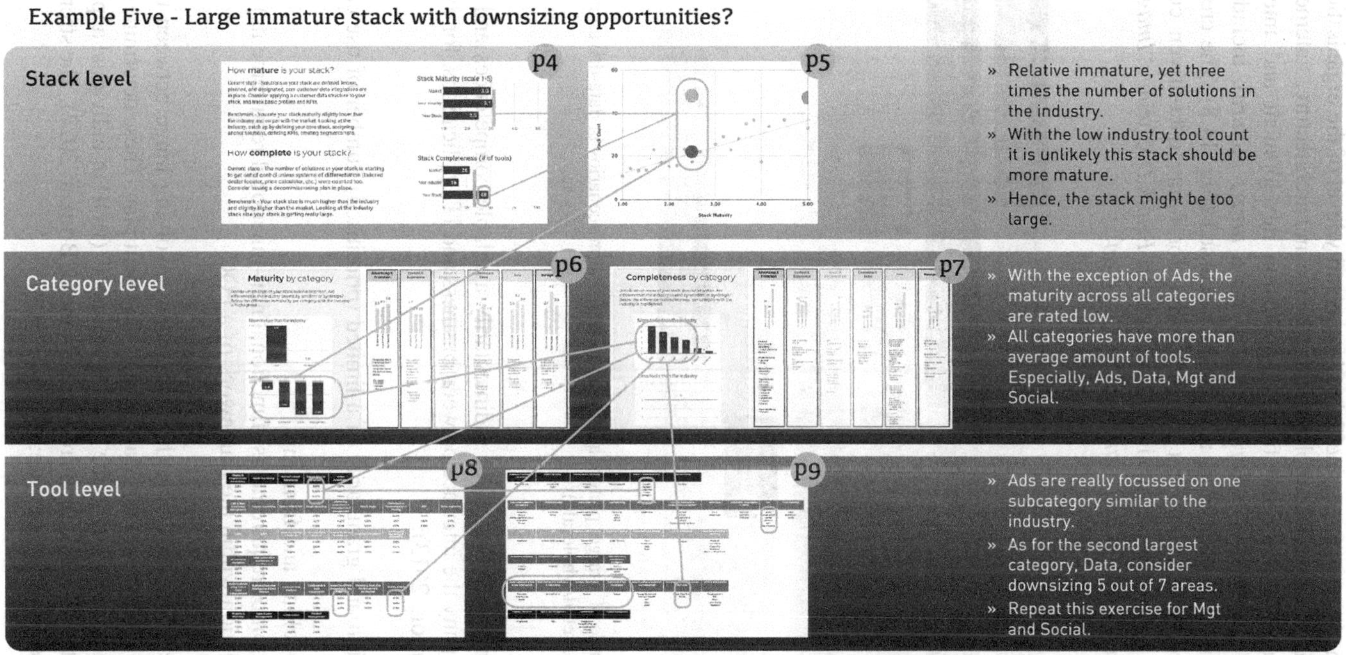

Fig. 14.7 Example of benchmarking—extensive tool landscape with downsizing options (project example: consumer goods manufacturer)

applicable, existing constraints are considered, as well as existing contractual situations, competence gaps, or inefficiencies (maturity level of the organisation).

By comparing the existing application landscape and architecture, statements can be made about the fit of the further application development and integration scenarios into the *master construction plan* (as a *target picture*), including the interfaces required in each case, and can be discussed (Fig. 14.8). The credo: not so much PowerPoint charts, but rather a vision for future data-driven customer interaction . . . following the maxim of brand expert *Frank Dopheide*: "*Imagination is the beginning of everything—and not the exit plan*".

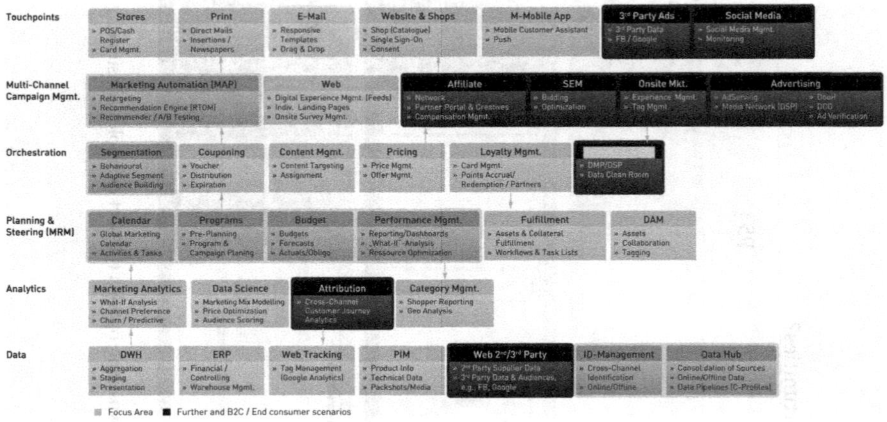

Fig. 14.8 Example of a target picture according to application scenarios in data-driven marketing (project example: retail/wholesale)

The challenge: only rarely or rudimentarily available competences and experience to accompany the interface between business and IT applications, for example, regarding (Vernon, 2013):

- The definition and granularity of a limited (prioritised) number of use cases, as well as
- Process modelling and from this
- The derivation of requirements (functional/non-functional requirements) or
- Their translation within the framework of a POC

Use cases are thus basically the permanently evolving hinge between the customer journey analysis and the MarTech development plan. These determine content and prioritisation according to the "business impact" (ROI) of individual application scenarios and the IT applications required for them (Brinker, 2022). The strengths of modelling based on use cases are:

- The vivid showcasing of which actors (should) interact with the system following which use cases
- The transparency for smaller models and
- The broad acceptance for a first draft to represent individual sub-aspects in an even more complex process landscape

The high-priority ("must-have") use cases and requirements can be placed directly against selected providers in the same methodical procedure (*fit gap analysis*) in order to determine directly in detail which applications have the greatest coverage or in which detailed requirements customising expenses will arise or have to be completely covered by third-party extensions (Fig. 14.9).

The analysis based on a benchmarking database and the subsequent fit gap analysis allows the reduction of a project's duration by 35–40%.

Q#	Must-Haves	Team 1	Team 2	Team 3
A1	Our future email editor can best be described as = HTML Editor + Basic building blocks	Yes, filterable	HTML Editor + Basic building blocks	HTML Editor + Basic building blocks
A2	Our future landing page / form editor can best be described as = Template based + Custom Build	Template based + Custom Build	Template based + Custom Build	Template based + Custom Build
A3	Our future campaign flow editor can best be described as = Template based + Custom Build	Custom Build	Template based + Custom Build	Template based + Custom Build
A6	We futurely use custom objects as = Limited Custom Objects for specific Entities	Custom Object Configuration	None	Limited Custom Objects for specific entities
A10	Our future in-app messaging requirements can best be described as = Website, Webshop & app	None	Website, Webshop & app	Website, Webshop & app
B2	Our future list & segment management capabilities are = Static + Dynamic	Yes, Static + Dynamic	Yes, Static + Dynamic	Yes, filterable
B3	Our future merging lists capabilities are: = Multiple data sets	Yes, contacts only	Yes, contacts only	Yes, contacts only
B8	Our future lead assignment / distribution is = Via workflow to sales reps (external CRM)	Manual	Automated, Internal + external	Workflow / Rule driven Internal + external
B12	Our future campaign/lead nurture automation capabilities are facilitated through/by = Advanced	Advanced. Includes filters & decision trees	Advanced and incl external channels (i.e. social)	Advanced and incl external channels (i.e. social)
B14	Our future campaign execution drivers are = Manual/Scheduled & trigger-based & adaptive	Manual/Scheduled & trigger-based & adaptive (curn, throttling, time-based	Manual/Scheduled & trigger-based	Manual/Scheduled & trigger-based & adaptive (curn, throttling, time-based)
B15	Our future reporting & analysis capabilities include = Basic Email Statistic	Includes external acquisition (social, PPC)	Includes external acquisition (social, PPC)	Includes external acquisition (social, PPC)
B22	Our future automating appointment scheduling will be = Native	Not available	Native	Native
C8	Our future MS Dynamics CRM integration is facilitated through/by = Native	Thru API Integration	Thru iPaaS Integration	Native
C10	Our future cdp integrations are = Yes	API	API	Yes
D1	Our future implementation + set up ownership is with = Ops/Admin	IT	Ops/Admin	Marketing
D2	Our future automation flow configuration is = DIY	DIY	Expert Assisted	Expert Assisted
F2	Our future solution is bought by = IT	IT	Marketing	Marketing

Team comparison
not covered
Partially covered
New skills required

Fig. 14.9 Database-supported fit gap analysis in the field of marketing automation (project example: food retail)

References

Brinker, S. (2022, February). It's not the size of your MarTech stack, it's your range of use cases. *Chiefmartec*.

Byrne, T., & Gingras, J. (2017). *The right way to select technology*.

De Libero, G. (2022, March 14). How to unlock the power of your marketing technology. Do it right and you increase your chances of successful digital transformation. *MarTech*.

Nieto-Rodriguez, A. (2016, December 13). How to prioritise your company's projects. *Harvard Business Manager*.

Strauß, R. E. (2019). *Digitale transformation*.

Userlane. (2023, March). *The state of digital adoption report*.

Vernon, V. (2013). *Implementing domain-driven design*.

Index

R. Strauss, *Data-Driven Customer Engagement*,
https://doi.org/10.1007/978-3-031-64295-1

9783031642944